Narrating Peoplehood amidst Diversity

Narrating Peoplehood amidst Diversity

Historical and Theoretical Perspectives

Edited by
Michael Böss

AARHUS UNIVERSITY PRESS

Narrating Peoplehood amidst Diversity
MatchPoints2
© the authors and Aarhus University Press
Typeset by Narayana Press
Cover design by Jørgen Sparre
Printed by Narayana Press
Printed in Denmark 2011

ISBN 978 87 7934 569 0
ISSN 1904-3384

Published with the financial support of
The Aarhus University Research Foundation

Aarhus University Press

Århus
Langelandsgade 177
DK – 8200 Århus N

København
Tuborgvej 164
DK – 2400 København NV

www.unipress.dk

INTERNATIONAL DISTRIBUTORS:
Gazelle Book Services Ltd.
White Cross Mills
Hightown, Lancaster, LA1 4XS
United Kingdom
www.gazellebookservices.co.uk

The David Brown Book Company
Box 511
Oakville, CT 06779
USA
www.oxbowbooks.com

Contents

■ Notes on contributors

Michael Böss is Associate Professor of History and Social Science and Director of the Canadian Studies Centre at Aarhus University, His research interests are political theory, the history and theory of nationalism, nationhood and the nation-state. He is currently doing comparative studies in Canadian and Australian debates on national identity and multiculturalism. He has published widely on Irish history and culture. His most recent books are *Forsvar for nationen: Nationalstaten under globaliseringen* (In Defence of the Nation: The Nation-state under Globalisation) (2006), *The Nation-state in Transformation: Economic Globalization, Institutional Mediation and Political Values* (2010) and *Republikken Danmark: Oplæg til en ny værdipolitisk debat* (The Republic of Denmark: Towards a New Value Politics) (2011).

Leo Chavez is a professor in the Department of Anthropology at the University of California, Irvine. His research examines various issues related to transnational migration, including immigrant families and households, labor market participation, motivations for migration, the use of medical services, and media constructions of "immigrant" and "nation." He is the author of *Shadowed Lives: Undocumented Immigrants in American Society* (1992, 1997 2nd edition) and *Covering Immigration: Popular Images and the Politics of the Nation* (2001), among others. His recent book, *The Latino Threat: Constructing Immigrants, Citizens, and the Nation* (2008), examines the role of media spectacles in helping shape how Latinos are constructed as a threat to the nation and for undermining claims of citizenship.

Andrew Cohen is a professor of journalism and international affairs at Carleton University in Ottawa. He is a syndicated columnist and a bestselling author. Among his most recent books are *The Unfinished Canadian: The People We Are* (2007) and *Extraordinary Canadians: Lester B. Pearson* (2008).

Francis Fukuyama is Olivier Nomellini Senior Fellow at the Freeman Spogli Institute for International Studies (FSI), resident in FSI's Center on Democracy, Development, and the Rule of Law. Dr. Fukuyama has written widely on issues relating to questions concerning democratization and international political economy. His book, *The End of History and the Last Man,* was published by Free Press in 1992 and has appeared in over twenty foreign editions. His most recent books are *America at the Crossroads: Democracy, Power, and the Neoconservative Legacy*, and *Falling Behind: Explaining the Development Gap between Latin America and the United States*. His latest book, *The Origins of Political Order: From Prehuman Times to the French Revolution* will be published in April 2011.

Jack Granatstein taught Canadian history in Toronto for thirty years, is a Senior Research Fellow of the Canadian Defence and Foreign Affairs Institute, and was Director and CEO of the Canadian War Museum. He has written extensively on all aspects of Canadian national history and on topics such as citizenship and war and multiculturalism and its impact on foreign policy.

Mark Haugaard is founding editor of the *Journal of Political Power* (Routledge), Chair of the IPSA Research Committee on Power (RC 36) and Senior Lecturer at the National University of Ireland, Galway. He has published numerous books and articles on power and social theory, including: (2010) 'Democracy, Political Power and Authority', *Social Research*, vol 77; (2010) 'Power: A Family Resemblance concept' (2010), *European Journal of Cultural Studies*, 13; (2010) 'Power and Social Critique', *Critical Horizons* 11 (1); Haugaard Mark and S. Clegg (ed.) (2009) *The Sage Handbook of Power*, Sage; Haugaard and S. Malesevic (2007) *Ernest Gellner and Contemporary Social Thought*, Cambridge: Cambridge University Press. He is currently working on a new book, provisionally entitled, *Rethinking Power*.

Martin O. Heisler is Professor Emeritus of Government and Politics at the University of Maryland. He has also taught at the University of Illinois, Aarhus University, the Institut d'Études Politiques (Paris) and Lewis and Clark College. His degrees in Political Science are from the University of California at Los Angeles. Recent publications include "Academic Freedom and the Freedom of Academics" (2007); and, as editor and contributor of two articles, *The Politics of History in Comparative Perspective* (2008). His current projects include "Negotiating Narratives, Not 'History'" in domestic and international politics and a book on "Migration, Governance, and Transformations of World Politics."

Richard Jenkins is Professor of Sociology at the University of Sheffield, UK. Trained as a social anthropologist at Queen's University Belfast and the University of Cambridge, he has undertaken field research in Northern Ireland, England, Wales and Denmark, looking at a range of topics, but most consistently looking at various identity-related issues. Among his recent publications are *Social Identity* (Routledge, 3rd edition 2008), *Rethinking Ethnicity* (Sage, 2nd edition 2008) and *Being Danish* (Museum Tusculanum Press, 2011).

Bernard Eric Jensen is Associate Professor of History and History Didactics at Danish School of Education, Aarhus University, Denmark. Fields of research include the history of historical thinking, the theory of history and the uses of history (public history, memory studies etc.).

Tomás R. Jiménez is an assistant professor of sociology at Stanford University and author of Replenished Ethnicity: Mexican Americans, Immigration, and Identity (University of California Press, 2010). His research has been published in the American Journal of Sociology, Ethnic and Racial Studies, Social Science Quarterly, DuBois Review, and the Annual Review of Sociology. Professor Jiménez has also taught at the University of California, San Diego. He has also been an Irvine Fellow at the New America Foundation. Before that, he was the American Sociological Association Congressional Fellow in the office of Rep. Michael Honda (CA-15). His writing on policy has appeared in reports for the Immigration Policy Center, and he has written opinion-editorials on the topic of immigrant assimilation in several major news outlets, including the Los Angeles Times, CNN.com, and the San Diego Union-Tribune. He holds a B.S. in sociology from Santa Clara University and A.M. and Ph.D. degrees in sociology from Harvard University.

Claus Møller Jørgensen is Associate Professor at the Department of History and Area Studies, Aarhus University, holding a chair in historical theory and method. He has published books and articles on Danish and European historiography in the 19th and 20th century, and articles on historical theory and method. He is currently working on an article on the 1848 revolutions as a European and transurban phenomenon.

Desmond King holds the Andrew W Mellon Chair of American Government at the University of Oxford and was formerly Professor of Politics at St John's College, Oxford. His publications include: *Making Americans Immigration, Race and the Origins of the Diverse Democracy* (2000), *The Liberty of Strangers* (2005), *The Unsustainable American State* (2009, coedited with Lawrence Jacobs) and *Still A House Divided: Race and Politics in Obama's America* (2011, with Rogers M Smith). He is a Fellow of the British Academy.

Ove Korsgaard is a professor in the Faculty of Arts, University of Aarhus. His main research interests are the history of education, philosophy of education, and national identity. His books include *The Struggle About the Body: The Danish History of Body Culture through 200 Years* (Gyldendal 1982), *The Struggle About the Light. The Dansih History of Adult Education through 500 Years* (Gyldendal 1997), *The Struggle for the People. Five hundred Years of Danish History seen through an educational Perspective*

(Gyldendal 2004), *The Struggle for the People: Five hundred Years of Danish History in Short* (Danmarks Pædagogiske Universitetsforlag 2008).

Eric Rauchway is professor of history at the University of California, Davis, and the author of *Blessed Among Nations: How the World Made America* and *The Great Depression and the New Deal: A Very Short Introduction*, among other books.

Rogers M. Smith is Christopher H. Browne Distinguished Professor of Political Science at the University of Pennsylvania and Chair of the Penn Program on Democracy, Citizenship, and Constitutionalism. He is the author or co-author of numerous articles and six books, including *Stories of Peoplehood: The Politics and Morals of Political Membership*, and *Still a House Divided: Race and Politics in Obama's America* (with Desmond S. King). He is a Fellow of the American Academy of Arts and Sciences and the American Academic of Political and Social Science.

Inés Valdez is a political theorist and will complete her PhD at the University of North Carolina at Chapel Hill in the summer of 2011 and take a position as Max Weber Postdoctoral Fellow at the European University Institute in Florence. She is interested in immigration, sovereignty, and democratic theory. Her work is forthcoming in *Political Studies*.

1 Stories of Peoplehood: An Approach to the Study of Identity, Memory, and Historiography

Michael Böss

The purpose of this book is to describe, analyze, and theorize the nature and history of "stories of peoplehood" and their implications for national identities, public culture, and academic historiography in societies characterized by cultural and social diversity. It offers theoretical reflections on the narrative character of national identities and empirical studies of the contexts in which they emerged. The book also raises normative issues such as: To what extent does peoplehood make sense today? Can plural societies tell "national stories" without marginalizing their minorities? Should historians be concerned with stories of peoplehood? In this introduction, I will present the individual contributions to the collection against the background of preliminary considerations of the book's major concepts and themes.

"Stories of peoplehood," the key concept, comes from a work by the political scientist Rogers M. Smith, who is one of the contributors to this book. In *Stories of Peoplehood: The Politics and Morals of Political Membership* (2003), Smith defines stories of peoplehood as "persuasive historical stories that prompt people to embrace the valorized identities, play the stirring roles, and have the fulfilling experiences that political leaders strive to evoke for them, whether through arguments, rhetoric, symbols, or "stories of a more obvious and familiar sort."[1] Smith believes that the creation of a relatively enduring sense of political community requires accounts, narratives, or stories of peoplehood that successfully inspire feelings of both belonging and trust in a population. He distinguishes between three types of stories: "economic" stories, "political power" stories, and "ethically constitutive" stories. Stories of peoplehood "proclaim that members' culture, religion, language, race, ethnicity, ancestry, history, or other such factors are constitutive of their very identities as persons, in ways that both affirm their worth and delineate their obligations."[2] Stories of peoplehood thus contribute significantly not only to the constitution of a political community, but also to the definition of its ethical and

---

1. Rogers M. Smith, *Stories of Peoplehood: The Politics and Morals of Political Membership* (Cambridge: Cambridge University Press, 2003), 45.
2. Ibid., 65.

cultural values. Smith's definition has been used as a common source of inspiration for the contributors to this book. However, we have agreed that we may either adopt it in its original form or elaborate on it.

A story of peoplehood is not in itself a social and cultural phenomenon, but should rather be understood as an analytical tool for interpreting social and cultural phenomena, first of all cultural, political, and public discourses and symbols. In introducing the chapters of the book, I intend to demonstrate how, as I see it, this concept may be used to cast light on the identities, memories, and histories of individuals and communities.

Narrative identity: The self-awareness of individuals and groups

While the concept of "national character" goes back to the Enlightenment, it was not until the mid-1950s that the word "identity" was used to refer to collectivities such as nations. The inspiration came from psychology, and was primarily a result of the great influence of Erik H. Erikson.[3] Erikson was interested in the way social conditions give rise to certain traits in the individual, especially how they may afflict adolescents to cause a "crisis of identity." In *Childhood and Society* (1950), Erikson accepted that the notion of identity might also be used to discuss groups, but he did not attempt to do so. In a survey of Erikson's work in 1955, the anthropologist Margaret Mead supported this idea, predicting that, given the great changes in social development occurring at the time, identity was likely to become one of the "burning problems of the present age."[4] And indeed it was: since then, identity has preoccupied sociology and psychology as well as cultural studies.

The social anthropologist Richard Jenkins, who is among this book's contributors, explains how individual and collective identities are a result of ongoing processes in which relations of difference and similarity are established between the individual and the group and his and its "others"; identities should therefore be seen as dynamic and flexible processes of "identification" constructed through social interaction.[5] This dynamic conception of identity is reflected in modern psychology, which, to a great extent, has been inspired by the philosopher Paul Ricoeur's thoughts about the "narrative" character of identity.[6] Ricoeur explained in

---

3. Erik H. Erikson, *Childhood and Society* (New York: Norton, 1950). I was made aware of this while reading James Curran and Stuart Ward, *The Unknown Nation: Australia after Empire* (Melbourne: Melbourne University Press, 2010), 17.
4. Curran and Ward, *The Unknown Nation.*, ibid.
5. Richard Jenkins, *Social Identity*, 2nd ed. (London: Routledge, 2004).
6. Paul Ricoeur, *Time and Narrative*, transl. Kathleen Blarmey and David Pellauer, 3 vols (Chicago and London: University of Chicago Press, 1988). Originally published as *Temps et Récit* (Paris: Seuil, 1983-85).

1983-84 that it is only by structuring time as a narrative that an individual is able to see meaning and coherence in his life and the world around him. An individual constructs continuity between the past and present when she structures her experiences as a sequence of causes and effects. This time-line reflects the individual's self-interpretation. But because she keeps acting and experiencing throughout her life, new elements will constantly be added to the self-narrative. Jerome Bruner picked up this idea when he broke with the earlier view of the individual self as an unchanging entity.[7] He argued that, instead, we should understand individual identity as a result of a genetic faculty to render experiences into a narrative structure. In *Time, Narrative and History*, David Carr used Ricoeur's philosophy for a theory in which individual and collective identities were connected through the concept of narrativity. Carr argued that there is a narrative aspect to all intentional individual acts. Due to the teleological character of an act, the individual will necessarily look toward the future, i.e. towards some possible and intended state of affairs. Since actions are motivated by personal reasons, however, he will also look backward to the past and to the events that brought him to the present situation from which he acts. The present moment of acting is thus the point at which the individual's sense of his past history, present situation, and future possibilities merge. It is this temporal aspect which endows the intentional act with a narrative structure, and acts are in themselves enactments of a narrative in progress:

> We are constantly striving with more or less success to occupy the storyteller's position with respect to our own actions. [...] Such narrative activity [...] has a practical function in life [as] a constitutive part of action, and not just as an embellishment, commentary, or other incidental accompaniment [...]
>
> The actions and sufferings of life can be viewed as a process of telling ourselves stories, listening to those stories, and acting them out or living them through. [...] To be an agent or subject of experience is to make the constant attempt to surmount time in exactly the way the storyteller does. It is the attempt to dominate the flow of events by gathering them together in the forward-backward grasp of the narrative act.[8]

Thus, individual identity does not only evolve as the individual relates to her past and to others, but also as a result of her interaction with an environment of meanings, i.e. a web of the historically determined symbols, codes, and narratives of her culture and lifeworld.[9]

---

7. Jerome Bruner, *Actual Minds, Possible Worlds* (Cambridge, MA: Harvard University Press, 1986) and *Acts of Meaning* (Cambridge, MA: Harvard University Press, 1990).
8. David Carr, *Time, Narrative, and History* (Bloomington and Indianapolis: Indiana University Press, 1986), 61-62.
9. Cf. Clifford Geertz, *The Interpretation of Cultures* (New York: BasicBooks, 1973) and Anthony P. Cohen, *Self-Consciousness* (London: Routledge, 1994).

We develop self-perception by interacting with the symbolic system of our cultural environment, and our individual self-narratives are therefore closely bound up with various "cultural narratives," which may be based on language, ethnicity, nationality, family, gender, class, race, territory, or region, and so on. This does not mean that the individual self is predetermined by the narratives of his group or cultural environment. However, they do set certain limits to personal agency. As Seyla Benhabib puts it: "Our agency consists in our capacity to weave out of those [cultural] narratives our individual life stories, which make sense for us as unique selves."[10]

We only have that capacity because, apart from the faculty to organize temporal experiences as narratives, we are endowed with the faculty to remember. But memory, too, is only partially individual.

Memory, group identity, and collective stories

Memory and narrative are two sides of the same coin, because we remember in and through narrative. And as our self-narratives are informed by the narratives of our lifeworlds and the groups to which we belong, so are our memories. The sociologist Maurice Halbwachs once observed that family memories are particularly important to an individual's memories and sense of identity.[11] He claimed that what the individual thought of later in life as personal memories had in fact been constructed from the stories she had been told. Memories that an individual may believe to be authentic may thus be based on family memory and family story telling. Halbwachs also thought that personal self-awareness was shaped by the individual's identification with other social groups, not least that of the nation. This view has later been adopted by oral historians. Alistair Thomson, for example, has shown how Australian veterans from the First World War later remembered their war experiences through narratives that reflected the Anzac myth, Australia's major story of peoplehood.[12]

All groups – from families to local communities and nations – have stories and myths they "live by."[13] Collective identities are based on their members' mutual interaction, common experiences and relationships with groups they consider their "others." The national group's shared memories – and the stories by which they are both retained and constructed – ensure continuity from one generation to the

10. Seyla Benhabib, *The Claims of Culture* (Princeton: Princeton University Press, 2002), 15.
11. Maurice Halbwachs, *On Collective Memory* (Chicago: Chicago University Press, 1992).
12. Alistair Thomson, "Anzac Memories: Putting Popular Theory into Practice in Australia," in *The Houses of History*, ed. Anna Green and Kathleen Troup (Manchester: Manchester University Press, 1999), 239-52.
13. Cf. Dan P. McAdams, *The Stories We Live By: Personal Myths and the Making of the Self* (New York and London: The Guilford Press, 1993).

next, thus rendering it possible for later generations to re-imagine their cultural identities and maintain collective awareness.[14] Through "acts of memory", that is, collective memories ritually acted out in a public space, a nation is reminded of its triumphs and defeats, heroes and martyrs. Acts of memory may take various forms, including national holidays, festivals, pilgrimages, burials, and the unveiling of statues and plaques, but they all serve to enhance a people's sense of living in a political community whose values and cultural identity have been formed by historical experiences and the narratives by which they are retained.

In accordance with this line of thinking, which has been developed by historians such as Pierre Nora and Paul Connerton, Bernard Eric Jensen describes nations as "communities of memory."[15] In his present contribution, "Re-imagining a People: Towards a Theory of Peoplehood as Social Imaginary," Jensen explores the question of how self-interpretation interacts with man's nature as a social, cultural, inter-subjective, and language-using being and how it contributes to the making and re-making of a people. Although he uses Benedict Anderson's theory of imagined communities as a starting point for his discussion, he suggests that Anderson never succeeded in clarifying the ontological status of an imagined community. If this is to be done, Jensen argues, it demands the transposition of Anderson's theory from its historical materialist setting into a more clear-cut social constructivist framework. Jensen outlines his own theory of peoplehood as social imaginary by drawing on a set of pivotal insights he has derived from Charles Taylor, Stuart Hall, and David Carr.

It almost goes without saying that if we understand stories of nation and people-hood in this broader perspective, as I think we should, then they are much more than a people's "myth of common descent" or its "historical memories."[16] As Jensen suggests, they should be seen as part of what Taylor describes as a "social imaginary," i.e. "the kind of common understanding that enables us to carry out the collective practices that make up our social life."[17] For my own part, I define stories of peoplehood as narratives and other symbolizations of shared social and political experiences that inform national awareness, shape values, motivate political action, and legitimize institutions of society and state.

However, the consensual character of many such stories today should not make us blind to the fact that they may be contested, and that they may have evolved from conflicting processes in the past.

---

14. Jan Assmann, *Das kulturelle Gedächtnis. Schrift, Erinnerung und politische Identität in frühen Hochkulturen* (Munich: Beck, 1992).

15. Bernard Eric Jensen, *Historie – livsverden og fag* [History – Lifeworld and Academic Discipline] (Copenhagen: Gyldendal, 2003).

16. Cf. Anthony D. Smith's definition of an ethnic community, e.g. in *National Identity* (London: Penguin 1991), 21.

17. Charles Taylor, *Sources of the Self: The Making of Modern Identity* (Cambridge: Cambridge University Press, 1989) and *Modern Social Imaginaries* (Durham and London: Duke University Press, 2004), 24.

Contested stories

Stories of nationhood have frequently been contested because, though they claim to speak for the whole people, they may have served particular social and political interests. Nation- and state-building processes are connected, but since this connection may lead to unequal distributions of power, stories of nation and peoplehood have at times been more hegemonic than agreed upon. In contemporary nation-states alternative stories and past conflicts may still be glossed over when the nation's history is taught and represented in schools and museums and other nation-building public institutions. However, the tendency today is to represent the people's past with more complex and plural narratives. This change came about when historians began to turn away from political history and towards social history, including the history of marginalized groups. A recent source of inspiration for the pluralization of national histories has been the experience of immigration, a subject which is given special emphasis in this book. As the political scientist Martin Heisler points out in "Our Stories, Our Selves: Collective Identities and the Dialogics of Narrative," contemporary patterns of immigration have made it even more difficult to base national identities on culturally exclusionary narratives. The question of whose stories are "Our Stories" may at least require us to revise our national narratives. And as Richard Jenkins argues in "Citizenship, Belonging and Identification: The State of Denmark," modern "multi-ethnic collectivities" necessitate explorations of alternative perspectives on the relationship between citizenship and national identity, since the "historical" aspect of nationality may no longer "fit."

It may be doubted, however, whether citizenship provides enough glue for the liberal democratic state to be functional, and whether total state neutrality towards values and stories of cultural identity can ensure the collective allegiance of citizens. In "Identity and Nationalism in a Global World: Some Theoretical Reflections," Mark Haugaard argues that nationalism served the liberal state well in the past, but that it is losing its effectiveness as a source of identity since it is being challenged by other identities in an increasingly globalized world. The question for political theorists and policy-makers is therefore: To what extent should the state reinforce these new identities and support education directed at creating alternative identities? Haugaard doubts that a liberal night-watchman state will command the same collective allegiance of its citizens as the nation-state, in which citizens imagined the state as an heirloom. Hence, he finds it necessary for the state to embrace new alternative identities that enable modern individuals to identify with it. He thinks that multicultural identities have a potential to strengthen liberal democracy against nationalism and other identities that tend toward comprehensiveness. However, he is also aware of the danger that "some of these identities may themselves pose as comprehensive identities" which provide answers to all life's questions. Liberal democracy should not encourage identities which "re-describe the world in its entirety to the exclusion of other descriptions."

Traditional stories of peoplehood are questioned and challenged as a result of political, economic, cultural, and social changes. It may argued, however, that this is not big news. In the East, too, notions of national identity were subject to re-interpretation under novel circumstances. In the United States, one major factor was immigration. Mass immigration from the mid-1880s onwards challenged the Founding Fathers' story of the American people. In "Nation, Region, and Immigra-tion," Eric Rauchway explores how, in the 1800s, immigration was to affect different parts of the United States in different ways. He argues that what was in time to be thought of as a national narrative, which included the story of immigration in the larger story of America, was in reality the result of a triumphant regional narrative that occurred mid-century.

In "From a Shining City on a Hill to a Great Metropolis on a Plain? American Stories of Immigration and Peoplehood," Rogers M. Smith argues that even before the nation's founding, Americans had woven accounts of immigration into their narratives of peoplehood. American proponents and critics of immigration both did so while insisting that the United States was a uniquely great nation that should serve as an example to, or as the actual leader of, all humanity. In the twenty-first century, Smith concludes, Americans – once again – need to adjust their story. In the light of the new international order, they will have to recognize that, though they have many reasons to take pride in their nation, they should embrace a more moderate sense of peoplehood conducive to multilateral, cooperative efforts to ad-dress the world's problems.

In his controversial book *Who Are We? America's Great Debate* (2005), Samuel P. Huntington argued that the notion of America as an immigrant nation was a twentieth-century myth constructed by politicians and academics. Referring to Franklin D. Roosevelt's challenge in 1938 to the Daughters of the American Revo-lution that all Americans were "descended from immigrants," Huntington found Roosevelt "totally wrong": "Their ancestors were not immigrants but settlers, and in its origins America was not a nation of immigrants, it was a society, or societies, of settlers who came to the New World in the seventeenth and eighteenth centu-ries. Its origins as an Anglo-Protestant settler society have, more than anything else, profoundly and lastingly shaped American culture, institutions, historical development, and identity."[18] Huntington's central argument was that the central elements of Anglo-Protestant culture, traditions and values ended up defining the "American Creed with its principles of liberty, equality, individualism, representative

---

18. Samuel P. Huntington, *Who Are We? America's Great Debate* (New York: Simon and Schuster, 2004), 39.

government, and private property," and subsequent generations of immigrants were assimilated into that culture.[19] Although they also contributed to it and modified it, they did not change it fundamentally, because it was this culture - and the political liberties and economic opportunities it produced - that kept attracting immigrants. But this pattern, Huntington claimed, was changed with the third wave of immigration since the 1960s, and particularly the large immigration from Mexico now challenges the creed and the "story" - or stories - of America on which it is based.

This thesis is contested in the contributions to this book by Leo R. Chavez, Tomás R. Jimenez, Desmond King, and Ines Valdez. In "From Workers to Enemies. National Security, State Building and America's War on Illegal Immigrants," King and Valdez argue that since the mid-1980s immigration policy toward illegal immigrants has assumed the character of a war expressed by growing border militarization and fortification, greater numbers of enforcement officers both at the border and away from it, and an enhanced domestic program of prosecution against undocumented immigrants, who have become "illegal aliens" or "illegals" in popular discourse. These immigrants today comprise an estimated 12 million people. King and Valdez trace the institutional transformations of immigration enforcement into a militarized endeavor and immigrants into security threats by identifying seven stages of a war-like strategy characterized by a build-up that precedes yet supports the process of state building that has taken place in the post-9/11 period. This process of state building is coupled and supported by exclusionary narratives of peoplehood that prevent the opening of political spaces in which immigrants' rights may be claimed for and a response may be given to the militarization of the realm of immigration. These narratives exclude immigrants, potentially affecting the entire Latino/a population in the United States, stigmatizing and marking them as perpetual outsiders, King and Valdez argue.

In "Narratives of Nation and Anti-Nation: The Media and Construction of Latinos as a Threat to the United States," Leo Chavez examines the US public discourse about Latinos, or Hispanics, and their representation as a problem for the nation. The representation of Latinos as a threat to the nation is problematic because its hyperbolic nature obscures more balanced characterizations of Latinos. This makes arriving at a consensus on immigration reform difficult. The following questions frame Chavez's chapter: What is meant by nation? How are Latinos represented as a threat to the American nation and American nationality? And how accurate are the representations of Latinos? To answer these questions, Chavez's chapter examines popular discourse on the nation, Latinos, and immigrants as reflected in national news magazines in the United States over more than forty years.

---

19. Ibid., 41.

In "Immigration and the Intersection of Ethnic and National Narratives: The Case of Ethnic Mexicans in the United States," Tomás Jimenez draws on in-depth interviews and observations with later generation Mexican Americans, showing how ongoing Mexican immigration shapes the ethnic identity of these descendants of early Mexican immigrants. Interviews and observations also illustrate how immigration defines Mexican ethnicity – the Mexican ethnic "narrative" – in ways that prevent all people of Mexican descent from being written into an American national narrative rooted in *historical*, not contemporary or ongoing immigration. Jimenez argues that the "nation of immigrants" is an ideal. In reality, the role that immigration plays in America's national identity suggests an amended version of its narrative: the United States is a nation of *descendants of immigrants* who overcame the hardships of immigration and assimilation.

As one of Europe's oldest states, Denmark cannot meaningfully be described as a nation of immigrants. Still, 8 % of Denmark's population today consists of immigrants and the descendants of immigrants. Two of the contributions to this book, Ove Korsgaard's "Grand Narratives in Danish History" and Claus Møller Jørgensen's "History-writing and National Identity," exemplify how some Danish historians grapple with the issue of making sense of Danish peoplehood, the former for the writing of national history, and the latter in light of globalization and immigration.

History and peoplehood

The two historians share a dynamic and non-essentialist conception of nationhood, although Møller Jørgensen doubts the meaningfulness of categories such as the "Danish people" and the "nation-state" as a basis for writing the history of Denmark.

Møller Jørgensen's chapter falls into three parts. It begins with a very brief introduction to traditional Danish national history writing until about 1970. In the second section, entitled "Denmark in context," recent general contributions to the history of Denmark are analyzed with respect to their "methodological nationalism," which is the assumption that the nation-state is a natural research object, and that it can be seen in isolation from the surrounding world. Møller Jørgensen concludes that the contextualization of the history of Demark seems to vary according to the period under study. Only recently, with a collective work on the history of Denmark and Norway (1997-98), has the first important step been taken in analyzing Denmark as part of the wider context of the Danish Conglomerate state, which is not defined by the backward projection of the Danish nation-state. On the other hand, histories are still written in which Denmark is treated in isolation from European cultural and intellectual currents. The final section is entitled "Danish identity" and contains an analysis and critical discussion of recent contributions to the history of Danish national identity. These can be divided into two types. The first type presents modern Danishness as the cumulative outcome of historical processes in the form of a stable, harmonic, and uniform Danish national identity. The second version does not view Danishness as stable or harmonic, but as an object of ongoing discursive struggle. Epochal hegemonic identifications can be discerned, but they are never undisputed and as national identifications are related to other social identifications they are never uniform. The article concludes with a discussion of recent trends in Danish historical scholarship. A call is made for a transnationalization of history writing and a pluralization of the writing of the history of Danish national identity.

In "Grand Narratives in Danish History: From Functional Identity to Problematic Identity," Ove Korsgaard theorizes the concept of "people," situating the historical meanings of the concept in a Danish context and the notion of a Danish "grand narrative." The war in 1864 and the loss of Slesvig and Holstein played an extremely important role in the formation of a Danish identity. Out of the collapse of the old multinational and multilingual state a new Danish nation state emerged which came close to fulfilling the ideal, i.e. a complete overlap of state, nation, language, and ethnicity. Danish identity became rooted in two grand narratives, one about the peasants and another about the workers. "People" is a core concept for both narratives. However, these narratives are no longer functional to the same extent as they used to be, first of all because they do not include a European or a multicultural perspective. The Europeanization process has raised the question of whether it is possible or desirable for Danes to belong to a European "people." The migration process has raised questions about whether it is possible or desirable for immigrants to belong to a Danish people, and what it means to belong to a Danish people today.

In the decades after ca. 1970, many historians declared national history dead, it having been the dominant genre, indeed almost a *raison d'être*, for historians for more than 150 years. Historians no longer saw themselves as guardians of the nation-state. But other factors complicated the issue: the advent of social-science history (New History); the fragmentation of history into sub-disciplines; and from the 1980s, postmodern critiques of objectivism, historical narrative, and traditional notions of "what history is." All over Europe, there were historians who claimed that it was not only impossible, but also irrelevant to write national histories. As the Danish historian Søren Mørch wrote in *Den sidste Danmarkshistorie* (The Last Danish History):

Danish history belongs to a box of ideological elements we are in the process of shelving. Neither I myself nor my many thousand colleagues will be able to narrate it in the way it could be done in the past, because it is no longer coherent. Instead we are able to tell many different stories. What comes of this book is my version. What I aim to discover, is how Denmark became a nation-state, and why things are different now.[20]

That Danish historians were more likely to declare national history dead than other European historians may be explained as a result of a general intellectual critique of what had hitherto been an almost unquestioned master narrative of Denmark's smooth modernization and socio-cultural homogeneity and harmony. In all fairness it must be granted that there was indeed a need for more nuances and complexities in the writing of Danish history. However, in hindsight Mørch's both nostalgic and light-hearted prediction appears premature. Although Mørch's "conflictual" perspective has retained its edge, as is documented in Møller Jørgensen's chapter, postmodern historians' worst onslaught and politicization of history as an academic discipline has not, neither in Denmark nor in the rest of Europe and the United States.[21] From both America and Britain came well-argued and reasoned defences.[22] The public was assured that historians could generally be trusted, and that the writing of history still had important social functions. More than ever, there was a "public demand for history," including histories that constructed national identities.[23]

But commercial publishers already knew this; in Denmark, for example, the market has for the past ten years been flooded with short introductions to Danish history and "stories" from the nation's past. Both here and in most of the rest of the Western world citizenship tests now require applicants to have both civic knowledge and an insight into the prospective nation's history, culture, and values, and therefore books and guides are being produced that replicate largely consensual stories of peoplehood.[24]

It appears, then, that Europeanization, globalization, and immigration have had the opposite effect than was expected back in the early 1990s, having created new social, political, and individuals' demands for collective stories of nationhood that contribute to social cohesion, political allegiances, and ontological security.

---

20. Søren Mørch, *Den sidste Danmarkshistorie* (Copenhagen: Gyldendal, 1992), 15.
21. E.g., Keith Jenkins, *Re-thinking History* (London: Routledge, 1991) and *On 'What Is History?'* (London: Routledge, 1995). For a Danish assesment of the impact of postmodern history, see *Historiefaget efter Postmodernismen*, thematic issue of *Den jyske Historiker*, 88 (April 2000).
22. E.g., Richard J. Evans, *In Defence of History* (London: Granta Books, 1997), Willie Thompson, *What Happened to History?* (London: Pluto Press, 2000), and Joyce Appleby, Lynn Hunt, and Margaret Jacob, *Telling the Truth About History* (New York and London: Norton, 1994).
23. E.g., David Cannadine (ed), *What Is History Now?* (London: Palgrave, 2002), 12.
24. See, e.g., *Discover Canada; The Rights and Responsibilities of Citizenship* (Ottawa: Government of Canada, 2009) and *Danmark før og nu* [Denmark – Then and Now] (Copenhagen: Ministeriet for Flygtninge, Indvandrere og Integration, 2007).

A need for both story and history?

Many political scientists today concur with Francis Fukuyama that liberal, pluralist states need common ground and shared stories of peoplehood. In "National
Identity, American and Otherwise," Fukuyama argues that there is an inherent
tension in all democratic societies between their need for national identity and
the democratic principles on which they are founded. All workable democratic
societies must be bounded in some way by a community of shared culture if
there is to be collective action and commitment to the political system. On the
other hand, the boundaries of that community must necessarily be defined on
the basis of pre- or non-democratic principles like language, ethnicity, religion,
or other shared cultural attributes. Today's successful democracies are stable
because they have been built upon national communities forged through often
non-democratic means before the rise of modern democracy. American national
identity is contested on precisely these grounds. One version of this argument is
given by Seymour Martin Lipset: that American identity is essentially political,
based on allegiance to the US Constitution and the Constitution's democratic
principles. Another version has been articulated by Samuel Huntington, who argued that American identity was formed by the Anglo-Protestant culture specific
to the religious and ethnic group that first settled North America. The chapter
argues that while the Huntington interpretation is historically correct, its religious
and ethnic roots have been universalized, and that American identity has evolved
once more into the Lipset version of affairs.

In "Who Are We Now? A Multicultural Canada in the Twenty-First Century,"
Canadian historian Jack Granatstein argues that the decision of Canadian governments since 1971 to define a Canadian people with its own history and "story" has
failed not only to integrate the various regions of Canada, but also to make a unity
of its population, thus failing the social needs of its immigrants. However, paradoxically, what attracts immigrants to Canada in the first place is their perception of a
particular peoplehood based on a unique historical experience. Immigrants choose
Canada because it has its own history and its own institutions, its own record of
fighting for democracy and freedom, its own story of hard-won tolerance. But when
they arrive and send their children to school, they learn almost nothing of the new
country. Both native-born and immigrant Canadians seem to learn that Canada has
no past worth studying. Why then assimilate or integrate into such a society? Why
then not retain the old country's culture? In its effort to de-anglicize Canada and heal
the old division between francophones and anglophones, the federal government
adopted a policy of multiculturalism that was to be the country's unifying identity
and tried to sell this idea to the citizens. However, the problem with this policy,
Granatstein argues, is that it only succeeded in fragmenting Canadians more than

ever. What Canadians need now, he concludes, is awareness of their history as a nation.

The journalist and commentator Andrew Cohen supports Granatstein's argument. He argues that Canada not only needs a unifying story, but that Canadians also need to know their history. Historical ignorance is a challenge to national cohesion. Hence, the state should see to it that history is taught in schools, that historic places are preserved, that anniversaries are marked, that leaders are remembered, and that new museums are created. And, he argues, there would be an enthusiastic audience. The challenge is not demand, but supply. It is demanded because there is a deep desire, in a world of that is changing, to understand some of the fundamentals of one's country.

The book ends with my own chapter, "Narratives of Peoplehood, National History, and Imagined Nations amidst Diversity." Here I use some reflections on the Irish revisionist debate in the 1980s and 1990s as a point of departure for a concluding discussion of the nature of stories of peoplehood in relation to the conceptualization of nationhood and historical master narratives. I end my chapter by considering the ethics of narrating peoplehood in plural societies and its implications for the professional historian.

Bibliography

Appleby, Joyce, Lynn Hunt, and Margaret Jacob. *Telling the Truth About History*. New York and London: Norton, 1994.

Assmann, Jan. *Das kulturelle Gedächtnis. Schrift, Erinnerung und politische Identität in frühen Hochkulturen*. Munich: Beck, 1992.

Benhabib, Seyla. *The Claims of Culture*. Princeton: Princeton University Press, 2002.

Bruner, Jerome. *Actual Minds, Possible Worlds*. Cambridge, MA: Harvard University Press, 1986.

Bruner, Jerome. *Acts of Meaning*. Cambridge, MA: Harvard University Press, 1990.

Cannadine, David ed. *What Is History Now?* London: Palgrave, 2002.

Carr, David. *Time, Narrative, and History*.Bloomington and Indianapolis: Indiana University Press, 1986).

Cohen, Anthony P. *Self-Consciousness*.London: Routledge, 1994.

Curran, James and Stuart Ward. *The Unknown Nation: Australia after Empire*. Melbourne: Melbourne University Press, 2010.

Danmark før og nu [Denmark – Then and Now]. Copenhagen: Ministeriet for Flygtninge, Indvandrere og Integration, 2007.

Discover Canada; The Rights and Responsibilities of Citizenship. Ottawa: Government of Canada, 2009.

Erikson, Erik H. *Childhood and Society*. New York: Norton, 1950.

Evans, Richard J. *In Defence of History*. London: Granta Books, 1997.

Geertz, Clifford. *The Interpretation of Cultures*. New York: BasicBooks, 1973.

Halbwachs, Maurice. *On Collective Memory*. Chicago: Chicago University Press, 1992.

Historiefaget efter Postmodernismen. Thematic issue of *Den jyske Historiker*, 88 (April 2000). Huntington, Samuel J. *Who Are We? America's Great Debate*. New York: Simon and Schuster, 2004.

Jenkins, Keith. *Re-thinking History*. London: Routledge, 1991.

Jenkins, Keith. *On What Is History?* London: Routledge, 1995.

Jenkins, Richard. *Social Identity*, 2nd ed. London: Routledge, 2004.

Jensen, Bernard Eric. *Historie – livsverden og fag* [History– Lifeworld and Academic Discipline] Copenhagen: Gyldendal, 2003.

McAdams, Dan P. *The Stories We Live By: Personal Myths and the Making of the Self*. New York and London: The Guilford Press, 1993.

Mørch, Søren. *Den sidste Danmarkshistorie*. Copenhagen: Gyldendal, 1992.

Ricoeur, Paul. *Time and Narrative*, transl. Kathleen Blarmey and David Pellauer, 3 vols. Chicago and London: University of Chicago Press, 1988. Originally published as *Temps et Récit*. Paris: Seuil, 1983-85.

Smith, Anthony D. *National Identity*. London: Penguin 1991.

Smith, Rogers M. *Stories of Peoplehood: The Politics and Morals of Political Membership*. Cambridge: Cambridge University Press, 2003.

Taylor, Charles. *Sources of the Self: The Making of Modern Identity*. Cambridge: Cambridge University Press, 1989.

Taylor, Charles, *Modern Social Imaginaries*. Durham and London: Duke University Press, 2004).

Thompson, Willie. *What Happened to History?* London: Pluto Press, 2000.

Thomson, Alistair. "Anzac Memories: Putting Popular Theory into Practice in Australia," in *The Houses of History*, edited by Anna Green and Kathleen Troup, 239-52. Manchester: Manchester University Press, 1999.

2 Re-imagining a People: Towards a Theory of Peoplehood as Social Imaginary

Bernard Eric Jensen

> *Nations and states are of our own making and can be remade according to other images.*
> *– Richard Kearney, Postnationalist Ireland, 1997*

The question of peoplehood in plural societies can be approached in two interrelated ways. We can set out to study past history in order to determine the present state of affairs with regard to peoplehood in plural societies, and we can also explore how prevailing conditions could be changed with a view to making history through an act of intervention. To the extent that we want to meet the latter challenge, we have to employ an approach to politics that throws light upon the process of how people's identities are shaped and re-shaped.[1]

In 1989, Stuart Hall and Martin Jacques published a collection of essays entitled *New Times: the Changing Face of Politics in the 1990s*. One of these essays deals with the political significance of shaping and re-shaping people's identities. In her essay *The Politics of Identity* Rosalind Brunt wrote:

> The question of identity is at the heart of any transformatory project. [... It is] a politics whose starting point is about recognising the degree to which political activity and effort involves a continuous process of making and re-making ourselves – and our selves in relation to others. [...] And unless and until we have an adequate recognition of the ways identities work, we are not going to be that effective at world-changing.[2]

Thus, one of the questions to be addressed is: What does it take to re-imagine a people? The concept of an imagined community appears to be very attractive here because if a political community is something imagined, then it also should be possible to re-imagine – that is, to re-shape – such a community. However, in this

---

1. Bernard Eric Jensen, "History and the Politics of Identity: Reflections on a Contested and Intricate Issue," in *Bruk og misbruk av historien*, ed. Sirkka Ahonen et al. (Trondheim: NTNU, 2000), 43-67.
2. Rosalind Brunt, "The Politics of Identity," in *New Times: The Changing Face of Politics in the 1990s*, ed. Stuart Hall and Martin Jacques (London: Lawrence & Wishart, 1989), 150-153.

case we not only need to understand its constituent components; we need to have insight into how it is established and functions in everyday life.

Benedict Anderson's achievement and shortcomings

It is now more than 25 years since Benedict Anderson (b. 1936) published his influential book *Imagined Communities: Reflections on the Origin and Spread of Nationalism*. It first appeared in 1983, a second revised and enlarged edition came out in 1991, and a third revised and enlarged edition in 2006. It has been published in 33 countries and in 29 languages. Moreover, its publication has been seen at times as a deliberate attempt to make history. For example, George Soro's Open Society Institute decided to fund translations of this book into Eastern European languages specifically to further the establishment of pluralist democracies in Eastern Europe.

Over the past 25 years Anderson's book has exerted a remarkable influence upon the theoretical frameworks employed in ongoing research on the building of nation-states and the formation of national identities. Its impact has been due, in part, to the fact that scholars from many disciplines have come to see his way of defining a nation as a very fertile one. The key formulation in *Imagined Communities* is now almost a classic definition:

> The nation [...] is an imagined political community. [...] It is imagined because the members of even the smallest nation never know most of their fellow-members, meet them, or even hear of them, yet in the minds of each lives the image of their communion.[3]

The feature highlighted in this definition appears – on reflection – to be a rather obvious one, once the point has been made. Yet, it is Anderson's achievement to have generated insight into this very basic and salient feature of human communities and to have made their imagining the starting-point of an eye-opening analysis of one of the distinct communities in modern times.

In defining the nation as an imagined community, Anderson succeeds in identifying one of its constituent features. But he does not go on to develop a theory of imagined communities, as such. As Ernesto Laclau has noted, the reader of Anderson's book is frequently uncertain as to whether he "[...] is referring to the nation as a specific imagined community or whether he is speaking of any imagined community."[4] It transpires that Anderson's analysis has two crucial shortcomings.

---

3. Benedict Anderson, *Imagined Communities: Reflections on the Origin and Spread of Nationalism*, rev. ed. (London: Verso, 2006), 6.
4. Ernesto Laclau, "On Imagined Communities," in *Grounds of Comparison: Around the Work of Benedict Anderson*, ed. Pheng Cheah and Jonathan Culler (New York: Routledge, 2003), 23.

It does not address the question of how an imagined community is actually constructed in any detailed way, nor does it provide a satisfactory explanation of its ontological status.

Anderson has important things to say about how a community is imagined. He formulates the principle that "communities are to be distinguished [...] by the style in which they are imagined," and goes on to pinpoint the characteristic features of a nation: it is imagined as limited, sovereign, and as a community.[5] He also makes the related point that a nation is to be understood as "a cultural artefact of a particular kind," but has nothing specific to say about how such an artefact is constructed. The reason why he side-steps this issue follows from the manner in which he explains the initial emergence of nations:

> To understand [nations] properly we need to consider carefully how they have come into historical being [...] I will be trying to argue that the creation of [the nation as a cultural artefact] towards the end of the eighteenth century was the spontaneous distillation of a complex 'crossing' of discrete historical forces.[6]

Anderson identifies the set of discrete historical forces that account for the initial emergence of a national political community: the printing press, a new concept of time and space, the use of vernacular languages, etc. But he does not clarify how these forces merged and were able to generate a new kind of imagined community. The attempt to explain this achievement as "a spontaneous distillation" merely begs the question. However, once the nation was established, Anderson explains the successive emergence of nations by a process of imitation – or, using Anderson's own terms, "the transplanting of a modular."

Anderson also describes an imagined community as a form for human "self-consciousness" but has nothing much to say about the character or functions of human consciousness. It is indeed surprising that Anderson sets out to explore the character of a specific kind of political community without referring at any point to debates in the human and social sciences about how to understand human collectives. Is such a community to be understood as an aggregate of individuals (atomism/individualism) or as something trans-individual (holism/collectivism)?[7] Thus, Anderson's first theoretical shortcoming is that he does not deal satisfactorily with the question of how an imagined community is constructed.

This shortcoming may plausibly be explained by the rather eclectic theoretical framework of *Imagined Communities* – a fact that Anderson openly acknowledges in

---

5.   Anderson, *Imagined Communities*, 6-7.

6.   Ibid., 4.

7.   Cf. Philip Pettit, *The Common Mind: An Essay on Psychology, Society and Politics* (New York: Oxford University Press, 1996).

the postscript to the 2006 edition of his book.[8] In the main, the analysis is based upon a variant of historical materialism, but he opts, so to speak, to import a social constructivist notion into this materialist framework when defining an imagined community as a cultural artefact. Moreover, this eclecticism helps to explain the book's other shortcoming, concerning the ontological status of an imagined community.

The term "imagined" is a tricky word in the English language. According to the *Oxford English Dictionary*, it can refer to (i) something that is invented, planned or designed – i.e. an artefact that forms an integral part of the real world. However, it also can refer to (ii) something that is merely conceived by the human mind and is therefore only supposed or fancied – i.e. that which has no real existence. It is clear from Anderson's critique of Ernest Gellner's position that he wishes to distance himself from the second usage of the term "imagined."[9] Yet he does not wholeheartedly endorse the first usage. This ambiguity becomes clear in the postscript to the 2006 edition when he makes the following point:

> The concept of 'imagined community' [... is] something unsettling, neither 'imaginary' as in 'unicorn', nor matter-of-factly 'real' as in 'TV set', but something analogous to Madame Bovary and Queequeg, whose existence stemmed only from the moments Flaubert and Melville imagined them for us.[10]

Anderson here places an imagined community ontologically on a par with Flaubert's realist fiction, thereby implying that people have not only been willing to kill, but also to die for the sake of something equivalent to a fictional story. Rather than accept this implication, I want to suggest that the theoretical ambiguity at issue is a corollary of the materialist ontology that forms the backbone of Anderson's analysis. It is this ontology that prevents him from exploring the character, status, and functions of human imagining.

Amending Benedict Anderson's shortcomings

I wish to outline a theoretical argument in favour of the notion of imagined communities that is more coherent and sound than the one found in Benedict Anderson's book. If this is to be done, it demands – I suggest – that this notion is lifted out of its historical materialist setting in *Imagined Communities* and re-placed it in a more clear-cut social constructivist framework. I will do this by drawing upon

---

8.   Anderson, *Imagined Communities*, 227.
9.   Ibid., 6.
10. Ibid., 227.

sets of insights put forward by three scholars: (i) the Canadian philosopher Charles Taylor (b.1931), (ii) the British-Jamaican sociologist Stuart Hall (b.1932), and the US philosopher David Carr (b.1940).

What do Taylor, Hall, and Carr have in common? As I see it, each of them (i) bases their present-day thinking upon a social constructivist understanding of human life. That is, they understand social life as being constructed and re-constructed continuously through people's meaningful actions and interaction. Each of them (ii) assigns a fundamental importance to people's signifying practices – the ongoing making and re-making of networks of meaning. Moreover, each of them (iii) understands narrative to be a constituent feature of human living. That is, they conceive of narrative as a constituent feature of a lived life and therefore of any adequate social ontology.

In recent years, Taylor in particular has employed Anderson's notion of an imagined community in his own work, notably in *Modern Social Imaginaries* (2004) and *A Secular Age* (2007). Taylor speaks very favourably about Anderson's work. However, as I see it, he distances himself – at least indirectly – from Anderson when it comes to the question of the ontological status of the imagined. While Anderson places the imagined on a par with realist fiction, Taylor wants to give it a rather different status. Towards the end of *Modern Social Imaginaries*, the following point is made:

> Like all forms of human imagination, the social imaginary can be full of self-serving fiction and suppression, but it also is an essential constituent of the real. It cannot be reduced to an insubstantial dream.[11]

At no point was Anderson willing to see the imagined as "an essential constituent of the real." It is his materialist ontology – I surmise – that prevents him from doing so. It is because Taylor is working within a social constructivist framework that he can do so. Within such a framework the imagined is understood to be an essential component of social reality since it decisively influences the shaping and re-shaping of human action and interaction. Human imagining is nothing less than a formidable and dynamic force in the life of humans, a pre-condition of human action and interaction.

Of all the attempts to develop Anderson's notion of an imagined community, I find Taylor's recent work to be the most promising. The premise of his *Modern Social Imaginaries* is that social imaginaries play a decisive role in human social life, and he therefore wants to clarify their nature and functions.

---

11. Charles Taylor, *Modern Social Imaginaries* (Durham: Duke University Press, 2004), 183.

By social imaginaries, I mean [...] the ways people imagine their social existence, how they fit together with others, how things go on between them and their fellows, the expectations that are normally met, and the deeper normative notions and images that underlie these expectations.[12]

Taylor's concept of social imaginary is not only complex, it is a multi-layered and intersectional concept. Thus, it attempts to identify crucial points of intersection between the minds and actions of humans. It seeks to integrate within a single framework: (i) the tacit and thematized dimensions of human consciousness; (ii) its descriptive, metaphorical, and normative dimensions; (iii) its emotive and cognitive dimensions; (iv) its narrative and theoretical modes of operating; and (v) the realizing of plans through human action and interaction. Attempting to include so many dimensions within a single concept may appear to be a hazardous undertaking. However, it can be argued that the merging or intersecting of these dimensions is precisely what goes on in and between people when they perceive and conceive, act and interact, in everyday life.

Employing social imaginaries is not – to use one of Taylor's favourite phrases – "an optional extra." It is rather to be understood as a pre-condition of being able to function socially in so far as social imaginaries enable people to interact with other human beings and navigate social settings. A culture comprises a repertory of social imaginaries that people use to shape and re-shape their ongoing processes of meaning-making, and an imagined community is shaped by the set of social imaginaries that its members employ and share.

Moreover, a theory of social imaginaries has a broader range of application than a theory of nationhood or peoplehood. The notion of social imaginary is related to that of peoplehood in the following way (see Fig. 1):

The figure highlights the following points: (i) whereas a nation is based upon a notion of peoplehood, not all forms of peoplehood are conceived of as nations; (ii) whereas a people is an imagined community, there are also imagined communities that do not conceive of themselves as constituting a people; and (iii) whereas any imagined community will employ social imaginaries, there are also imaginaries that concern humans as distinct individuals rather than as members of a group.

---

12. Ibid., 23.

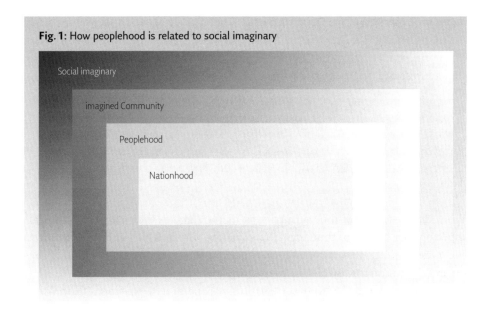

Fig. 1: How peoplehood is related to social imaginary

Social imaginary

imagined Community

Peoplehood

Nationhood

Towards a theory of social imaginary

The thrust of Taylor's analyses in *Modern Social Imaginaries* (2004) and *A Secular Age* (2007) seeks to identify the new set of interrelated social imaginaries, which together have come to constitute the self-understanding that forms the foundation of the present-day moral order in the Western world. I will be moving in a different direction by attempting to clarify the underlying assumption of any conception of social imaginary. For that reason, I will not concern myself with the issue of whether or not the imaginaries in question are pre-modern, modern or postmodern. The following theorems are to be highlighted:

1. Culture is a constitutive condition of social life.
2. Humans are language-using animals.
3. Humans are social animals.
4. Humans are self-interpreting animals.
5. Humans are inter-subjective animals.
6. Human are animals with cultural identities.
7. Humans are story-telling animals.
8. Culture is a crucial way of regulating human affairs.

Stuart Hall was part of the Open University Team that published a six-volume study of *Culture, Media and Identities* in 1997. This work is based on the idea of a circuit of culture, rendering culture a crucial constituent of all dimensions of social life. Hall addresses a pertinent issue about "The Centrality of Culture":

> [...] a major conceptual revolution is in the making in the human and social sciences. [...] It refers to an approach to contemporary social analysis which has made culture a constitutive condition of existence of social life, rather than a dependent variable, provoking a paradigm shift in the humanities and social sciences in recent years which has come to be known as the 'cultural turn'. Essentially, the 'cultural turn' began with a revolution in attitudes towards language.[13]

What Hall describes as the "cultural turn" is the same as the emergence of social-constructivist modes of thinking. It "signals the way in which culture creeps into every nook and crevice of contemporary social life, creating a proliferation of secondary environments, mediating everything."[14]

The assertion that "culture is a constitutive condition of existence of social life" is an apposite formulation of one of the main assumptions of social-constructivist thinking. The phrase "constitutive condition" not only implies that cultural activity is an indispensable element of all social life, it also means that cultural activity is understood to be a dynamic and mobilizing force in human life. It is culture that shapes and re-shapes the lives of humans.

I now want to pinpoint some anthropological assumptions that can ground the idea of culture as being a constitutive condition of social life. By identifying what appear to be the characteristic features of human animals, I will also be singling out some of the key issues for the agenda when the question of the viability of a social-constructivist approach is under discussion.

Humans are not the only animals to use "language" when communicating with conspecifics, and some of the ways in which humans use language are similar to those of other higher mammals. However, Taylor also makes the point that humans use language in distinctly human ways, including what he terms a constitutive use of language. This refers to the creative use of language – one that not only "makes possible its own content," but is also able to transform the ways in which people live their lives.

> Linguistic beings [i.e. humans] are capable of new feelings which affectively reflect their richer sense of their world: not just anger, but indignation; not just desire, but love and admiration. [...] Gregarious apes may have what we call a 'dominant male', but only language beings can

13. Stuart Hall, "The Centrality of Culture: Notes on the Cultural Revolutions of Our Time," in *Media and Cultural Regulation*, ed. Kenneth Thompson (Milton Keynes: Open University, 1997), 220.
14. Ibid., 215.

distinguish between leader, king, president, and the like. Animals mate and have off-spring, but only language beings define kinship.[15]

The idea of a constitutive use of language is crucial when it comes to clarifying how an imagined community is established. Hall makes a somewhat similar point employing a different terminology. Where Taylor talks of a constitutive use of language, Hall speaks of signifying practices, yet both are describing how meaning-making gives the life of humans its distinct character. Hall explains it in the following way:

> In a sense, culture has always been important. [...] Human beings are meaning-making, interpretive beings. [...] Systems or codes of meaning give significance to our actions. They allow us to interpret meaningfully the actions of others. Taken together, they constitute our 'cultures'. They help to ensure that all social action is 'cultural', that all social practices [...] are 'signifying practices'.[16]

The theorem that humans are language-using animals is closely related to that which states that humans are social animals. In the former, it is implicitly assumed that people learn the distinct or different languages they employ – their use of gestures, sounds, images, signs, spoken, and written words – through interactions with other people. The latter theorem goes a step further by making the social-constructionist point that humans only become functioning persons by becoming part of a group – that is, by being members of a community. In *Sources of the Self* (1989), Taylor puts it this way:

> [...] one cannot be a self on one's own. I am a self only in relation to certain interlocutors. [...] A self exists only within [...] 'webs of interlocution'. It is this original situation which gives its sense to our conception of 'identity', offering an answer to the question of who I am through a definition of where I am speaking from and to whom [...that is with] reference to a defining community.[17]

Understanding the social embeddedness of humans in this way can be described as holistic individualism,[18] because it stresses that humans cannot become fully human without – at least for a time – being a part of and thus participating in a community. However, by distinguishing between formal ("we are always socially embedded") and material modes of social embeddedness (the specific social imaginaries employed in a given instance), holistic individualism also makes it possible

---

15. Charles Taylor, *Philosophical Arguments* (Cambridge, MA: Harvard University Press, 1997), 105-106.
16. Hall, "The Centrality of Culture," 208.
17. Charles Taylor, *Sources of the Self: The Making of Modern Identity* (Cambridge: Cambridge University Press, 1989), 36.
18. Cf. Taylor, *Philosophical Arguments*, 301.

to understand that communities may be highly collectivist as well as distinctly individualist in orientation. The specific orientation depends on the social imaginaries that are employed.[19]

To the foregoing three theorems, I now want to add a fourth: that humans are self-interpreting animals. This is one of the themes Taylor has returned to over the years, and it is essential when seeking to clarify how an imagined community functions. In *Human Agency and Language* (1985), Taylor writes:

> [...] the slogan that human beings are self-interpreting animals [means] that there is no such thing as what they are, independently of how they understand themselves. To use Bert Dreyfus' evocative term, they are interpretations all the way down.[20]

The point being made here is a standard one within the hermeneutic-phenomenological tradition: one cannot adequately understand human action and interaction without attending to the ways in which the actors themselves understand these activities. Yet it may guard against a possible misunderstanding if it is mentioned that self-interpreting here refers to the full range of human consciousness, from a tacit-performative level right through to a thematized-explicated self-understanding. Thus, self-interpretation also includes the largely unstructured and inarticulate understandings that people have of themselves and the world in which they live and act.

The tacit-performative levels of consciousness are especially important when dealing with people's social imaginaries because – as Taylor points out – "humans operated with a social imaginary, well before they ever got into the business of theorizing about themselves."[21] Thus, "the ways people imagine their social existence, how they fit together with others, how things go on between them and their fellows" become pertinent issues in describing how an imagined community functions in everyday life.[22]

A further theorem to the effect that humans are also inter-subjective animals needs to be added to this list. In a recent study of human evolution, the point is made that "what originally differentiated the human species from other primates was our extended capacity to read each others' intentions and mental states – our capacity for inter-subjectivity, or mind-reading."[23] The focus here will be on how the issue of human inter-subjectivity clarifies the manner in which an imagined community functions.

Among the existing attempts to explain how a human community is constructed

---

19. Charles Taylor, "The Great Disembedding," chap. 3 in *A Secular Age* (Cambridge, MA: Harvard University Press, 2007).

20. Charles Taylor, *Human Agency and Language* (Cambridge: Cambridge University Press, 1985), 191.

21. Taylor, *A Secular Age*, 173.

22. Taylor, *Modern Social Imaginaries*, 23.

23. Jerome Bruner, *Making Stories: Law, Literature, Life* (Cambridge, MA: Harvard University Press, 2002), 16.

and maintained, I consider that presented by David Carr in *Time, Narrative, and History* (1986) to be the most persuasive. He argues for the existence of forms of trans-individual subjectivity without implying the existence of anything in the nature of a "group mind" or a "supra-personal subject." Carr first presented his analysis in an article entitled "'Cogitamus Ergo Sumus': The Intentionality of the First-Person Plural" (1986) – mentioned here because that title indicates the thrust of his entire argument.[24] While it is standard procedure within phenomenological research to undertake analyses from a first-person perspective, Carr argues that humans do not only perceive, act, and interact as first-person subjects – that is, as an *I*. Humans also perceive, act and interact as parts of a group – that is, as parts of a *we*, or what he terms a "we-subject."

> We are saying that individuals, in their sense of and use of 'we', certainly take [groups] to exist and that their taking them to exist in a sense makes it so. In saying 'we' the individual identifies himself with the group and thus, in a Husserlian sense of the word, constitutes the group as comprising those who similarly, in the relevant context, say 'we'.[25]

The starting point of his analysis is groups of people that know each other face-to-face – for instance, a family or a football team. But Carr goes on to analyze how a community of people who do not know each other face-to-face is established and functions – understood as a mental projection of the same kind of inter-subjective consciousness that is operative in a group whose members do know each other face-to-face. Carr at no stage employs the term "imagined community," but his analysis of how such communities are established provides the missing link in Benedict Anderson's *Imagined Communities* (1983/2006), namely, the theoretical clarification of how an imagined community is constructed.

It should also be noted that most people are, most of the time, members of a plurality of groups and they will therefore employ a plurality of we-subjects in their everyday lives. Humans do not have one identity, but a multiplicity of identities. This is not least true in regard to their inter-subjective identities – that is, the identities they share with other people. Whether such identities are relatively stable or precarious is an open question.

I will now move on to the sixth theorem, which states that humans are animals with cultural identities. It is one of the key tenets of social-constructivist thought that human identities are socially constructed. For this reason Taylor stresses that "social embeddedness is [...] partly an identity thing."[26] In explaining how an imagined community functions, it is people's shared or inter-subjective identities

---

24. Reprinted in David Carr, *Interpreting Husserl* (Dordrecht: Martinus Nijhoff, 1987), 281-295.

25. David Carr, *Time, Narrative, and History* (Bloomington: Indiana University Press 1986), 133.

26. Taylor, *A Secular Age*, 149.

that are the important ones. However, the formation of human identities – whether shared or individual – takes place through a complex set of signifying processes (for instance, the process of identification), and in that way the available cultures become internalized by the people living in these cultures. Parts of these cultures become – so to speak – part of their identities. This process can be described in the following way:

> [A] crucial feature of human life is its dialogical character. We become full human agents, capable of understanding ourselves, and hence of defining our identity, through the acquisition of rich human languages of expression. [...] The genesis of the human mind is [...] not monological, not something each person accomplishes on his or her own, but dialogical. [...] We define our identity always in dialogue with, sometimes in struggles against, the things our significant others want to see in us.[27]

Human identities are the outcome of ongoing dialogues and struggles between people. However, they also have a built-in narrative structure, which brings us to the seventh theorem stating that humans are story-telling animals.

As I see it, the most penetrating analysis of the narrative dimension of human life is found in David Carr's *Time, Narrative, and History* (1986), in which narrative is seen as an integral part of an adequate social ontology. Carr argues that:

> [...] narrative activity [...] has a practical function in life, that is, it is often a constitutive part of action, and not just an embellishment, commentary, or other incidental accompaniment. [... Stories] are told in being lived and lived in being told. The actions and suffering of life can be viewed as a process of telling ourselves stories, listening to those stories, and acting them out or living them through.[28]

What is crucial in the present context is the fact that many of the social imaginaries employed by people are stories about their *we*-subjects. It is by means of the ongoing use of such stories – it is argued – that inter-subjective identities are formed, thereby establishing a community and enabling it to function as such.[29] But at the same time it should be noted that "[...] a community is often characterized not by a single story of its origins, unity, and tasks, on which all agree, but by rival and conflicting stories.[30]

Struggles about storied social imaginaries, told and queried at a given time and place, bring us to the eighth and last of the theorems to be addressed, which states

---

27. Taylor, *Philosophical Arguments*, 230.
28. Carr, *Time, Narrative, and History*, 61.
29. Cf. Taylor, "Modes of Narration," chap. 12 in *Modern Social Imaginaries*.
30. Carr, *Time, Narrative, and History*,152.

that culture is one of the crucial ways of regulating human affairs. When culture is seen as being a constitutive condition of social life, the corollary is that one of the main ways of exerting power in social life will be by regulating and controlling existing signifying practices. Stuart Hall, in particular, has attended to this dimension of social constructivist thought and analysis. In order to handle this issue, he has coined the phrase "governing by culture." He wants to make it manifestly clear that cultural politics is one of the central arenas in which the wielding of power takes place today. Cultural politics is a key site of power struggles.

> [...] we [have] come to recognize that 'culture' is no soft option. It can no longer be studied as some unimportant, secondary or dependent variable in what makes the modern world move and shake, but has to be seen as something primary and constitutive, determining its shape and character as well as its inner life.[31]

Governing by culture also takes the form of governing through identities,[32] and it therefore follows that there is a need to focus attention on the complex set of issues involved in elucidating the ways in which the storied social imaginaries of a given society are presented, used, legitimated, or opposed in ongoing processes of acculturation.

Re-imagining a people

In her review article on *The Politics and Perils of Peoplehood* (2006), Sheila Croucher highlights what she describes as "the muddy theoretical waters" of peoplehood.[33] I have tried here to find a way of navigating our way out of such a theoretical morass. I have argued that if this is to be achieved, we need, first, to move Benedict Anderson's key concept out of its materialist framework – as expounded in his book on *Imagined Community* – and to reposition this concept within a clear-cut social constructivist framework. As the next step, we need to explore in detail how a people becomes established and functions through their employment of social imaginaries. Peoplehood can be then understood as having the following characteristics:

- ▶ It is a special form of human inter-subjectivity.
- ▶ It is grounded in shared forms of we-consciousness.
- ▶ It has an ontological status somewhat similar to that of the human self.

---

31. Hall, "The Centrality of Culture," 215.
32. Cf. Stephen Lawler, "Becoming ourselves: governing and/through identities," chap. 4 in *Identity: Sociological Perspectives* (Cambridge: Polity Press, 2008).
33. Sheila Croucher, "The Politics and Perils of Peoplehood," *International Studies Review* 8 (2006): 77-89.

▶ It is constituted by its members perceiving their life-world from a first-person *we*-perspective and acting in this world while employing such a perspective.

▶ It is shaped by the repertory of storied social imaginaries that its members employ in their everyday self-interpretations.

▶ It forms a complex network of meanings that – to a greater or lesser extent – is shared and used by its members.

I now want to return to my opening question: What does it take to re-imagine a people? It is certainly possible to re-imagine a people and this probably happens all the time. This much is clear from the analyses presented in, for instance, Charles Taylor's books on *Modern Social Imaginaries* (2004) and *A Secular Age* (2007). At times, it transpires that re-imagining has been intentional, the result of people's pursuit of specific projects. At other times, it appears rather to have been unintended.

However, the fact that it is possible to re-imagine a people does not mean that it is easy to plan or control such a process of re-imagining. Employing social imaginaries in our everyday lives is not optional; this, it would seem, is part of the human condition. But we can – to a degree – exert control over the specific social imaginaries that we do employ in our everyday lives.

At least two challenging tasks have to be faced with regard to a projected re-imagining of a people. The first is that it is never possible to start – so to speak – at a zero point. Seeking to modify a specific imagined community entails re-working or even dismantling the social imaginaries that are being employed at a given time and place. This is a formidable task, the reason for which is given in the following:

[…] identity is memory. As Hegel put it, 'das Wesen ist das Gewesene'. 'What is is what it has become'. Or more simply, the past is always present.[34]

Our past is sedimented in our present, and we are doomed to misidentify ourselves, as long as we can't do justice to where we came from. This is why the narrative is not an optional extra.[35]

The continuing appeal of and allegiance to that which Michael Ignatieff in *Blood and Belonging* (2000) terms "ethnic nationalism" illustrates just how difficult it is to dismantle one of the imagined communities that continues to exert a decisive influence in our present-day world.[36] It has been able to hold its sway over many people's social imaginaries in everyday life long after the theoretical justification of such a manner of thinking has been undermined within the academic world.

The second task is equally difficult. It concerns the construction of a new or a

---

34. Richard Kearney, *On Stories* (London: Routledge, 2002), 81.
35. Taylor, *A Secular Age*, 29.
36. Michael Ignatieff, *Blood and Belonging: Journeys into the New Nationalism* (London: Vintage, 2000).

modified imagined community. This task calls for nothing less than a re-interpretation of the available repertory of social imaginaries or the invention and diffusion of some new ones. It also includes the task of working out the metaphors and story lines that will form integral parts of an imagined community at a future point in time. This task is no less formidable than the first. Thus, although it is possible to re-imagine a people, it is exceedingly difficult to do so, at least in the short term.

Bibliography

Anderson, Benedict. *Imagined Communities: Reflections on the Origin and Spread of Nationalism*. Rev. ed. London: Verso, 2006.

Bruner, Jerome. *Making Stories: Law, Literature, Life*. Cambridge, MA: Harvard University Press, 2002.

Brunt, Rosalind. "The Politics of Identity," in *New Times: The Changing Face of Politics in the 1990s*, edited by Stuart Hall and Martin Jacques, 150-159. London: Lawrence & Wishart, 1989.

Carr, David. *Time, Narrative, and History*. Bloomington: Indiana University Press, 1986.

Carr, David. *Interpreting Husserl: Critical and Comparative Studies*. Dordrecht: Martinus Nijhoff, 1987.

Croucher, Sheila. "The Politics and Perils of Peoplehood." *International Studies Review* 8 (2006): 77-89.

Hall, Stuart. "The Centrality of Culture: Notes on the Cultural Revolutions of Our Time." In *Media and Cultural Regulation*, edited by Kenneth Thompson, 207-238. Milton Keynes: Open University, 1997.

Ignatieff, Michael. *Blood and Belonging: Journeys into the New Nationalism*. London: Vintage, 2000.

Jensen, Bernard Eric. "History and the Politics of Identity: Reflections on a Contested and Intricate Issue." In *Bruk og misbruk av historien*, edited by Sirkka Ahonen et al., 43-67. Trondheim: NTNU, 2000.

Kearney, Richard. *Postnationalist Ireland: Politics, Culture, Philosophy*. London: Routledge, 1997.

Kearney, Richard. *On Stories*. London: Routledge, 202.

Laclau, Ernesto. "On Imagined Communities," in *Grounds of Comparison: Around the Work of Benedict Anderson*, edited by Pheng Cheah and Jonathan Culler, 21-28. New York: Routledge, 2003.

Lawler, Steph. *Identity: Sociological Perspectives*. Cambridge: Polity Press, 2008.

Pettit, Philip. *The Common Mind: An Essay on Psychology, Society and Politics*. New York: Oxford University Press, 1996.

Taylor, Charles. *Human Agency and Language*. Cambridge: Cambridge University Press, 1985.

Taylor, Charles. *Sources of the Self: The Making of Modern Identity*. Cambridge: Cambridge University Press, 1989.

Taylor, Charles. *Philosophical Arguments*. Cambridge, MA: Harvard University Press, 1997.

Taylor, Charles. *Modern Social Imaginaries*. Durham: Duke University Press, 2004.

Taylor, Charles. *A Secular Age*. Cambridge, MA: Harvard University Press, 2007.

3 Citizenship, Belonging and Identification: The State of Denmark

Richard Jenkins

One of the founding principles of modern geo-politics is that national identity and citizenship should, in principle at least, more or less overlap, each finding mutually reinforcing expression in a nation-state's culture and institutions.[1] This assumption reflects an axiomatic acceptance of the nation-state as *the* definitive modern form of polity on the one hand, and a loosely cultural, or ethnic, definition of national identity on the other. As conventional academic wisdom, it was the context for the long-standing emphasis in academic debate upon citizenship and social stratification, inspired by Marshall.[2] Increasingly, however, this assumption has been called into question as the focus has gradually shifted towards an engagement with the realities of globalization.[3] The question now is what happens to citizenship predicated upon national identity when national borders are no longer, as they once apparently were, relatively secure political containers, and nation-states may increasingly no longer be sovereign political entities?

The internal affairs of states are still bound up with this issue, of course: another question that has received some attention in the contemporary literature is what happens when there is an endogenous "disconnect" between citizenship and national identity. The paradigmatic examples of this kind of problem seem to be found in multi-ethnic or multicultural states, in which nominal universal state citizenship exists without at least some kind of unified ethno-national identity, the central concern being the rights and protection, and sometimes the responsibilities, of minorities.[4]

1. For an example of a tussle about the relationship between nationality and citizenship in the context of an expanding and integrating Europe that is simultaneously struggling to cope with non-EU immigration, see the debate between Delanty and Rex. G. Delanty, "Beyond the Nation-State: National Identity and Citizenship in a Multicultural Society – A Response to Rex," *Sociological Research Online* 1 (1996): 3, www.socresonline.org.uk/socresonline/1/3/1.html; J. Rex, "National Identity in the Democratic Multi-Cultural State," *Sociological Research Online* 1 (1996): 2, www.socresonline.org.uk/socresonline/1/2/1.html.
2. T.H. Marshall, *Citizenship and Social Class and Other Essays* (Cambridge: Cambridge University Press, 1959).
3. D.I. Miller, *Citizenship and National Identity* (Cambridge: Polity Press, 2000); R. Munch, *Nation and Citizenship in the Global Age: From National to Transnational Ties and Identities* (Basingstoke: Palgrave Macmillan, 2001); T.K. Oommen, *Citizenship and National Identity: From Colonialism to Globalism* (London: Sage, 1997).
4. W. Kymlicka, *Multicultural Citizenship: A Liberal Theory of Minority Rights* (Oxford: Oxford University Press, 1996).

There are arguments to be had about the nature of state borders, the wisdom of treating the nation-state as our axiomatic baseline, the reality of the nation-state's apparent decline, and the notion that multi-ethnic collectivities are anything other than the historical and contemporary norm, but I cannot address them here.[5] Instead, in this chapter I shall explore an alternative perspective on the relationship between citizenship and national identity, and suggest that we should not, in fact, expect that, in any specific political context, modern citizenship and national identity should "fit" each other. They are historically and politically two rather different kinds of "belonging" and may potentially be disagreeable bedfellows. This holds good even in those western European and northern American democracies in which the image of "citizenship-cum-national-identity" has developed.

Citizenship

If we buy into the well-known political and intellectual genealogy of the notion of citizenship that reaches back to the Greek city-states of antiquity, then what it means to be "a citizen" seems clear and straightforward: it's a matter of membership in a "common society."[6] Stripped down to its bare bones, citizenship is the bundle of rights and responsibilities that accrues to those who are politically participant members of a polity.[7] It is a contractual relationship between, on the one hand, concrete human individuals and, on the other, those more or less abstract collectivities that are organized to distribute resources and to defend the territory, hearth and home, to which they belong.[8] In order to bring this definition into focus some further comments, none of which are spectacularly original, are necessary.

First, the practical meaning of political participation is historically and locally variable; it is sometimes even variable *within* polities. Simply focusing on "the vote" for purposes of illustration, there is a broad spectrum of modern enfranchisement and electoral systems: from the complexities of various kinds of proportional representation to the apparent clarity of first-past-the-post systems, taking in local specialities such as electoral colleges, primaries, and so on *en route*. What's more, being a "participant member" does not necessarily mean voting in public, more or

5. See R. Jenkins, *Rethinking Ethnicity: Arguments and Explorations*, 2nd ed. (London: Sage, 2008), 26-41; R. Jenkins, *Social Identity*, 3rd ed. (London: Routledge, 2008), 18-27.
6. J.M. Barbalet, *Citizenship* (Milton Keynes: Open University Press, 1988), 1.
7. I use the broad expression "polity" here in order to allow consideration of the pre-modern and modern versions of citizenship without becoming bogged down in discussions about the nature of "the state" in different eras.
8. See J.M. Barbalet, *Citizenship*; K. Faulks, *Citizenship* (London: Routledge, 2000); and B.S. Turner, ed., *Citizenship and Social Theory* (London: Sage, 1993) for general discussions of citizenship that have informed this opening discussion.

less transparent elections to a legislature. It certainly didn't in Athens or Rome, and it doesn't in contemporary Saudi Arabia, Brunei, or Myanmar, for example. All that is meant by the expression is an accepted right to express a public opinion in an appropriate forum about how local affairs should be run.

Second, who can be a participant member is also important. Until the very recent modern era, even in those polities with a category of membership that resembled citizenship, citizens were a minority, and sometimes a tiny minority. Participant citizenship, however it is defined locally, has never been the only possible way of belonging to a polity. Full inclusion in the category "citizen" depended, and in some respects and places still depends, upon gender (citizenship for women is a twentieth-century phenomenon, which is not yet globally universal), legal status (slavery, serfdom, bonded labour or imprisonment are all conditions that may compromise or deny citizenship), ethnicity or "race" ("native peoples" or colonial subjects may be excluded from, or restricted in, their citizenship rights), age status (the acquisition of legal rights and responsibilities, not least political rights, is often a threshold of adulthood), and intellectual and psychological competence (incapacity of one sort or other may be a disqualification). In late nineteenth-century France, for example, women, prisoners, Muslim Algerians, minors and mad people may have been considered "French," in one way or another, but they were French without full French citizenship rights. To take another example, it is not unheard of for non-nationals to be able to vote in some states, in some circumstances; this does not, however, make them citizens. There are degrees of belonging, and of participation; they need not map on to each other. It is important, therefore, to distinguish between the specific political category "citizenship" and general ethno-national membership and identification, as they are not necessarily entailed in each other.

Third, and allowing for what I have just said, the twentieth century did witness convergences between citizenship and national identity, as specified in this chapter's opening sentence. In the western democracies this happened because successful campaigns for universal suffrage created a need for an inclusive criterion that could determine who should be entitled to citizenship rights;[9] nationality more or less fitted the bill. In other kinds of polity – and even, to be fair, in some "democracies" – these two categories of group membership have overlapped only in part; the relationship between them can vary enormously, according to local circumstances and practices. This suggests that in a more thoroughgoing analysis than I have space for here we should need at least three, only partly and contingently overlapping,

---

9. It is worth remembering that even "universal" citizenship may in practice compromise the citizenship rights and responsibilities of some citizens (for example, those who have been authoritatively categorized as incompetent in one way or another).

categories: the *citizenship* of politically participant membership, the *nationality* of the passport, and *national identity* as an ethnic category.

Fourth, the existence of citizenship does not actually presuppose or require that all citizens should be equal. Apart from the bald fact of participation rights – which may mean very little in practice – there are no other implications of equity, whether in terms of status, welfare, income, or effective power. Participation in political decision-making offers no guarantees of effective representation or influence, and the responsibilities of citizenship – most obviously liability for military service and taxation – are not necessarily in proportion to the accompanying rights. Once again, there is much that is locally variable.

Fifth, there has been no continuous "progressive" evolution of the notion of citizenship. The genealogy referred to earlier is discontinuous and – as with all genealogies, perhaps – mythical. The concept of citizenship, such as it was at the time, vanished along with the western Roman Empire, reappearing in an attenuated form in some of the city-states of medieval Europe, before being locally influential during some of the political conflicts of the Reformation (in England and Geneva, for example). The eighteenth-century American and French Revolutions marked the beginnings of the modern hegemony of citizenship as the basis for organizing politics, and while knowledge of ancient Greece and Rome may have been a useful rhetorical resource during those struggles, it stretches the facts to claim that modern citizenship is directly descended from the *politeia* of ancient Greece. "Citizenship" has since become the axiomatic global political membership category – rivalled only by "identity"[10] – and is perhaps the dominant political discourse of the contemporary world. However, it is not clear, coherent, nor agreed upon, but a fuzzy abstract symbol, capable of achieving precision only in its many local definitions.

Finally, as a consequence of local political histories, variations in the meanings and practices of citizenship, and contemporary geo-political realities, there is no necessary homology or overlap within any modern state between definitions and understandings of national membership and of citizenship. This is not just a matter of contradictions between aspirational universal citizenship and the messy multi-ethnic realities of many modern states (although those contradictions are real enough, and consequential). Other things may be significant as well. I will mention only two – there are doubtless others – which may co-exist and reinforce each other. First, the contractual basis of the relationship between the *individual* citizen

---

10. For staunch critiques of the contemporary political significance of "identity," in particular the ideological notion that "identity" is a collective and individual good, the nurture and defence of which cannot be questioned and the imperatives of which are irresistible, and of the complicity of social science in reproducing this see S. Malešević, *Identity as Ideology: Understanding Ethnicity and Nationalism* (Basingstoke: Palgrave Macmillan, 2006).

and the state may not fit easily alongside a narrative of collective identity that is framed in more or less ethno-national terms and privileges members of a certain ethnic *group* or groups. Second, the continuing vitality of long-standing national "symbolic constructions", which – apparently anachronistically, but nonetheless meaningfully and powerfully – dramatize relationships between *subjects* and the state (embodied, perhaps, in the person of a ruler), may sit uneasily alongside the emphasis on rights and responsibilities that is so central to the relationship between *citizens* and the state.

So the normal – as opposed to the normative – relationship between national identity and citizenship should not be taken for granted as axiomatically close. There is no necessary reason why, in any given polity, the meanings and practices of citizenship and national identity should map on to each other in anything other than the most imperfect fashion. Next, although it is possible, and necessary, to talk in general ideal-typical terms about both citizenship and national identity, each should always be thought of in local plurals: we live in a world of citizenships and national identities, and it is these local meanings and practices that matter. Lastly, citizenship and ethno-nationality are both matters of group membership, one aspect of which is belonging. It is to belonging that I now turn.

Belonging

Citizenship is frequently talked about in terms of belonging.[11] But what does "belonging" mean? Simply put, belonging is a matter of being in the right place, with the right people, whether that place and those people are a family, a friendship network, a workplace, a community, an organisation, or a nation (or any other collectivity that you might think of). Or, rather, it is a matter of the *perception* of being in the right place, with the right people. Even more accurately, perhaps, it is a matter of the *sense* that one is in the right place, with the right people. Put thus, belonging, rather than being clear-cut or precisely bounded and defined, is likely to be a somewhat fuzzy business. This is a generic proposition that applies to more than the British fuzziness delineated by Robin Cohen:[12] all belonging and identification are, to a greater or less extent, routinely imprecise and contingent.

Anthony Cohen's writings about belonging and community may help us to

---

11. E.g. A. Baumeister, "Ways of Belonging: Ethnonational Minorities and Models of 'Differentiated Citizenship'," *Ethnicities* 3 (2003): 393-416; S. Castles and A. Davidson, *Citizenship and Migration: Globalization and the Politics of Belonging* (London: Routledge, 2000); J. Hampshire, *Citizenship and Belonging: Immigration and the Politics of Demographic Governance in Postwar Britain* (Basingstoke: Palgrave Macmillan, 2005); J. Shotter, "Psychology and Citizenship: Identity and Belonging," in *Citizenship and Social Theory*, ed. B.S. Turner (London: Sage, 1993).
12. R. Cohen, "Fuzzy Frontiers of Identity: The British Case," *Social Identities* 1 (1995): 35-62.

understand better this fuzziness and imprecision.[13] Drawing his inspiration in equal parts from Durkheim and Barth, thus combining two rather different approaches to understanding groups, Cohen argues that belonging and community are "symbolically constructed". A symbol is anything that more or less abstractly represents or stands for something else. What we hear and what we see are at the heart of symbolism. Communities are represented to, and by, their members through shared symbols, which can be anything from a flag, to a sports team, to an annual ceremony, to a personage, to a religion, to a language. It is in relationships to, and between, shared symbols that the meanings and practices of belonging are to be found.

Cohen then argues that belonging to, in, or with, a "community" – defined simply as a group that matters to its members – has nothing to do with the similarity, or equality, of its members. In fact, the reverse might almost be said to be true: belonging to a community works because its members *differ* from each other (as all individual humans must). The cohesive – or adhesive – power of symbols rests in the fact that they condense within them a range of meanings, not all of which will harmonize with each other. They do not have to; this is the whole point of symbols. The Christian cross, for example, may simultaneously evoke, to different people, God's sacrifice of His only Son in the interests of the salvation of humanity, Christian mercy and charity, the doctrine of "love thy neighbour as thyself", the Inquisition, the Crusades, the power of the Vatican, and fundamentalist protestant exclusivity. It is a palimpsest of love, mercy, tolerance, ideological conformism, violence, authority, and insubordination, each potentially illuminating and simultaneously obscuring the others. To take a modern, secular example, the iconic image of Elvis Presley stands for the youthful power of the original Sun recordings, trivially bad movies, "Crying in the Chapel," the black leather of the 1968 comeback, the ignominy of death-by-hamburger, and Graceland Inc. In principle, one can be a Christian or an Elvis fan, belonging to a community of Christians or Elvis fans, without having to accept all of these meanings and images, dwell upon your differences from other members, or venerate the symbols in the same practical fashions.

Their complex, condensed polysemy means that shared symbols belong to many different people, for whom they may mean different things and evoke different practices. Yet all these people can stand together in the shade or light of those symbols and "belong" without necessarily having to explore what might otherwise divide them. They are together and apart, similar and different. Consensus is not

---

13. A.P. Cohen, *Belonging: Identity and Social Organisation in British Rural Cultures* (Manchester: Manchester University Press, 1982); *The Symbolic Construction of Community* (London: Tavistock, 1985); *Symbolising Boundaries: Identity and Diversity in British Cultures* (Manchester: Manchester University Press, 1986); R. Jenkins, *Social Identity*, 132-144.

necessary, nor is conformity. What's more, people can belong to, and in, many different communities, and it is routine that they do, whether by drawing on some minimally shared symbolism or quarantining incompatible symbolic representations from each other. One might be an "Elvis fan for Jesus," in which case Elvis's gospel recordings would be an obvious point of shared reference (or reverence), or a Christian *and* an Elvis fan, in which case the two might be "kept in different boxes." Finally, because symbols mean different things to different people their meanings can never be regarded as finished business: different interpretations and constituencies may come and go, and all meanings are political.

The final major dimension of Cohen's model, for which he draws heavily on Barth,[14] is that community, and community membership, becomes most obvious to members – because all other things being equal it will be taken for granted – at its boundary. In other words, it is during dealings with non-members that members come to realize that they *are* members. It is also in interactions across boundaries that collective symbols are, so to speak, waved or paraded most vigorously. Although this point of view underplays the importance of interaction and relationships between members within the community – shared symbols can, for example, be both means and end in factional politics – it has one significant implication. Since collective boundaries are encountered during, and in some senses emerge out of, interaction, the contingencies of interaction mean that they are unlikely to be hard-edged or straight-lined. Symbols and communal belonging are practical matters of interaction, as are their meanings. Rather than being engraved on tablets of stone – or even *when* they are engraved on tablets of stone – their meanings and observances are, at least potentially, negotiable and changeable over time. Once again, "fuzzy" might be a good word.

For the purposes of the present discussion, one supplementary theme should be added to this understanding of the symbolic construction of community. Symbols do not merely have the capacity to reconcile incompatible or conflicting meanings and practices and to allow a diversity of individuals to feel a sense of belonging together; they also seem to be capable of making belonging, community, and identification *matter* to people, whether individually or collectively. Particularly when symbols are part of ceremonial or ritual,[15] they appear to be capable of touching the emotions, reaching hearts as well as minds; this is how belonging becomes a matter of *being* as well as *knowing*. It need not necessarily happen, and it is likely to do so to

14. F. Barth, "Introduction," in *Ethnic Groups and Boundaries: The Social Organisation of Culture Difference*, ed. Fredrik Barth (Oslo: Universitetsforlaget, 1969).
15. P. Connerton, *How Societies Remember* (Cambridge: Cambridge University Press, 1989); E. Durkheim, *The Elementary Forms of the Religious Life*, trans. J. W. Swain (London: George Allen and Unwin, 1976); R.L. Grimes, *Deeply into the Bone: Re-inventing Rites of Passage* (Berkeley: University of California Press, 2000); W.V. Turner, *The Ritual Process: Structure and Anti-Structure* (Harmondsworth: Pelican, 1974).

differing degrees, depending on local contingencies of history, circumstance and practice, but when it does it is not to be underestimated. *Why* this "affect effect" works is not at all well understood. As to *how* it works, however, if we want to understand these enchantments better we should probably look to shared rituals and ceremonies – the collective experience of events and occasions, particularly if people have been socialized into them, and have learned the appropriate emotional registers, early in life – rather than to anything that might inhere in symbols *per se*. That they do work should not, however, be in doubt: rulers, politicians, religious leaders, and generals have understood their effectiveness for millennia.

From this perspective, "belonging" – and by extension "community" – is fundamentally fuzzy, imprecise and perhaps even ambiguous. This is not just a matter of the language that we use to talk about belonging, either: it is definitive of the phenomenon itself. Without this imprecision, it wouldn't work at all. Perhaps the most telling tribute to this inherent fuzziness is how much work is required by nation-states, and indeed other organizations, to keep their collective boundaries as clear-cut as possible. It is for this reason that modern belonging, especially perhaps large-scale belonging, is so massively over-determined.

Fuzzy boundaries and indeterminacy should not, however, be mistaken for insignificance or weakness. The robustness and resonance of the symbolic construction of community and belonging, and the capacity of belonging to strike genuine emotional chords, must be recognized; they may, indeed, actually derive in part from fuzzy indeterminacy. Much depends, if nothing else, on *which* collectivities people belong to – although even relatively trivial affiliations, when viewed from outside, may sometimes be surprisingly powerful – but when belonging matters, it can *really* matter. This is not a defence of primordialism or essentialism. Brubaker and Malešević,[16] for example, are right to insist that that there is nothing inevitable or irresistible about the demands of belonging and identity. What I am saying is that we need to look at why, and how, belonging comes to matters *when* it matters, and that in order to do so we need, *inter alia*, to look at the construction and organization of emotion in the symbolization of belonging.

---

16. R. Brubaker, *Ethnicity Without Groups* (Cambridge, MA: Harvard University Press, 2004); S. Malešević, *The Sociology of Ethnicity* (London: Sage, 2004), and *Identity as Ideology: Understanding Ethnicity and Nationalism* (Basingstoke: Palgrave Macmillan, 2006).

Identification

"Identity" and "identification" are often used as if they are synonymous with belonging. Identity is also often mentioned in the same breath as citizenship.[17] If we are to understand better the relationship between citizenship and national identity we need to look more closely at what we mean when we talk about identity.[18] Identity is a matter of knowing "who's who," and is vital if we are to know "what's what." This is a fundamental human competence, without which the human world as we know it would simply not be possible.

The working principle of identity is the interplay between two criteria of comparison, similarity and difference: you and I are different from each other as individuals, but we may in some contexts appear to be sufficiently similar that "we" can mark our difference from "them." In yet another context, however, "we" and "they" may all find enough in common to differentiate ourselves from another set of Others. These relationships of resemblance and differentiation are symbolically constructed, rather than "objective" or given, and may change from situation to situation. Similarity and difference are, what's more, unthinkable in isolation. Each needs the other to make sense: "I" and "we" only come into focus in the presence of "you" and "them" (and *vice versa*).

Properly speaking, however, it is not "identity" with which we are concerned here but "identification," which is a process, that people *do*, rather than some*thing* that they *have*. Reification of the latter kind should be resisted. Even so, Brubaker's insistence that we should expunge the term "identity" altogether,[19] in favour of a root-and-branch use of "identification," goes too far; in the first place, we need to talk about identity in order stay in touch with everyday discourse, and, in the second, substituting one noun for another does not necessarily solve the problem. We simply need to remember that when we talk about identity, we are referring to a process.

Among the reasons why this is important is that identity-as-a-thing allows us to talk about it as if it were solid, if not utterly fixed and immutable, whereas identity-as-process leaves the door open to the acknowledgement of change and mutability and the interplay of similarity and difference. This is not to say, in the spirit of postmodernism, that all that is identity can melt into air - human life is not in perpetual flux, and it would be unliveable if it were - but it is to recognize

---

17. E.F. Isin and P.K. Wood, *Citizenship and Identity* (London: Sage, 1999); Shotter, "Psychology and Citizenship"; Y.S. Soysal, "Citizenship and Identity: Living in Diasporas in Postwar Europe," in *The Postnational Self: Belonging and Identity* (Minneapolis: University of Minnesota Press, 2002); C. Tilly, ed., *Citizenship, Identity and Social History* (Cambridge: Cambridge University Press, 2002).
18. See R. Jenkins, *Social Identity*, for a more detailed account of what follows.
19. Brubaker, *Ethnicity*, 28-63.

that how people are identified and how they identify themselves may change during interaction and over the course of their lives. Such transformations are actually routine and unremarkable. That said, however, there are also routine limits to change; the major constraints are physical embodiment, the availability of resources, the strength and nature of internalized self-identification, and the attitudes taken by significant others.

The last two items alert us to the fact that identification is a two-way street: identity, whether individual or collective, emerges interactionally in the ebb and flow between self-identification and external categorisation by others. While this is to make an orthodox symbolic interactionist point, it also recognizes the importance of power. Which side of the "internal-external dialectic of identification" is the more influential in deciding "who's who" is not random, nor is the playing field always level. For most people, much of the time, there may be an unexamined and taken-for-granted appearance of a reasonable fit between presentation of self and audience perception. However, how we are externally categorized by others may differ from our own self-identification; that difference may also be very consequential. This is particularly so in the case of organizational identification: modern organizations, whether public or private, are enormously influential categorizers of "who's who," possessing the authority or power to make resources and penalties follow those categorizations and thus to make their identifications of others count, and stick. So much so that external categorizations may become internalized as the self-identifications of those who are labelled.

This brings me to the relationship between identification and belonging. Belonging is a sub-set of the broader field of identification: it involves identification *with*, which may be emotional and/or strategic, as well as identification *of*, which is cognitive, a matter of classification. Here we are again at the heart of current debates about identity:[20] should identification be understood as a purely cognitive, classificatory matter, or are other factors in play? It should be clear by now that my reply to the second part of that question is in the affirmative. However, as already suggested, those "other factors" are not independent of classification. "Identification with," for example, is impossible without "identification of," so there is a sense in which classification is the bottom line of identification. Classification is also essential for belonging in another respect. It is one thing to feel that one belongs, but unless that self-identification is validated by the classificatory work of others – others who "belong," and are therefore potential fellows – it will count for very little (as any child starting the school day in a strange playground can tell you).

---

20. E.g. Brubaker, *Ethnicity*, 64–87.

Another meeting point is that criteria of similarity and difference, as suggested earlier, are fundamental to both belonging and classification. In addition, belonging and classification both involve dialectical relationships between self-identification and external categorization. In the case of belonging there is, as already mentioned, a categorizing audience to satisfy. In the case of classification, one may classify self as well as others (or, collectively, fellow group members and Others, insiders and outsiders). Finally, because "knowing who's who" and "knowing what's what" are mutually entailed in each other, classification is generally no more disinterested or aloof from the everyday human world than belonging. Too much hangs on it. So it seems that "identification with" (belonging) and "identification of" (classification) both matter to human beings, albeit perhaps in different ways, or from different directions.

The last point to make about identification in this context concerns clarity. As I have already suggested, belonging is necessarily somewhat imprecise and fuzzy. The symbolic construction of "we-ness" depends on a degree of indeterminacy if all of the disparate individuals who constitute "us" are to feel included; belonging is not a matter of peas in a pod. Classification, however, although it is never set in stone and is likely to vary according to who is doing the classifying, in which circumstances, and why, may appear to be the more precise art. In any specific context there is, in principle, an either/or classificatory logic and even anomalies should be definitively classifiable as such.

This is where modernity comes in. Perhaps the most important, maybe even the only, modern transformation of identification that one can name with any confidence is the increased significance of categorization by others, specifically organizational categorization. As organizations have become ever more ubiquitous, resource-intensive and influential – and we should think of nation-states as organizations – so too has their capacity to influence the identification of individuals and collectivities become more far-reaching and more consequential. If we accept the broad brush-strokes of Weber's and Foucault's arguments about bureaucracy, discipline and the relationship between power and knowledge, part of this historical trend is an impetus towards the ever more detailed and precise classification of persons. Whether we are talking about social statistics, population registration, educational and occupational qualifications, criminal justice systems, border controls, medical oversight, or financial record-keeping, the direction of travel, aided by ever larger-scale and apparently more sophisticated surveillance and information technologies, is unmistakeable. There is nothing invincible about this – humans can, and will, resist, and all systems are fallible, intrinsically and in their reliance upon human operators – but it does mark a significant break with the past.

The state of Denmark

At this point, after more than four thousand words, some readers may be wondering when I am going to get to the point about citizenship and national identity. Well, we are here. Nation-states have often embarked on enormous long-term projects of more or less successful symbolic reconstruction aimed at harmonizing citizenship and national identity, and not only in the causes of modernization and industrialization (for France and England, see Weber and Colley,[21] respectively). One reason why these efforts have been necessary, and why citizenship and national identity do not always easily fit together, is that national identity, in the ethno-cultural sense that I use the expression, is in the first instance about the imprecision of belonging. Citizenship, by comparison, is, once again in the first instance, a political classification: a more straight-edged organizational category of the state. Note that each is a matter of emphasis, however, in the *first* instance: citizenship, for example, may well evoke a sense of belonging in individual citizens, in its own right and more distantly with respect to national identity. Similarly the national identity of individuals may be a matter of both official and everyday vernacular categorization by others. Everything depends on local histories and current circumstances.

At which point a paradox presents itself. Under some circumstances dual citizenship is perfectly straightforward, although it is not common; dual national identity in the ethno-cultural sense, while it may be common, is, however, anything but straightforward. Faced with the latter we talk about people being "between cultures" or improvise hyphenated "new identities" in order to mitigate the confusion. Either way, it is often seen as a problem. Given my earlier comments about the fuzziness of belonging and the clarity of citizenship one might expect it to be the other way round. The conundrum is more apparent than real, however. It is exactly *because* modern citizenship is a precisely defined bureaucratized identity that dual citizenship may be possible: if that option exists in the rules of particular states, then so be it, and if it does not exist then it simply cannot happen. There is no room for manoeuvre, no fuzziness at all. National identity, however, is both imprecisely defined and emotionally charged; the possibility of two simultaneous national identities exposes that imprecision to the cruel light of day – rather than the comfortable twilight of axiomatic doing-rather-than-reflecting – and may also arouse emotions. Neither of these is politically or interactionally desirable. The only solution is a new, and fuzzy, category.

Given local variability, there is no good reason for examining one case rather than

---

21. E. Weber, *Peasants into Frenchmen: The Modernisation of Rural France, 1870-1914* (Stanford: Stanford University Press, 1976); L. Colley, *Britons: Forging the Nation 1707-1837* (New Haven: Yale University Press, 1992).

another. The United States, for example, a settler state built on immigration, will offer one perspective on these issues and the Russian Federation, the substantial remains of a multi-ethnic empire, another (and both characterizations are, I am well aware, simplifications). That I have chosen to look briefly at Denmark is a consequence of where I have been doing research since the mid-1990s.[22] In the context of the present discussion, however, Denmark is not completely uninteresting.[23]

The Danish mid-nineteenth century was marked by two major landmarks: the first Constitution, a reluctant retreat from absolutism on the part of a king who saw the writing of the 1848 revolutions on the wall, and some military success against the Prussians, in defence of Danish rights to Slesvig and the Holstein duchies. Both were misleading; by the mid-1860s Prussia had trounced the Danes militarily and occupied half of Jutland, and politically the rest of the century was a constant battle between a revanchist monarchy and the right wing on the one hand, and a gradually organizing, although anything but united, alliance of small farmers and urban workers on the other. The citizenship that had been granted by the 1849 Constitution still had to be struggled for. Not until the third decade of the twentieth century did the Germans quit North Slesvig, as part of the post-war rearrangement of Europe, and a durable constitutional settlement finally emerged in Denmark, underpinning the eventual emergence of a social democratic welfare state on Nordic lines.

Modern Danish national identity – a nineteenth-century construction for the most part – developed within this history, in large part as a grassroots movement. Particularly in the aftermath of the 1864 war, small farmers began to develop better farming techniques and reclaim land, and to organize themselves into co-operatives, encouraged by the earlier development of self-help education in the folk high schools. This movement for the "enlightenment of the people" so that they could take advantage of the possibilities for political participation, inspired by the teachings of Grundtvig, was fiercely nationalistic and rooted in a Romantic

---

22. For further details see R. Jenkins, "Not simple at all: Danish identity and the European Union," in *An Anthropology of the European Union: Building, Imagining and Experiencing the New Europe*, ed. I. Bellier and T.M. Wilson (Oxford: Berg, 2000); "Modern monarchy: a comparative view from Denmark," *Sociological Research Online* 7 (2002); "The forest and the trees: images of social change in Denmark," *Ethnos* 71 (2006): 367-89; "Inarticulate speech of the heart: Nation, flag and emotion in Denmark," in *Flag, Nation and Symbolism in Europe and America*, ed. T.H. Eriksen and R. Jenkins (London: Routledge, 2007); and *Rethinking Ethnicity*, 147-67.

23. For English-language sources for this account of Denmark in addition to my own research, see: R.T. Anderson, *Denmark: Success of a Developing Nation* (Cambridge, MA: Schenkman 1975); H. Branner, H. and M. Kelstrup, eds., *Denmark's Policy Towards Europe After 1945: History, Theory and Options* (Odense: University Press of Southern Denmark, 2003); J.L. Campbell, J.A. Hall, and O.K. Pedersen, eds., *National Identity and the Varieties of Capitalism: The Danish Experience* (Montreal and Kingston: McGill-Queen's University Press, 2006); K.J.V. Jespersen, *A History of Denmark* (Basingstoke: Palgrave Macmillan, 2004); and U. Østergård, "Peasants and Danes: The Danish National Identity and Political Culture," *Comparative Studies in Society and History* 34 (1992): 3-27.

understanding of the primordial cultural unity of "little Denmark" and the Danes. By the early 1900s, this small-nation nationalism had combined with the nascent socialism of the urban labour movement and a rural post-peasant ideology of radical egalitarianism, producing a national narrative emphasizing Danish cultural and social homogeneity and resourceful, sturdy self-help in the face of adversity.

This story – "We are all the same, none better than any other, and must pull together" – faced no serious challenge for most of the rest of the twentieth century, providing a symbolic charter for local social democracy, a lens through which to interpret the mixed experience of German occupation 1940-45, a permissive framework for the post-war modernization of the monarchy, an ideological ground on which established politics could meet the post-1968 demands of women and the young, and an incentive for a considerable degree of consensus politics. It was also fundamental to the elaboration of a symbolic portfolio of modern Danish national identity (*danskhed*, or "Danishness"). Although in some respects this process had begun at least as early as the 1700s, it was spurred on by defeats in the Napoleonic Wars and the Prussian war of 1864, and the subsequent occupation of Jutland. By the end of the second German occupation in 1945, a rich and complex symbolic construction of Danish nationhood was in place.[24] Perhaps the three most consistent and important symbols in this complex are Dannebrog (the national flag), the monarchy, and the Danish language.

The national flag symbolizes, and can be applied to, pretty much everything that is considered to be Danish. Not least that, in its myth of origin, it dramatizes the state's antiquity. Dannebrog is particularly interesting in its egalitarian association with the secular life of civil society, which finds expression in an omnipresent spectrum of non-state, vernacular flagways, from marking family festivities to advertising special offers in supermarkets. The flag's popular association with happiness (*glæde*) is a core element in the emotional pull of Danish belonging.[25] The monarchy also symbolizes the ancientness of the kingdom, claiming a line of descent back to Gorm den Gamle (Gorm the Old) in the tenth century. Despite some rough water in the early 2000s, the royal house remains popular and has so far avoided serious scandal or the ambivalence accorded to its British cousins, and continues to manage a delicate balancing act between profane proximity and sacred remoteness.[26] The language symbolizes Denmark's uniqueness and difference from its neighbours, its history, and its altogether admirable smallness. That it is, apparently, "one of the most difficult languages in the world to learn" (as one is so often told) serves

24. I. Adriansen, *Nationale Symboler i Det Danske Rige 1830-2000* (Copenhagen: Museum Tusculanums Forlag, 2003).
25. Jenkins, "Inarticulate speech," 2007.
26. Jenkins, "Modern monarchy," 2002.

to include/exclude, while at the same time affording those who do speak it a flush of smug self-congratulation.

Other elements in the constellation have moved in and out of the limelight, depending on context. During the debates and campaigns leading to various referenda about the EU and the euro, the themes that have been stressed include the egalitarian "Danish way," the national currency, Nordic social democracy (an interesting example of a pan-national factor being incorporated into national identity), and the German bogeyman (an interesting example of the explicit use of "them" to define "us"). More recently, immigration and post-9/11 changed global realities have brought into sharp relief what was, perhaps, the most under-stated, if not completely unmarked, core symbol of Danishness: Christianity. Nearly 90 percent of the population subscribe to the national Lutheran church, and whether one can be authentically Danish and a Muslim is a question that is now beginning to be asked in public (and not only by the priest-politician Søren Krarup of the right-wing Dansk Folkeparti). The Muhammad cartoons affair has, in addition, brought into view freedom of speech as something that apparently ineluctably symbolizes an important facet of Danishness.

There are many other more or less minor elements in this particular symbolic system: from Hans Christian Andersen and the Little Mermaid, to the pastoral idyll of the summerhouse, the sea and the landscape, to Lego and "Danish Design". More intriguing perhaps than these, which are fairly obvious, is the "national song book," a corpus of Danish songs that young Danes learn and sing in kindergarten, at school, on special days in the annual cycle, and at parties and celebrations (at the latter they provide templates that everybody knows for texts that have been newly composed for the occasion). Singing together is regarded as "very Danish." Most of the songs are not particularly patriotic – although some are – but they are inclusive/exclusive, a tacit performative boundary of Danishness.

These then are some of the major moving parts of Danishness or *danskhed*, an imprecise and fuzzy sense of belonging to and in Denmark that is, ideally, the authentic claim of all Danes to national identity. Much of this symbolic construction is unremarked upon – people do not, for example, think much, if at all, about how they use Dannebrog or the "national song book" and few attend church for anything other than weddings and funerals (etc.) – and there is considerable leeway to take or leave this or that. Until the last quarter of the twentieth century – and allowing for the remaining fragments of empire, the Greenlanders, Faeroese, Icelanders (until 1940), and "home Germans" of Southern Jutland, for all of whom a niche could be found in the national story – there was an acceptably snug fit between "being Danish," albeit that its emphases might change according to circumstances, and being a Danish citizen. Any challenges to that fit were individual cases and could be resolved as such. After 1970 that began to change.

Three sources of this change, of which two have already been alluded to, are often mentioned in public discourse. The first is Denmark's accession to the European Community in January 1973. Second, from the early 1970s there was a gradual increase in immigration, and eventually undeniable permanent settlement, by visibly different foreigners, many of whom were Muslims, first as guest workers and subsequently as refugees and asylum seekers. Third, both of these can be folded together into a more general set of changes, which can be summed up as globalization: the increasingly unmistakeable impact of cultural influences from outside Denmark (and, indeed, outside Europe), the visible internationalization of the Danish economy, and the growing political international interdependence of the Danish state. Less visible in Danish public debate is a fourth aspect of this recent history, consumerism; material affluence and the successful marketing of lifestyle has transformed many Danish homes and expectations.[27]

As a result of this combination of events and processes, the established national narrative of "We are all the same, none better than any other, and must pull together" came under pressure from several directions at once. Ethnic similarity, cultural similarity, and socio-economic (class) similarity – no matter how imagined they might actually have been – no longer *looked* as settled, or as plausible, as they once did. If for no other reason, this was because they could no longer be taken for granted: externally and internally the boundaries of "us-them" became dramatized, and put up for relocation and renegotiation. One sign of this has been the publication, since the early 1990s, by intellectuals, journalists, and politicians, of a continuing string of books problematizing, or attempting to clarify, various aspects of *danskhed*, Danish national identity.[28] My own ethnography suggests that although ordinary Danes generally have other more urgent things to talk about, this is an issue with some currency in everyday life. The question at the heart of the matter is "Who is a Dane?" or, more precisely perhaps, "Who can be a Dane?" – which is a question about the relationship between ethno-national identity and citizenship.

---

27. Jenkins, "The forest and the trees," 2006.

28. Of which the following are only a sample: I. Adriansen, *Nationale Symboler i Det Danske Rige 1830-2000*, 2 vols. (Copenhagen: Museum Tusculanums Forlag, 2003); M. Böss, *Forsvar for nationen* (Aarhus: Aarhus University Press, 2006); O. Feldbæk, ed., *Dansk Identitetshistorie*, 4 vols. (Copenhagen: C.A. Reitzels Forlag, 1991-92); P. Gundelach, *Det er Dansk* (Copenhagen: Hans Reitzels Forlag, 2002); P. Gunelach, ed., *Danskernes særpræg* (Copenhagen: Hans Reitzels Forlag, 2004), P. Gundelach, H.R. Iversen, and M. Warburg, *I hjertet af Danmark* (Copenhagen: Hans Reitzels Forlag, 2008); A. Knudsen, *Fanden på Væggen: Verden efter Amsterdam-traktaten* (Copenhagen: Gunbak og Kaspersen, 1997); S. Krarup, *Kristendom og danskhed: Prædikener og foredrag* (Højbjerg: Hovedland, 2001); C.A. Larsen, *Nationale forestillinger* (Aalborg: Aalborg Universitetsforlag, 2008); U. Østergaard, *Dansk Identitet?* (Aarhus: Aarhus University Press, 1992); T. Saugstad Gabrielen and M.A. Séférian, eds., *Hvor Danske er Danskerne?* (Copenhagen: Forlaget Amanda, 1991); and "Danskhed," special issue, *Tidsskriftet Antropologi* 42 (2000).

There has been more to the matter than public debate and private conversations. The state has become involved. I will finish this account by looking briefly at policy developments in the field of education, but first a few words about Danish citizenship. To simplify the matter by ignoring some minor limiting cases, Danish citizenship is an automatic entitlement if you are born in Denmark to parents or a parent of Danish citizenship. It is also possible to apply for Danish citizenship by naturalization; candidates must renounce their previous nationality and satisfy residency, economic self-sufficiency, and "good character" provisions. Since 2007, however, it has also been necessary to pass a test of knowledge of Danish society, culture, and history. This latter is clearly an attempt to (re)assert a link between citizenship and national identity.

The real battleground in this particular culture war appears to have become education. For many years state schools inculcated Danishness implicitly, not to say "fuzzily," teaching Danish language, history, some degree of Christianity (religious education is, tellingly, known as *kristendomskundskab*), and the national songbook, and participating in the full spectrum of vernacular flagways. In 1994 the role of schools in the production and reproduction of Danishness was recognized explicitly when, for the first time, schools became legally obliged to ensure that young Danes were familiar with Danish culture. The law did not, however, define what Danish culture might actually be, and little changed; throughout the 1990s one would have looked in vain for a slot marked "Danish culture" in the curriculum.

Following the electoral victory in 2001 of a right-wing coalition – a victory made sustainable by the support, outside government, of the anti-immigrant Danish People's Party – the elaboration of education for national identity and citizenship proceeded apace. Following the introduction in 2003 of the beginnings of a national curriculum based on benchmarking and attainment targets, in 2004 the government established a committee of experts to determine the content of an authoritative Danish "cultural canon" (*kulturkanon*) to inform and guide teaching in state schools. The canon, which is composed of specialized subject canons, was published and came into effect in 2006; the books specified in the literature canon, for example, have to have been read by all pupils by the time they leave education.

Also in 2006, *kristendomskundskab* became a formally-examined subject and an official commission charged with strengthening the subject reiterated and underlined the centrality of the doctrine of the national Lutheran church. Finally, and once again as the result of a committee of experts, 2008 saw the publication of the official "democracy canon" (*demokratikanon*) for use in social studies teaching in state schools. Perhaps the most controversial of the canons – unofficial alternatives are in circulation – this codifies a body of historical and other knowledge that is believed to be essential to understand democracy (and to be a participating citizen in the Danish style).

These developments dramatize the disjuncture that has come to be perceived in Denmark – which is by no means exceptional in this respect – between citizenship and national identity, and the state's attempts to intervene, to bring them back into their "proper" relationship (of close fit). In terms of the arguments of this chapter, we can see an attempt by the state to render national identity – the "belonging" that inheres in Danishness – in less fuzzy terms, and to legislate for its components in a way that more closely resembles what might be expected for citizenship. Whether or not the fuzzy logic of belonging and identification can be manipulated in this way remains to be seen.

Three final points can be made in closing, to refer back to the theoretical discussion of earlier sections. First, membership of the European Union, immigration, globalization and consumerism caused the hitherto axiomatic relationship between national identity and citizenship to become a focus of attention, as problematic. It was not that there was a tight fit between them earlier in the twentieth century, but rather that it was simply not an issue (as it arguably had been during the nineteenth century, for example). Second, this is a symbolic (re)construction of national identity on a grand scale, which, once again, is not without its precedents in the nineteenth century (although that was largely a popular, not a state, initiative). The cultural and democracy canons, and the reconfiguration of Christianity within schools, are heavily symbolized and symbolic. Finally, the main object of these initiatives is probably not the integration of the immigrant Muslim population, whether they are citizens or not. It is, in fact, the integration of "ethnic Danes." It is *their* "identification with" and "belonging" that seems to be most at issue, and a refusal of multiculturalism as a local option that is the subtext.

Bibliography

Adriansen, I. *Nationale Symboler i Det Danske Rige 1830-2000*. 2 vols. Copenhagen: Museum Tusculanums Forlag, 2003.

Anderson, R.T. *Denmark: Success of a Developing Nation*. Cambridge, MA: Schenkman, 1975.

Barbalet, J.M. *Citizenship*. Milton Keynes: Open University Press, 1988.

Barth, F. "Introduction," in *Ethnic Groups and Boundaries: The Social Organisation of Culture Difference*, edited by F. Barth. Oslo: Universitetsforlaget, 1969

Baumeister, A. "Ways of Belonging: Ethnonational Minorities and Models of "Differentiated Citizenship." *Ethnicities* 3 (2003): 393-416.

Branner, H. and M. Kelstrup, eds. *Denmark's Policy Towards Europe After 1945: History, Theory and Options*. Odense: University Press of Southern Denmark, 2003.

Brubaker, R. *Ethnicity Without Groups*. Cambridge, MA: Harvard University Press, 2004.

Böss, M. *Forsvar for Nationen: Nationalstaten under globalisering*. Aarhus: Aarhus University Press, 2006.

Campbell, J.L., J.A. Hall, and O.K. Pedersen, eds. *National Identity and the Varieties of Capitalism: The Danish Experience*. Montreal and Kingston: McGill-Queen's University Press, 2006.

Castles, S. and A. Davidson, *Citizenship and Migration: Globalization and the Politics of Belonging*. London: Routledge, 2000.

Cohen, A.P., ed. *Belonging: Identity and Social Organisation in British Rural Cultures*. Manchester: Manchester University Press, 1982.

Cohen, A.P. *The Symbolic Construction of Community*. London: Tavistock, 1985.

Cohen, A.P., ed. *Symbolising Boundaries: Identity and Diversity in British Cultures*. Manchester: Manchester University Press, 1986.

Cohen, R. "Fuzzy Frontiers of Identity: The British Case." *Social Identities*, 1 (1995): 35-62.

Colley, L. *Britons: Forging the Nation 1707-1837*. New Haven: Yale University Press, 1992.

Connerton, P. *How Societies Remember*. Cambridge: Cambridge University Press, 1989.

Delanty, G. "Beyond the Nation-State: National Identity and Citizenship in a Multicultural Society – A Response to Rex." *Sociological Research Online* 1 (1996): 3. www.socresonline.org.uk/socresonline/1/3/1.html.

Durkheim, E. *The Elementary Forms of the Religious Life*. Translated by J.W. Swain. London: George Allen and Unwin, 1976.

Faulks, K. *Citizenship*. London: Routledge, 2000.

Feldbæk, O., ed. *Dansk Identitetshistorie*, 4 vols. Copenhagen: C.A. Reitzels Forlag, 1991-2.

Grimes, R. L. *Deeply into the Bone: Re-inventing Rites of Passage*. Berkeley: University of California Press, 2000.

Gundelach, P. *Det er Dansk*. Copenhagen: Hans Reitzels Forlag, 2002.

Gundelach, P., ed. *Danskernes særpræg*. Copenhagen: Hans Reitzels Forlag, 2004.

Gundelach, P., H.R. Iversen, and M. Warburg. *I hjertet af Danmark*. Copenhagen: Hans Reitzels Forlag, 2008. Hampshire, J. *Citizenship and Belonging: Immigration and the Politics of Demographic Governance in Postwar Britain*. Basingstoke: Palgrave Macmillan, 2005.

Isin, E.F. and P.K. Wood. *Citizenship and Identity*. London: Sage, 1999.

Jenkins, R. "Not simple at all: Danish identity and the European Union," in *An Anthropology of the European Union: Building, Imagining and Experiencing the New Europe*, edited by I. Bellier and T.M. Wilson. Oxford: Berg, 2000.

Jenkins, R. "Modern monarchy: a comparative view from Denmark." *Sociological Research Online* 7 (2002):1 www.socresonline.org.uk/7/1/jenkins.html.

Jenkins, R. "The forest and the trees: images of social change in Denmark." *Ethnos* 71(2006): 367-89.

Jenkins, R. "Inarticulate speech of the heart: Nation, flag and emotion in
Denmark." In *Flag, Nation and Symbolism in Europe and America*, edited by T.H. Eriksen and R. Jenkins. London: Routledge, 2007.

Jenkins, R. *Rethinking Ethnicity: Arguments and Explorations*. 2nd ed. London: Sage, 2008.

Jenkins, R. *Social Identity*. 3rd ed. London: Routledge, 2008.

Jespersen, K.J.V. *A History of Denmark*. Basingstoke: Palgrave Macmillan, 2004.

Knudsen, A. *Fanden på Væggen: Verden efter Amsterdam-traktaten*. Copenhagen: Gunbak og Kaspersen, 1997.

Krarup, S. *Kristendom og danskhed: Prædikener og foredrag*. Højbjerg: Hovedland, 2001.

Kymlicka, W. *Multicultural Citizenship: A Liberal Theory of Minority Rights*. Oxford: Oxford University Press, 1996.

Larsen, C.A. *Nationale forestillinger*. Aalborg: Aalborg Universitetsforlag, 2008.

Malešević, S. *The Sociology of Ethnicity*. London: Sage, 2004.

Malešević, S. *Identity as Ideology: Understanding Ethnicity and Nationalism*. Basingstoke: Palgrave Macmillan, 2006.

Marshall, T.H. *Citizenship and Social Class and Other Essays*. Cambridge: Cambridge University Press, 1959.

Miller, D.I. *Citizenship and National Identity*. Cambridge: Polity Press, 2000.

Munch, R. *Nation and Citizenship in the Global Age: From National to Transnational Ties and Identities*. Basingstoke: Palgrave Macmillan, 2001.

Oommen, T.K. *Citizenship and National Identity: From Colonialism to Globalism*. London: Sage, 1997.

Østergård, U. "Peasants and Danes: The Danish National Identity and Political Culture." *Comparative Studies in Society and History* 34 (1992): 3-27.

Østergård, U., ed. (1992b) *Dansk Identitet?* Aarhus: Aarhus University Press, 1992.

Rex, J. "National Identity in the Democratic Multi-Cultural State.".

Sociological Research Online 1 (1996): 2. ww.socresonline.org.uk/socresonline/1/2/1.html.

Saugstad Gabrielen, T. and M.-A. Séférian, eds. *Hvor Danske er Danskerne?*. Copenhagen: Forlaget Amanda, 1991.

Shotter, J. "Psychology and Citizenship: Identity and Belonging," in *Citizenship and Social Theory*, edited by B.S. Turner. London: Sage, 1993.

Soysal, Y.S. "Citizenship and Identity: Living in Diasporas in Postwar Europe." In *The Postnational Self: Belonging and Identity*, edited by U. Hedetoft and M. Hjort. Minneapolis: University of Minnesota Press, 2002.

Tidskriftet Antropologi. "Danskhed." Special issue, 42 (2000).

Tilly, C., ed. *Citizenship, Identity and Social History*, Cambridge: Cambridge University Press, 1996.

Turner, B.S., ed. *Citizenship and Social Theory*. London: Sage, 1993.

Turner, V.W. *The Ritual Process: Structure and Anti-Structure*. Harmondsworth: Pelican, 1974.

Weber, E. *Peasants into Frenchmen: The Modernisation of Rural France, 1870-1914*. Stanford: Stanford University Press, 1976.

4 Our Stories, Our Selves: Identities and the Dialogics of Narrative

Martin O. Heisler*

I. Introduction: Stories and the Structures and Dynamics of their Narration

All peoples have stories about the paths they travelled to become who they are today.[1] The broadest, most encompassing stories describe the foundations and basic character of collectivities such as tribes, ethnic groups, nations, or religions. In Rogers M. Smith's terms, these are not only "constitutive" (or "people-making") but "ethically constitutive" stories: they build communities in part by calling attention to the precepts that have guided, and should continue to guide, their course through history.[2] The precepts highlight the values and principles that shaped and continue to inform the collectivity's identity and distinctive character, and they help to differentiate it from other collectivities. They also influence relationships among members, as well as between them and outsiders.[3] Families and other primary groups – kin, friends, neighbours – instill such values and principles in their children through informal socialization; societies reinforce them through formal education. Since most newcomers enter collectivities through birth, such socialization has always been the predominant mode of incorporation.

---

*   Thanks to Michael Bøss for the invitation to participate in this project; Barbara Schmitter Heisler for sharing her greater knowledge of many aspects of migration theory; for access to printed sources, Torben Grøngaard Jeppesen; Watzek Library at Lewis and Clark College; and Dee Grimsrud at the Wisconsin Historical Society.

1.   Like Rogers M. Smith, whose seminal book, *Stories of Peoplehood: The Politics and Morals of Political Membership* (2003) stimulated my interest in this and related subjects, I want to avoid equating a "people" with any specific established type of human collectivity, such as nation, ethnic group, or "civilization" – at least in the initial part of the discussion. These are used so widely and loosely in the social sciences, humanities, and everyday language that it is difficult to free them from preconceptions about their referents. While the subjects of "stories of peoplehood" clearly resemble such collectivities (especially nations), not all of them exhibit the distinctive political and moral precepts of the sort at the core of the *political* peoplehood of interest to Smith or to me.

2.   Rogers M. Smith, *Stories of Peoplehood* (Cambridge: Cambridge University Press, 2003).

3.   To include some as members is, *per force*, to exclude others. Smith is aware of the problematic nature of this facet of the stories and processes involved in people-making (Smith, *Stories of Peoplehood*, 56 and passim).

The focus of this essay is on *connections between such stories or narratives* (a nuanced distinction, explained below) *and the formation or, better, transformation of the identities of immigrants* – those who enter the social, cultural, economic, and political spaces of collectivities as adults. Such connections are established over time, through complex exchanges with several voices, each usually telling partial or fragmented stories from its perspective. The process is dialogical: multiple voices speak and interact with each other in the same space and time. Each has its own history, interpretation, values and biases, and cognitive make-up. Although the transcription and analysis of actual dialogical discourses would be very complex and problematic,[4] they can be represented through *constructed types* – abstracted sketches that are reasonable approximations of empirical cases.[5] Outlines of the historical settings and conditions – including their cultural, structural, economic, political, institutional, spatial and other components – in which migrants and members of the collectivity interact can provide a sense of what (versions of) stories of that collectivity are likely to be told, as well as the positions and dispositions of the tellers and hearers of those stories.

The sketches presented in Section III below of early Danish immigrants to the American Upper Midwest in the third quarter of the nineteenth century and people from West Africa to the Paris region in recent times are not meant to be solid historical descriptions. Rather, they have two purposes: to give approximations of how and with what effects immigrants encounter stories or narratives of the places they enter; and to suggest why and how it was possible for early Danish immigrants to the Upper Midwest of the United States to integrate into the host society. The juxtaposition of their experiences with those of immigrants to France – like the United States, a "country of immigration" until recently – from West Africa and France's Afro-Caribbean overseas *départements* in two different periods of the twentieth century is intended as a reminder of the enormous differences between the migrants, host societies, structural conditions, and *Zeitgeists* – that is, to put the Danish case into temporal, spatial, and normative perspective.

Numerous challenges must be confronted before addressing these tasks directly. We need to ask a series of adverbial questions at the outset about stories: who tells them; where; when; what is told; why; how; who hears the stories; and under what circumstances are they heard? Of course, not all of these aspects of the transmis-

---

4. My notion of dialogical processes and their complexities derives from Edgar Morin's work of the past 60 years (see especially Edgar Morin, *Les idées*, vol. 4 of *La Méthode* (Paris: Éditions du Seuil, 1991), 111. Also see Edgar Morin, *On Complexity* (Cresskill, NJ: Hampton Press, 2008).

5. A "constructed type [is] a purposive, planned selection, abstraction, combination, and (sometimes) accentuation of a set of [characteristics] with empirical referents that serve as a basis for comparison of empirical cases." John C. McKinney, *Constructive Typology and Social Theory* (New York: Appleton-Century-Crofts, 1966), 3; italics omitted. It differs from Weberian ideal types in subtle but important ways that cannot be explored here.

sion and reception of stories can be explored in a short essay, but it is possible to broach several of the most important.

■ Whose stories are "Our Stories"?

The first, seemingly simple but actually deceptive and complex, question is *whose* story is being told – who are "the people"?"[6] For the newcomers to recognize on which elements of their new home they should focus, they need to know whose story is "our story,'"" who they are expected to become, and how their own identities might be affected. The common assumption is that "the people" are the population of a society, or perhaps a nation or potential nation. This is often accompanied by a corollary assumption that the population is coextensive with a country, or state, or territory. In turn, this leads to expectations that newcomers will focus on the nation, state, or country they have entered and will develop some sort of identitive relationship with it – perhaps even loyalty to it.

Yet most modern countries are, or have been until recently, populated by more than one people. They contain (or had in their well-remembered pasts) politicized ethnic groups or cultural or national minorities with their own stories, or people who may have sought autonomy – separateness or independence – from the dominant group. Such divisions and movements for autonomy have proliferated since the mid-nineteenth century, as has the proportion of *plural societies* among the world's countries since the middle of the twentieth.[7]Furthermore, since the mid-1970s, the rise of various forms of multiculturalism has buttressed arguments for the legitimate coexistence of multiple stories in many developed democracies.

It is especially difficult to specify "the people" in plural societies. Milton Gordon's definition of such a society is useful here. For Gordon a plural society is

> a national society in which various groups, *each with a psychological sense of its own historical peoplehood*, maintain some structural separation from each other in intimate primary group relationships and in certain aspects of institutional life and thus create the possibility of maintaining [...] some cultural patterns which are different from those of the 'host' society and of other racial and ethnic groups in the nation.[8] (italics added)

---

6. Ove Korsgaard problematizes this question in a similar fashion. Ove Korsgaard, "Grand Narratives in Danish History: From Functional Identity to Problematic Identity" (Paper presented at the International Seminar on Nationhood in Plural Societies, Aarhus University, 14-15 May, 2009), 2ff.

7. This is in part the consequence of the near four-fold increase in the number of independent countries in the world since the end of the Second World War.

8. Milton M. Gordon, "Models of Pluralism: The New American Dilemma," *Annals of the American Academy of Political and Social Science* 454 (March 1981): 181.

In the sections that follow I argue that in some ways both Danish immigrants in the upper Midwest of the United States in the mid- and late nineteenth century and Africans in the Paris region in recent times came to constitute such groups, although *in different ways, for different reasons, and with different consequences*. But, more importantly, both encountered partial and contested stories; and they formed impressions that reflected such complex, segmented, or even fragmented, images of the societies they entered. In short, the stories they heard were not fully indicative of the values and norms – the readings of history and expectations of the future – of the whole that, at some remove in time and place, might be termed "the story of America" or "the story of France."

The problems encountered in plural societies are compounded where multi-dimensional (linguistic, religious, ethno-cultural, and other) cleavages reinforce each other,[9] especially when these cleavages coincide with (sub-state) territorial or jurisdictional boundaries.[10] Is the story that will help to integrate immigrants who settle in, for instance, Quebec to be that of Anglo-dominated Canada; or is it to be the story of French Canada?[11] Long before Belgium became a federal state most immigrants from such francophone or partly francophone countries as Morocco, Congo/Zaire, and several other sub-Saharan African states settled in Brussels or in French-speaking Wallonia, reinforcing the differences – and tensions – between (to use the terminology of the Belgian constitution) the Flemish and French "cultural communities" and the three constitutionally specified regions of Flanders, Wallo-

---

9. In the social science literature there is a distinction between "plural societies" such as Belgium, Sri Lanka, Iraq, and even Canada, characterized by deep, often reinforcing cleavages, and "pluralistic societies" and polities like the contemporary United States, Germany, and Switzerland. See, for example, Joseph V. Montville,, ed., *Conflict and Peacemaking in Multiethnic Societies* (Lexington, MA: Lexington Books/D. C. Heath, 1990); Andreas Wimmer, *Nationalist Exclusion and Ethnic Conflict: Shadows of Modernity* (Cambridge: Cambridge University Press, 2002); cf. Alain G. Gagnon and James Tully, eds., *Multinational Democracies* (New York: Cambridge University Press, 2001); Martin O. Heisler, ed., *Ethnic Conflict in the World Today*, special issue, *Annals of the American Academy of Political and Social Science*, 433 (Sep. 1977). In many western countries, historically deep cleavages in what had been plural societies have been managed, sometimes peacefully, in other cases through conflict, and transformed into *pluralistic democracies*. Martin O. Heisler, "Ethnicity and Ethnic Relations in the Modern West," in *Conflict and Peacemaking in Multiethnic Societies*, ed. Joseph V. Montville (Lexington, MA: Lexington Books/D. C. Heath, 1990); Martin O. Heisler and Barbara Schmitter Heisler, "Citizenship – Old, New, and Changing: Inclusion, Exclusion, and Limbo for Ethnic Groups and Migrants in the Modern Democratic State," in *Dominant National Cultures and Ethnic Identities*, ed. Jürgen Fijalkowski, Hans Merkens, and Folker Schmidt (Berlin: Freie Universität, 1991). Most countries, democratic or not, are plural or divided by cleavages, but few meet even the least stringent criteria for pluralistic democracy. The problems of delineating a people, especially one with a coherent political ethos, are common and severe.
10. Formal jurisdictional divisions, such as those found in federations and confederations, can exacerbate the problem, since sub-state units often have at least partial control over education, cultural policy, and other socializing functions.
11. See e.g. *Canadian Ethnic Studies Journal* 34, no. 3 (Sep. 2002), entire issue.

nia, and Brussels.[12] Whose stories, and whose versions of history and political and cultural relations, were they likely to hear? What constitutes integration (however conceived) in the sub-societal milieu of Quebec or Wallonia, which are themselves not comprehensively integrated in their countries' institutions or dominant cultures?

Just as the societies immigrants enter are likely to be culturally and politically "plural," so too there may be deep cultural and political divisions – even mutual hostility – among the immigrants. Migrants may vary by region or culture of origin; education; skills; religion; and other forms of economic, political, and social capital, as well as by such visible markers as gender and skin color. Even those from what is ostensibly one country may not share a common identity; such identity is often projected onto them in and by the host society. Thus, in the nineteenth and early twentieth centuries, many Italian, German, Jewish, and other immigrants to the United States viewed their places of origin in regional, provincial, or local rather than national terms. Just as slaves from several parts of Africa in earlier times – with distinctive cultures, languages, religions, and identities – were molded into Africans in the New World and became, over time, African-Americans, Afro-Caribbeans, or Afro-Colombians, so too collective identities can be imposed on more recent migrants in their new societies.[13]

These are some of the reasons for delving into the make-up and nature of the collective "we" whose stories are the putative vehicles for affecting the identities of newcomers, as well as into some of the characteristics of the migrants themselves. If the question of whose stories are "our stories" – to whom the "we" in "who we are" refers – has no simple answer, neither does the question of "who" or "what am I."

---

12. See e.g. Martin O. Heisler, ed., *Ethnic Conflict in the World Today*, special issue, *Annals of the American Academy of Political and Social Science*, 433 (Sep. 1977); Martin O. Heisler, "Hyphenating Belgium: Changing State and Regime to Cope with Cultural Division," in *Conflict and Peacemaking in Multiethnic Societies*, ed. Joseph V. Montville (Lexington, MA: Lexington Books/D. C. Heath, 1990).

13. On African-Americans, see Ira Berlin, *The Making of African America: The Four Great Migrations* (New York: Viking, 2010), 30f., 45; and Nell Irvin Painter, *Creating Black Americans: African-American History and Its Meanings, 1619 to the Present* (Oxford & New York: Oxford University Press, 2006). On "whites," see Nell Irvin Painter, *The History of White People* (New York: W.W. Norton, 2010). People from Calabria, Catania, Sicily, Tuscany, and Piedmont who arrived in the United States from the newly unified Italy in the decades following the *Risorgimento* had to learn to think of themselves as Italian. See, e.g., Francis X. Femminella and Jill S. Quadango, "The Italian American Family," in *Ethnic Families in America: Patterns and Variations*, ed. Charles H. Mindel and Robert Haberstein (New York: Elsevier, 1976); also Berlin, *The Making of African America*, 45; and for West Africans in France today, Nicolas Jounin, *Chantier interdit au public: Enquête parmi les travailleurs du bâtiment* (Paris: Éditions du Découverte, 2008). Turks and Kurds who went to Germany as foreign workers in the last quarter of the twentieth century were not only culturally and ethnically distinct, they often regarded each other with suspicion, even hostility, given relationships between the Turkish majority and state and the country's Kurdish minority. Yet the distinction was commonly lost on their German hosts, who tended to regard them simply as Turkish well into the 1990s. Similarly, superimposing the generic label "Asian" on immigrants from South Asia in Britain blurred highly significant religious, political, and other differences among Indians, Pakistanis, and Bangladeshis; see, e.g., Muhammad Anwar, *Race and Politics: Ethnic Minorities and the British Political System* (London: Routledge, 1986).

■ When and where are the stories narrated?

If stories are to be effective tools for integrating a people, they must be rich in content and texture and substantively plausible.[14] Durability and continuity also matter. The absence of significant interruptions or gaps in the historical narrative is important.[15] The United States and France, the settings of the illustrative cases discussed below, differ from each other in this regard. In the former, as Robert Wiebe noted, "[e]ach generation has had to rediscover America, for its meaning has been a problem that could be neither ignored nor resolved. Americans pursued it so doggedly because so much depended upon an answer."[16] In one sense, continuity and durability have been elusive in France as well. After all, while the United States has had one constitution since 1789, in which – it could be argued, or at least pretended – even major changes over time have been in harmony with its basic tenets, France has had more than a dozen, many explicitly premised on the substantive as well as symbolic rejection of their predecessors. But in France, more than in the United States (especially if the Civil War is added to the segmentation and fragmentation at the core of Wiebe's thesis), the focus was on the country and nation as a whole, not on parts.[17] France was, in Ernest Renan's famous statement (expressed in the ripe, romantic trope of his time) a nation "with a soul [that was] an expression of a spiritual principle" and which "exhibited a commitment to living together and the will to continue to value its heritage" (my translation).[18]

---

14. This does not mean, of course, that they have to be wholly "factual." As Smith (*Stories of Peoplehood*) and many others have pointed out, such stories are invariably blends of evidence-based history, myth, legend, and outright fabrication. See, e.g., William J. McNeill, *Mythistory and Other Essays* (Chicago: Chicago University Press, 1986); Benedict Anderson, *Imagined Communities* (London: Verso, 1983); Joseph Mali, *Mythistory: The Making of a Modern Historiography* (Chicago: Chicago University Press, 2003); and cf. Peter Novick, *That Noble Dream: The "Objectivity Questions" and the American Historical Profession* (Cambridge & New York: Cambridge University Press, 1988).

15. Eviatar Zerubel, *Time Maps: Collective Memory and the Social Shape of the Past* (Chicago: Chicago University Press, 2003), 52ff. and passim; cf. David Carr, *Time, Narrative, and History* (Bloomington & Indianapolis: Indiana University Press, 1986), 23ff.

16. Robert H. Wiebe, *The Segmented Society: an Introduction into the Meaning of America* (New York: New York University Press, 1975), 90; but cf. Smith, *Stories of Peoplehood*, who, in that book, but not in much of his earlier and subsequent work on American political development, shows concern for continuity. Peter Katzenstein, "Walls Between 'Those People?' Contrasting Perspectives on World Politics," *Perspectives on Politics* 8 (March 2010): 16f. highlights the multiple competing or conflicting patterns in both the practices and principles that are emphasized over time in Smith's work on American political development. The relatively abstract formulation in *Stories of Peoplehood* points up what Smith sees as the country's *essential* history. Important questions regarding changes in the American story have been raised by the preeminent historian of early America, Edmund S. Morgan, e.g., in some of the essays reprinted in Edmund S. Morgan, *The Genuine Article* (New York & London: W.W. Norton, 2004). Also see Robert H. Wiebe, *Who We Are: A History of Popular Nationalism* (Princeton: Princeton University Press, 2002).

17. See, e.g., Frederick Brown, *For the Soul of France: Culture Wars in the Age of Dreyfus* (New York: A. A. Knopf, 2010).

18. Ernest Renan, "Qu'est-ce qu'une nation?" (Lectures delivered at the Sorbonne, March 11, 1882) http://ig.cs.tu-berlin.de/oldstatic/w2001/eu1/dokumente/Basistexte/Renan1882FR-Nation.pdf#2. Renan's conception of peoplehood in a nation is remarkably similar to Smith's notion of ethical peoplehood, although Renan is more

Notwithstanding such differences, the grand narratives of both countries *project* durability and continuity (centuries of collective life) onto their histories. But whether we examine variations in their "actual" histories or accept renditions that feature continuity, it is clear that *when*, as well as *where*, newcomers enter matters greatly to the stories they will hear. Thus (staying with my two illustrative "host societies"), Danes who entered the United States in the years before or after the Civil War would have been exposed to substantially different narratives of America, depending on whether they arrived in what became the Union side (as most did) or the states of the Confederacy. Similarly, West African immigrants in France before the 1960s – admittedly few in number and generally with levels of education equal to or greater than the French average – would have found a country and society that viewed them much more favorably than those – to be sure, far more numerous and generally with less human and cultural capital – who arrived in the latter decades of the twentieth century. And the many who alighted in the Paris region in recent times had a very different reception, encountering a very different France from those who went to other parts of the country in smaller numbers.

■ Who listens to the stories, and how do they hear them?

Much is known about the socialization of children into cultures, political systems, and identities; and there are many studies of the difficulties encountered by the second generation – the children of immigrants – in developing coherent, positive identities and in integrating into the host societies in Europe and North America. Considerably less is known about how migration affects the identities of adults. While there are some parallels in the ways children and adult newcomers relate to the stories of host societies, there are also significant differences. Here I consider the effects of stories of peoplehood and their normative precepts on immigrants' political identities. Assuming that such narratives influence the integration of those born into a society, do they exert similar influence on those who enter as adults and, if they do, how?

Like the question of whose stories should be of interest, the *how* in this *problématique* is much more complex than it may first appear: Do the stories foster identification with the new home country in ways that help to shape newcomers'

concerned with what it represents and assumes the universal membership of all citizens (which, in the French context, was not necessarily the same as all fellow nationals; but cf. Marcel Mauss, "La Nation," 1920; repr. *Année sociologique*, 3rd series (1953-4): 7-68), while Smith emphasizes *how* peoplehood is built and membership achieved. Also see Nikolaj Frederik Grundtvig's 1848 verse, which begins "People! what is a people?" Uffe Østergård, "Peasants and Danes: The Danish National Identity and Political Culture," *Comparative Studies in Society and History* 34, no:1 (Jan. 1992): 9-10.

political identities so that they move toward the political identities of members of the host society? If so, how, and through what social, political, and communicative processes is such influence exerted? And what of the identities of migrants before they moved from one society to another? I cannot answer these and related questions with confidence here, but it is possible to note some of the most obvious complexities.

First, adult immigrants carry the imprint of foundational stories and the normative messages indwelling them in their place of origin, and they generally arrive at their destination with preconceptions about it. Second, stories are narrated, written, or recounted *by people, to people*, in specific places and times; therefore the contexts in which they are told and heard – the where and when – matter greatly.[19] As I have suggested, if we want to gauge the impact and consequences of exposure to stories, we need to know who is telling them, to whom, how, when,[20] and in what circumstances.

Third, stories are mediated by social, cultural, and formal (institutional) filters before they reach their intended audience. Their content is filtered or refracted in ways that diminish, distort or even reverse their thrust. It is important, therefore, to examine the spaces, histories, institutions, and political arrays that lie between the emission of stories and their reception. Such mediating factors affect the impact of stories with national or societal messages on the identities of immigrants. This is especially true in plural or structurally divided societies, such as the United States was in the nineteenth century and contemporary France is in ways that bear on the concerns here.[21] There is a truism sometimes overlooked even by students of migration: while legally and formally immigrants enter a country, in practice they enter a specific place and connect with particular portions of that country's society. National policies toward immigration do not necessarily reflect – indeed, they frequently completely disregard realities on the ground. The histories, people,

---

19. Gregory Currie, *Narratives & Narrators: A Philosophy of Stories* (Oxford & New York: Oxford University Press, 2010).

20. The *when* of telling and hearing stories is an especially complex matter. In addition to the local or immediate settings in which they are recounted and heard, the broader *Zeitgeist* must also be taken into account. Thus, in some places and times (for instance, in one of the immigration-encouraging phases of a "country of immigration," such as the United States or Argentina in the nineteenth century), the stories may be expansive and welcoming, stressing the society's opportunities and integrative capacity, as well as an expectation that newcomers will assimilate or acculturate; at other times and/or places (e.g., Canada and the Netherlands from the mid-1970s to the mid-1990s), a prevailing multicultural ethos might have emphasized the possibilities for retaining the cultural distinctiveness of immigrants and downplayed the unique nation-generating histories and expectations of patriotic commitment to the new homeland. On Canada, see Elke Winter, "Die Dialektik multikultureller Identität: Kanada als Lehrstück," *Swiss Political Science Review* 15, no. 1 (2009).

21. My argument regarding the United States owes much to the work of a distinguished historian, the late Robert H. Wiebe (see, in particular, Wiebe, *The Segmented Society*). The segmentation of France today is rather different, as I suggest below, but it is no less segmented.

institutions, economic conjuncture, and other specifics of the places immigrants enter usually matter more in this regard than the general conditions or policies of the country or the qualities of the host society writ large.[22]

Fourth, adults are able to engage with the stories they encounter and shape their meaning; they have much greater agency than children. They can take an active part in critically evaluating and debating, accepting, or rejecting – or, most often, adapting – the stories to which they are exposed. Such capabilities of the individuals and groups toward whom stories are directed are often overlooked or insufficiently analyzed in writings on the transmission of foundational stories or grand narratives.[23] Finally, the normative and intellectual dispositions of the subjects (narrators and listeners), as well as those of observers and commentators (including ours, of course) matter greatly. Such dispositions are mixtures of the experiential, cultural, social, and psychological elements in the make-up of individuals; they influence the way stories are told and received.[24] As the experiences of Danish migrants in nineteenth century America and of West Africans who arrived in the Paris region recently illustrate, time, place, conditions, and normative dispositions – *Zeitgeists* – matter greatly.

■ A Note on the Approach Taken Here

These primitive formulations reflect my intellectual orientation – epistemological, analytical, and theoretical – to the subject of this essay. That orientation mirrors the treatment of history and people's relationships to it by philosophers who argued that historical knowledge is the product of encounters between personal experience (ordinary or "lived" life) and socially mediated observations and accounts. This position is particularly vivid in the work of three philosophers who concerned themselves with such relationships – Wilhelm Dilthey,[25] Paul

22. Martin O. Heisler, "Now and Then, Here and There: Migration and the Transformation of Identities, Borders, and Orders," in *Identities, Borders, Orders: Rethinking International Relations Theory*, ed. Mathias Albert, David Jacobson, and Yosef Lapid (Minneapolis: University of Minnesota Press, 2001); Daniel J. Hopkins, "Politicized Places: Explaining Where and When Immigrants Provoke Local Opposition," *American Political Science Review*, 104, no. 1 (Feb. 2010): 40-60.

23. See Currie, *Narratives & Narrators*, chap. 6. This oversight is also evident in much of the literature on collective memory. See Martin O. Heisler, "Cognitive and Philological Bases of Power in the Politics of Memory" (Paper presented at the annual meeting of the American Political Science Association, Washington D.C., 2005); Martin O. Heisler, "Power(s) in the Politics of Memory and Memorialization" (Paper presented at the annual meeting of the American Political Science Association, Philadelphia: 2006).

24. See Currie, *Narratives & Narrators*.

25. Esp. Wilhelm Dilthey, *Gesammelte Schriften*, vol. 7, *Der Aufbau der geschichtlichen Welt in den Geisteswissenshaften*; vol. 8, *Weltanschauungslehre, Abhandlungen zur Philosophie der Philosophie* (Göttingen: Vandenhoeck & Ruprecht, 1991-1992).

Ricœur,[26] and Edgar Morin.[27] It is partly paralleled in the work of a fourth, David Carr.[28]

Carr's interpretation of the thrust of Dilthey's and Ricœur's writings on those questions shows their relevance to the topic at hand. Dilthey provided a strikingly modern formulation of the interplay of personal and social elements in constructions of history, anticipating current thinking by a hundred years; Ricœur deepened and extended the analysis, adding a rich psychological dimension. Carr relates the gist of their arguments to a theory of narrative that helps in explorations of the meeting ground of immigrant identities and suggests that formulating stories as narratives may be analytically and theoretically useful. Although the analytic path I take here to the relationships between those identities and stories or narratives differs from Carr's, his ideas about the dynamics of narrative are similar to mine – especially in that we both view narrative as a dynamic and interactive process rather than static, unidirectional communication. But while Carr's goal is "to contribute to the philosophical understanding of history,"[29] thus entering philosophers' and historians' debates regarding the nature of history, I am interested in exploring immigrants' encounters with particular renderings of the history and destiny of the people among whom they find themselves and in the effects of those encounters on political identity.

By seeking to exploit the complexity of those encounters for analytic gain (rather than reducing them for the sake of parsimony), I use what Pierre Bourdieu and Loïc Wacquant termed "reflexive sociology," as applied to historical and literary "data."[30] Such reflexivity at the level of collectivities shows itself to be recursive for the individual and in individual identity. Here Edgar Morin's notion of recursivity is especially helpful.[31] He views identity as an ongoing negotiation between the external world and people's responses to it, based on their experiences and actual day-to-day lives.[32]

My thoughts about the dynamic nature of narratives and their influences on the

---

26. Esp. Paul Ricœur, *Time and Narrative* (Chicago: University of Chicago Press, 1984-88); Paul Ricœur, *Memory, History, Forgetting* (Chicago: University of Chicago Press, 2004).

27. See, e.g., among his more than 50 books: Edgar Morin, *Le vif du subject* (Paris: Éditions du Seuil, 1982); Edgar Morin, *La vie de la vie*, vol. 2 of *La Méthode* (Paris: Éditions du Seuil, 1985); Edgar Morin, *L'humanité de l'humanité*, vol. 5 of *La Méthode* (Paris: Éditions du Seuil, 2003).

28. Carr, *Time, Narrative, and History*.

29. Ibid., 7.

30. Pierre Bourdieu and Loïc D. Wacquant, *An Invitation to Reflexive Sociology* (Chicago: University of Chicago Press, 1992). Julie Kalman presents a lucid, well-grounded, historical study of the reflexivity of a collectivity's narrative of its identity and the shaping and reshaping of the self-concepts of a minority within its boundaries in *Rethinking Antisemitism in Nineteenth-Century France* (Cambridge and New York: Cambridge University Press, 2010).

31. Edgar Morin, *On Complexity*, 16 and passim.

32. Morin, *La vie de la vie*; Morin, *L'humanité*.

identity of immigrants are sketched in the next section. This is followed in Section III by illustrations of how such an approach might be applied to the seemingly strange selection of cases here: migrants from Denmark to nineteenth century America and West Africans in the Paris region in the twentieth century. The cases were chosen with three considerations in mind: (1) the differences that eras, places and their associated *Zeitgeists* make in the host society's narratives and in new-comers' encounters with them; (2) the effects of the cultures of migrants and host populations; ethnicity; "race;" religion; and other traits on relationships between immigrants and natives and on political identities; and (3) the influences of the major structural and processual features of social, economic, and political systems on those relationships and identities. Insights gleaned from the illustrative cases inform my conclusions regarding the dynamic connections between narratives and identities in Section IV.

II. Beyond Stories, Beneath Grand Narratives

Stories are told or written, and they are heard or read. But there is no direct, straight-forward way to ascertain how, if at all, their messages are received or what their impacts may be. Although there is no reason to think of a story as static, *the idea of story* does not invite dynamic, interactive, or reflexive analysis, either in its literal or its metaphoric sense.[33] Nor, generally, are its meanings, or the act of story-telling, viewed as contingent on context. Yet the processes through which people are engaged by, and in turn engage with stories are dynamic, interactive, and contingent on many contextual factors.[34]

As already noted, the ways immigrants encounter narratives about the places they enter and how they interact with them are varied and complex. And the stories are told and heard and engaged with in a *reflexive* fashion, requiring each actor (teller or hearer) to examine her or his position as well as those of the interlocutors in the exchanges that comprise the transmission and reception of a story. Stories

---

33. See Christian Salmon, *Storytelling: La machine à fabriquer des histoires et à formatter les esprits* (Paris: La Découverte, 2007), whose notion of storytelling in a multitude of fora is one-directional: from the source of the story to its target audience. He seems to assume that the audience simply absorbs the message of the story. In Currie's much more rigorously reasoned view, the exact opposite is the case (Currie, *Narratives & Narrators*).

34. This caveat can be extended to both stories of peoplehood and reifications of collective memory. See, e.g., Heisler, *Power(s)*; Jan Werner Müller, "Introduction: the Power of Memory, the Memory of Power and the Power over Memory," in *Memory and Power in Post-War Europe: Studies in the Presence of the Past* (Cambridge: Cambridge University Press, 2002); James W. Wertsch, *Voices of Collective Remembering* (Cambridge: Cambridge University Press, 2002); and for Pierre Bourdieu's more sweeping analytic perspective, see David Swartz, *Culture and Power: The Sociology of Pierre Bourdieu* (Chicago: University of Chicago Press, 1997). For an excellent recent philosophical treatment of the nature of stories and narratives see Currie, *Narratives & Narrators*.

in action – stories that do not simply reside passively on bookshelves or in people's minds – can thus be thought of as multiplex dialogues about messages flowing back and forth almost simultaneously among those doing the telling and the hearing. Such dialogues can be in "real time" – that is, actual exchanges in real time, or, at some remove, through, for instance, exchanges of "dueling essays" or speeches or texts. The perspectives of the people involved – their experiences, current situations, psychological states, and other factors that affect their cognitive processes – alter the interpretations and impacts of those messages in myriad ways, some small and others not so small.

It helps to conceptualize stories as *narratives*, a near-synonym, because the concept of narrative lends itself more readily to analysis in such dynamic terms. Two factors make it more useful than commonly understood notions of story: time – not only the passage of time but also the era in which it unfolds – and relationships or connections between the author or teller and her audience.[35] *A narrative is constructed through such connections or, more precisely, through relationships that are, in essence, interpersonal communications.*[36]

The communication processes by which narratives are constructed are not simply dyadic, however. They are mediated by many intervening factors – interpretations, reframings, and reconstructions. The cases here were selected in large part because they provide good illustrations of the salient types of context in which such mediation occurs.

Stories, as Smith (2003) envisions them, are essentially historical or diachronic grand or master narratives projected at the societal (or national or country) level.[37] But narratives actually unfold on many levels – ranging from all of humanity at the most inclusive down to the individual. (Multiple narratives can coexist even within the mind of a single individual, that is, at an intra-psychic level. At some stages in the migrant experience individuals may engage in internal dialogues regarding their identity, which is characterized by chronic ambivalence.[38]) The thoughts of migrants, whether voluntary or exiled, can accommodate simultaneous narratives focused on their current home *and* on their place of origin. This is especially common among transnational migrants in the modern world.[39] In this sense, the dialogical –

---

35. Carr, *Time, Narrative, and History*, 46; 46-65 passim.
36. Kenneth J. Gergen, Stuart M. Schraeder, and Mary Gergen, *Constructing Worlds Together: Interpersonal Communication as Relational Process* (Boston, MA: Allyn & Bacon, 2008).
37. As I noted earlier, this is so, even in the absence of explicit identification of that level.
38. See, e.g., the essays in André Aciman, ed., *Letters of Transit: Reflections on Exile, Identity, Language, and Loss* (New York: The New Press, 1999); a thorough scholarly analysis is provided in Jon Elster, ed., *The Multiple Self* (Cambridge & New York: Cambridge University Press, 1987).
39. There is a large and diverse literature on this subject. See, e.g., Franz Fanon, *Peau noire, masques blancs* (Paris: Éditions du Seuil, 1952); Heisler, "Now and Then"; David Jacobson, *Place and Belonging in America* (Baltimore

interactive, participatory – nature of narratives adds a synchronic dimension to the diachronic one of stories. Migrants, especially adults, *compare* the stories, as well as the realities, of the places they come from and those in the places in which they find themselves. For them, there is more than one story, and individuals, collectivities of various kinds, and sometimes institutions (such as churches, schools, and governments) must strive to manage the multiplicity of messages.[40]

The view of stories as grand narratives that unfold at the level of society, or a similarly large and broadly inclusive level, has important normative implications. Such stories can be seen as purposive, aimed at achieving and maintaining the cohesion of the population. They are devices for establishing and maintaining boundaries.[41] In order to perform those tasks effectively, they need to subsume smaller or less inclusive narratives.

A grand narrative is, in effect, what Giselle Bastin (2005) has termed a *metanarrative*. Conceiving of and working with stories at this level is clearly appropriate if we assume, as Smith and I do, that their principal function is the political integration of a population *along distinct, specifiable lines*: in terms of principles and norms such as those that delineate what Smith calls "ethical peoplehood." A corollary assumption is that such encompassing stories govern (*or should govern* and be superordinate to) stories encountered on lower, less inclusive or extensive levels, such as regions and local communities.

These considerations raise a series of questions. How do such grand narratives achieve the coherence necessary for subsuming less inclusive narratives – if, indeed, they can? For, as Bastin noted, not only are "history's metanarratives [...] always accompanied by other, 'smaller' histories, [but] the unity of metanarratives is made

---

& London: Johns Hopkins University Press, 2002), 167ff.; and Lok Siu, *Memories of a Future Home: Diasporic Citizenship of Chinese in Panama* (Stanford, CA: Stanford University Press, 2005). The "divided self" concept in Western literature can be traced to Goethe's *Faust* and some of the writings of Ralph Waldo Emerson, George Eliot, and others. The seed of W.E.B. DuBois's formulation of "double consciousness" may have been planted in his studies with William James. See Bruce D. Dickson Jr., "W.E.B. DuBois and the Idea of Double Consciousness," *American Literature* 64, no. 2 (June 1992). While the intra-psychic level may be apposite for considering identity, it is less central to the aims of this essay.

40. In the past 100-150 years, cross-national migrations have commonly been accompanied by the pull-and-tug of institutions (usually governments and churches), culture-based sentiments, and changes in – or changing assessments of – material conditions in the places of origin and destination. This vast subject cannot be explored here, but see, for instance, B.S. Heisler ("Sending Countries") for illustrations of the roles of institutions. Economic, cultural, familial and other factors are often noted in migrants' correspondence with those in the place of origin. For Scandinavians in nineteenth-century America, see, for example, Joan M. Jensen, *Calling This Place Home: Women on the Wisconsin Frontier, 1850-1925* (St. Paul, MN: Minnesota Historical Press, 2006); also Kristian Hvidt, *Flight to America: The Social background of 300,000 Danish Emigrants* (New York: Academic Press, 1975), esp. chap. 15.

41. Smith's (*Stories of Peoplehood*) "constitutive stories" are clearly of this sort.

constantly unstable by their presence."[42] Grand narratives and the principles and precepts associated with them are generally seen as instrumental in the formation of a people's collective identity; they are likewise presumed to be important in shaping (and, for immigrants, reshaping) the identities of individuals.

But what is the relative power of the metanarrative vis-à-vis more limited or particular narratives? How might less inclusive narratives – the stories of subsocietal peoples or a region, for instance, or the experiences of a given generation – affect the grand narrative?[43] Can less inclusive narratives persist in the presence of differing, even conflicting, grand narratives? In short, what is the relationship between narratives at various levels – the metanarrative (a story of peoplehood) and more particularistic narratives (stories of people in particular places, eras or circumstances)? Metanarratives aim to capture the public imagination regarding what a people is about,[44] but they are likely to succeed in this only if there is agreement on the basic principles and values the public can accept – or at least that large segments of the public do not reject or contest.[45]

Smaller, less inclusive, narratives may not be in direct conflict with a metanarrative; but because they are based on particular experiences – and are, therefore, presumably more concrete or specific – they may not be in harmony with it. This tension is a concern here because of my focus on two elements of *Zeitgeist*: *time* (era) and *place*, where place represents a particular culture and community as well as topographic and built space.[46] Era and place (or type of place) are significant sources of particular or smaller narratives; and they are keys to understanding the dialogical processes through which more inclusive narratives are framed, communicated, and grasped.

Finally, narratives are communicated and internalized by processes that are *political* in the most basic sense. They involve power relationships, based on status and authority, cultural and communicative resources, and so on; and they pass through

---

42. Giselle Bastin, "From *Grand Récit* to *Petit Histoire*: Exploring Historical Cleavage in Kate Grenville's *Joan Makes History*," *Limina – A Journal of Historical and Cultural Studies* 11 (2005): 28. Immigration policies provide good illustrations. The changing criteria for admitting immigrants into the United States have exerted frequent and very substantial changes in "who Americans are" or should be. For a sweeping overview of American immigration history, see Aristide Zolberg, *A Nation by Design: Immigration Policy in the Fashioning of America* (New York, Cambridge, MA & London: Russell Sage Foundation and Harvard University Press, 2006), and cf. Samuel P. Huntington, *Who Are We? The Challenges to America's National Identity* (New York: Simon and Schuster, 2004).
43. One can also conceive of influences on stories of peoplehood emanating from such more inclusive levels as the Muslim *umma*, Christendom, Catholicism, "Europe," *Norden*, "Western Civilization," etc.
44. Cf. Meili Steele, *Hiding from History: Politics and Public Imagination* (Ithaca & London: Cornell University Press, 2005), chap. 3.
45. Ibid., chaps. 4-5.
46. André Aciman, "Shadow Cities," in *Letters of Transit: Reflections on Exile, Identity, Language, and Loss* (New York: The New Press, 1999); Jacobson, *Place and Belonging*.

and are mediated by social and formal institutions. The cases sketched below can serve to illustrate such relationships and their influence on the transmission and internalization of grand narratives or stories of peoplehood.

III. Stories on the Pre-Modern American Prairie and in Post-modern Paris: Danes in America and West Africans in France[47]

The mid-nineteenth-century American Midwest and the Paris region 150 years later obviously differ greatly, as did the people of Danish and African origin who migrated to these places. Understanding some of these differences will help explain the kinds of narratives with which the newcomers might have made contact and how that contact unfolded. These differences are crucial, of course, from the point of view of the *substance* of what is recounted and heard, but also for how such com-munications take place. Considering the contextual factors that can influence the content of the narrative and the ways in which it might be received yields a better understanding of the *processes* by which stories reflect and influence identities – in this case, those in the host society and the migrants with whom they interact. These cases can illustrate – albeit at a general and abstract level (especially for historical Danish migration) – more particular contexts or "smaller narratives" that are more directly relevant to migrants than metanarratives of entire societies over long spans of time; and they also provide more useful insights into the sorts of influence that exchanges about stories can exert on newcomers.

■ Danes in the Upper Midwest, 1850-1875[48]

The settlement of Scandinavian immigrants in the Upper Midwest in the mid-nineteenth century typically followed one of two patterns. They either joined other Danes or Scandinavians to establish communities in small towns or, especially after the advent of the Homestead Act of 1862, they lived on individual homesteads in rural areas, interspersed with locally established Americans, many of whom had recently migrated from the eastern part of the country. The towns – whether populated mainly by native-born Americans or by early immigrants – tended to be

---

47. Recall that these sketches are constructed types: simplifications, abstractions, and generalizations intended to sharpen analytic points (see note 5 above). They are distillations from illustrative cases, anecdotes and such primary sources as news accounts and letters, rather than "history" supported by systematic evidence.
48. This period extends by five years what Torben Grøngaard Jeppesen termed the "early immigration" of Danes to the United States. Torben Grøngaard Jeppesen, *Danske i USA, 1850-2000 – en demografisk, social og kulturgeografisk undersøgelse af de danske immigranter of deres efterkommere* (Odense: Odense Bys Museer, 2005), chap. iv.

culturally, linguistically, and ethnically homogeneous.[49] (Those created by immigrants are usually termed enclaves or "colonies" in the literature on migration.[50]) If the first pattern led to the creation of enclaves or colonies, the second reflected the stereotypical farmstead depicted in both historical and fictional accounts of the peopling of the American Midwest, especially in the immediate aftermath of the Homestead Act and the Civil War.

Largely homogeneous Danish or Scandinavian communities in Wisconsin, Iowa, and Nebraska were formed along the lines of the first pattern.[51] While some may not have been entirely self-sufficient economically, they did serve as cultural cocoons for new arrivals; and they created opportunities for teachers, clergy, and other "idea workers," migrants who could influence ideas and reinforce the culture of the homeland and identity with it. In the words of Morawska and Spohn, "[o]rganized communities of fellow nationals were practically the only place where these people could find jobs [...]."[52]

The looseness of the American legal structure and the decentralized nature of life in these western states and territories, coupled with prevailing norms and practices and the relative sparseness of the population, made it possible to approximate and maintain many of the important qualities of Danish life, at least for one or two generations. Schools, churches, and other institutions sustained language and most familiar values.[53] Those values and principles could be characterized

---

49. These early settlements seemed homogeneous when contrasted with contemporaneous cities in eastern and southern United States, as well as with most of the country in later periods. Scandinavians joined what Milton Gordon termed the "subsociety of [the] white Protestant group" in nineteenth-century America. Milton M. Gordon, *Assimilation in American Life: The Role of Race, Religion, and National Origin* (New York & Oxford: Oxford University Press), 78, 116ff..

50. The concepts "enclave" and "colony," as well as their empirical referents, were similar, though not identical. Enclaves are more or less comprehensive functionally, so that most of the services and many of the products used by their populations are provided internally. Alejandro Portes and Robert D. Manning, "The Immigrant Enclave: Theory and Empirical Examples," in *Competitive Ethnic Relations* (New York: Academic Press, 1986); Alejandro Portes and Leif Jensen, "What's an Ethnic Enclave: The Case for Conceptual Clarity," *American Sociological Review* 52, no. 6 (Dec. 1987). "The word colony – or settlement – [...refers to] a compact Danish group setting in an area, where there is in addition established some form of Danish organization such as a church, social organization or the like." Torben Grøngaard Jeppesen, *Dannebrog on the American Prairie* (Odense: Odense City Museum, 2000), 45.

51. See the rich descriptions, enlightening analyses, and helpful bibliography in Grøngaard Jeppesen (*Dannebrog*). Also see Steffen Elmer Jørgensen, "A Scattered People? Danish Settlement Structure and Community Transplantations in the Midwest," in *On Distant Shores: Proceedings of the Marcus Lee Hansen Immigration Conference; Aalborg, 29 June-1 July 1992*, ed. Birgit Flemming Larsen, Henning Bender, and Karen Veien (Aalborg: Danes Worldwide Archives; Danish Society for Emigration History, 1993).

52. Ewa Morawska and Willfried Spohn, "Moving Europeans in the Globalizing World: Contemporary Migrations in a Historical-Comparative Perspective (1955-1994 v. 1870-1914)," in *Global History and Migrations* (Boulder, CO & Cumner Hill, Oxford: Westview, 1997), 49.

53. Henrik Brednose Simonsen, *Kampen om danskhed: tro og nationalitet i de danske kirkesamfund i Amerika* (Aarhus: Aarhus University Press, 1990); Østergård, "Peasants and Danes."

as broadly Grundtvigian in spirit, even for those Danes who did not explicitly associate with that movement. The spirit of Grundtvigism, as summarized by Uffe Østergård, "underlin[ed] [...] the unity of land, country, God, and people."[54] Grundtvig also assumed "that culture and identity are embedded in the unity of life and language."[55] And one of its core values was (and remains, a century and a half later in Denmark, although some believe it is eroding) a fundamental egalitarianism and solidarity.

The stories Danes in such communities heard were not simple or straightforward narratives of the history and nature of America, and they did not emanate from a central, authoritative source. What follows is abstracted from the layers of narratives about America that early Danish immigrants likely encountered. Danes' experiences in Wisconsin in the 1850s can be gleaned from the archives of local newspapers,[56] and for the period 1850-1875 from numerous memoirs and scholarly reconstructions.[57] While historical evidence from primary sources can help to identify the major elements and structures of the dialogics of narrative, the processes that bring them to life can only be surmised.

What they heard was inflected by contextual factors, having passed through several varied filters before reaching their audience. The first set of those filters were the stories about America that migrants encountered before leaving Denmark. These had multiple sources and presumably reflected diverse perspectives. The letters and public writings of (in Torben Grøngaard Jeppesen's periodization) the "pioneering Danes" who arrived before 1850, as well as tales told by those who returned to Denmark, provided descriptions and impressions of the New World. These stories were eagerly received and widely circulated.[58] Thus, the expectations

---

54. Østergård, "Peasants and Danes," 18.

55. Ibid., 10.

56. Those consulted include *The Blair Press of Alma Center; The Blair Press of Taylor; The Janesville Democrat; The Janesville Gazette;* and *The Weekly Jeffersonian.*

57. See, e.g., Halvdan Helweg, *An Early History of the West Denmark Colonization [Optegnelsen om grundlæggelsen den danske koloni West Denmark, Wisconsin i USA]* (Luck, WI: West Denmark Lutheran Church, 1963/1907); extensive quotes from the correspondence of early pioneers such as Rasmus Sørensen in Frederick Hale, *Danes in Wisconsin,* rev. and expanded ed. (Madison, WI: Wisconsin Historical Society Press, 2005); as well as Thomas P. Christensen, "Danish Settlement in Wisconsin," *The Wisconsin Magazine of History* 12, no. 1 (1928): 19-40; Erik H. Pedersen, "Danish Farmers in the Middle West," *The Bridge* 5 (1982): 51-68; Enok Mortensen, "The Acculturation of the Danish Immigrant," *The Bridge* 3 (1980): 83-91; and especially Niels Peter Stilling and Anne Lisbeth Olsen, *A New Life: Danish Emigration to North America as Described by the Emigrants Themselves in Letters, 1842-1946,* 2nd ed., (Aalborg: Danes Worldwide Archives, in collaboration with the Danish Society for Emigration History, 1994).

58. Steffen Elmer Jørgensen, "Ideal or Counter-Image? Aspects of the American Cultural Impact on Denmark, 1776 to 1995," in *Images of America in Scandinavia* (Amsterdam & Atlanta: Rodopi, B.V., 1998).

formed before people set off on their momentous journeys were the first filters through which they viewed their new homes.[59]

Since it is not likely that they had all read or heard the same stories of America before departure, they doubtless exchanged their ideas of what lay ahead on their journey. Such discussions were, in essence, *dialogues about imaginaries* of the United States and perhaps also of the particular place that was their destination. Preconceptions encountered others' preconceptions; imaginaries met; and those dialogues affected the initial expectations about America that had been formed when they decided to emigrate. This was a second filter.

The early enclave or colony-like settlements were a third, and perhaps the most important, factor affecting the content and form of the narratives of America. Although new and small, such communities were complex social systems, with their own cultural, political, and economic structures. Personal reputation or prestige and social standing (even among a relatively egalitarian people) gave greater or lesser weight to the views or interpretations of some regarding their new environment. Discussions, even debates, about the meanings of initial experiences, as well as stories about America – its nature, norms, people, and institutions – were doubtless a regular part of life. The settler community served to shape, reshape, and, in general, again to filter those messages and impressions. The most important dialogues about the meanings of America may have thus taken place when early individual or collective contacts with people and institutions outside the community were discussed among its members and in this way put through the filter of the collectivity's internal cultural, social, and interpersonal processes, especially in the schools, churches, and other institutions led by fellow Danes.

In the second pattern of settlement, outside towns, encounters between earlier settlers and newly arrived outsiders were *per force* noteworthy for both. The sparse population in the countryside of the Upper Midwest in the mid-nineteenth century made it difficult for residents to ignore newcomers; and the latter, of course, could only interact with the established residents and each other.[60] Contact was eventful – literally remarkable – for both Americans and Danes. The experience of

---

59. Cf. Poul Houe and Sven Hakon Rossel, eds., *Images of America in Scandinavia* (Amsterdam & Atlanta: Rodopi, B.V., 1998).

60. For analytic convenience, I am using the simplifying assumption here that the earlier settlers were English-speaking, mostly Protestant, Americans and that the newcomers were Danes or other northern Europeans. But depending on specific periods and locales (e.g., counties or towns), the mix may have been different. Thus, for instance, the earliest Danish arrivals comprised a miniscule portion of European immigrants in Wisconsin. Drawing on the 1850 US census, Mark Wyman found thousands of Germans, Irish, English, and Norwegians, as well as 146 Swedes in the state, but only 88 Danes. Mark Wyman, *The Wisconsin Frontier* (Bloomington & Indianapolis: Indiana University Press, 1998), 189. But by 1860 there were 1,160 Danes and by 1870 more than 5,000 in Wisconsin alone.

meeting and adjusting to life near new arrivals, especially from other countries, was interesting for Americans.[61] For Scandinavians, the people, landscape, language, and customs of the established populations were clearly consciousness-raising events. The letters of early settlers living outside enclaves focused on the hardships of daily life, earning a living, and family matters, but they included comments on American and other neighbors as well.

Such encounters appear to have produced little tension and virtually no conflict.[62] Several factors facilitated adjustment between the indigenous and immigrant populations. First, as already noted, both had moved into what was a frontier region. In-migration and settlement were expected and seen as normal; it was a major element of the *Zeitgeist*. Second, although some would eventually "pull up stakes" and move further west if, as the cliché of the time had it, they could see the smoke from their neighbor's chimney, population density was low; and while there was doubtless competition for the most desirable locations, land was abundant and cheap, compared with the home country or the more densely populated East. Culturally abrasive contacts or conflicts over land seem to have been infrequent. In towns, the greater linguistic and cultural homogeneity that characterized immigrant enclaves smoothed relationships even in the presence of higher population density. Third, functional (e.g., economic, security-related) necessity militated in favor of civil and cooperative relationships. Mutual need and benefit conduced to building communities together, and doing so also involved politics.[63] In the end, however, it becomes difficult – and probably unnecessary – to separate cultural and sentimental ties on the one hand, and "rational" or interest-based links on the other.[64]

Cultural harmony did not mean, however, that there was no political activity in such towns, since neither differences in economic interests and values nor competition for leadership or influence were absent or avoidable. Unfortunately, there is little direct evidence of the content of either such internal politics or political connections with people and groups outside the enclaves for this early period.[65]

Relationships among those living in more or less homogeneous communi-

---

61. Heisler, "Now and Then," esp. 227-229; also see Zolberg, *A Nation by Design*, 16.

62. This observation is based on a perusal of letters Danish arrivals sent home, local newspapers, and memoirs. These remarked on the arrival and activities of Scandinavians in matter-of-fact ways and reported few if any conflicts. See, for instance, Helweg (*An Early History of the West Denmark*); and Niels Peter Stilling and Anne Lisbeth Olsen, *A New Life*.

63. Compare "economically constitutive stories" in Smith (*Stories of Peoplehood*). On the edges of the frontier, concerns about security vis-à-vis the forces of nature as well as Native Americans ("Indians") also created shared interests.

64. James S. Coleman, "Social Capital in the Creation of Human Capital," *American Journal of Sociology* 94 (1988): 95-120.

65. There are indirect indications, noted below, of the long-term influence of the political aspects of Scandinavian culture on the normative and practical political lives of the communities and regions in which they settled, particularly in the Upper Midwest.

ties fostered what is termed *bonding social capital in the social science literature.*[66] Bonding social capital is conducive to high levels of trust, attributable largely to members' connections through many links, such as ethnic and family relationships and interdependence in daily life. These mutually reinforcing ties tend to produce high levels of mutual loyalty. A betrayal of trust would likely carry heavy penalties, such as ostracism by others in the community whose approbation is important; it would impinge on friendships and economic and other relationships.[67]

The high levels of bonding social capital characteristic of the sorts of (relatively small) enclaves formed by Danes in the Upper Midwest in the mid-nineteenth century had a two-fold effect on how – and what sorts of – stories of America reached the immigrants. First, narratives passed through the screen of the community and its institutions before they reached individuals and families. Individuals and families could interrogate the contents and meanings of the narratives and doubtless did so in countless exchanges, but even if a grand narrative of America was available to those in more established communities, it did not reach recent arrivals directly. Second, the smaller histories, the particularities of the people who comprised the enclave, and their places of origin and circumstances (e.g., family situation, economic resources, education, the location and conditions of their community in America) all inflected the metanarrative, but in a fashion that put a premium on relating individual interpretations to some common rendering of it. Thus, *whatever story of America was "out there," its impact on the individual identity of the Danish immigrant was likely to be indirect.*

Social capital was also created by those who settled outside enclaves or colonies (the second pattern), but in different ways and forms. They interacted with Americans – often also recent settlers in the area – as individuals or households, rather than as members of a collectivity. If distance and circumstances made it possible, they could establish links with other Danish (or Scandinavian) immigrants; but, since they did not live in close-knit, culturally homogeneous, and more or less self-contained communities, their contacts with Americans were likely to be more regular and significant. The relationships established through such contacts tended to be based on practical, mundane needs rather than linguistic, national, or cultural affinities. Such relationships were conducive to *bridging social capital.*[68]

The differences between the two kinds of social capital associated with these different patterns of settlement had important ramifications for identity formation. In Robert Putnam's words, bonding social capital is "inward looking and tend[s] to

---

66. Robert D. Putnam, *Bowling Alone: The Collapse and Revival of American Community* (New York: Simon & Schuster, 2000); also see Coleman, "Social Capital.".

67. Coleman, "Social Capital.".

68. Putnam, *Bowling Alone*; Coleman, "Social Capital."

reinforce exclusive [in this case Danish] identities and homogeneous groups. [...] *[B]ridging social capital can generate broader identities and reciprocity, whereas bonding social capital bolsters our narrower selves*" (italics added).[69]

Those who took advantage of land grants under the Homestead Act of 1862, Americans and immigrants alike, faced similar challenges in establishing homes and developing farms. They shared concerns and had opportunities to discuss them at markets and social gatherings and to exchange opinions formed in settings that were new to both. The historical scholarship on the period and region suggests that discussions among citizens and recent arrivals were likely to occur on a wide range of public issues. They shared stories. Language differences were not insuperable. As early as 1848 Rasmus Sørensen could boast that "I speak English almost as well as I speak Danish now;"[70] and by the 1860s there were institutionalized efforts to learn the language: "[I]n Racine,... the Dania Society was founded in 1867. According to its constitution, [it] was to promote music, debates and language study.... Its cultural activities featured evening courses in English."[71]

Americans in the mid-nineteenth-century Upper Midwest could and did narrate their understanding of the country *as they perceived it*; *newcomers listened to those stories and recounted their own*. Relationships between them tended to develop on the basis of relative equality.

It does not require a great leap of imagination to suppose that Danes and Americans thought about and commented on each other's stories; they both took active parts in such dialogues. The stories that emerged tended to emphasize the local, particular, and practical implications of the tenets of Americanism and the nature of America – but not necessarily at the expense of its national, general, and principled qualities. The local was embedded in the national; and, given the latter's general and rather abstract qualities, it could readily embrace the various local and particular narratives.

The dialogical processes through which these early Danish immigrants encountered the story/ies of America and by which their identities were (re)shaped reflected more directly the impact of the *lived lives*, not received abstractions. Those in (more or less) homogeneous communities could experience and interpret the New World in shared cultural settings, through collective perceptions, while settlers on individual homesteads, outside such enclaves or communities and in the company of mostly

---

69. Putnam, *Bowling Alone*, 22-23.
70. Hale, *Danes in Wisconsin*, 49.
71. Ibid., 34. As Frederick Hale noted, "Partly because Danes were numerically weak in Wisconsin before the Civil War, they appear to have assimilated American ways rapidly. Learning English was a crucial part of most newcomers' adaptation, and those from Denmark were no exception." Ibid., 15. Also consider Helweg's reference to "a German-born wife of a Danish pioneer" who "spoke... in the most peculiar language, a colorful mixture of Danish, German, and English" (Helweg, *An Early History of the West Denmark*, 12).

American neighbors, negotiated their identities day by day. Their interactions with dissimilar settlers necessitated individual (or familial) interpretations of the "text" of America in more direct and immediate circumstances.[72]

The influence of the story/ies of America in the (re)shaping of Danish immigrants' identities followed from concrete experiences and interpretations of the import of those stories that were produced jointly by Danes and non-Danes. One could argue that this *is* the story of America, that in a land of immigration the integration of immigrants creates a story that is an amalgam of the histories, myths, and memories of members of the host society and of later arrivals. In this sense, the morphing of Danish identities into American identities is a joint and dialogical process that, in the nineteenth-century Upper Midwest was less direct and perhaps completed a generation or two later for those who settled in largely Danish or northern European communities than for homesteaders who mingled with Americans on the prairie.

■ West Africans in the Paris region[73]

The population of the vast urban agglomeration that is modern Paris is remarkably heterogeneous, with greatly varying cultural, linguistic, economic, and other attributes, and in some cases legal status. Both casual encounters (in the streets or in shops and public transportation) and more structured interactions (at the workplace, in schools or government offices) entail frequent (usually unavoidable, though often impersonal) meetings with the Other. Such encounters are not supposed to be remarkable in a place long regarded as the epitome of cosmopolitanism. The norms associated with urban life in modern western democracies call for routine, matter-of-fact reactions, even when meeting people differ markedly in physical appearance or dress from the dominant cultural majority. Yet those encounters are often jarring, tense, and occasionally even conflict-bearing.[74]

This situation differs markedly from that of Paris and most of urban France in the first 60 or so years of the twentieth century. Then *some* people of color may have felt

---

72. In this view, following Dilthey, *Gesammelte Schriften*; Morin, *Le vif du sujet*; and, less directly, Carr, *Time, Narrative, History, lived lives* shape narratives of a people or place – of history, or collective experiences and memories – into socially constructed reality.

73. For directly related research findings, see Claude-Valentin Marie, "Les Antillais en France: une nouvelle donne," *Hommes & Migrations* 1237 (May-June 2002): 26-38; and Mar Fall, *Le destin des Africains noirs en France: discrimination, assimilation, repli communautaire* (Paris: L'Harmattan, 2005).

74. Angèle Nyer-Malbet, "Migritude," *Cahiers d'anthropologie et biométrie humaine* 13 (1995): 3-4; Ida Simon-Barouh and Pierre-Jean Simon, *Les Étrangers dans la ville: Le regard des sciences sociales* (Paris: L'Harmattan, 2000); Stefan Goodwin, *Africa in Europe, Vol. II: Interdependence, Relocations, and Globalization* (Lanham, MD & Plymouth, UK: Lexington Books, 2009), 308ff.; also see Heisler, "Now and Then," 227ff.

more welcome there than in most other parts of the world. More specifically, *some* migrants from Africa and those of African ancestry arriving from the French Antilles, the United States, and elsewhere were notable in Paris in the 1920s and1930s and in the years after World War II, not because there was cultural friction between them and the dominant cultural majority but, rather, because they were valued for their intellectual luminosity and cultural contributions to the larger society. They were writers, poets, artists, doctors, lawyers, and scholars; many were major public figures in their homelands as well as in France. And, rather than clashing with that majority, they approximated closely what were perceived to be its highest ideals.[75]

By coming to France, such migrants validated two of the most cherished elements in the idea of France, the story it had told itself since at least the advent of the Third Republic (if not the Revolution): (1) embodiment of the ideals of the Enlightenment in the quest for freedom of beliefs and expression, knowledge, and the arts; and (2) extending welcome to those whose pursuit of such values was stymied elsewhere.[76] The arrival of those who sought to embrace such ideals or to escape from places where they were denied served to reinforce the collective self-concept of the French. Such cosmopolitan reception greeted those who were "somebody," who stood out in ways valued by the host society, those who came with large amounts of such cultural capital. The most distinguished among them could convert that cultural capital into social and political (and often economic) capital – within limits. Notwithstanding such welcome, however, they, and certainly "ordinary people" of color, were not accepted unconditionally.[77] Being well-received by segments of French society did not make them immune to treatment as actual or potential threats to public order or to surveillance by police.[78] Ideals and practice were often at odds.[79]

The French collective self-image as cosmopolitan champions of freedom, reason, openness, and tolerance has been challenged frequently by traumatic events, most

---

75. Dominique Chathuant, "L'émergence d'une élite politique noire dans la France du premier 20e siècle?," *Vingtième Siècle* 101 (2009/1); Philippe Dewitte, *Les mouvements nègres en France, 1919-1939* (Paris: L'Harmattan, 2004).
76. Jennifer Anne Boittin, "Black in France: The Language and Politics of Race in the Late Third Republic," *French Politics, Culture & Society* 27, no. 2 (Summer 2009), 781-792.
77. Mary Dewhurst Lewis, *The Boundaries of the Republic: Migrant Rights and the Limits of Universalism in France, 1918-1940* (Stanford: Stanford University Press, 2007).
78. See, e.g., Carole Reynaud Paligot, *Races, racisme et anti-racisme dans les années 1930* (Paris: Presses Universitaires de France, 2007); Jennifer Anne Boittin, *Colonial Metropolis: The Urban Grounds of Anti-Imperialism and Feminism in Interwar France* (Lincoln, NE: University of Nebraska Press, 2010); Dewitte, *Les mouvements*, 21ff. As recently as the late 1960s or early 1970s, police in France, as well as in many other western and central European countries, commonly lumped matters related to foreigners and criminals (often more specifically those suspected of violations of drug or vice laws) into one category or department.
79. Eugen Weber opened the chapter on foreigners in his book on the 1930s in France with the observation that "[t]he more the twentieth century advanced, the more France was to attract foreigners, benefit from them, resent them, reject them." Eugen Weber, *The Hollow Years: France in the 1930s* (New York & London: W.W. Norton, 1994), 87.

notably the Dreyfus affair; the policies and actions of the Vichy regime and individual collaborators; and the wars of decolonization in Indochina and Algeria. Those wars and the subsequent, almost entirely peaceful, moves to independence by France's African colonies were followed by the influx of, first, hundreds of thousands, then millions of immigrants who were visibly different from the white European, overwhelmingly Christian population. Added to these waves of immigrants (including large numbers of foreign workers recruited from southern Europe and North Africa) were smaller numbers of *de jure* but not always *de facto* citizens of color from Overseas Departments (DOMs) and Territories (TOMs),[80] as well as refugees and expatriates from Indochina, the United States, the Soviet Union, Eastern Europe, and elsewhere.

The criteria I used earlier to analyze salient elements in the relationships of Danish immigrants to America in the nineteenth century can serve to illuminate the stark differences between the experiences of the earlier migrants in France and those who arrived more recently. The characteristics of the migrants, changes in the French metanarrative and general *Zeitgeist*,[81] the structural, cultural, and institutional circumstances – and *the numbers of migrants* – in the two periods need to be taken into account, as do smaller, local stories affecting the way migrants related to the French metanarrative and to essential elements of being or becoming French. The patterns of settlement of the two waves of migrants to France are also important as analytic dimensions, as they are in considering modes of Danish settlement. Those patterns have direct bearing on the mutual orientations of migrants and host societies and on the ways the French metanarrative might have affected individual and collective identities.[82] Sketches in the following paragraphs of the immigration of elites in the earlier period and of the more recent entry of larger numbers of "ordinary people" provide illustrations.

The early migrants from West Africa and the French Afro-Caribbean territories entered the *Métropole* with a commitment to highly valued qualities at the core of

---

80. See Michel Giraud, "The Antillese in France: Trends and Prospects," *Ethnic and Racial Studies* 27, no. 4 (July 2004): 622-640. Some overseas territories did not accept recent revisions in their status and now are referred to as *collectivités d'outre-mer* (COM).

81. This is not the place to describe such changes; but two diametrically opposed developments affecting attitudes, policies and behavior regarding people of African, Asian, and Jewish origin in France in the second half of the twentieth century need to be taken into account. First, anti-immigrant, and often explicitly racist, views crystallized into political movements, most notably the *Front National*, which was founded in 1972, and gained strength in the next 30 years. Second, significant social and political movements came into being in this period, supporting the rights of ethnic and racial minorities and of immigrants of all kinds. The largest, most durable and important of these is *SOS Racisme*. See, for example, Philippe Bataille and Michel Wieviorka, eds., *Racisme et xénophobie en Europe* (Paris: La Découverte, 1994); and Jérémy Robine, "SOS Racisme et les ghettos des banlieues: construction et utilizations d'une representation," *Hérodote* 113, no 2 (2004): 134-151.

82. Recall my earlier suggestion that the American story has shown more discontinuity over time than the French.

the French metanarrative and possessed cultural resources – bridging social capital – necessary for establishing ties to both formal and social institutions. In a sense, they could be said to have integrated before or on arrival. Very few of the hundreds of thousands of migrants from those regions in the late twentieth century possessed such attributes. Lacking the resources necessary for integrating into an advanced industrial economy and society, they found themselves isolated geographically (in terms of where they could find housing), culturally, and economically, and without effective political voice. Virtually none had attributes useful as social capital for establishing links – "bridges" – to the institutions of modern France; and, for the most part, the bonding capital they were able to find was of a sort that impeded eventual integration into the larger society. If they were able to integrate into a sub-societal population, it was that of other recent or relatively recent arrivals from the Third World – a population that was characterized first and foremost by its isolation. Such association or integration *engendered an oppositional orientation* to the story of France: "we" are the "exclus;" "they" are to be regarded as hostile.[83] Such an orientation was fueled by: un- or under-employment; inferior living conditions and educational opportunities; poverty and a strong sense of relative deprivation; feeling disenfranchised; conflictive relationships with public institutions, especially law enforcement; pessimistic outlook regarding economic or social progress; and constant manifestations of discrimination in various forms.[84]

The differences between the two types of migrants and their relationships to French society can be seen by comparing the experiences of three notable personalities (two immigrants from what were then colonies in French West Africa and an "internal migrant" from an overseas *Département* in the Caribbean) in the earlier era and those of more recent, "ordinary" people from former French West Africa and the Caribbean DOMs. They illustrate the possibilities for integration into French political and social life by those who are both able and willing to embrace the prin-

---

83. On the general syndrome and theory, see Jane Mansbridge and Aldon Morris, eds., *Oppositional Consciousness: The Subjective Roots of Social Protest* (Chicago: University of Chicago Press, 2001).

84. For evidence, see, *i. a.*, Maurice Blanc, "Social Integration and Exclusion in France: Some Introductory Remarks from a Social Transaction Perspective," *Housing Studies* 13, no. France, special attention was given to "the black population of Paris in 1776, and [...] Muslims in Provence and Protestants in Alsace, [and all] foreigners, at least in Paris" (Peter Sahlins, *Unnaturally French: Foreign Citizens in the Old Regime and After* (Ithaca & London: Cornell University Press, 2004), 263-264, and 406, n. 143). 16 (Nov. 1998): 781-792; Jacques Chevrier, "Afrique(s)-sur-Seine: Autour de la Notion de 'Migritude'," *Notre Librairie* 155-156 (July-Dec. 2004): 13-17; Fall, *Le destin*; Giraud, "The Antillese,"; Faïza Guélamine, *Action sociale et immigration en France: Repères pour l'intervention* (Paris: Dunot, 2008); Loïc Wacquant, "Urban Outcasts: Stigma and Division in the Black American Ghetto and the French Urban Periphery," *International Journal of Urban and Regional Research* 17, no. 3 (1993): 366-383; Michel Wieviorka, *L'espace du racisme* (Paris: Éditions du Seuil, 1991). For additional theoretical insights related to the French situation, see Martine Xiberras, *Les theories de l'exclusion* (Paris: Arman Colin, 1998) and Michel Wieviorka, *La différance* (Paris: Balland, 2001).

ciples and conventions highlighted in the French metanarrative. They also point to the difficulties faced by "ordinary" people to form a positive orientation to the story of French peoplehood, to be accepted by the dominant cultural majority and the country's institutions – to become French – at the end of the twentieth century. The biographical sketches of the three luminaries are taken from the public record; the sketches of the three – I believe representative – recent "ordinary" migrants are based on extensive and repeated conversations.

■ "Black exemplars of Frenchness"[85]

Three of the distinguished immigrants of African origin who were exemplars *par excellence* of French society's image of itself, illustrate the possibility of achieving political membership in the French people. *They integrated successfully because they had assimilated – internalized – the central elements of that story even before arriving in the Métropole.* They were Léopold Sédar Senghor, Félix Houphouët-Boigny, and Gaston Monnerville, exceptional characters, to be sure, but not the only strangers accepted as "French at heart."

Senghor was born in Senegal. He received his higher education in France and subsequently taught literature there. He became a French citizen at the age of 25; fought with the French forces in World War II; taught literature at the university level; and was subsequently elected to the French National Assembly. After the war, he was the co-founder of the influential cultural and intellectual movement of Négritude. His achievements as a writer and poet, coupled with the impact of his creative and consequential philosophical writings, earned the respect and admiration of French political, social, and intellectual élites. He served as Senegal's president from the country's independence, in 1960, until 1980. Houphouët-Boigny, from Côte d'Ivoire, was a medical doctor, labor and community organizer, and for many years a member of the French National Assembly. He served in several cabinets in the Fourth Republic and in the first government of the Fifth, leaving those posts to become the first president of the Côte d'Ivoire and arguably the most influential political leader in newly independent West Africa.

A third luminary, Gaston Monnerville, was born in French Guyana, the grandson of slaves. He went to the University of Toulouse to complete his legal studies; was subsequently elected to the French National Assembly; served in the navy; and, following France's surrender in 1940, joined the Free French resistance. After the war he was elected to the Council of the Republic from Lot and then to its presidency for the duration of the Fourth Republic. The Fifth Republic's constitution

---

85. This is how these three men were characterized by a mid-level French civil servant and sociologist of Afro-Caribbean origin in the course of an interview with me in November, 1991.

transmuted the Council into the Senate, over which he continued to preside until he resigned, in 1968, to protest what he saw as de Gaulle's constitutional overreach. The presidency of the Senate made him Vice-President of the Republic. He finished his governmental career in his mid-80s as president of the Constitutional Council; and in retirement he took the leadership of a nationwide organization fighting racism and anti-Semitism.

These men clearly had exceptional educational, intellectual, and personal qualities. And they were quintessentially French, in terms of the criteria of ethical peoplehood. *They chose to be French*, even those who never lost sight of – and eventually returned to – their places of origin.[86] In some respects, they were much more French than most of those commonly seen as French – except for the huge difference of their places of origin and skin color, factors discussed further below. They reinforced many of the positive elements of the French story; they validated that story and made French people proud to be French.

Myriad others – artists, performers, and writers, political dissidents from Asia, the Americas, and Eastern Europe, as well as Africa – moved to Paris in the decades before and after World War II, seeking freedom of expression or opportunity to plot against their home regimes – or even France.[87] They may have been seeking to escape from a racist or homophobic atmosphere in their homeland,[88] or a chance to flourish artistically and benefit from the critical mass of creative people from around the world who congregated there. While such emigrés and expatriates were not accepted unconditionally, those who appeared to pursue lives that conformed to prevailing French values were at least tolerated and in many instances were seen to enhance and validate the cosmopolitan self-image of the country.

The cultural assets such individuals brought with them served as bridging capital. Their origins and skin color were not impediments to integration into the intelligentsia, and into elites in general – *as individuals*. But such integration was made possible by the stratification of French society in terms of social class, education, and world views. The prominent immigrants of color identified with and integrated into higher strata of French society, not into the society as a whole, except to the

---

86. Elsewhere I have argued that "peoplehood is a political state of being" requiring "conscious association, based on reflection, not simply propinquity...; [and] it provides some degree of volition or choice." Martin O. Heisler, "Challenged Histories and Collective Self-Concepts: Politics in History, Memory, and Time," *Annals of the American Academy of Political and Social Science* 617 (May 2004): 204.

87. See Dewitte, *Les mouvements*, esp. chaps. viii-ix. As Ho Chi Minh demonstrated, it was much easier to plot against French colonial rule in Paris than in the colonies.

88. Notable examples were the American performer Josephine Baker and the writers Richard Wright and James Baldwin. Jazz musicians and visual artists also moved from the United States to France for shorter or longer periods for these reasons. See Michel Fabre, *From Harlem to Paris: Black American Writers in France, 1840-1980* (Urbana & Chicago: University of Illinois Press, 1991) and William A. Shack, *Harlem in Montmartre: A Paris Jazz Story between the Great Wars* (Berkeley & Los Angeles: University of California Press, 2001).

extent that that society valued intellectuals and people with extraordinary qualities. They were French, but "special," just as they were special as immigrants. Their daily lives seldom intersected with those of "the masses." There were few occasions for "jarring encounters" of the sort alluded to above, something that characterized interactions between the far more numerous "ordinary" immigrants of color and the host society.

Migration had a curious effect on the identities of such individuals: in some respects they were returning home. They fit better in the culture, society, and polity of France – or at least into its elite strata – than in the places they had left behind. Their attributes and aspirations were probably valued and appreciated more highly in the former than in the latter and their talents could be put to better use. Sojourns in France increased the social and political (and often economic) capital of those who returned to their places of origin – not only Senghor and Houphouët-Boigny but also many artists, writers, and political dissidents.

■ Mass migration from West Africa and the Caribbean DOMs

That was then. Immigrants of color since the 1970s entered a very different France; and, equally or more importantly, they differed greatly from the well-educated, sophisticated, skilled individuals who had been accepted by French society and institutions in the earlier period. Although most recent arrivals could speak French (with considerable variation in dialect and proficiency), few arrived with appreciable human and social (not to mention economic) capital. Most important, they came with little or no cultural capital. Unlike the three men noted above, they had not internalized the elements of the metanarrative of France that added up to the normative qualities expected of and by the French. They were and are judged wanting in these qualities, even if these qualities are lacking in many, if not most, native-born white Frenchmen and women.

By European standards, they were not well educated; and they were certainly not sophisticated in ways recognized and valued in France. They were not trained in the liberal professions or sciences; they were not prepared to join – and probably not very interested in joining – discussions on most public issues of the day; nor did they readily fit into mainstream institutions. A large majority were poor or very poor, and if they had connections with people already in France, they were likely to be with people who also lacked appreciable resources.[89] *And while they may have chosen to be in France, few if any had chosen to be French.* They were in France by default; and many of those who subsequently moved toward French identity

---

89. Therefore they were dependent in varying degrees and forms on public assistance, ranging from housing subsidies to remedial education for their children, at least for some years after their arrival (Guélamine, *Action sociale*).

and full, active, citizenship may have also done so to make the best of relatively circumscribed situations: it was the most (or only) attractive option among the few they had. They did not reinforce the positive self-images of French people.

Where the earlier elite migrants were able to use their education, talents and cultural luminescence as bridging capital to relate to prominent individuals and important institutions, the more recent arrivals were encapsulated in a heterogeneous but fairly rigidly bounded sub-society of poor, ill-housed people often disdained by the dominant cultural majority.[90] Social discrimination and poverty reinforced cultural disadvantages, leading to the formation of large tracts of poorly maintained and serviced mid-rise buildings occupied almost exclusively by relatively recent arrivals from sub-Saharan and North Africa. Geographic concentration and poverty fostered shared perceptions of disadvantage and discrimination among residents of those areas. The perceptual boundaries between them and what many viewed as "French society" were crystallized by real and perceived policies and actions of discrimination by public institutions (e.g., the police) and portions of the society in general. Developing a sense of belonging and identity with those who shared the milieu was the path of least resistance for many. This bonding capital created solidarity within and an oppositional stance toward other people and what came to be seen as "their" institutions. Such bonding, which arguably stemmed from isolation imposed by limitations of housing, finances, and marketable skills as well as by a perception of openness in the larger society, was interpreted as a will to stand apart – to resist integration and to embrace fully (or to try to achieve) French identity.

In 1991 I began a series of conversations in the Paris region with a large number of adult immigrants from West and North Africa and Portugal, as well as a few native-born French citizens of color from France's Antillean overseas *départements*. The aim of the study was to learn about the influences of social institutions (such as friendship networks and neighborhood circles) and formal organizations (immigrants' associations, religious institutions, and public agencies) on individuals' identities and orientations to France.[91] Most of the individuals and immigrants' associations I sought out were located in the "popular" (i.e., modest, poor, disadvantaged) neighborhoods of Paris and its surround. The trajectories of three of the individuals – "Michel," "Nicolas," and "Aimée"[92] – whose lives in, and relationships to, France I followed for many years illustrate the differences between "notables" in earlier times and more recent "ordinary" arrivals.[93]

---

90. See, e.g., Wacquant, "Urban Outcasts.".

91. The project, entitled "The Normative and Institutional Construction of Identity," was initially supported by an international fellowship from the Centre National de la Recherche Scientifique (CNRS).

92. These are pseudonyms, but the characteristics and life stories are those of three specific individuals.

93. The formal phase of the interviews was concluded in 2001, while I was a visiting professor at the *Institut d'Études Politiques* in Paris. Since then I have stayed in touch intermittently with some of the persons involved, but difficulties

Michel arrived in France in 1987 from Senegal under the provisions of a statute for family reunification; he married a French citizen of Senegalese origin. He was 21 at the time, she 20. On his entry application he stated that he planned to work as a taxi chauffeur (once he was licensed), in the firm that employed his father-in-law. He also planned to further his education. His spoken French was excellent; but his education, after eight years in, and a diploma from, a Senegalese vocational school, was relatively limited. He tried to qualify as a taxi chauffeur but failed the written test three times; subsequently he accepted work as a general assistant at the taxi firm, which employed a number of immigrants from Senegal. His diligence so impressed the management that it provided him with the opportunity to further his education. He was eventually promoted to a clerical position in the company; and in 1999 was hired by a large freight hauling firm as assistant to the director of operations, dealing largely with employee-related matters. He and his wife (who worked in a pre-school as an aide) had two children, moved out of their small apartment in a rent-subsidized building (in a poor and dangerous area) and into a three-room rental apartment in the 20th *arrondissement* of Paris – an area with an increasingly upwardly-mobile, middle class population, with a relatively large but generally upwardly-mobile West African population. In the course of his first fifteen years in the country he shed (*je m'ai débarassé*) most of his friends in the housing project in which they had lived until then and stopped pretending to be a devout Muslim. He became a French citizen in 2001 and, in a conversation in 2010, mentioned that he and his wife had saved enough money to try to buy an apartment.

When I asked whether he thought of himself as French he responded that he did, "but France and French people did not allow him to forget that he was 'French with a difference.'" He volunteered that he felt he might fall between his "community" (i.e., that of Muslim immigrants of color who lived in relatively isolated suburbs) and "the French."[94]

Nicolas arrived in the Paris region in 1990 from Mali, but under very different circumstances. Originally from a small, isolated village, he passed through the Malian capital, Bamoko, but had never before lived in that or any other city. He was literally a stereotypical "sans-papier," an undocumented immigrant, without passport, visa, residence permit or any other identity documents. He was 17 years old; his formal education was limited to six years of intermittent schooling; and while he could speak a relatively "informal" French (with a small vocabulary), he

in maintaining contact over the years with most drastically reduced their number. The most recent conversations with "Michel" and "Nicolas" took place in early June, 2010; I lost contact with "Aimée" in 2003; according to mutual acquaintances, she returned to Guadeloupe to resume her teaching career.

94. Charles Tilly, *Identities, Boundaries and Social Ties* (Boulder & London: Paradigm, 2005).

was not comfortable with any written language. For nearly 10 years he worked as a casual clandestine laborer, mainly in construction. In late 1999 he was arrested on suspicion of having committed a petty crime and kept in custody once his immigration status was discovered. In the course of several months of inquiries by police and interviews with social workers tasked with working with young offenders and gangs he was exonerated of the crime; eventually he received provisional residence and work permits. In early 2000 he was hired by the local government of the suburb in which he lived to counsel recent young, mainly African, arrivals and was encouraged to further his education. His residence status was formalized in 2005 and the next year he was certified as a youth counselor, a position he still occupied in 2010. From 2001 through my last meeting with him, in 2010, I asked him (in varying forms) whether he felt himself to be French; he usually responded that he worked and lived with people who were not permitted to be French. He attended a mosque located in an apartment in his building but did not think of himself as very religious. In our last conversation he offered that he saw his task as "getting France to listen" to the concerns of his community.

Aimée came to the *Métropole* in 1989 from the overseas *département* of Guadeloupe, in the French Antilles. She was 25, a native-born citizen, trained (and certified, according to the standards of the French Ministry of Education) as a special education teacher, and had been engaged while still in Guadeloupe to teach in two small schools in the central city of Clermont-Ferrand, in Auvergne. Her stay there was unhappy from the start. She perceived both racial and professional discrimination by the parents of her pupils as well as by some colleagues and administrators in the school system. She had difficulty in finding satisfactory housing and felt socially isolated as a young single woman of color. In 1991 she was able to move to one of the eastern suburbs of Paris with a high North and sub-Saharan African population. She felt more effective professionally, related better to her pupils, and found more personal acceptance. She shared a flat with a colleague also of Antilles origin and had a modicum of success in establishing social relationships. Nonetheless, in four conversations over the course of nine years (between late 1991 and early 2001) I sensed a progressive disenchantment with or alienation – both personal and professional – from life in France. Her social relationships proved unstable, which she attributed to "the ghetto mentality" of the people in her life, "the pull of the ghetto", and being in the thrall of Islamic ideas among the men she dated. From our first meeting to the last she indicated a strong resistance to "being pulled in" – into what she perceived as the self-defeating, self-isolating, and self-pitying "mentality" of the North and sub-Saharan populations with whom she worked and among whom she lived. She observed a number of her Antilles acquaintances being drawn into that milieu and identifying with non-citizens of color. While she claimed solidarity with those in that world, she feared losing her personal and professional self – in her words, "ceding what I had earned through hard work," for the sake of belonging. She returned to Guadeloupe in 2003.

IV. Conclusion: Blending Identities Then and Fragmenting Identities Now

From a theoretical point of view, there is an interesting difference between the processes and outcomes of settlement and the identity-influencing effects of exposure to the stories of the two host societies – the United States in the mid-nineteenth century and France in the earlier and later twentieth. Danes who settled in largely homogeneous towns with fellow Danes or Northern Europeans fostered ties – "bonding social capital" – that reinforced elements of the culture and values carried across the ocean. This pattern of settlement may have slowed full integration or assimilation by a generation or two, in comparison with those who homesteaded in open country alongside American settlers. The latter stimulated "bridging social capital" and probably somewhat more rapid integration. Such differences between bonding and bridging social capital are observable in the French case as well. But there the patterns of settlement – while consequential in one respect, to which I shall return forthwith – were not the only important influences.

Early Danish migrants to America and the immigrants to France in the middle third of the twentieth century – the "Black exemplars of Frenchness" – possessed ideal, or at least highly desirable attributes for successful settlement and eventual integration. For the former, one of the most important attributes was a willingness and aptitude for hard work of a practical sort – work not entirely unlike that which they had performed in Denmark, albeit under very different circumstances. A second useful trait was commitment to sacrifice, with a view to reaping future benefits. These qualities were highlighted in the stories of America the migrants encountered even before their arrival: an important part of the American narrative (probably more then than in recent times) emphasized plentiful *opportunity* for those who could and would work hard – America was perceived as "a land of opportunity." The letters and other communications home from early migrants indicated clearly that a good life could be had, but it was not guaranteed. Many succeeded, some did not. Both shared the fortunes of native-born Americans and others who had moved to the Upper Midwest.

Settlers in largely Danish or Scandinavian "colonies" had greater social support (bonding social capital) and perhaps a cushion of time as regards integration. They benefited from some of the *collective opportunities* promised by the American story, especially the freedom to surround oneself with important aspects of the culture of origin. In effect, they became prototypical "hyphenated Americans": for two or more generations they were Danish in America, before becoming Americans of Danish origin – until, in many or most cases, that qualifier melted into the mixture that is American identity.

Other attributes Danish immigrants to America shared (not only in the nineteenth century, of course) were being white and almost exclusively Protestant, and speaking a Germanic language closely related to English. In a pluralistic society that is also a plural society – in terms of skin color, language, and, until the last generation or two, religion – Danes were in a comparatively advantageous position to achieve fairly swift and unhindered integration. Finally, while neither the United States nor Denmark were full and mature democracies in the mid-nineteenth century, several dimensions of equality and political activity were expected in both, at least for adult white males. The participatory elements in Danish culture and political culture helped the early immigrants to play active roles in relating to the (local or regional as well as comprehensive) stories of America and in the sculpting of their identity. Manifestations of these aspects of political culture brought by Danes and other Scandinavians to the Upper Midwest and Pacific Northwest in the United States were evident 100 years later in the politics of those regions. Thus, these qualities not only stood the early immigrants in good stead and helped their integration, they also left durable marks on the American polity.[95]

Migrants from West Africa and the Antilles and others of color did not possess all of these felicitous attributes when they entered France, either in the earlier part of the twentieth century or more recently. They were inescapably visibly different, with all of the negative connotations most people attached to such differences in virtually all European societies. The first cohort discussed above, however, arrived with very substantial cultural capital, capital that could redound to their social and political advantage in many cases. Whether from French colonies or overseas territories or from other places such as the United States, their cultural assets connected with the flattering self-concept of France as a cosmopolitan country open to all who resonated to its story. For at least two of the three luminaries, Senghor and Houphouët-Boigny, however, the French identity embraced was of a hyphenated sort, since they returned to their countries of origin not as Frenchmen but as Senegalese and Ivorian. But it is plausible to argue that, had they chosen to remain in France, unqualified French identity was available to them – at least as far as elites and relatively highly educated and sophisticated French people were concerned.

The recent waves of immigrants, documented or undocumented, to France from sub-Saharan Africa carried most of the negatives and few of the positively valued attributes French people associate with the French metanarrative. But, arguably,

---

95. See, e.g., Daniel J. Elazar, *American Federalism: A View from the States* (New York: Crowell, 1966).

this is an indirect source of the difficulties in integration and in aspiring to French identity. The times, and the numbers of migrants, have changed. Large-scale immigration today is a political, economic, and cultural irritant almost completely independent of the attributes of the migrants.[96]

In France, as in many other European countries, the cumulative disadvantages of poverty, relatively low levels of education, visible difference, and belonging to a religious minority have led to the *de facto* residential segregation of many immigrants. Such segregation creates asymmetrical or incomplete enclaves or colonies beside more integrated mainstream communities. The enclaves are asymmetrical in that they do not provide all of the functions – the services and goods – needed by the community; they are manifestly not self-sufficient. Nor do they have a degree of autonomy or self-rule associated with many enclaves in other places and periods – such as, for instance, some of the largely Danish and/or Scandinavian communities in nineteenth-century America. Thus, even if the populations of such enclaves shared substantial cultural and normative orientations, they would not have opportunities to make and enforce their own rules or to gain greater control over their daily lives. Populations such as those in the eastern suburbs of Paris have created a sense of solidarity based on a sense of exclusion, discrimination, and victimhood. The choice for most recent immigrants to France from Africa (North, as well as sub-Saharan) is, therefore, either cultivating bonds with others in similar situations based on opposition to the dominant culture or leaving the community, perhaps severing bonds (losing their "bonding social capital"), and striving to integrate into the larger society.

Danish immigrants to the United States have never had to make such choices. Compared with modern migrants to virtually any part of the world, and compared with many – especially non-Northern European – migrants to nineteenth-century America, the path to integration into the mainstream society was relatively smooth and easy. The story of America was plastic and accommodating. The evolution of American identity was (and remains) also remarkably swift. Retaining a sense of Danish origins was and remains a matter of personal and familial choice for most, not a dictate of the surrounding society or circumstances. For this reason, if for no other, it is important to view the Danish experience in America in a perspective that is comparative across societies and time.

---

96. Martin O. Heisler, "Contextualizing Global Migration: Sketching the Socio-Political Landscape in Europe," *UCLA Journal of International Law and Foreign Affairs* 3, no. 2 (Fall/Winter 1998/99): 557-593; Martin O. Heisler, "Now and Then"; Martin O. Heisler and Zig Layton-Henry, "Migration and the Link between Social and Societal Security," in *Identity, Migration and the New Security Agenda in Europe*, ed. Ole Wæver, Barry Buzan, Morten Kelstrup, and Pierre Lemaitre (London: Pinter, 1993).

Bibliography

Aciman, André, ed. *Letters of Transit: Reflections on Exile, Identity, Language, and Loss*. New York: The New Press, 1999.

Aciman, André. "Shadow Cities," in Aciman, *Letters of Transit*.

Anderson, Benedict. *Imagined Communities*. London: Verso, 1983.

Anwar, Muhammad. *Race and Politics: Ethnic Minorities and the British Political System*. (London: Routledge, 1986).

Bataille, Philippe, and Michel Wieviorka, eds. *Racisme et xénophobie en Europe*. Paris: La Découverte, 1994.

Bastin, Giselle. "From *Grand Récit* to *Petit Histoire*: Exploring Historical Cleavage in Kate Grenville's *Joan Makes History*." *Limina – A Journal of Historical and Cultural Studies* 11 (2005): 28-37. Accessed May 4, 2009. http://limina.arts.uwa.edu.au.

Berlin, Ira. *The Making of African America: The Four Great Migrations*. New York: Viking, 2010.

Bille, John H. *A History of the Danes in America*. Vol. XI of *Transactions of the Wisconsin Academy of Sciences, Arts, and Letters*. (March 1896).

Blanc, Maurice. "Social Integration and Exclusion in France: Some Introductory Remarks from a Social Transaction Perspective." *Housing Studies* 13, no. 6 (Nov. 1998): 781-792.

Boittin, Jennifer Anne. "Black in France: The Language and Politics of Race in the Late Third Republic." *French Politics, Culture & Society* 27, no. 2 (Summer 2009): 23-46.

Boittin, Jennifer Anne. *Colonial Metropolis: The Urban Grounds of Anti-Imperialism and Feminism in Interwar France*. Lincoln, NE: University of Nebraska Press, 2010.

Brown, Frederick. *For the Soul of France: Culture Wars in the Age of Dreyfus*. New York: A. A. Knopf, 2010.

Canadian Ethnic Studies Journal 34, no. 3 (Sep. 2002). Entire issue.

Carr, David. *Time, Narrative, and History*. Bloomington and Indianapolis: Indiana University Press, 1986.

Chathuant, Dominique. "L'émergence d'une élite politique noire dans la France du premier 20e siècle?" *Vingtième Siècle* 101, no. 1 (2009).

Chevrier, Jacques. ""Afrique(s)-sur-Seine: Autour de la Notion de 'Migritude'." *Notre Librairie* 155156 (Juil.-Dec. 2004): 13-17.

Christensen, Thomas P. "Danish Settlement in Wisconsin." *The Wisconsin Magazine of History* 12, no. 1 (1928): 19-40.

Coleman, James S. "Social Capital in the Creation of Human Capital." *American Journal of Sociology* 94 (Supplement, 1988): S95-S120.

Currie, Gregory. *Narratives & Narrators: A Philosophy of Stories*. Oxford and New York: Oxford University Press, 2010.

Dewitte, Philippe. *Les mouvements nègres en France, 1919-1939*. Paris: L'Harmattan, 2004.

Dickson, Bruce D., Jr. "W. E. B. DuBois and the Idea of Double Consciousness." *American Literature* 64, no. 2 (June 1992): 299-309.

Dilthey, Wilhelm. *Gesammelte Schriften*, vol. 7, *Der Aufbau der geschichtlichen Welt in den Geisteswissenschaften*; vol. 8, *Weltanschauungslehre, Abhandlungen zur Philosophie der Philosophie*. Göttingen: Vandenhoeck & Ruprecht, 1991-1992 [1910-1911].

Elazar, Daniel J. *American Federalism: A View from the States*. New York: Crowell, 1966.

Elster, Jon, ed. *The Multiple Self*. Cambridge and New York: Cambridge University Press, 1987.

Fabre, Michel. *From Harlem to Paris: Black American Writers in France, 1840-1980*. Urbana and Chicago: University of Illinois Press, 1991.

Fall, Mar. *Le destin des Africains noirs en France: discrimination, assimilation, repli communautaire*. Paris: L'Harmattan, 2005.

Fanon, Franz. *Peau noire, masques blancs*. Paris: Éditions du Seuil, 1952.

Femminella, Francis X., and Jill S. Quadango. "The Italian American Family," in *Ethnic Families in America: Patterns and Variations*, edited by Charles H. Mindel and Robert W. Haberstein. New York: Elsevier, 1976.

Gagnon, Alain G., and James Tully, eds. *Multinational Democracies*. New York: Cambridge University Press, 2001.

Gergen, Kenneth J., Stuart M. Schraeder, and Mary Gergen. *Constructing Worlds Together: Interpersonal Communication as Relational Process*. Boston, MA: Allyn & Bacon, 2008.

Giraud, Michel. "The Antillese in France: Trends and prospects." *Ethnic and Racial Studies* 27, no. 4 (July 2004): 622-640.

Goodwin, Stefan. *Africa in Europe, Vol. II: Interdependence, Relocations, and Globalization*. Lanham, MD and Plymouth, UK: Lexington Books, 2009.

Gordon, Milton M. *Assimilation in American Life: The Role of Race, Religion, and National Origin*. New York and Oxford: Oxford University Press, 1964.

Gordon, Milton M. "Models of Pluralism: The New American Dilemma." *Annals of the American Academy of Political and Social Science* 454 (March 1981): 178-188.

Grøngaard Jeppesen, Torben. *Dannebrog on the American Prairie*. Odense: Odense City Museum, 2000.

Grøngaard Jeppesen, Torben. *Danske i USA, 1850-2000 – en demografisk, social og kulturgeografisk undersøgelse af de danske immigranter og deres efterkommere*. Odense: Odense Bys Museer, 2005.

Guélamine, Faïza. *Action sociale et immigration en France: Repères pour l'intervention*, 2nd ed. Paris: Dunot, 2008.

Hale, Frederick. *Danes in Wisconsin*. Rev. and expanded ed. Madison, WI: Wisconsin Historical Society Press, 2005.

Heisler, Barbara Schmitter. "Sending Countries and the Politics of Emigration and Destination." *International Migration Review* 19, no. 3 (Autumn 1985): 469-484.

Heisler, Martin O., ed. *Ethnic Conflict in the World Today*. Annals of the American Academy of Political and Social Science, 433 (Sep. 1977).

Heisler, Martin O. "Managing Ethnic Conflict in Belgium." *Annals of the American Academy of Political and Social Science*, 433 (Sep. 1977): 32-46.

Heisler, Martin O. "Ethnicity and Ethnic Relations in the Modern West," in *Conflict and Peacemaking in Multiethnic Societies*, edited by Joseph V. Montville. Lexington, MA: Lexington Books/D. C. Heath, 1990.

Heisler, Martin O. "Hyphenating Belgium: Changing State and Regime to Cope with Cultural Division," in *Conflict and Peacemaking in Multiethnic Societies*, edited by Joseph V. Montville. Lexington, MA: Lexington Books/D. C. Heath, 1990.

Heisler, Martin O. "Contextualizing Global Migration: Sketching the Socio-Political Landscape in Europe." *UCLA Journal of International Law and Foreign Affairs* 3, no. 2 (Fall/Winter 1998/99): 557-593.

Heisler, Martin O. "Now and Then, Here and There: Migration and the Transformation of Identities, Borders, and Orders," in *Identities, Borders, Orders: Rethinking International Relations Theory*, edited by Mathias Albert, David Jacobson and Yosef Lapid. Minneapolis: University of Minnesota Press, 2001.

Heisler, Martin O. "Cognitive and Philological Bases of Power in the Politics of Memory." Paper presented at the annual meeting of the American Political Science Association; Washington, DC, September 1-4, 2005.

Heisler, Martin O. 2006. "Power(s) in the Politics of Memory and Memorialization." Paper presented at the annual meeting of the American Political Science Association; Philadelphia, August 31-September 3.

Heisler, Martin O. "Challenged Histories and Collective Self-Concepts: Politics in History, Memory, and Time." *Annals of the American Academy of Political and Social Science* 617 (May 2008): 199-211.

Heisler, Martin O. and Barbara Schmitter Heisler. "Citizenship – Old, New, and Changing: Inclusion, Exclusion, and Limbo for Ethnic Groups and Migrants in the Modern Democratic State," in *Dominant National Cultures and Ethnic Identities*, edited by Jürgen Fijalkowski, Hans Merkens, and Folker Schmidt. Berlin: Freie Universität, 1991.

Heisler, Martin O. and Zig Layton-Henry. "Migration and the link between social and societal security," in *Identity, Migration and the New Security Agenda in Europe*, edited by Ole Wæver, Barry Buzan, Morten Kelstrup and Pierre Lemaitre. London: Pinter, 1993.

Helweg, Halvdan. *An Early History of the West Denmark Colonization*. [*Oplegnelsen om grundlæggelsen den danske koloni West Denmark, Wisconsin i USA*.] Luck, WI: West Denmark Lutheran Church, 1963 [1907].

Hopkins, Daniel J. "Politicized Places: Explaining Where and When Immigrants Provoke Local Opposition." *American Political Science Review* 104, no. 1 (Feb. 2010): 40-60.

Houe, Poul, and Sven Hakon Rossel, eds. *Images of America in Scandinavia*. Amsterdam and Atlanta: Rodopi B.V, 1998.

Huntington, Samuel P. *Who Are We? The Challenges to America's National Identity*. New York: Simon and Schuster, 2004.

Hvidt, Kristian. *Flight to America: The Social Background of 300,000 Danish Emigrants*. New York: Academic Press, 1975.

Jacobson, David. *Place and Belonging in America*. Baltimore and London: Johns Hopkins University Press, 2002.

Jensen, Joan M. *Calling This Place Home: Women on the Wisconsin Frontier, 1850-1925*. St. Paul, MN: Minnesota Historical Society Press, 2006.

Jørgensen, Steffen Elmer. "Ideal or Counterimage? Aspects of the American Cultural Impact on Denmark, 1776 to 1995." In Houe and Rossel, *Images of America in Scandinavia*, 38-82.

Jørgensen, Steffen Elmer. "A Scattered People? Danish Settlement Structure and Community Transplantations in the Midwest," in *On Distant Shores: Proceedings of the Marcus Lee Hansen Immigration Conference; Aalborg, 29 June-1 July, 1992*, edited by Birgit Flemming Larsen, Henning Bender, and Karen Veien. Aalborg: Danes Worldwide Archives; Danish Society for Emigration History, 1993.

Jounin, Nicolas. *Chantier interdit au public: Enquête parmi les travailleurs du bâtiment*. Paris: Éditions du Découverte, 2008.

Kalman, Julie. *Rethinking Antisemitism in Nineteenth Century France*. Cambridge and New York: Cambridge University Press, 2010.

Katzenstein, Peter J. "'Walls between 'Those People?' Contrasting Perspectives on World Politics." *Perspectives on Politics* 8, no. 1 (March 2010): 11-25.

Korsgaard, Ove. "Grand Narratives in Danish History: From Functional Identity to Problematic Identity." Paper presented at the International Seminar on Nationhood in Plural Societies, Aarhus University, Aarhus, May 14-15, 2009.

Lewis, Mary Dewhurst. *The Boundaries of the Republic: Migrant Rights and the Limits of Universalism in France, 1918-1940*. Stanford: Stanford University Press, 2007.

Mali, Joseph. *Mythistory: The Making of a Modern Historiography*. Chicago: University of Chicago Press, 2003.

Mansbridge, Jane, and Aldon Morris, eds. *Oppositional Consciousness: The Subjective Roots of Social Protest*. Chicago: University of Chicago Press, 2001.

Marie, Claude-Valentin. "Les Antillais en France: une nouvelle donne," *Hommes & Migrations* 1237 (mai-juin 2002): 26-38.

Mauss, Marcel. "La Nation." 1920. Reproduced in *Année sociologique*, 3rd series (1953-54): 7-68. Accessed October 13, 2008. Electronic facsimile at http://www.uqac.uquebec.ca/zone30/Classiques des sciences sociales/index.html.

McKinney, John C. *Constructive Typology and Social Theory*. New York: Appleton-Century-Crofts, 1966.

McNeill, William J. *Mythistory and Other Essays*. Chicago: University of Chicago Press, 1986.

Montville, Joseph V., ed. *Conflict and Peacemaking in Multiethnic Societies*. Lexington, MA: Lexington Books/DC Heath, 1990.

Morawska, Ewa, and Willfried Spohn. "Moving Europeans in the Globalizing World: Contemporary Migrations in a Historical-Comparative Perspective (1955-1994 v. 1870-1914)." In *Global History and Migrations*, edited by Wang Gungwu. Boulder, CO and Cumnor Hill, Oxford, 1997.

Morgan, Edmund S. *The Genuine Article*. New York and London: W.W. Norton, 2004.

Morin, Edgar. *Le vif du sujet*. Paris: Éditions du Seuil, 1982 [1969].

Morin, Edgar. *La vie de la vie*. Vol. 2 of *La Méthode*. Paris: Éditions du Seuil, 1985.

Morin, Edgar. *Les idées*. Vol. 4 of *La Méthode*. Paris: Éditions du Seuil, 1991.

Morin, Edgar. *L'humanité de l'humanité*. Vol. 5 of *La Méthode*. Paris: Éditions du Seuil, 2003.

Morin, Edgar. *On Complexity*. Cresskill, NJ: Hampton Press, 2008 [1994]. [*La complexité humaine*. Paris: Flammarion, 1994.]

Mortensen, Enok. "The Acculturation of the Danish Immigrant," *The Bridge* 3 (1980): 83-91.

Müller, Jan-Werner. "Introduction: the power of memory, the memory of power and the power over memory." In *Memory and Power in Post-War Europe: Studies in the Presence of the Past*, edited by Jan-Werner Müller. Cambridge: Cambridge University Press, 2002.

Novick, Peter. *That Noble Dream: The "Objectivity Question" and the American Historical Profession*. Cambridge and New York: Cambridge University Press, 1988.

Nyer-Malbet, Angèle. "Migritude." *Cahiers d'anthropologie et biométrie humaine* 13, nos. 3-4 (1995): 369-375.

Østergård, Uffe. "Peasants and Danes: The Danish National Identity and Political Culture." *Comparative Studies in Society and History* 34, no. 1 (Jan. 1992): 3-27.

Painter, Nell Irvin. *Creating Black Americans: African-American History and Its Meanings, 1619 to the Present*. Oxford and New York: Oxford University Press, 2006.

Painter, Nell Irvin. *The History of White People*. New York: W. W. Norton, 2010.

Pedersen, Erik H. "Danish Farmers in the Middle West." *The Bridge* 5 (1982): 51-68.

Portes, Alejandro, and Leif Jensen. "What's an Ethnic Enclave: The Case for Conceptual Clarity." *American Sociological Review* 52, no. 6 (Dec. 1987): 768-771.

Portes, Alejandro, and Robert D. Manning. "The Immigrant Enclave: Theory and Empirical Examples," in *Competitive Ethnic Relations*, edited by Susan Olzak and Joane Nagel, 47-68. New York: Academic Press 1986.

Putnam, Robert D. *Bowling Alone: The Collapse and Revival of American Community*. New York: Simon & Schuster, 2000.

Renan, Ernest. "Qu'est-ce qu'une nation?" Lecture delivered at the Sorbonne, 11 March 1882. Accessed June 4, 2009. http://ig.cs.tu-Berlin.de/oldstatic/w2001/eu1/dokumente/Basistexte/Renan1882FR-Nation.pdf#2.

Reynaud Paligot, Carole. *Races, racisme et anti-racisme dans les années 1930*. Paris: Presses universitaires de France, 2007.

Ricœur, Paul. *Time and Narrative.* 3 vols. Translated by Kathleen Blamey and David Pellauer. Chicago: University of Chicago Press, 1984-88.

Ricœur, Paul. *Memory, History, Forgetting*. Translated by by Kathleen Blamey and David Pellauer. Chicago: University of Chicago Press, 2004.

Robine, Jérémy. "SOS Racisme et les ghettos des banlieues: construction et utilisations d'une représentation." *Hérodote* 113, no. 2 (2004): 134-151.

Salmon, Christian. *Storytelling: La machine à fabriquer des histoires et à formater les esprits*. Paris: La Découverte, 2007.

Shack, William A. *Harlem in Montmartre: A Paris Jazz Story between the Great Wars*. Berkeley and Los Angeles: University of California Press, 2001.

Simon-Barouh, Ida, and Pierre-Jean Simon, eds. *Les Étrangers dans la ville: Le regard des sciences sociales*. Paris: L'Harmattan, 2000.

Simonsen, Henrik Brednose. *Kampen om danskheded: tro og nationalitet i de danske kirkesamfund i Amerika*. Aarhus: Aarhus University Press, 1990.

Siu, Lok. *Memories of a Future Home: Diasporic Citizenship of Chinese in Panama*. Stanford, CA: Stanford University Press, 2005.

Smith, Rogers M. *Stories of Peoplehood: The Politics and Morals of Political Membership*. Cambridge and New York: Cambridge University Press, 2003.

Steele, Meili. *Hiding from History: Politics and Public Imagination*. Ithaca and London: Cornell University Press, 2005.

Stilling, Niels Peter, and Anne Lisbeth Olsen. *A New Life: Danish Emigration to North America as Described by the Emigrants Themselves in Letters, 1842-1946*. 2nd ed. Aalborg: Danes Worldwide Archives, in collaboration with the Danish Society for Emigration History, 1994.

Swartz, David. *Culture and Power: The Sociology of Pierre Bourdieu*. Chicago: University of Chicago Press, 1997.

Tilly, Charles. *Identities, Boundaries and Social Ties*. Boulder and London: Paradigm, 2005.

Wacquant, Loïc. "Urban Outcasts: Stigma and Division in the Black American Ghetto and the French Urban Periphery." *International Journal of Urban and Regional Research* 17, no. 3 (1993): 366-383.

Weber, Eugen. *The Hollow Years: France in the 1930s*. New York, London: W.W. Norton, 1994.

Wertsch, James W. *Voices of Collective Remembering*. Cambridge: Cambridge University Press, 2002.

Wiebe, Robert H. *The Segmented Society: an introduction into the meaning of America*. New York: Oxford University Press, 1975.

Wiebe, Robert H. *Who We Are: A History of Popular Nationalism*. Princeton: Princeton University Press, 2002.

Wieviorka, Michel. *L'espace du racisme*. Paris: Éditions du Seuil, 1991.

Wieviorka, Michel. *La différance*. Paris: Balland, 2001.

Wimmer, Andreas. *Nationalist Exclusion and Ethnic Conflict: Shadows of Modernity*. Cambridge: Cambridge University Press, 2002.

Winter, Elke. "Die Dialektik multikultureller Identität: Kanada als Lehrstück." *Swiss Political Science Review* 15, no. 1 (2009): 133-168.

Wyman, Mark. *The Wisconsin Frontier*. Bloomington and Indianapolis: Indiana University Press, 1998.

Xiberras, Martine. *Les théories de l'exclusion*. Paris: Armand Colin, 1998.

Zerubavel, Eviatar. *Time Maps: Collective Memory and the Social Shape of the Past*. Chicago: University of Chicago Press, 2003.

Zolberg, Aristide R. *A Nation by Design: Immigration Policy in the Fashioning of America*. New York, Cambridge, MA, and London: Russell Sage Foundation and Harvard University Press, 2006.

5 Identity and Nationalism in a Global World: Some Theoretical Reflections

Mark Haugaard

In normative political theory, and in much of everyday life, identity claims are considered normatively powerful. If an actor argues that a given set of social relations violate or fail to affirm their identity, this is frequently considered a legitimate basis for critique of those institutions as morally reprehensible. As globalization advances and people of different cultures cohabit to a greater extent than before, these normative claims will become more prevalent. They are claims that may be competing with each other, and their content could be contrary to the basic principles of liberal democracy. Consequently, the basis for these claims has to be interrogated rather than taken for granted.

My method of resolving some of these issues will be based on moving between *is* and *ought*. I will examine the sociological basis of identity and use that to interrogate the legitimacy of identity claims relative to the conditions of possibility for liberal democracy.

The common everyday view of identity is singular. This is particularly the case with nationalist identity claims. In reality, of course, being Irish or Danish is only one aspect of identity. For instance, as argued by Sen, the author is male, an atheist, a university lecturer, heterosexual, and a keen sailor.[1] However, the categories of Irish, Danish, or European are relevant to power relations and define conditions of possibility in politics, which is possibly why they frequently first come to mind as sources of identity. This is not some universal truth of social life, but reflects a specific historical conjuncture. Over the last two hundred years or so the nation-state has haunted the imagination of politics in Western societies. Prior to the seventeenth century (and in much of the contemporary Islamic world) being an atheist would probably constitute a more significant part of identity than nationality. If globalization is to be taken seriously, we should expect nationality to be one of a number of competing identity claims. The emergence of new social movements, which assert the rights of different sexualities, ethnicities, life-style choices, and so on, suggests that this is indeed the case. The re-emergence of religion as a source

---

1. A. Sen, *Identity and Violence* (London: Allan Lane, 2006).

of identity suggests the same. We are entering a world of overlapping and multiple identities, all of which are claiming their right under the sun. The question is how seriously should we take these competing claims?

At one end of the spectrum there is the perception that identity is some kind of normative "trump card." As ideal types, this is frequently based upon two possible and opposing fallacious perceptions of the self. The first can be characterized as a liberal radical individualist view in which the identity of a person is considered something unique to them. This uniqueness is something to be protected from the tyranny of the majority. The individual is seen as an individual creator of meaning of self, who is prior to, or separable from, the social world, and is thus vulnerable to violation by it. This is identity as individuality. The unique individual is something which is fundamental to the liberal idea of the authentic self.[2] It arose in the early nineteenth century as part of a changed perception of art. Previously, the object of art was mimesis, the representation of an external world. This is replaced by art as an act of creation that comes from within the creator. Consistent with this, the self is considered unique and any claim to the effect that this individuality is being crushed out of existence is a normatively powerful one. However, this position is premised upon an under-socialized concept of the self.

There is a second view of identity as a trump card that is implicit in postmodern theory. As speaking subjects we are essentially social beings. Social agents are constituted through their ability to impose meaning upon the world, and that capacity is communal. If a set of political arrangements force people to negotiate politics through meanings which are alien to them, these arrangements are a violation of their being-in-the world. A person can be expected to compromise on specific external desires, such as wealth or party preference, but you cannot ask them to compromise on who they are. Because social agents are members of communities, and their interpretative powers derive from that membership, they cannot be asked to step outside themselves. In postmodern thought this is represented by the so-called 'death of the author'. In Foucault and Derrida we are interpretative beings who express ourselves through the reproduction of systems of meaning that we have little capacity to transcend.[3] Communities are interpretative groups, and forced membership of a community of which you are not a part constitutes a violation of what it is to be human. If identity is defined as group membership, violation of a person's identity is violation of their humanity. Thus it constitutes a normative non-negotiable. The fundamental flaw here is that this view of identity is based upon an over-socialized concept of the self.

---

2. C. Taylor, *The Ethics of Authenticity* (Cambridge, MA: Harvard University Press, 1991).
3. M. Foucault, *The Order of Things* (London: Routledge, 1970); J. Derrida, *Writing and Difference* (Chicago: University of Chicago Press, 1978).

Both the radically liberal and postmodern communitarian positions are essentialist. In the liberal version there is an essence prior to socialization, which has to be protected from it, while the radical postmodern communitarian version presupposes that the essence of self is exhausted by, and coterminous with, socialization in groups. What both positions ignore is the constructed, negotiated, and interactive aspects of the constitution of self. Once we take account of these, the normative case becomes much more complex.

As social agents we are interpretative beings, who use our interpretative horizons to make sense of the world. We look upon the world and order it, and that ordering is essential to our being in the world as ontological entities. We see the world as a series of relational similarities and differences. To take an example which Kuhn used to explain the nature of paradigms:[4] Imagine a father takes a child for a walk in the park; the child sees a pond full of birds and says "bird," and the father explains that these birds are "ducks." A little later she sees some geese and says "duck," and the father corrects the child with an explanation of the difference between geese and ducks, along the lines that geese are larger than ducks, etc. Shortly after the child sees some swans and says "geese" and a further category of similarity and difference is supplied to the child surrounding the words "swan" and "goose." The child who leaves the park is a different interpretative being from the one who entered it. The child has internalized an external socially constructed ordering of the physical world that has fundamentally altered the way she sees it. She has been changed by the experience and is a different being-in-the-world who perceives reality through an altered way of ordering it.

The external world, which is also part of the self, includes not only physical things but also other agents. The "furniture" of the world includes not only ducks and geese, but "Danes," "women," "geriatrics," and so on. These labels are every bit as much part of an agent's sense-making vocabulary. She learns that Danes and Irish people have specific characteristics, and this knowledge facilitates an actor's sense-making capacity. As observed by Jenkins,[5] in that sense stereotypes are inescapably part of our interpretative frameworks and who we are as social beings. Like other forms of ordering they give the world predictability and, in turn, constitute an integral element of ontological security.[6]

This interpretative scheme not only relates to the outside world of people and things; it is self reflective in so far as these interpretative individuals see themselves in it. The child in the park is not only a homo sapiens, but she may also be

4.   T. Kuhn, *The Essential Tension* (Chicago: University of Chicago Press, 1977), 311.
5.   R. Jenkins, *Social Identity*, 2nd ed. (London: Routledge, 2004), 124-30.
6.   A. Giddens, *The Constitution of Society* (Cambridge: Polity Press, 1984).

"a middle-class Dane," "Irish," and "a daughter." However, the placing of the self into the furniture of the world is never unproblematic, and it is not a solipsistic act because it cannot be accomplished in isolation from others. It is dialogic, and others may well resist the signifiers we apply to ourselves (the author of this text has frequently been rejected as either Irish or Danish and my preferred European identity is considered valid by few). Others may think that an identity should not apply to us, or they may judge that the signifier refers to a different set of concepts than we do. Alternatively, reversing the process, the subject may also find themselves having a signifier placed upon them, which they may wish to reject. This signifier can be a negative one, as in labeling. However, having an identity forced upon one can also take place when identities are recognized as some kind of "emancipatory act" whereby people are forced to choose a ready-made set of ascribed identities. This can happen with "group rights" and consociational democracy.

Having an identity implies having certain meaning as an agent. If the meaning in terms of which a subject wishes to define their identity does not match external reality, this has the potential to be traumatic and affect their self-esteem. This fact has led Taylor to argue that there is a moral imperative for recognition by others.[7] This is given added force by the implicit argument that different socializations and constitution of habitus, or interpretative horizons, constitute the essence of our identity. If we ask another person to embrace a different identity, we are essentially asking them to abandon "their" interpretative horizon, which is who they are. This is true to some extent, and constitutes a powerful argument for multiculturalism. However, we must be careful not to make the elision whereby identity and our sense of self are telescoped into one. As already observed, we can have many identities and, I want to argue, the plurality of these is essential to the constitution of liberal democracy. In fact, part of socialization is a learning curve in which we inhabit multiple identities which are constantly being negotiated.

It has often been argued by social theorists, such as Giddens,[8] that identity is a modern phenomenon. What he means is that the reflexive construction of self is modern, while traditional selves were constituted through assigned roles and identities. As Jenkins has correctly observed, this belief is part of a self-congratulatory view of modernity in Enlightenment terms as an increase in reason.[9] Modern and traditional societies entail different constraints, while negotiating these entails different strategies, and there is no *prima facie* reason to think that the former

7. C. Taylor, *The Ethics of Authenticity* (Cambridge, MA: Harvard University Press, 1991), and "The Politics of Recognition," in *Multiculturalism*, ed. Amy Gutmann (Princeton: Princeton University Press, 1994).
8. Giddens, *The Constitution of Society*.
9. Jenkins, *Social Identity*, 34.

entails a greater level of reflexivity than the latter. As is apparent from Barth, in traditional societies identities are also complex and negotiated, which implies reflexivity. However, that said, liberal industrial societies did significantly change the nature of identity construction.

One of the elements of this change was the emergence of what Gellner termed the transition from single-stranded to multi-stranded thinking.[10] In multi-stranded thinking various ways of interpreting the world were fused. In particular, normative and empirical thought were continuous with each other: there was no distinction between *is* and *ought*. So, for instance, if the local priest said "it is going to rain tomorrow," this was not simply an empirical assertion which one could disagree with based upon fact. It was also a normative assertion concerning mutual ties and obligations.[11] Possibly, a better example than Gellner's is provided by the resistance by the Catholic Church to the Copernican idea that the sun, not the earth, was the centre of the solar system. The issue was not one of fact in a modern scientific sense, it was a normative and moral issue concerning man's place in the universe. If we were no longer at the centre of the universe, then it was no longer "for us." Relative to this moral fact concerning the ordering of the universe, Galileo's observations by telescope were "beside the point."

Single-stranded logic entails massive methodological bracketing. For the sake of a specific scientific problem, all moral considerations are put to one side. Gellner primarily thought of the ability to think using single-stranded logic in terms of the distinction between moral and empirical reason. I would like to extend his argument in a Weberian way and argue that what is central to modernity is the ability to interpret the world single-strandedly along several dimensions. As social agents we constitute interpretative beings. We make sense of the world by imposing meaning upon it. Going back to the example of the child in the park, the orderedness of ducks, geese, and swans in the pond presupposes the imposition of meaning upon these creatures by an interpretative being. This interpretative being has, following Heidegger, an interpretative horizon by which she makes sense of the world. The same object can appear as different things depending upon which interpretative horizon is imposed upon it. This is the quality of gestalt pictures, whereby the same object or drawing appears as one thing and then another; it is also an underlying principle of many jokes. In the first half of a story the listener thinks of something as one thing and then suddenly it becomes another. With the sharper division of life into work-time and free-time, public and private, and so on, social actors were expected to adopt different identities depending upon circumstances, and these identities constituted vantage points for seeing the world differently.

---

10. E. Gellner, *Plough, Sword and Book* (Chicago: University of Chicago Press, 1988).
11. Ibid., 47.

Identities do not simply entail different rules of behavior, as is suggested by social roles; they entail two fundamental cognitive shifts. On the one hand the person is seen in a particular way as a carrier of meaning. In becoming a "teacher," "seller," "tax official," or "doctor," the individual becomes a signified for a specific signifier. Their ontological status in the world changes, and with that the subject's orientation towards others alters and becomes specific. These behavioral patterns entail certain interpretative horizons, which enable actors to behave predictably relative to each other. If I am a "university lecturer," the other is a "student" with whom I am expected to interact in a particular way. I can engage in a two-hour monologue about the finer points of sociological theory, but cannot confide to her the details of my personal life and must refrain from seeing her in a sexual way. If I do so, I am no longer acting as a "lecturer" and may lose my position. If the students are taking exams, I must methodologically bracket any friendship I may have with them and mark their examinations with the impartiality of a stranger. Of course, this methodological bracketing of different ways of seeing others is far from perfectly achieved in real life, but it is still a norm which is aspired to. When I go home in the evening, I am not expected to talk at my family for two hours at a stretch. If I do so, I am behaving socially incompetently in seeing my wife and child as students, and I will in all probability find myself divorced – which is the equivalent of getting fired at a university. Social competence within modernity entails a complex ability to negotiate different social identities in a multiplicity of social circumstances. None of these identities singly constitute my sense of self. It is their composition, plus the creative ability to balance them against each other, that makes us who we are in terms of a self.

This ability to methodologically bracket according to a singular logic is an essential prerequisite for modern bureaucratic administration. If we take Bauman's account of *Modernity and the Holocaust* seriously,[12] this ability made it possible for the efficient bureaucrat to methodologically bracket the humanity of the Jews being transported on trains, transforming them into "numbers" or "units" to be administered. However, seeing other people as numbers to be administered is not always a source of injustice, if for instance, the other is a student in an examination. The methodological bracketing, which turns Jews into numbers and dead women and children into "collateral damage," is a source of both the morally worst and finest achievements of modernity. It facilitates both bureaucratic indifference to suffering and liberal justice.

Rawls' description of the self in the "original position" as someone behind a "veil of ignorance" who does not know their class, status, natural assets, abilities,

---

12. Z. Bauman, *Modernity and the Holocaust* (Cambridge: Polity, 1989).

and so on,[13] and is conscious only of what resources are necessary for a good life in general, has frequently been criticized as being sociologically untenable.[14] However, I would argue that it is substantially more empirically based than it may appear at first sight. Of course, it is not a description of any concept of the *self*, but it is characteristic of precisely the type of single-stranded methodological bracketing which characterizes a specific form of identity necessary to modern perceptions of justice.

In everyday conversation, if one person tries to convince the other of the rightness of an outcome, central to that argument has to be the claim that it is argued from a neutral position. If Plato or Socrates were to argue today that philosophers should be kings, they would have to convince their modern interlocutors that holding this belief had nothing to do with the fact that they happened to be philosophers. Kant's essay "What is Enlightenment?" constitutes a powerful endorsement of the idea that knowledge must be divorced from the authority.[15] Any modern moral justification entails a distancing of the circumstance of the speaker from the statement in a way which was not characteristic of the multi-stranded logic of traditional societies. As observed by Gellner, the authoritative position of the priest makes the statement "It's going to rain" more true.

The liberal self who methodologically brackets their sense of class and so on is cut of the same cloth as the person acting out the complex set of roles demanded by modernity. Modern identity derives from this complex set of identities. The modern self is not a singular self for whom all of social life can be reflected against one interpretative horizon. We are complex beings with a multiplicity of signifiers to denote who we are and local interpretative horizons which go with each of these ways of being in the world. Sometimes these come into conflict and this creates cognitive dissonance. The office party is one such instance: how do we negotiate colleagues becoming friends? What do we do if are in the local pub with our "mates" and our "boss" walks in? If we introduce him, does he then become a "mate"? How should we behave in the morning – as if the night before did not happen?

The identity that goes with the Rawlsian veil of ignorance is the "citizen" as the carrier of political rights. This modern political self has its counterpart in the economic sphere of everyday life: the "consumer." If we go into a shop we can consume what we like irrespective of our class, status, and history, as long as we have sufficient money to pay. With each of these signifiers goes a different interpretative horizon. Just as with "lecturer" and "student," there are certain perceptions of the

---

13. J. Rawls, *Theory of Justice* (Oxford: Oxford University Press, 1971), 136-7.
14. For instance, M. Sandel, *Liberalism and the Limits of Justice* (Cambridge: Cambridge University Press, 1982).
15. I. Kant, "An Answer to the Question 'What is Enlightenment?'" in *Political Writings* (Cambridge: Cambridge University Press, 1970 [1784]).

world that entail specific norms. As a consumer I can argue that my consumer rights have been infringed if, while there is a general notice declaring that everything is 15 percent off, I am told that this discount does not apply to a specific item that I wish to purchase, either because of the nature of the item or because of who I am. My consumer rights have been violated by my being denied a reduction, even though the amount involved may be minimal. However, if I were to walk into the shop 15 cents short of the purchase price of a loaf of bread, my consumer rights would not be violated even if I were starving because the rights of a consumer are not related to need, which constitutes a methodological bracketing that makes no sense relative to multi-stranded logic.

The modern state is responsible not only for justice and politics but also for socialization. As observed by Gellner, the modern state is defined not only by its monopoly on violence and taxation but also by its control over education. Mass education entails mass socialization. The question then arises: Whose culture should we be socialized into? In Denmark the answer largely entails middle-class Copenhagen Danish speech and behavior, while in the case of the UK it is Englishness. This of course has both a centrifugal and a centripetal effect. In the case of Denmark it is largely centrifugal, while in Great Britain it is largely centrifugal on the main island, but largely centripetal with regard to the island of Ireland.

The centripetal result comes about when an alien interpretative horizon is forced upon the Irish other, while coupling it with a demeaning perception of identity. Irishmen should become Englishmen. As is argued by Gellner in his account of nationalism, what made the subaltern cultural group nationalistic was the added insult that when they absorbed the behavioral patterns of the dominant group, they were still considered inferior.[16] The natural reaction for the middle classes was the creation of their own state in which being "Irish" was not a badge of inferiority.

National identity solves a number of functional problems for the modern liberal state. The idea of being a citizen is not substantive enough or thick enough to absorb most people's loyalties. The person under the "veil of ignorance" is a relatively lifeless entity for which most people are willing to make few sacrifices. However, except for an entirely minimal state, a properly functioning liberal democracy actually presupposes certain levels of distributive justice in the form of welfare, which entail substantive (by historical standards) taxes. Most actors are only willing to give to others with whom they have some kind of collective identity. If it cannot be kinship, then the "nation" provides a collective identity through the "imagined community."[17] Just as our many social identities entail specific local interpretative

---

16. E. Gellner, *Nations and Nationalism* (Oxford: Blackwell, 1983).
17. B. Anderson, *Imagined Communities* (London: Verso, 1983).

horizons which go with these roles, so, too, the nation has its interpretative horizon, which is created through the educational system.

The imagined community of the nation also solves many other functional problems for the liberal state, the most obvious being the problem of limiting the state's responsibilities. Scandinavians do not have to feel too guilty for their high standard of living and welfare entitlements, relative to the plight of sub-Saharan Africa. Our entitlements are for "us" and not for "them." Liberalism, on the other hand, has to be universalistic in its logic. If a person's ethnicity or place of birth should be under a "veil of ignorance," then it makes no sense to exclude people from sub-Saharan Africa from the Danish welfare system as they have a much greater need than most Danes. However, just as the consumer in the shop does not have rights based upon need, so, too, the need of others applies only to Danes. Of course, this is not entirely correct. Many Danes do decry the global inequalities and Denmark does contribute aid to the developing world. This is similar to the cognitive dissonance felt between treating the "boss" in bureaucratic mode and "mate" mode. Danes are both citizens with liberal views in which ethnicity and birth are irrelevant, and "Danes" for whom the world is divided into members of the imagined community, who constitute "us," and those outside who are "them." However, the "them and us" distinction is absent not only in the liberal mode but also in many other modern identities. The world is full of fellow "consumers" and "workers." The competent social actor is a member of many imagined communities of "citizens," "consumers," "professionals," "sports enthusiasts," and so on.

The modern actor who is capable of this variety of ways of being in the world is in many respects a fragmented being who is frequently subject to cognitive dissonance in moving from one situation to the other. However, the ability to keep these interpretative horizons together is the basis of competent social interaction. There are of course psychological conditions in which the individual cannot accomplish this.

Balance between interpretative horizons, social roles, and identities is not always inevitable. Because they are in tension, and frequently incommensurable, the dominance of one way of being can effectively annihilate the other. While nationalism provides for the functional needs of the modern state in certain respects in which liberalism cannot, the extension of nationalism into a comprehensive interpretative horizon invariably entails the end of liberalism. Hannah Arendt argued that Nazism was effectively a fusion of nationalism with natural science, in the form of misappropriated Darwinian theories of natural selection.[18] The result was a nationalism in which the state had the right to direct the socialization, reproduction, and

---

18. H. Arendt, *The Human Condition* (Chicago: University of Chicago Press, 1958).

survival of the Aryan German species. In Ireland during the 1950s and 60s, there was a fusion of nationalism with Catholicism which, in essence, created a single comprehensive worldview supported by both state and church to the exclusion of basic liberal premises, as is evidenced by the increasingly loud testimony of single mothers and "illegitimate" children who experienced those years.

My general hypothesis is not that only nationalism has this potential to destroy the basis of a liberal society. As has been argued by Weber and Habermas, the over-extension of a bureaucratic rationality will also stultify democracy. The emergence of the modern self, made up of conflicting roles and identities, is absolutely essential to the maintenance of modern liberal societies. There are four interrelated reasons for this.

Firstly, as we have been arguing, the act of methodologically bracketing various interpretations, which single-stranded thought presupposes, is a form of internal constraint which is particular to modern agency. The liberal self, as described by Rawls, presupposes a massive act of methodological bracketing. The ability to adopt the "veil of ignorance" is not something that comes naturally to people in all types of society. Rather, it presupposes a self who is used to behaving as a competent single-stranded social agent in a complex modern world.

This ability to carry off a multiplicity of identities does not only facilitate a particular form of identity which is central to liberalism; the constant ability to change interpretative horizon is significant in that it socializes people into the view that things can have many descriptions. As noted by Rorty, the liberal self is an ironic self for whom there are no ultimate descriptions, only better and worse ones.[19] The world becomes a contingent place in which there is no ultimate referent or description of things provided by an ultimate vocabulary. The liberal self is a person who has come to terms with the contingency of meaning and has given up the search for final vocabularies, and in so doing becomes fundamentally tolerant of difference and the liberty of others.

The multiplicity of ways of seeing the world is central to liberal autonomy. The liberal idea of the authentic self as self-creating is sociologically untrue. We cannot transcend meaning entirely and create it for ourselves. However, the post-modern view whereby we are caught in webs of meaning that we cannot escape is also flawed. Social agents do not need some transcendental viewpoint from which to judge reality in order to be creatively autonomous. They do not need a rock of certainty; rather, they can move from description to description and mirror them off each other. The wonder of language is its capacity to move a finite number of sounds and words to an infinity of ideas and concepts. This comes not simply from

---

19. R. Rorty, *Contingency, Irony, Solidarity* (Cambridge: Cambridge University Press, 1989).

words relationally but from the fact that multiple descriptions and re-descriptions are possible. The autonomous creative agent does not have to "invent" a "private language" for themselves, but can distance themselves from one set of signifiers, mirroring one local language against another. While working in the transport office in Nazi Germany it may have been the norm to see Jews as "numbers," but it was also possible to see them as "persons." When at war it may be possible to see the other as "the enemy," "collateral damage," "human beings," "women," "men," "children," "fellow workers," "terrorists," "an inferior race," or "victims of genocide." The social agent who is used to switching interpretative horizons will be able to exercise autonomy and is less likely to be overcome by the collective group thinking and singular descriptions of the "nation at war" because they continually move from one of these descriptions to the other. Our multiplicity of descriptions allows us to reflect ways of "seeing" the world against each other.

The self who can consciously methodologically bracket various interpretations of the same signified, recognizing them all as valid but relative to different contexts, has the capacity to live with contingency. However, the capacity for this kind of internal pluralism, by consciously using multiple interpretative horizons to make sense of the world, belongs to a fairly rare type of social agent in historical terms. They are a product of a specific felicitous conjunction when political theory (what is considered normatively right) and social order (what is empirically observed) are in tandem with each other. It is my sincere concern that this conjunction will not endure because of a failure to realize how unique it is. A truly liberal society does not only allow a multiplicity of local cultures to flourish, it also encourages a kind of internal pluralism. One of the weaknesses of some forms of multiculturalism, which encourage groups to look inward by educating themselves, is precisely that by looking inward those social agents becomes singular in their interpretative horizon. In so doing, they lose the ironic quality of seeing meaning as constructed and plural.

One reason why this uniqueness is not fully appreciated is the tacit historicist view that history progresses from lower to higher forms of reasoning – the "end of history hypothesis." Thus it seems inconceivable that, in the long run, societies may become less liberal and democratic.

In a globalizing world, nationalism is losing its automatic effectiveness as a source of identity and is being challenged by other identities. The question for political theorists and policy-makers is to what extent the state should reinforce these new identities. Most acutely, should the state support education directed at creating alternative identities?

The answer is a complex fusion of multiculturalism and liberalism. As we have already observed, nationalism is not entirely benign but can be functional to the liberal democratic state, which is also the case with these new identities.

It should be clear that total state neutrality, while sounding very liberal, is not the answer. The night-watchman state will not have the collective allegiance of its citizens. They will become disaffected from it as they cease to think of it as "theirs." I think the current disaffection with politics in most Western democracies comes precisely from this sense that the state is not for them. It is disengaging from its citizen's lives under the influence of neo-liberalism.

Taylor's point that the validation of identities is significant for self-esteem and the liberal notion of authenticity has some moral force.[20] However, it is not an absolute moral imperative. Modernity entails many identities, and part of socialization is learning how to perform these parts adequately. Rejection as well as affirmation are the stuff of everyday interaction. There should be no singular identity which is sacred. Getting your first job is a complex conjuncture of affirmation and rejection of structuration practices; this cut and thrust of identity building which applies to the self as an employee applies equally with regard to other identity creation acts. There is no *prima facie* reason why the normal rules of social interaction should be suspended in one specific sphere. However, that said, it must be conceded that affirmation is preferable to rejection and negative identification should be avoided. But this does not entail that all identities should be affirmed in every respect.

If being a "citizen" is not enough, and being a Dane or an Irishman is not sufficient, it is necessary for the state to embrace and validate new alternative identities. We have argued that multiple identities are central to the conditions of possibility of modern liberal democracy. It follows that these new identities have the potential to add to this multiplicity of ways of seeing the world. In that sense, multicultural identities have a clear potential to strengthen liberal democracy against nationalism or any other identities that have a tendency towards comprehensiveness.

Against these positive aspects, there is a danger that some of these new identities may themselves pose as comprehensive identities, apparently becoming, like multi-stranded thought, answers to all the questions of life. In liberal democracy, identities should not be encouraged which re-describe the world in its entirety to the exclusion of other descriptions. They must be commensurable with and tolerant of the multiple and fractured self of modernity. It must be possible to read the story of Genesis and study Darwin's theory of evolution and, through single-stranded logic, understand that the former is a metaphor for the spiritual world while evolution is a falsifiable fact of the empirical world.

In education, state policy directed at the challenges of identity must bear in mind the importance of knowing how to "methodologically bracket" and think

---

20. Taylor, *The Ethics of Authenticity*.

single-strandedly. Simultaneously, students should learn that there are multiple descriptions of the world and no single transcendent one that trumps the rest.

In conclusion, new multicultural identities are functional to liberal democracy, though in a qualified way.

Bibliography

Anderson, B. *Imagined Communities*. London: Verso, 1983.

Arendt, H. *The Human Condition*. Chicago: University of Chicago Press, 1958.

Bauman, Z. *Modernity and the Holocaust*. Cambridge: Polity, 1989.

Derrida, J. *Writing and Difference*. Chicago: University of Chicago Press, 1978.

Foucault, M.. *The Order of Things*. London: Routledge, 1970.

Gellner, E. *Nations and Nationalism*. Oxford: Blackwell, 1983.

Gellner, E. *Plough, Sword and Book*. Chicago: University of Chicago Press, 1988.

Giddens, A. *The Constitution of Society*. Cambridge: Polity Press, 1984.

Jenkins, R. *Social Identity*. 2nd ed. London: Routledge, 2004.

Kuhn, T. *The Essential Tension*, Chicago: University of Chicago Press, 1977.

Kant. I. "An Answer to the Question 'What is Enlightenment?'" in *Political Writings*, edited by H.S. Reiss and translated by H.B. Nisbet. Cambridge: Cambridge University Press, 1970 [1784].

Rawls, J. *A Theory of Justice*. Oxford: Oxford University Press, 1971.

Rorty, R. *Contingency, Irony, Solidarity*. Cambridge: Cambridge University Press, 1989.

Sandel, M. *Liberalism and the Limits of Justice*. Cambridge: Cambridge University Press, 1982.

Sen, A. *Identity and Violence*. London: Allan Lane, 2006.

Taylor, C. *The Ethics of Authenticity*. Cambridge, MA: Harvard University Press, 1991.

Taylor, C. "The Politics of Recognition." In *Multiculturalism*, edited by Amy Gutmann. Princeton: Princeton University Press, 1994.

6 Nation, Region, and Immigration in US History, 1864-1924

Eric Rauchway

Whenever we think about national narratives, we also need to think about regional narratives: most nations of any substantive size contain regions distinct for reasons of history and geography, possessing different economies and often different political institutions as well as cultures. Indeed, for many countries a so-called national narrative is really a particular regional narrative that happens at the moment to prevail over others: perhaps the cities are in the ascendant, or possibly the farms; maybe the port interests prevail for a time over those of the manufacturing centers, and so forth. And the importance of subnational regions becomes especially clear when we think about the influence of immigration on a people's sense of themselves. When we think about the implications of immigration for plural societies' sense of themselves, we need to think about regional narratives for at least three clear reasons.

First, immigrants generally don't arrive or settle evenly dispersed throughout a country. Although official data often discuss migrants as a proportion of total national population, this method of calculating the foreign presence in a society is virtually meaningless; migrants neither arrive evenly spread over a country nor do they disperse to achieve a uniform diffusion. Instead migrants cluster around port cities where they arrive, and move along established routes of travel through the country seeking, normally, economic opportunity. So different parts of a country have different experiences of immigration owing to the differing patterns of regional settlement.

Second, many plural societies have federal institutions that give political representation to place. The Australian, Canadian, and US Senates, the German Bundesrat and other like institutions award political power in federal capitals based arbitrarily on location without attention to population. Such institutions have the effect of amplifying the importance of the first reason to attend to subnational regions: if different regions have different experiences of immigration and in addition those regions have political representation, the national government will have to take account of these various experiences. Federal capitals will play host to politicians from regions both rich and poor in their understanding of immigration's impact.

Perhaps no such institution is quite so firmly devoted to representation of place as the US Senate, which allots two senators to each state irrespective of whether anyone lives there. In England before the 1832 reform bill, they called a place like that a "rotten borough"; in America, we call it Wyoming. But even if the US is peculiarly devoted to representation of subnational regions, the general point stands: institutions often permit representation of place and thus give voice to different experiences of immigration.

Third, many plural societies were originally settler societies: Australia, Canada, Brazil, Argentina, and other New World nations like the US owe their modern shape to the European practice of establishing colonies and displacing or mixing with the native populations (or both). That is to say, they trace their national story to a founding date and place, a starting-point or two from which the society expanded, often violently.

Such settler societies therefore have older and newer regions. These newer regions were once regarded as frontiers, and for a settler society a frontier is the font from which national narratives spring. The frontier is where the nation manufactures its future; it's the national narrative made material, in the stuff of roads and farms carved from a retreating wilderness. Settlers who live on frontiers enjoy the privilege, or suffer the burden, of embodying the national progression toward modernity; their fellow countrymen look to the frontiers to describe where the country is, perhaps literally, going.

Because the US was settled mainly East to West, the West is this newer region. But in the US we maybe have a slightly special case among settler societies because the older part of the country is not simply "the East" but rather is divided into North and South, approximately along the lines drawn by the perceived necessity of chattel slavery in the early nineteenth century.

Even considering this peculiarity, to which we will return, the US experience of settlement applies elsewhere: frontiers are where the peculiar national version of modernity gets made, and the presence and role of immigrants on the frontier necessarily plays a role in the peculiar national version of modernity.

So, special features of the US case aside, we can draw three broadly generalizable observations from it: (1) immigrants don't arrive or settle evenly dispersed; (2) institutions of representation often give representation to places, thus (considering (1)) ensuring contentious debates over the place of immigrants; and (3) settler societies have a special stake in the role of immigrants on the frontier. So even though in this essay I discuss US history, what I have to say about regions and American narratives of nationhood should apply, to greater or lesser degrees, to plural societies elsewhere.

And the story we can see when we consider the influence of regions on the reception of immigration into a national narrative is this one: that while you can see American debates over immigration as a clash of conflicting visions, with one or another attaining preeminence at one time or another, what you're often seeing is in fact not the strength of one narrative over another, but the political rise and fall of various regions and their influence at the national level.

The regions, or sections, of the United States differed substantially from each other even before the nineteenth-century era of mass overseas immigration, and they already had characteristic and distinct narratives about themselves. The classic account of these regional narratives is Constance Rourke's 1931 study of regional archetypes in Americans' vernacular culture, archetypes that derived from the specific experience of each section.

The earliest such archetypes emerged from the contrast, increasingly drawn in the years just after the revolution, between the New England and the Old. Royall Tyler's 1787 play *The Contrast* employed a stock comic type, the Yankee Jonathan, who spoke plainly and had little regard for finer ideas of manner. Jonathan survived Tyler's play and became a staple of American comic theater, growing wilier and lankier, appearing increasingly as a peddler and a sharp dealer. Before too much time had passed, Jonathan – increasingly known as Brother Jonathan and then Uncle Sam – became the personification of the American nation itself, or at least, he did for people prepared to see the country as primarily commercial and worldly.

If the Yankee archetype was cruder than the Englishman with which he contrasted himself, he nevertheless still had commerce with the world and an acquaintance with its people, though he occupied himself principally with besting them. Strip away these minor refinements and you got an American figure even more novel, distinct, and assertive: the backwoodsman. Based on the real lives of frontiersmen like Daniel Boone and David Crockett, the American backwoodsman was principally a figure of violence, someone who fought and killed to justify his existence, whose job was to defend and extend American settlements. The American backwoodsman gave archetypal definition to the West: instead of facing the Old World, he looked deep into the heart of the continent, promising to extract from it by whatever violence was necessary the trappings of a suitable New World.

Were it not for slavery, the Yankee and the backwoodsman might have been sufficient to define American character. But this peculiar institution necessitated a third figure: the minstrel, the great lie of slavery – the bondsman who enjoys his toils. Called on with increasing frequency to defend their practice of holding their fellow men in chains, Americans not only concocted but valorized the cheerful thrall.[1]

When immigrants came to the US, they came not to an America, but to a part of America where one of these figures dominated the culture, and vied for control of the national narrative.

---

1. Constance Rourke, *American Humor: A Study of the National Character*, ed. W.T. Lhamon Jr. (Tallahassee: University Presses of Florida, 1986 [1931]).

The US Civil War is of course the great example of regional conflict in the US, and it began as a conflict between the North and the South over what the West should look like – whether the Yankee or the minstrel would accompany the backwoodsman into the West. Abraham Lincoln, often depicted as an archetypal backwoodsman (the "railsplitter") was elected president in 1860 not to abolish slavery but to keep it out of the West. Almost immediately thereafter, eleven southern states seceded rather than see the West closed to slavery and plantation labor. And although it took four years for the United States to defeat the southern rebellion, secession itself ensured that the South lost the battle to tell the story of the new lands. For no sooner had the southern representatives left Congress than the Republican majority among the remaining lawmakers began sketching the map of the new West.

One of the major draftsmen of this plan was a Yankee, Justin Morrill of Vermont, who had a clear narrative of American nationhood that drew on his worries about America's place in the world. In Morrill's story, immigrants played a major part. Morrill saw an America providentially blessed with natural resources, but profligately frittering them away through incautious use of the soil. As the US exhausted its endowment, European nations, using scientific agriculture, had taught their farmers to replenish the soil. The Old World thus threatened to surpass the New, as Morrill explained in 1862:

> European nations [...] all seem eager to place their people ahead in the great race for [...] mastery. [...] we are doomed to be dwarfed in national importance, and not many years can pass away before our ships will be laden with grain not on their outward but homeward voyage. Then, with cheap bread no longer peculiar to America, our free institutions may be thought too dear by those of whom even empires are not worthy – the men with hearts, hands, and brains – vainly looking to our shores for life, liberty, and the pursuit of happiness.[2]

Morrill argued that unless Americans planned better uses of their West, they would fall behind in the progress of nations and no longer attract the best people from overseas. This worry informed Republican policies passed by Congress during the war. They subsidized a Pacific Railway to enable swift passage to the West. More importantly, they established the Homestead Act, enabling farmers willing to migrate – including from overseas – to find a small parcel of land cheaply in the West, thus filling the new territories with hardy independent farmers, rather than large, southern-style plantations: ensuring it was the backwoodsman, and not the minstrel, who remained the characteristic figure of the American frontier. And they passed Morrill's own college legislation, to provide for research and instruction in the replenishment of American soil.

---

2. Justin Morrill, Speech in Congress on behalf of land-grant college bill. Cong. Globe, 37th Cong., 2nd Sess. Appendix (6/6/1862).

Morrill, his Yankee eye gimlet-fixed on international competition, believed the US in danger of losing its traditional edge: "We are doomed to be dwarfed in national importance, and not many years can pass away before our ships will be laden with grain not on their outward but homeward voyage." The only way to keep the American advantage was to realize of the new land to the West the same kind of open, mobile market in goods and talents in which Yankees had always excelled. Morrill especially liked the idea of education to promote mobility; his policies would "obliterate state lines [...] Sedentary life is anti-American," he claimed.[3]

In Morrill's story, mobility included immigrants coming from overseas, who would, like his proposed colleges, replenish the land by supplying a scarce commodity: people. Immigrants must come, he claimed; there were not enough people in the East to settle the Western territories: "If they suddenly make drafts upon the old States [...] the aggregate wealth and power of the country is weakened, for not so much is contributed to the new as has been subtracted from the old." The territories therefore required "[f]oreign emigration."[4] In the Yankee mind, immigrants – at least, immigrants properly educated and provided with land and access to markets – were simply more settlers.

Nor was this solely Morrill's story. In his annual message of 1863, Lincoln called for "a system for the encouragement of immigration. Although this source of national wealth and strength is again flowing with greater freedom than for several years before the insurrection occurred, there is still a great deficiency of laborers in every field of industry, especially in agriculture and in our mines, as well of iron and coal as of the precious metals."[5] The Republican platform of 1864 resolved "That foreign immigration [...] has added so much to the wealth, development of resources and increase of power to the nation" and therefore needed encouragement.[6] Lincoln in his Thanksgiving Proclamation expressed gratitude to God for having "augmented our free population by emancipation and by immigration."[7] In his annual message of 1864, he said, "I regard our immigrants as one of the principal replenishing streams which are appointed by Providence."[8]

In all these pronouncements we see the idea of immigration as a vital source

3. Justin Morrill, Speech in Congress on behalf of land-grant college bill. Cong. Globe, 42nd Cong., 3rd Sess., 558 (12/5/1872).
4. Ibid., 258.
5. Abraham Lincoln, Third Annual Message (12/8/1863), accessed 2/20/2011. UCSB American Presidency Project, http://www.presidency.ucsb.edu/ws/?pid=29504.
6. Republican Party (6/7/1864), 2/20/2011. UCSB American Presidency Project, http://www.presidency.ucsb.edu/ws/?pid=29621.
7. Abraham Lincoln, Thanksgiving Proclamation (10/20/1864), accessed 2/20/2011, UCSB American Presidency Project, http://www.presidency.ucsb.edu/ws/?pid=69998.
8. Abraham Lincoln, Fourth Annual Message (12/6/1864), accessed 2/20/2011, UCSB American Presidency Project, http://www.presidency.ucsb.edu/ws/?pid=29505.

of renewal to America's endangered resources, a means of restoring the United States to a condition of health. The Yankee, as ever, faced the world, and for a time during the Civil War the Yankee sensibility commanded the economic policy of the Republican Party. Immigrants must flood in – particularly, Lincoln noted, to agriculture and mining; which is to say, particularly into the West – to ensure the frontier would look as the United States' war aims would have it look, like the North rather than the South, a land of prudent, independent citizens, not arrogant and luxurious slavemasters sustained by oppressed bondsmen. The US Congress made policy from this story in 1864 with An Act to Encourage Immigration.[9] The law supplemented existing efforts to publicize the availability of western lands to immigrants by endowing a commissioner of immigration with a budget of $25,000 to assist in securing transportation for immigrants to the West by rail and the establishment of an office of immigration in New York asked to care for immigrants' possessions, arrange their passage to the West, and ensure their good treatment at the hands of future employers.

And in the wake of the war the spinners of this tale looked on it with satisfaction. Morrill reported in 1867 that the influx of immigrants to the United States "vastly more than supplies our losses during the late war."[10]

But before long, unanticipated obstacles changed the course of Morrill's story. Together with his Republican colleagues, who represented the political clout and economic ambitions of the industrial North, Morrill had crafted a plan for western settlement during the Civil War, while the representatives of the South had forcibly absented themselves from the nation's capital. And this plan looked as it did in large measure because Morrill and his colleagues hoped to keep the institutions and habits of the South out of the new republic that would emerge from the war and include the new states of the West.

Then, at the war's end, the South returned swiftly to the Union and the representatives of the South returned to the halls of Congress, and southern stories began to compete for their place in the national narrative about immigration. The southern contribution to the national vernacular identity was the minstrel, a happy bonded laborer – but now the politics of Reconstruction and the enfranchisement of African Americans threatened that myth. To white southern leaders, then, the prospect of immigration looked different from how it did to northerners. Where to the Yankee the immigrants replaced the citizens lost in the war and filled the West with desirable independent farmers, to the southerner the immigrant looked like a possible new source of bonded labor.

---

9.   13 Stat. 385 (1864).
10. Justin Morrill, "The Currency" (Congressional speech published as a pamphlet, 12/11/1867), 8.

The US commissioner of immigration reported in 1866 that from the South

this bureau has received numerous letters requesting authority to bring into the south East Indian or coolie laborers. The writers have been informed that the whole policy of the government is opposed to such propositions, and that the introduction of new races bound to service and labor, under contracts similar to those in the West Indies, is contrary to the true interests, as it is to the laws, of the United States. If proper and profitable contracts cannot be made with the freedmen who are used to the peculiar labor of the southern States, there is no doubt but that a free, foreign immigration will supply all their necessities.[11]

Over time white southerners remained captivated by the prospect of importing Chinese labor. As one wrote in 1869,

[...] even if the present labor element among us could be utilized and profitably employed, it would still be utterly inadequate to the wants of the Southern and South- western States, and that we not only have ample room and superior inducements to offer to European immigration, but that it is also desirable and necessary to look to the teeming population of Asia for assistance in the cultivation of our soil and the development of our industrial interests; and that China, especially, is capable of supplying us with a class of laborers peculiarly adapted to our circumstances [...]. [12]

That thin euphemism, "peculiarly adapted to our circumstances," featuring the loaded word "peculiar" – slavery in America was often called the "peculiar institution" – appears to support the commissioner of immigration's worry that the desire for Chinese immigration to the South represented a desire to reestablish slavery in all but name.

Now, as long as immigrants came freely to the United States to establish themselves as farmers in the West, they fit the Civil War storyline of a nation made stronger by the addition of foreign elements to its population. But if they were to come as indentured laborers, with the expectation that they would fit themselves to the peculiar needs of southern agriculture for forced labor, they threatened the whole purpose for which the Civil War had been fought – to keep bondsmen and the peculiar institution out of the West. So to those Americans who had subscribed to the northern narrative of the West, it became clear that indentured laborers must be kept out of the West – and, as the commissioner of immigration wrote, "East Indians" or "coolie[s]" were seen as likely sources of bonded labor.

---

11. Secretary of State, Letter transmitting the report of the Commissioner of Immigration of the expeditures, & c., since the establishment of the bureau, Serial Set vol. no. 1256, session vol. no. 8, 39th Cong., 1st Sess., H.Exec. Doc. 66 (3/9/1866), 6.
12. *Memphis Daily Avalanche*, July 16, 1869. "To supplement the Negro," in vol. 9 of John Commons, ed., *A Documentary History of American Industrial Society* (Cleveland, Ohio: The Arthur H. Clark Co., 1910), 81.

This observation helps us to understand how the West became a region largely opposed to immigration. The settlers who homesteaded on the frontier often imagined themselves as hardy American backwoodsmen, fighting off nature and Indians to make an American civilization in the wilderness. But they did not come alone, or even first, to the frontier they imagined. The railroads and the mining, timber, and other extractive industry ran alongside or preceded them, taking the land or the rights to the land, and bringing laborers – often Chinese – as well as, at least briefly, capital to the region. The would-be backwoodsmen imagining a vacant prairie found instead a region rich in claimed land and competition.

And for reasons of both climate and geology, the settlers got from this new land not the steady harvest Morrill in his brighter moments envisioned and promised, but floods and ebbs of boom and bust. Boom and bust in turn begot consolidation: whenever drought brought smaller farms low, the owners of bigger farms would buy them; whenever a mining outfit exhausted its seam, smaller operators bowed out and bigger companies bought their stakes. The consolidation of western holdings proceeded so that by 1900 many of the states with the largest average farm sizes were western states: so much for the dream of the homesteader civilization. And by the same time, many of the states with the highest proportions of foreign-born residents were also western states.

The bursting of the homesteader bubble created a class of the discontented in the West, and as this class grew, so too did a new story about immigration and the American nation. Now, instead of replenishing scarce resources, as in the vision propounded by Morrill, the immigrants were competing for them. And as long as the immigrants were chiefly Chinese, and could be cast as members of a people bound for "coolie" status, imported by wily operators and worked at substandard wages, white workingmen in the West could frequently fixate on the foreigners when seeking someone to blame for their troubles. A Congressional report of 1877 found

> a bitterly hostile feeling toward the Chinese, which has exhibited itself sometimes in laws and ordinances of very doubtful propriety and in the abuse of individual Chinamen and sporadic cases of mob violence. [...] As long as there is a reasonable hope that Congress will apply a remedy for what is considered a great and growing evil, violent measures against the Chinese can be restrained.[13]

Where the Yankee saw in immigration a promise of renewing America's premier position as a commercial power, where the purveyors of the minstrel image saw in immigration a promise of renewing the caste of bonded labor, the frustrated

---

13. Joint Special Committee to Investigate Chinese Immigration, Serial Set vol. no. 1734, Session vol. no. 3, 44th Cong., 2nd Sess., Senate Report 689, v (2/27/1877).

backwoodsmen of the new West saw a threat. And increasingly, Congress seemed willing to oblige the westerners, protecting the country from their doubtful laws and brutal vigilantism by excluding immigrants either from the country altogether or at least from the body politic.

A few years later, in 1882, Congress passed the first Chinese Exclusion Act, which opened,

> Whereas [...] the coming of Chinese laborers to this country endangers the good order of certain localities within the territory thereof: Therefore [...] until the expiration of ten years next after the passage of this act, the coming of Chinese laborers to the United States be, and the same is hereby, suspended. [...] That hereafter no State court or court of the United States shall admit Chinese to citizenship[.][14]

Congress appears to have reasoned, with considerable frankness, that the bigotry of white westerners was such that they could not live alongside Chinese immigrants without distorting the law or disrupting social order. Thus, the appropriate measure was to exclude the Chinese.

What began with the Chinese in 1882 continued later to other populations. As Japanese immigration replaced Chinese immigration, white western pressure required the adoption of a Japanese exclusion policy, this time by executive agreement, in 1907. Furthermore, in the decades following Chinese exclusion, the language of opposition to "coolie" labor spread to other nationalities. Observing the increase of European immigration in the first decade of the twentieth century, Samuel Gompers, president of the American Federation of Labor, wrote in 1911 of "stimulated artificial immigration," brought over to displace American workers and drive down wages by calculatingly importing the "ignorant classes."[15]

So the story of sections and American immigration began in the era of the Civil War with the North extending to the West a new national strength supported by immigrant sinews, a tale explicitly told to counter the possibility of extending southern-style, peculiarly bonded labor to the West. In the course of western settlement, the fear of bonded labor shifted quickly to a fear of immigrant, "coolie," labor, a fear placated by the exclusion of Asian peoples.

By 1917, these exclusions extended to cover others. The original complaint about immigrants was that they were too well adapted to the brutal system of industrial labor in the US, and could out-compete the native-born worker, doing hard tasks for low wages. But in the late nineteenth and early twentieth centuries, Americans increasingly voiced a different objection, fretting now that immigrants were "likely

---

14. 22 Stat. 58 (1882).
15. A.T. Lane, "American Trade Unions, Mass Immigration, and the Literacy Test, 1900-1917," *Labor History* 25, no. 1 (1984): 10.

to become a public charge" – that they were unfit to compete in the industrial system and would of necessity land on the charities and (admittedly meager) welfare rolls of American cities. The American immigration bureaucracy increasingly began excluding immigrants for health reasons – though reasons allegedly to do with "health" often included vague reasons such as "poor physique" and increasingly corresponded to negative stereotypes about immigrant nationalities.[16] By 1915, nearly 70 percent of immigrants barred from entry were excluded for medical reasons. Afraid first of the "yellow peril," Americans worried now about the merely sallow peril.

Fear of disease-bearing immigrants was peculiarly, if not exclusively, a middle-class person's fear. For in the decades around 1900, American cities that saw a large number of immigrants arrive – cities located chiefly in the North – grew increasingly worried (not entirely, though partly, irrationally) about the health risks such immigrants posed, and thus spent more money on public health policies. Immigration, once the middle-class Yankee American's fond desire because it lowered the cost of labor, now hit that same middle-class American in the pocketbook because of his increased taxes. Southern cities, possessed by the much more irrational idea that black people posed a similar health threat, also spent a great deal on public health measures and their white citizens entertained similar fears of the immigrant threat.[17]

Thus even before the World War brought fresh reasons to fear foreigners, northern middle-class fears of immigrants and of southern worries about blacks and immigrants grew. The early 1910s saw a convergence of concerns among a variety of native-born people: working-class whites, white westerners and southerners, and middle-class Americans. These overwhelmed the relatively weaker pro-immigration sentiment of prospective employers, cosmopolitans, and whatever visionaries still clung to the Yankee dream of the 1860s. In consequence the US enacted increasingly strict anti-immigration laws in 1917, 1921, and 1924.

If we consider only the shift from the 1864 act to encourage immigration to the 1924 act to discourage immigration, we might see only the triumph of anti-immigrant over pro-immigrant sentiment; we see an inclusive narrative of American nationhood, in which immigrants replenish scarce re sources, eclipsed by an exclusive narrative in which immigrants sap vital resources. And if we look only at that story of eclipse, we might despair at the absolute displacement of optimism by pessimism.

But if we pay attention to the subnational regions and their various experiences

16. Howard Markel and Alexandra Minna Stern, "The Foreignness of Germs: The Persistent Association of Immigrants and Disease in American Society," *Milbank Quarterly* 80, no. 4 (2002), 757-788.
17. Eric Rauchway, *Blessed Among Nations: How the World Made America* (New York: Hill & Wang, 2006), 85-121.

of immigration, this story appears far too simple: in fact that eclipse occurred at a superficial level only. Beneath it you can see that immigration engendered different expectations in different regions because it fit differently in different regional narratives, and the effects of immigration met or thwarted those expectations in different ways. Anti-immigrant sentiment came to dominate the national political discourse only through a patchwork of cross-class and cross-regional concerns.

And this coincidence of concerns proved tenuous, and susceptible of revision. Before much more than a decade had passed, the American narrative about immigrants shifted yet again, as the political exigencies of the New Deal and World War II brought new sectional configurations to the fore in American politics. But that's another, further story – even if it's also one that can only be properly told if we pay close attention to the differential impact of immigration across regions and the way in which those differential impacts get translated into a precariously national sense of self.

Bibliography

Joint Special Committee to Investigate Chinese Immigration. Serial Set vol. no. 1734, Session vol. no. 3, 44th Cong., 2d Sess., Senate Report 689 (2/27/1877).

Lane, A.T. "American Trade Unions, Mass Immigration, and the Literacy Test, 1900-1917." *Labor History* 25, no. 1 (1984): 5-25.

Lincoln, Abraham. Third Annual Message (12/8/1863). Accessed 2/20/2011. UCSB American Presidency Project, http://www.presidency.ucsb.edu/ws/?pid=29504.

Lincoln, Abraham. Thanksgiving Proclamation (10/20/1864). Accessed 2/20/2011. UCSB American Presidency Project, http://www.presidency.ucsb.edu/ws/?pid=69998.

Lincoln, Abraham. Fourth Annual Message (12/6/1864). Accessed 2/20/2011. UCSB American Presidency Project, http://www.presidency.ucsb.edu/ws/?pid=29505.

Markel, Howard, and Alexandra Minna Stern. "The Foreignness of Germs: The Persistent Association of Immigrants and Disease in American Society." *Milbank Quarterly* 80, no. 4 (2002): 757-788.

Memphis Daily Avalanche. 7/16/1869. "To supplement the Negro." In vol. 9 of *A Documentary History of American Industrial Society*, edited by John Commons (Cleveland, Ohio: The Arthur H. Clark Co., 1910).

Morrill, Justin. Speech in Congress on behalf of land-grant college bill. *Congressional Globe*, 37th Congress, 2nd Session (6/6/1862), Appendix.

Morrill, Justin. "The Currency." (Congressional speech published as a pamphlet, 12/11/1867).

Morrill, Justin. Speech in Congress on behalf of land-grant college bill. *Congressional Globe*, 42nd Congress, 3rd Session (12/5/1872).

Rauchway, Eric. *Blessed Among Nations: How the World Made America*. New York: Hill & Wang, 2006.

Republican Party. (6/7/1864). Platform. Accessed 2/20/2011. UCSB American Presidency Project, http://www.presidency.ucsb.edu/ws/?pid=29621.

Rourke, Constance. *American Humor: A Study of the National Character*. Tallahassee: University Presses of Florida, 1986 [1931].

Secretary of State. Letter transmitting the report of the Commissioner of Immigration of the expeditures, &c., since the establishment of the bureau. Serial Set vol. no. 1256, session vol. no. 8, 39th Congress, 1st Session, H.Exec.Doc. 66 (3/9/1866).

7 From the Shining City on a Hill to a Great Metropolis on a Plain? American Stories of Immigration and Peoplehood

Rogers M. Smith

In *The Uprooted* (1951), a Pulitzer Prize-winning work of history that reads like a novel, Oscar Handlin famously began, "Once I thought to write a history of the immigrants in America. Then I discovered that the immigrants *were* American history."[1] Today this statement may sound politically incorrect, because it seems to dismiss the indigenous peoples who populated the territory that is now the United States; but it is also true that this territory did not become "America" until Europeans came and gave the continent that name. In conceiving this essay I thought to write on "the impact of immigration on stories of peoplehood in the United States," but I found myself in a position much like Handlin's – in the United States, there have never been stories of peoplehood that were not in one way or another stories of immigration.

I was therefore tempted to take the framework for analyzing stories of peoplehood laid out in my 2003 book of that title and show how the various competing accounts of immigration and American nationhood visible in US history were well explained by it. And I will do a little of that; but frankly it seems too obvious, and tediously taxonomic. So my thesis here is different. I will argue that common to virtually all the stories of immigration and American peoplehood that have been politically influential in US history – despite their otherwise diverse economic, political, cultural, and religious goals and uses – has been one theme that, in the twenty-first century, Americans need to change. That theme is the notion, going back to Puritan John Winthrop and the Massachusetts Bay Colony, that America is the most historically important, the most special, potentially if not actually the greatest nation in the world today and probably in all world history – a shining city on a hill that should at least serve as an example to all nations, if it is not indeed actively to lead them. I believe it is time, and past time, for Americans instead to think of themselves with some justified pride in their wealth, their power, and the

---

1. Oscar Handlin, *The Uprooted: The Epic Story of the Great Migrations that Made the American People*, 2nd ed. (Boston, MA: Little, Brown, & Co., 1973 [1951]), 3.

real achievements of their institutions and ways of life, while recognizing that all this makes America no more than one accomplished nation among many others, and a nation that needs in the twenty-first century to pursue increased economic, political, cultural, and yes, demographic interconnections with other nations and peoples on an egalitarian basis – to go from seeking to be a shining city on a hill to being instead a great metropolis on a global plain.[2] Today's American immigrants have great potential to contribute to such a transformation in American stories of peoplehood; but for reasons I will explain, it will not happen easily, and despite the election of the son of an African immigrant, Barack Obama, it is not clearly happening today.

I. Stories of Peoplehood, Settlers, and Immigrants

Let me begin by rehearsing some of the premises on which my argument depends.

I use the term "political people" broadly to include any group of human beings – whether defined in ideological, religious, linguistic, cultural, racial, ethnic, ancestral, territorial, or other terms – whose proponents assert that obligations to their group and its defining features legitimately trump many of the demands made on its members in the name of other human groups or associations. I presume that no political peoples are natural or primordial. All are creations of human beings in history. They are created via asymmetrical political processes in which leaders lead – but only under the great constraint that they must attract and keep followers. Leaders do so both through coercive force that intimidates potential members into obedience, and persuasive stories that prompt voluntary embrace of the worth of the communal life leaders offer as well as trust in the success of their group endeavors. Those stories are my concern here.

All forms of political peoplehood are subjects of continuing and sometimes intense contestation, both internal and external, and so aspirants to leadership are always crafting and re-crafting stories to inspire and maintain allegiance to their visions of peoplehood, as well as to their own leadership. Those stories always build to some degree on pre-existing senses of identity, interests, and values, but they also always re-shape those pre-existing conceptions to some degree in light of new circumstances. The degrees of continuity with past stories depend on what those circumstances are: those engaged in revolutions stress the new more than the old,

---

2. This argument seems to me largely consistent with, and is partly inspired by, the "brief on behalf of the 'cosmopolitan' strain of 'liberal egalitarianism,' tempered by a dose of realism," which concludes Aristide Zolberg's magisterial *A Nation by Design: Immigration Policy in the Fashioning of America* (Cambridge, MA.: Harvard University Press, 2006), 452-453.

though even they usually seek to show that what is new realizes what is best in the old. All stories of peoplehood also contain three types of elements, though with differing emphases: promises of economic well-being; promises of political power sufficient to insure personal security and a measure of political influence; and what I have termed "ethically constitutive" themes, i.e. accounts depicting membership in a people as having intrinsic normative worth. Both leaders and followers may be especially motivated by any one of these elements, but no form of peoplehood is likely to endure if a critical mass of members do not believe that through it they are receiving adequate shares of economic and power benefits and doing so in ways that seem to them normatively legitimate, if not indeed commendable.[3]

This perspective leads me to partial concurrence and partial disagreement with a distinction that the late Samuel Huntington used to critique the Handlin quotation with which I began. In *Who Are We: The Challenges to America's National Identity*, Huntington insisted that at its origin, America was not a nation of immigrants but a nation of "settlers." Immigrants, in his view, arrive generally as individuals or families who are leaving one society and seeking to join another that already exists and to which they must, to a considerable degree, adapt. Settlers instead see themselves as creating a colony in a new location to which they carry much of the culture and values of their homeland. Their colonies either occupy empty spaces or displace, rather than joining, the communities already present.[4] Huntington contended that the overwhelmingly British and Protestant settlers of colonial America created the nation to which millions have since immigrated, and he noted correctly that despite claims that the US is a "nation of immigrants," from 1820 until the present never had much more than 10 % of its population has been foreign-born – keeping it, in his view, far more an Anglo-Protestant "settler" nation.[5]

My partial disagreement with this part of Huntington's argument is to insist that from the standpoint of the politics of peoplehood I have sketched, the distinction between settlers and immigrants is necessarily one of degree. Both those Huntington sees as settlers and those he sees as immigrants play roles that are in some ways similar in the continuing, contested processes of crafting conceptions and institutions of political community, of political peoplehood; and they both pursue maintenance *and* modification of their existing values and identities, though to differing extents. However much they may wish to maintain continuity with their preexisting forms of political community, the members of settler colonies must

---

3. Rogers M. Smith, *Stories of Peoplehood: The Politics and Morals of Political Membership* (New York: Cambridge University Press, 2003), 19-71.
4. Samuel P. Huntington, *Who Are We? The Challenges to American National Identity* (New York: Simon and Schuster, 2004), 39-41.
5. Ibid., 46.

inevitably modify those forms in some ways because of the different ecological, economic, demographic, and political circumstances of their new environments – and many settlers, including the Massachusetts Puritans to whom I will turn next, actively seek to build societies that are significantly novel, that break from what they see as undesirable, obsolete, even corrupt in the community they have left. Many immigrants, on the other hand, seek not simply to adapt to what they find preexisting in their new community, but to contribute to reshaping it in ways that often reflect values they have brought from their societies of origin. There are elements of continuity and adaptation in each case, just in different proportions.

But those differences do matter. Huntington was correct to say that the original British settlers claimed for themselves the distinctive role of founding the template for American peoplehood with which later arrivals would have to engage. In so doing, I suggest, the first colonists also constructed the underlying common theme in most of the subsequent accounts of the relationship of immigrants to America, both pro- and anti-immigration, that native-born Americans and immigrant Americans alike would offer. This theme – that the community they were creating had a special and potentially exalted place among the nations of the earth – is visible, as I have already suggested following many others, in the sermon "A Model of Christian Charity," that Massachusetts Bay Company Governor John Winthrop gave to his fellow colonists in 1630 as their ship, the Arbella, first approached the shores of the New World. Referencing the Gospel of Matthew, chapter 5, verse 14, which states, "you are the light of the world. A city that is set on a hill cannot be hidden," Winthrop told his company members that, while they still had all the duties that they had had in England, they now had "to do more service to the Lord" and keep themselves "better preserved from the common corruptions of this evil world." If they did so, he promised:

> The Lord will be our God, and delight to dwell among us, as His own people [...] He shall make us a praise and glory that men shall say of succeeding plantations, 'may the Lord make it all like that of New England.' For we must consider that we shall be as a city upon a hill. The eyes of all people are upon us. So that if we shall deal falsely with our God in this work we have undertaken [...] we shall be made a story and a by-word through the world.[6]

It may seem absurd to think that the eyes of the world were on the passengers of the Arbella; and for those who do not share Winthrop's theology, it also seems unlikely that God intended to make the New Englanders His special people and dwell among them if they were faithful. But this was a religious "ethically constitutive" story of peoplehood, involving both continuity and change, that served to

---

6.   Governor John Winthrop, "A Model of Christian Charity" (1630), accessed May 6, 2009, http://religiousfreedom. lib.virginia.edu/sacred/charity.html.

inspire a sense of the enormous normative worth of the new form of community the Puritans were seeking to establish, as well a sense of trust that, despite the huge difficulties they faced, they would succeed. Since Winthrop did not rely on coercion, and he could not offer his fellows much in the way of economic benefits, and he also proved unwilling to share much political power, this promise of being part of either a glorious story if the colonists embraced his vision, or a degraded one if they did not, was crucial to the Puritan settler project.

Seven years later, Winthrop made clear that he believed New England's new Puritan people had the right to dictate the terms on which immigrants would join them and to exclude the unwanted. In "A Defense of an Order of the Court," Winthrop justified refusing religious dissidents entry into the colony by arguing first, that no "commonwealth can be founded but by free consent" of its members, and second, that "persons so incorporating have a public and relative interest in each other [...] and in all the means of their welfare so as none other can claim privilege with them but by free consent." Insisting that "a commonwealth is a great family," Winthrop maintained that "as a family is not bound to entertain all comers, no not every good man (otherwise than by way of hospitality) no more is a commonwealth."[7] In response, Henry Vane, Winthrop's rival for colonial leadership, argued that the Christian nature of the Massachusetts commonwealth meant that it could not exclude everyone, certainly not "eminent Christians," since "Christ bids us not to forget to entertain strangers."[8] Winthrop, then, claimed powers to refuse immigrants in order to ensure that the colony's divine mission would be fulfilled; Vane argued that this mission demanded an open door, at least for Christian strangers who sought to join them. But common to both these anti- and pro-immigrant positions was the belief that America must be as the Biblical city on a hill and act accordingly, whatever those requirements might be.

With varying degrees of sincerity, Americans from Thomas Paine to George W. Bush and beyond have argued that America has a special providential world mission ever since, as I'll detail. First, let me note that from early on, many Americans defined this mission in less religious, more political and economic terms. Hector St. John Crèvecoeur, the naturalized French immigrant who published the first widely read book by an American author, *Letters from an American Farmer*, in London in 1782, praised his adopted country as "the asylum of freedom, as the cradle of future nations, and the refuge of distressed Europeans," but not because of its service to Winthrop's Protestant God.[9] Crèvecoeur instead rejoiced that because

---

7. Sue Davis, *American Political Thought: Four Hundred Years of Ideas and Ideologies* (Englewood Cliffs, NJ: Prentice Hall, 1996), 34-35.
8. Ibid., 36.
9. Moses Rischin, ed., *Immigration and the American Tradition* (Indianapolis: Bobbs-Merrill, 1976), 21-22.

in America "all sects are mixed as well as all nations," Americans were becoming "less zealous and more indifferent in matters of religion," as he himself was.[10] In his telling, Americans were Europeans who had "become men" due to "new laws, a new mode of living, a new social system" in a land with rich resources that inspired them, through labor, to pursue prosperity and enjoy freedom in a country that gave them "land, bread, protection, and consequence."[11]

Similarly – though the deist Paine's great 1776 revolutionary pamphlet, "Common Sense," did not hesitate to suggest to Protestant America that its discovery had preceded the Reformation "as if the Almighty graciously meant to open a sanctuary to the persecuted in future years" – it was the fact that the revolutionaries were championing the economic and political "natural rights of all mankind" that made the "cause of America" in Paine's eyes "in a great measure the cause of all mankind."[12] And when George Washington wrote in the 1780s to Irish and Dutch admirers that America should be "open to receive not only the Opulent and respectable Stranger, but the oppressed and persecuted of all Nations And Religions," making it "an Asylum" for "the needy of the Earth," his stress was on economic opportunities as well as republican political and religious freedoms, not on the new nation as the home of Winthrop's God.[13] These were stories of peoplehood stressing economic and political power themes more than religious ones.

Even so, all these accounts still suggested that the "new ideas" of the Americans concerning human economic and political rights meant that America had a uniquely leading role to play both as an example to the world and as a haven for the world's, or at least Europe's, oppressed peoples. And though the receptivity to immigrants expressed by Crèvecoeur, Paine, and Washington may well have been driven by the need of the young nation for more Europeans to join in building the economy, defending against enemies including African slaves, and acquiring further land from the native tribes and an unyielding nature, their rhetoric still imbued their economic and political appeals with a sense that it was America's distinctive fate to play a signal role in the relief and emancipation of all the world.

That same more secular sense of America's special place, which served as a basis for welcoming immigrants in these writers, could also serve as a source of opposition to large-scale immigration much like that of John Winthrop. In his *Notes on the State of Virginia* written in the 1780s, Thomas Jefferson expressed great concern that European immigrants raised under "absolute monarchies" would bring with them "the principles of the governments they leave, imbibed in their early youth; or,

---

10. Ibid., 28-29.
11. Ibid., 24-26, 32-33.
12. Merrill Jensen, ed., *Tracts of the American Revolution 1763-1776* (Indianapolis: Bobbs-Merrill, 1967), 402, 424.
13. Rischin, *Immigration and the American Tradition*, 43-44.

if able to throw them off, it will be in exchange for an unbounded licentiousness." They would then infuse into American law "their spirit, warp and bias its direction, and render it a heterogeneous, incoherent mass."[14] Their coming should not be encouraged.

Though Jefferson later proved willing to see the French revolutionaries at their best as partners in what he saw as the global cause of human enlightenment and emancipation, he never doubted that, as he wrote shortly before his death, the creation of the American republic was indeed for all the world "the signal of arousing men to burst the chains under which monkish ignorance and superstition had persuaded them to bind themselves, and to assume the blessings and security of self-government."[15] Though less stridently than some, he, too, advanced a story of America's special place in world history. But he also eventually welcomed immigrants – because they proved for the most part to vote for Jeffersonian Republicans.

II. The Varieties of American Pro- and Anti-Immigrant Stories

As Jefferson's shift on immigration shows, the stories of peoplehood and immigration that Americans subsequently advanced were often bound up with partisan political struggles, though immigration issues have also often cut across party lines. The history is complex, and this is not the place for a comprehensive review of the accounts of immigration and national identity advanced by various political actors, parties, and advocacy groups throughout American history, much less the treatments of these themes in popular journalism, literature, art, music, theatre, films, television, and more. I do want to stress that influential accounts of immigration and American nationality can be found in all these venues, including works like the 1836 nativist fiction, *The Awful Disclosures of Maria Monk*; Israel Zangwill's play *The Melting Pot* (1908); the landmark Al Jolson film *The Jazz Singer* (1927), and the 1945 song and Academy Award-winning short film *The House I Live In*, featuring Frank Sinatra, among many others. These cultural creations all generated concepts and narratives that provide the materials on which political advocates have drawn to develop resonant stories of peoplehood. But while acknowledging their contributions, my aim here is to provide illustrative evidence of how throughout US history since the revolutionary generation, both political proponents and opponents of immigration in the US have defined and defended their positions in terms of

---

14. Quoted in Thomas Jefferson, *Notes on the State of Virginia*, ed. William Peden (Chapel Hill: University of North Carolina Press, 1955), 85.

15. Joyce Appleby and Terence Ball, eds., *Thomas Jefferson: Political Writings*. (Cambridge: Cambridge University Press, 1999), 149.

accounts that shared an emphasis on the special providential or world-historical nature, role, and destiny of America.

From the very first Congress, American leaders began debating whether the United States should see itself as the "asylum" for the world's oppressed, as Washington had urged, or whether that policy was too risky to be maintained. Conservative Federalists like Theodore Sedgwick of Massachusetts claimed that Americans were more "wise and virtuous" and "better qualified" for republican government than any people on earth; but they were so as a result of their "early education," and Sedgwick doubted that "republican character" could be formed any way "but by early education." Hence if Americans were to remain uniquely capable of the world's highest and most just form of governance, immigration and naturalization of adult foreigners should be discouraged, as Federalists like Sedgwick would go on to do via the notorious Alien and Sedition Acts of 1798.[16] Both sides of the 1790s debates over naturalization and alien rights accepted that the new American republic was the freest and best political society in the world, but they disagreed sharply over whether this meant it must remain the place of refuge for all humanity or whether it would lose its special qualities should those not born and bred to American republicanism gain entry in large numbers.

That debate became more acute from the early 1830s through the 1850s as immigration rose, especially Catholics from Ireland and Germany along with Scandinavian and British Protestants. In 1835 the American inventor and painter Samuel F. B. Morse published the seminal statement of American anti-immigrant nativism, "Imminent Dangers to the Free Institutions of the United States Through Foreign Immigration," which took as its epigraph the passages from Jefferson I have quoted. Like Paine, Morse argued that *the onward march of the world to liberty*," first set in motion by the Protestant Reformation, had then been "more completely developed in this land of liberty, and exhibited perpetually to the gaze of all the world."[17] In response, Morse believed, monarchists and Catholics in Europe were conspiring to destroy American by sending hordes of (often covertly) anti-republican immigrants to American shores. Morse's story of American peoplehood thus combined religious and republican themes in asserting the nation's special historic significance, now even more strongly in opposition to immigration. The response from Jacksonian Democrats, who like their predecessors the Jeffersonians benefited from immigrant votes, was again not to deny America's special status but to argue from it to more open policies. Thus Democratic pamphleteer Henry E. Riell wrote in 1840, "As a

---

16. Rogers M. Smith, *Civic Ideals: Conflicting Visions of Citizenship in U.S. History* (New Haven, CT: Yale University Press, 1997), 160-63.
17. Samuel F. B. Morse, *Imminent Dangers to the Free Institutions of the United States through Foreign Immigration* (New York: Arno Press, 1969 [1835]), 5, 7.

native American, I exult in the triumphant truth that the country which gave me birth is destined, both politically and physically, to be the free asylum for the oppressed and the distressed of the universal world."[18]

But many native-born Americans no longer shared Riell's exultation, and as nativism grew especially among American Protestants, the Whig party, the successor to Sedgwick's Federalist Party, disintegrated in the 1850s over both the issue of slavery and the issue of immigration. The anti-slavery cause proved sufficient to unite many former Whigs with "free soil" Democrats under the umbrella of the new Republican Party. The man who became its first great leader, the former Whig Abraham Lincoln, regularly rejected the anti-immigrant sentiments that many of his fellow Republicans still harbored. A devotee of the Declaration of Independence, Lincoln contended that if nativists had their way, that founding document would read "all men are created equal, except negroes, *and foreigners, and catholics*"; and Lincoln said in that case he himself would prefer to emigrate "to some country where they make no pretence of loving liberty."[19]

That did not mean, however, that Lincoln in fact regarded America as at bottom a nation like all others. He believed instead that America was the world's exemplary case of republican government, history's test case for the possibility of a nation dedicated to realizing the proposition that all men are created equal; and so when he proposed a plan for compensated emancipation of slaves in 1862, Lincoln termed the endeavors of the United States to end slavery and save its Union "the last, best hope of earth."[20] In this he echoed the German-born Republican leader Carl Schurz, who had argued in 1859 that "America and Americanism" had long appeared to him "the last depositories of the hopes of all true friends of humanity." The reason, Schurz explained, was that "true Americanism" meant realizing "the great cosmopolitan idea" that, because all deserve to be free and self-governing, America should clasp "mankind to its great heart," welcoming immigrants while leading the world to freedom.[21]

But in the late nineteenth century, many of the political heirs of Lincoln and Schurz concluded that America's special mission in the world required it to ban many immigrants after all. In 1882, Republican Senator John Miller of California introduced the first Chinese Exclusion Act, urging:

[...] the surest way to popularize and extend the blessings of civil liberty, free government, and American institutions is by example. Let us keep pure the blood which circulates through

---

18. Rischin, *Immigration and the American Tradition*, 93.
19. Ibid., 115.
20. Abraham Lincoln, "Annual Message to Congress," (1862), in vol. 6 of *The Writings of Abraham Lincoln*, ed. Arthur Lapsley (New York: Lamb Publishing Company, 1906), 179-211.
21. Rischin, *Immigration and the American Tradition*, 118, 129-30.

our political system [...] preserve our national life from the gangrene of oriental civilization; foster American institutions in their grandeur and purity [...] in fine, let our civilization be progressive and make free governments in the United States a perfect success, and an example will be furnished the world which will light the fires of liberty in every civilized land.

Miller insisted, however, that America could not play its exemplary role if it experienced "the debasement of our civilization through the injection in to the body-politic of a poisonous, indigestible mass of alien humanity, or the admixture of antagonistic races."[22] On political, economic, cultural, and especially on racial grounds, Miller found Chinese immigration abhorrent and demanded its end. In response, fellow Republican William Moore of Tennessee argued:

The establishment of such a precedent by the United States, the recognized champion of human rights – the nation of all others in the world whose chief pride and glory it has been to truly boast of being known and recognized everywhere as the home of the free, the asylum of the oppressed, the land where all men, of all climes, all colors, all conditions, all nationalities, are welcome to come and go at will, controlled only by [...] laws applying equally alike to the people of every class – is one that does so much violence to my own sense of justice that I cannot, under any stress of evident passion, consent to aid in establishing it.[23]

In this clash Miller prevailed, and Chinese exclusion, justified partly in terms of a racial story of American peoplehood, became the first in a long history of race-based immigration restrictions that would last in one form or another until 1965. America's global role was to be an example to those races capable of its high level of civilization, which Miller believed the Chinese could never attain. But again, common to his position and that of Moore's response, invoking the vision of America as the asylum of the oppressed, was the belief that in one way or another, the United States had a kind of premiere status among all the nations of the world.

And soon, the often racially as well as religiously defined accounts of American national identity that proliferated in the late nineteenth century were used not just to argue for the United States as example or asylum but for a third choice: America as world ruler. In 1898 the nation's leaders sought to extend the American settler project in a new imperial form, via the conquest of overseas colonies in the Spanish-American War. For some, that was only the beginning. In urging that the inhabitants of Puerto Rico, the Philippines, and the other Spanish-American War acquisitions should not receive constitutional rights, Republican Senator Albert Beveridge of Indiana contended in 1900 that

---

22. John Miller, "Chinese Exclusion," *Congressional Record*, vol. 13, pt. 2 (1992): 1481-1488.
23. Quoted in Smith, *Civic Ideals: Conflicting Visions of Citizenship in U.S. History*, 360.

God has not been preparing the English-speaking and Teutonic peoples for a thousand years for nothing but vain and idle self-contemplation and self-admiration. No! He has made us the master organizers of the world to establish system where chaos reigns [...] And of all our race He has marked the American people as His chosen nation to finally lead in the regeneration of the world. This is the divine mission of America, and it holds for us all the profit, all the glory, all the happiness possible to man.[24]

For Beveridge, it was appropriate for the US to govern racially diverse populations globally, but not on a basis of republican civic equality. Beveridge's positions denying equal rights to non-white residents of the new American colonies were then adopted by the Congress and the US Supreme Court; and the United States would also govern most of its domestic black, Latino, and Asian populations on that basis for more than half the twentieth century. After the Philippines proved hard to govern, Americans did back away from Beveridge's vision of direct imperial global domination. Instead, they embraced racial immigration restrictions even more fully. The chief author of the race-based national origins quota system adopted in the 1920s, Rep. Albert Johnson of Washington, insisted that

our capacity to maintain our cherished institution stands diluted by a stream of alien blood, with all its inherited misconceptions respecting the relationships of the governing power to the governed [...] It is no wonder, therefore, that the myth of the melting pot has been discredited [...]The day of indiscriminate acceptance of all races has definitely ended.[25]

Four decades later, however, the modern American civil rights movement succeeded in winning congressional and judicial invalidation of the systems of racial hierarchy and discrimination that had previously so pervasively structured American life, including ending the national origins immigration quota system in 1965 – developments well discussed in outstanding recent scholarship from Desmond King (2000), Daniel Tichenor (2002), Mae Ngai (2004), Aristide Zolberg (2006), and others.[26] Opposing those changes, Democratic Senator Robert Byrd of West Virginia sounded once again the dangers of "immigration of persons with cultures, customs, and concepts of government altogether at variance with those of the basic American stocks." He maintained,

---

24. Ibid., 431.
25. Quoted in Roger Daniels, *Coming to American: A History of Immigration and Ethnicity in American Life* (New York: HarperCollins, 1990), 55.
26. Desmond King, *Making Americans: Immigration, Race, and the Origins of the Diverse Democracy* (Cambridge, MA: Harvard University Press, 2000); Daniel J. Tichenor, *Dividing Lines: The Politics of Immigration Control in America* (Princeton, NJ: Princeton University Press, 2002); Mae Ngai, *Impossible Subjects: Illegal Aliens and the Making of Modern America* (Princeton, NJ: Princeton University Press, 2004); Aristide R. Zolberg, *A Nation by Design: Immigration Policy in the Fashioning of America* (Cambridge, MA: Harvard University Press, 2006).

We must not throw open the gates to areas whose peoples would be undeniably more difficult for our population to assimilate and convert into patriotic Americans. The alien inflow to America from potential waiting lists of applicants from Jamaica, Trinidad, Tobago, Indonesia, India, Nigeria, and so forth can profoundly affect the character of the American population and, in the long run, can critically influence our concepts of government.[27]

But Democratic President Lyndon Johnson condemned "the harsh injustice of the national quota system" because it "violated the basic principles of American democracy – the principle that values and rewards each man on the basis of his merit as a man," so that it was "un-American in the highest sense [...] untrue to the faith that brought thousands to these shores even before we were a country."[28] This time, proponents of more inclusive American stories of immigration and people-hood prevailed.

It is the consequences of the 1965 Immigration Act, which generated far more extensive Latino and Asian immigration than most of its authors anticipated, which have set the stage for current American debates over immigration. Though those debates have been intense, and in response to growing numbers of both documented and undocumented resident aliens, the US has passed laws restricting the eligibility of non-citizens for governmental social aid and has heightened efforts to police, especially, its border with Mexico, so far all efforts to reduce the overall official ceiling on legal immigration have failed. One reason is that although conservative Republicans form the heart of the anti-immigration movement in modern America, their greatest leader, Ronald Reagan, always celebrated legal immigration. He did so perhaps most memorably in his remarks at the 1986 Statue of Liberty Centennial Celebration, where he said "it's good to know that Miss Liberty is still giving life to the dream of a new world where old antagonisms could be cast aside and people of every nation could live together as one." Reagan continued by recalling, as he so often did, John Winthrop's vision of the Puritan colony as "a shining city upon a hill," and he stirred the crowd by elaborating:

> Call it mysticism if you will, I have always believed there was some divine providence that placed this great land here between the two great oceans, to be found by a special kind of people from every corner of the world, who had a special love for freedom and a special courage that enabled them to leave their own land, leave their friends and their countrymen, and come to this new and strange land to build a New World of peace and freedom and hope.[29]

---

27. Robert Byrd, "The Immigration Bill," *Congressional Record*, vol. 111 (1965): 23793-23795.
28. Lyndon B. Johnson, "Remarks at the Signing of the Immigration Bill," in vol. 2 of *Public Papers of the President: Lyndon B. Johnson* (Washington, DC.: Government Printing Office, 1966), 1038.
29. Ronald Reagan, "Remarks at the Opening Ceremony of the Statute of Liberty Centennial Celebration," (1986), accessed July 13, 2010, http://www.reagan.utexas.edu/archives/speeches/1986/70386d.htm.

Reagan's message here, as it was most often, was meant to be one of inclusion, even if his account gave no attention to those African-Americans whose ancestors had been brought to the New World in chains, or the Native Americans whose tribes had been conquered by the arriving Europeans. Note, however, that its indication that the immigrants who came to this country voluntarily had a special courage and a special love for freedom still suggested the inherent superiority of Americans to those who chose to stay behind; and Reagan also continued the longstanding theme that the nation the Americans built was intended by God as an example to all the world. By now it should be clear why it is not surprising that others in Reagan's party have turned this sense of America's special character and role into the kinds of arguments for immigrant exclusion advanced by American conservatives of all parties from Theodore Sedgwick through Samuel F. B. Morse, through John Miller to Robert Byrd to Congressman Thomas Tancredo and broadcaster Lou Dobbs today.

It may be more surprising, perhaps, to recognize that even in post-1965, more multicultural America, liberals who champion relatively generous immigration policies in American politics still often do so by invoking conceptions of America's special status. In a 1998 speech on how to "strengthen the bonds of our national community" as immigration made the nation "more racially and ethnically diverse," President Bill Clinton argued that America's "ability to lead" the world "rests in no small measure on our ability to be a better place here in the United States that can be a model for the world," and he maintained that "More than any other nation on Earth, America has constantly drawn strength and spirit from wave after wave of immigrants."[30] While Clinton portrayed immigrants as desirable contributors, not as burdens, he both claimed for America a unique impact from immigration that, as Huntington noted, is belied by the facts, and he continued to presume that this unique history was part of America's role as the world's leader and the world's model.

In these regards he is followed by the first American President to be a son of a temporarily resident immigrant, Barack Obama. Obama has a history of voting in favor of receptive immigration policies, but he, too, has done so while stressing that immigration has allowed Americans "to form a multicultural nation the likes of which exists nowhere else on earth."[31] And he has repeatedly won cheers from American audiences by contending that, though he has "brothers, sisters, nieces, nephews, uncles and cousins, of every race and every hue, scattered across three continents [...] for as long as I live, I will never forget that in no other country on

30. William Clinton, "Speech on Diversity, Portland State University," (1998), accessed July 12, 2010, http://www.thesocialcontract.com/pdf/eight-four/clinton.pdf.
31. Barack Obama, *The Audacity of Hope: Thoughts on Reclaiming the American Dream* (New York: Three Rivers Press, 2006), 232.

Earth is my story even possible."[32] Although neither Clinton nor Obama would publicly proclaim the providential status of America's identity and national mission as many other American political leaders have done, their rhetoric, even when stressing American inclusiveness toward immigrants, also still stresses how special and uniquely commendable the United States is.

III. The Case for Climbing Down from the City on a Hill

At this point many American readers may be thinking, OK, there is substantial evidence that both pro- and anti-immigration accounts of American national identity often celebrate America as a special, world-leading nation. But what's the problem with that? Here there can be no definitive answers, only more or less persuasive normative arguments.

In *Stories of Peoplehood*, I argue that especially in the twenty-first century, it is desirable to try to foster "moderate" forms of political community – societies that assert some significant claims on the loyalties of their members and some significant authority over various phases of their lives, without asserting absolutely sovereignty over all aspects or primacy over all alternative communities to which their members may also belong. Most people do require relatively stable forms of community with effective, enduring institutions if they are to be able to lead fulfilling lives. Weak, unstable communities do little to help meet their members' material and psychological needs. But strong forms of peoplehood that assert that the governments of a people are entitled to exercise absolute rule over all aspects of their members' lives obviously have great potential for repression, and to endure they usually need to be justified by chauvinistic doctrines that easily lend themselves to brutal and imperialist treatment of outsiders.[33] Those circumstances, I believe, have always been true; and in addition, in the twenty-first century we face numerous economic, environmental, security, and demographic challenges that cannot easily be met by the unilateral actions of policymakers who see themselves as acting only on behalf of the interests of their sovereign states. Many of the challenges facing humanity require multilateral responses through new institutions that limit the absolute sovereignty of particular nations and that need to be supported by more moderate senses of peoplehood that are more receptive to their constituents having multiple, overlapping, interconnected memberships.[34]

---

32. Barack Obama, "A More Perfect Union," (2008), accessed July 13, 2010, http://www.constitutioncenter.org/amoreperfectunion/docs/Race_Speech_Transcript.pdf.

33. Smith, *Stories of Peoplehood*, 130.

34. Ibid., 164-174.

It will be readily evident, I think, that the deep-rooted and longstanding American claims to special world-historical status work against the willingness of American leaders and citizens to accept a more moderate sense of their own peoplehood. Americans saw during the administration of President Obama's predecessor, President George W. Bush, ample evidence of the dangers of an excessively strong and assertive sense of their nation's special nature and destiny. In fairness, these dangers were heightened by understandable impulses to national self-affirmation and protection in the wake of the September 11, 2001 attacks. Those impulses were visible in a bevy of conservative patriotic books that came out soon thereafter, reasserting claims of America's special greatness and distinctive role in world history. In *Why We Fight*, for example, former Secretary of Education William Bennett wrote that:

> [...] we have provided more freedom to more people than any nation in the history of mankind [...] a greater degree of equality to more people than any nation in the history of mankind [...] brought more justice to more people than any nation in the history of mankind [...] our open, tolerant, prosperous peaceable society is the marvel and envy of the ages.[35]

Conservative pundit Dinesh D'Souza wrote similarly in *What's So Great about America* that the US was "the greatest, freest, and most decent society in existence,"[36] while constitutional scholar Walter Berns contended in *Making Patriots* that "Our lot is to be the one essential country, 'the last, best hope of earth,' and this ought to be acknowledged, beginning in our schools and universities, for it is only then that we can come to accept the responsibilities attending it."[37]All these authors cited Lincoln to insist that America was indeed Earth's last, best hope.

Similar themes also dominated the public discourse of President George W. Bush. Studies of presidential rhetoric by a number of scholars including me have shown that Bush argued more frequently and insistently than any of his predecessors, exceeding even Reagan, that America had a providential "mission to promote liberty around the world," a mission in which "that greater power who guides the unfolding of the years" had selected the United States to "lead the cause of freedom" globally. He concluded "we can be certain that the author of freedom is not indifferent to the fate of freedom."[38] In his 2004 State of the Union speech, Bush argued, again like Reagan, that "God has planted in every human heart the desire to live in freedom," and he assured Americans that they would fulfil their "mission" to "lead the cause of freedom" because "that greater power who guides the unfolding of the years" had

35. William J. Bennett, *Why We Fight: Moral Clarity and the War on Terrorism* (New York: Doubleday, 2002), 150-51.
36. Dinesh D'Souza, *What's so Great about America* (Washington, DC: Regnery Publishing Inc., 2002), 94.
37. Walter Berns, *Making Patriots* (Chicago: University of Chicago Press, 2001), ix-x.
38. George W. Bush, "Remarks at the 20th Anniversary of the National Endowment for Democracy," (2003), accessed May 21, 2007, http://www.whitehouse.gov/news/releases/2003/11/20031106-2.html.

"called" them to do so.[39] Bush's belief in his nation's providential mission, however sincere, accompanied America's undertaking of the only acknowledged first-strike war in its history as well as repressive measures toward those suspected of terrorism that most of the world, and now the Obama administration, have repudiated. It also stood in the way of pursuing new and effective multilateral policies and institutions to address a wide range of international problems, including global warming; peace and security in the Middle East; harmonious economic and political relationships between the US and Europe; needed reforms at the United Nations; and multinational efforts to address immigration challenges, among many other concerns. I believe the United States would have done better in the past and can do better in the future by accepting a more moderate sense of political peoplehood that is more conducive to working cooperatively with other states and non-governmental political actors in crafting and institutionalizing many more kinds of regional and global associated responses to these transnational challenges.

Whether or not that is right, what I have argued here raises a prior question: Can some more moderate sense of American peoplehood ever win enough political support to be pursued by American policymakers? To use the metaphor with which I have entitled this essay, can Americans be content with seeing themselves not as the world's shining city on a hill, but simply as one great metropolis among others on the flat world plain that Thomas Friedman depicts – a metropolis that is complex, exciting, with deep problems but genuine glories, but with no special manifest destiny? I acknowledge fully that, as the analysis in *Stories of Peoplehood* indicates and as American history confirms, stories proclaiming America's special status have enormous political strengths, so they are not easily abandoned or overcome.

But that analysis and history also suggest that acceptance of more moderate senses of peoplehood is facilitated when more people see themselves as having multiple, interrelated memberships and affiliations that they value. They are likely to prefer forms of political community that permit them to pursue as many of those affiliations as possible, to move among them as fluidly as possible, and to negotiate the conflicts in the obligations they generate as peaceably and productively as possible. Immigrants are people who are especially likely to have such senses of multiple identities and memberships. They therefore may be most inclined to support moderate senses of political peoplehood. It is precisely because that is true, I think, that so many American leaders throughout history have been suspicious of immigrants and have imposed upon them either high demands for assimilation or severe restrictions.

---

39. Quoted in Rogers M. Smith, "Religious Rhetoric and the Ethics of Public Discourse: The Case of George W. Bush," *Political Theory* 36 (2008): 272-300.

Recent scholarship by Irene Bloemraad and others indicates, however, that more multicultural policies toward immigrants that assist them in preserving a measure of their distinctive cultural identities comfortably in their new land actually facilitate political integration and loyalty therein, rather than promoting separatism.[40] Domestically as well as internationally, policies of assertive national sovereignty that demand strict conformity to very strong senses of peoplehood often promote alienation instead of willing assimilation. Consequently, I see in America's current influx of immigrants – driven, to be sure, primarily by economic interests on both sides of the immigration flows – the potential for building a broader coalition in favor of the sort of more moderate senses of American peoplehood and the more multilateral policies and institutions I believe current problems require. There are no guarantees, to be sure, that such a constituency will emerge or that American leaders will mobilize it on behalf of more moderate and globally-minded positions. As I have noted, Barack Obama has chosen, probably for both political and personal reasons, to wrap his very important celebrations of America's multiculturalism within a larger story that still stresses America's unique greatness.

Yet his political success does at a minimum reveal the potential to build support for the kind of acceptance of multiple affiliations and allegiances and multilateral policies and institutions that I have suggested are needed by America and the world. Obama is a successful politician in part because he speaks effectively to both sides on many issues – race, religion, the economy – and he has done so in regard to senses of American peoplehood as well. He has invoked traditions of America's unique, special character, while also urging Americans to embrace internal diversity and to reject the strongly unilateral focus of his predecessor's foreign policies. And in so doing, he has already brought change, the ultimate extent of which we cannot foresee.

So I will close simply by observing that whether or not Americans will soften their allegiance to conceptions of their own unique greatness, and will do so in salutary ways in the years ahead, will depend a great deal on the directions pursued by this remarkable political story-teller, with an extraordinary multi-racial and multi-national background, who perhaps significantly chose to move to the land of Lincoln and build his career not in the nation's leading city but in the midst of a great, immigrant-filled metropolis on America's plains. Whether Obama and others will take such experiences as a guide for where American should go, and whether they will be able to lead their nation successfully whilst moving in that direction, are central questions for the next chapter in America's stories of immigration and peoplehood.

---

40. Irene Bloemraad, *Becoming a Citizen: Incorporating Immigrants and Refugees in the United States and Canada* (Berkeley, CA: University of California Press, 2006).

Bibliography

Bennett, William J. *Why We Fight: Moral Clarity and the War on Terrorism*.New York: Doubleday, 2002.

Berns, Walter. *Making Patriots*. Chicago: University of Chicago Press, 2001.

Bloemraad, Irene. *Becoming a Citizen: Incorporating Immigrants and Refugees in the United States and Canada*. Berkeley, CA: University of California Press, 2006.

Daniels, Roger. *Coming to American: A History of Immigration and Ethnicity in American Life*. New York: HarperCollins, 1990.

Davis, Sue. *American Political Thought: Four Hundred Years of Ideas and Ideologies*. Englewood Cliffs, NJ: Prentice Hall, 1996.

D'Souza, Dinesh. *What's so Great about America*. Washington, DC: Regnery Publishing Inc., 2002.

Governor John Winthrop, "A Model of Christian Charity" (1630). Accessed May 6, 2009. http://religiousfreedom.lib.virginia.edu/sacred/charity.html.

Handlin, Oscar. *The Uprooted: The Epic Story of the Great Migrations that Made the American People*. 2nd ed. Boston, MA: Little, Brown, & Co, 1973 [1951].

Huntington, Samuel P. *Who Are We? The Challenges to American National Identity*. New York: Simon and Schuster, 2004.

Jensen, Merrill, ed. *Tracts of the American Revolution 1763-1776*. Indianapolis: Bobbs-Merrill, 1967.

King, Desmond. *Making Americans: Immigration, Race, and the Origins of the Diverse Democracy*. Cambridge, MA: Harvard University Press, 2000.

Morse, Samuel F. B. *Imminent Dangers to the Free Institutions of the United States through Foreign Immigration*. New York: Arno Press, 1969 [1835].

Ngai, Mae M. *Impossible Subjects: Illegal Aliens and the Making of Modern America*. Princeton NJ: Princeton University Press, 2004.

Obama, Barack. *The Audacity of Hope: Thoughts on Reclaiming the American Dream*. New York: Three Rivers Press, 2006.

Rischin, Moses, ed. *Immigration and the American Tradition*. Indianapolis: Bobbs- Merrill, 1976.

Smith, Rogers M. *Civic Ideals: Conflicting Visions of Citizenship in U.S.History*. New Haven, CT: Yale University Press, 1997.

Smith, Rogers M. *Stories of Peoplehood: The Politics and Morals of Political Membership*. New York: Cambridge University Press, 2003.

Smith, Rogers M. "Religious Rhetoric and the Ethics of Public Discourse: The Case of George W. Bush." *Political Theory* 36 (2008): 272-300.

Tichenor, Daniel J. *Dividing Lines: The Politics of Immigration Control in America*. Princeton, NJ: Princeton University Press, 2002.

Zolberg, Aristide R. *A Nation by Design: Immigration Policy in the Fashioning of America*. Cambridge, MA: Harvard University Press, 2006.

8 From Workers to Enemies: National Security, State Building, and America's War on Illegal Immigrants

Desmond King and Inés Valdez[1]

War and State Building

In this chapter we argue that since the mid-1980s immigration policy toward *illegal* immigrants has assumed the character of a war expressed in growing border militarization and fortification, expanded numbers of border guards, and an enhanced internal program of prosecution of "illegal aliens," which today comprise an estimated 12 million people (see Graph 1).[2] New agencies have been created and the number of security forces deployed increased substantially. Both Presidents Clinton and Bush supported building a wall against the foe of *illegal* immigrants, which if completed will constitute the longest barrier between two countries not undergoing violent conflict.

The fight against *illegal* immigrants is not an isolated event but fits onto a state-building trajectory rooted in quasi-military strategies and a language of war deployed increasingly since the 1960s. Once the language of war was embraced by the executive – notably in Lyndon Johnson's "war on poverty" – its usage set a precedent for how subsequent presidents might approach apparently dramatic problems. Declaring war on human or inanimate enemies serves multiple purposes for presidents.[3]

---

1. We acknowledge comments and feedback on previous versions of this chapter by Michael Jones-Correa and Rogers M. Smith. Previous versions of this chapter were presented at the Conference "Stories of Nationhood in Plural Societies," at Aarhus University (Denmark) in May 2009, at the Oxford University Centre for the Study of Inequality and Democracy Workshop Series (UK) in November 2009, and at the Institute for Government Quality University of Gothenburg (Sweden) in June 2010. We are grateful to the participants at those seminars who offered valuable comments on the paper; any errors remain the authors' responsibility.

2. We are aware of the problems of the term "illegal," and we agree with the reasons why some scholars eschew it. We employ it because in the context of our argument it is the most appropriate term – that is, it is the term of choice for naming an enemy. We nonetheless retain the quotation marks to remind the reader of its contested use.

3. Desmond King, "Mimicking War: How Presidents Coordinate the American State," *Working Paper No 74, TranState Working Papers Series*, Bremen (2008); Desmond King and Robert C. Lieberman, "Ironies of State Building: A

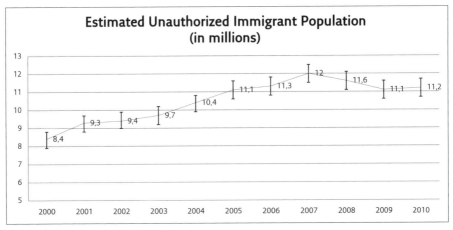

Estimated Unauthorized Immigrant Population (in millions)

△ **Graph 1**

Source: Pew Hispanic Center, "Unauthorized Immigrant Population: National and State Trends," *Pew Hispanic Center Report* CXXXIII (2011), table 2, page 9. Available at http://pewhispanic.org/ files/reports/133.pdf (accessed 03/12/2011). Estimates with 90% confidence intervals. Available Department of Homeland Security estimates exist for 2000 and 2005-2008 only and fall within the confidence intervals of Pew estimates except in 2009 and 2010, for which DHS estimates 10.8 million. Michael Hoefer, Nancy Rytna, and Bryan C. Baker, "Estimates of the Unauthorized Immigrant Population Residing in the United States: January 2010," *Population Estimates* February 2011. Available at http://www.dhs.gov/xlibrary/assets/statistics/publications/ois_ill_pe_2010.pdf (accessed 03/12/2011).

Wars articulate and focus domestic policy agendas around an immediate priority. This agenda setting sends a message to bureaucrats about where resources ought to be concentrated and what sort of policy requests will receive favorable responses. A war also sends a signal to Congress about presidential priorities. For the president, employing the rhetoric and language of a quasi-war strategy facilitates a direct appeal to voters. It concentrates attention on the political center and justifies significant decisions about how to allocate and spend money to expand state capacity in a polity considered constitutionally hostile to enhanced state power.[4] It empowers an executive in a polity whose fiscal constraints are constantly challenged,[5] and in which the struggle between federal and state interests is dynamic and nonlinear.[6]

Comparative Perspective on the American State," *World Politics* 61 (2009): 547-588; and Jennifer Light, *From Warfare to Welfare* (Baltimore: Johns Hopkins University Press, 2003).

4. Gary G. Hamilton and John R. Sutton, "The problem of control in the weak state: Domination in the United States 1880-1920," *Theory and Society* 18 (1989): 1-46.

5. W. Elliot Brownlee, ed., *Funding the modern American state 1941-1995* (Cambridge: Cambridge University Press, 1996), and Julian E. Zelizer, "The Uneasy Relationship: Democracy, Taxation and State Building since the New Deal," in *The Democratic Experiment*, ed. Meg Jacobs, William J. Novak and Julian E. Zelizer (Princeton: Princeton University Press, 2003).

6. Gary Gerstle, "The Resilient Power of the States across the Long Nineteenth Century: An Inquiry into a Pattern of American Governance," in *The Unsustainable American State*, ed. Lawrence Jacobs and Desmond King (New York: Oxford University Press, 2009).

Thus as a complement to waging real war, political executives controlling the American state have used similar language in respect to domestic problems for reasons elaborated upon below. In resorting to this strategy presidents find resonance in America's distinct militarist and religious culture.

Militaristic aspects of US political culture accommodate the idea of a nation at war domestically and abroad. In the two decades after 1945 many events had the potential to make the Cold War turn hot, and resulted in such domestic measures as the construction of a national highway system for efficient movement of military weaponry, the development of dispersal population policies in large urban areas,[7] civil defence, and the initiation of school children into the mores of hiding from nuclear attack.[8] The Armed Forces – in its various branches including the National Guard and state troopers – were a powerful presence in US society throughout the 1950s, 1960s, and 1970s. They were called on to protect Black American children judicially entitled after 1954 to enter integrated schools, to restore public order in those impoverished urban centres which erupted into flames and mayhem in the 1960s, and to hold back white opponents of the Supreme Court designated busing programs in the 1970s.[9] The end of the Cold War gave Americans only a putative breather from the salience of military preparedness, quickly pushed aside by an unwanted "war" against extremist terrorism and a potentially unctuous Americanism flamed by an expansive global anti-Americanism. Institutional executive power to engage in war has grown with President George W. Bush's extended use of signing statements, an authority President Obama plans to retain but to use differently.

The US is also a religious society and polity.[10] An apparently rigid constitutional separation of church and state sets an enduring barrier against the pursuit or institutionalization of theocratic tendencies in state law.[11] But religious images and language permeate politics, stemming from John Winthrop's famous "city on a hill" image of 1630 representing the US as a new nation, which is cited repeatedly by national leaders and was repackaged by Ronald Reagan as "a shining city upon a hill whose beacon light guides freedom-loving people everywhere."

This ubiquitous religiosity is conducive to the use of war as a metaphor in domestic politics.[12] It has featured historically in hostile responses to immigrants in

7. Jennifer Light, *From Warfare to Welfare*.
8. Andrew Grossman, *Neither Red Nor Dead* (New York: Routledge, 2001).
9. Michael D. Doubler, *Civilian in Peace, Soldier in War* (Lawrence KS: University Press of Kansas 2003).
10. John Micklethwait and Adrian Woolridge, *The Right Nation* (New York: Penguin, 2004).
11. This separation is not complete, however. There are many exemptions, including tax exemptions enjoyed by religious organizations, which incur controversy. Nonetheless some politicians and commentators have complained about a "war on religion," such is the discrimination experienced by religious organizations.
12. The Pew Research Center reports that among Americans, 70%, polled in 2007 agreed that the most important quality in a president was to "hold strong religious beliefs" comparable to results of public opinion about the same

the United States. Only a few decades after settling in America, Puritans feared the arrival of liberal members of Protestant sects from Europe and developed arguments for restricting their entry.[13] In the nineteenth and twentieth centuries, revulsion toward Catholics – Irish and Germans in the nineteenth and early twentieth century, and Latinos afterwards – drove restrictionists' advocacy of exclusionary national policies.[14] Religion helped structure American attitudes during the Cold War, with both fundamentalist doctrine and high religious commitment prompting citizens to hold anti-Soviet attitudes and support greater spending.[15] The connection between religion and foreign policy continued in the 1980s, when churches and synagogues provided sanctuary to Central American refugees who were routinely denied refugee status by the INS.[16] These migrants, who were fleeing El Salvadoran death squads and Guatemalan counter-insurgency campaigns, were faced with American government reluctance to acknowledge that their home governments were violating human rights, because of their alliance with them as a proxy of anti-communist struggle. A revival of this movement has been launched by Protestant and Catholic churches to protect and protest the deportation of *illegal* immigrants, although its reach is not comparable.[17] It was also in this era that Christian conservatives forged an alliance with secular conservatives, with President Reagan articulating the anti-communism of the Christian right, and announcing his moralistic and militant position against communism, the "evil empire," in a convention of conservative evangelicals.[18]

The growth and increasing political involvement of the Christian right was salient

issue in 2000 and 2004. The Pew Research Center and The Pew Forum on Religion & Public Life, "Religion in Campaign '08," *Survey Report September 06* (Washington DC: The Pew Research Center, 2007). Available at http://people-press.org/report/353/clinton-and-giuliani-seen-as-not-highly-religious-romneys-religion-raises-concerns, accessed 09/14/2010.

13. John Winthrop, "A Defense of an Order of Court (1637)," in *The Puritans in America*, ed. Alan Heimert and Henry Delbanco (Cambridge, 1985), 164-167.

14. John Higham, *Strangers in the Land. Patterns of American Nativism 1860-1925* (New Brunswick, 1966) and Samuel Huntington, *Who are We? America's Great Debate* (New York, 2004). In this chapter we use "Latino" and "Hispanic" interchangeably, as they are the most common descriptors for populations of Spanish-speaking ancestry in Latin America and the Caribbean. We are aware of the contestation that exists regarding these terms and we do not imply homogeneity in the groups described under these names. See Victoria Hattam, *In the Shadow of Race* (Chicago: University of Chicago Press, 2007) and Cristina Beltrán, *The Trouble with Unity: Latino Politics and the Creation of Identity* (Oxford: Oxford University Press, 2010).

15. James L. Guth, Cleveland R. Fraser, John C. Green, Lyman A. Kellstedt, and Corwin E. Smidt, "Religion and Foreign Policy Attitudes: The Case of Christian Zionism," in *Religion and the Culture Wars. Dispatches from the Front*, ed. John C. Green, James L. Guth, Corwin E. Smidt, and Lyman A. Kellstedt (Lanham, 1996), 331.

16. Susan Gzesch, "Central Americans and Asylum Policy in the Reagan Era," in *Migration Information Source* (Washington DC, 2006). Available at http://www.migrationinformation.org/Feature/ display.cfm?ID=384, accessed 05/26/3009.

17. Alfonso Serrano, "Churches Providing Sanctuary to Immigrants," in *CBS News* (2007). Available at http:// www.cbsnews.com/stories/2007/05/10/national/main2786988.shtml, accessed 05/26/2009.

18. Michael Lienesch, *Redeeming America. Piety and Politics in the New Christian Right* (Chapel Hill, 1993), 211.

during the presidency of George W. Bush, but the beginning of their activism can be traced to the post-Vietnam era, partly as a reaction to Christian liberals' opposition to the war.[19] Furthermore, Evangelicals have an active involvement with foreign policy, from the Middle East to the use that developing countries make of American aid.[20]

Beyond social movements, groups as diverse as think tanks and university intellectuals, officials working in state and municipal administration, parts of the media and political parties all have some interest in "war as metaphor"-type mobilizations aimed at entrenching and strengthening the American state. The metaphor concentrates minds and political resources. We apply this proposition in this paper to the evolution of policy toward *illegal* immigrants.

The New War

"People came to me and said, 'Father, when did we become the enemy?'"
Rev Gary Graf, Roman Catholic from Waukegan (IL)[21]

In addition to enhancing executive authority and resources, the war on *illegal* immigrants accommodates the process of state building by structuring the definition of enemies of the state. The declaration and process of war obversely defines more clearly who belongs to the state. In the case of immigrants, the lack of citizenship status renders them an ideal enemy, in opposition to which citizens can define themselves.[22] *Illegals* are an easy and legally vulnerable target and are supposedly clearly discernible from *real* citizens.

---

19. Robert Wuthnow, *The Restructuring of American Religion. Society and Faith Since World War II* (Princeton, 1988), 200-201.
20. William Martin, "The Christian Right and American Foreign Policy," *Foreign Policy* 114 (1999): 66-80. See also Lienesch, *Redeeming America*, 224-225; Guth et al., "Religion," 336; Robert C. Lieberman, "The 'Israel Lobby' and American Politics," *Perspectives on Politics* 7 (2009): 235-257; and in the same volume John J. Mearsheimer and Stephen M. Walt, "The Blind Man and the Elephant in the Room: Robert Lieberman and the Israel Lobby," *Perspectives on Politics* 7 (2009): 259-272 and Robert Lieberman "Rejoinder to Mearsheimer and Walt," 275-281.
21. Julia Preston, "Facing Deportation but Clinging to Life in U.S." *The New York Times* January 18, 2008. Available at http://www.nytimes.com/2008/01/18/us/18hide.html, accessed 03/12/2011.
22. On the complex relationship between immigration and citizenship in the United States see Ina Newton, *Illegal, Alien or Immigrant* (New York: New York University Press, 2008); Clare Sheridan, "Contested Citizenship: National Identity and the Mexican Immigration Debates of the 1920s," *Journal of American Ethnic History* 21 (2003): 3-35; and Rogers M. Smith, *Civic Ideals* (New Haven: Yale University Press, 1997).

While the legislative changes that suspended civil liberties and criminalized immigrants were in place before September 11, the febrile nationalism that followed these attacks proved empathic to the waging of war against immigrants. Immigration enforcement consumes substantial portions of the resources and manpower at the post-9/11 Department of Homeland Security; this allocation suggests that – just like the War on terror – the war on immigration is an unconventional one fought with all the tools available.

Given this antagonistic context, the massive immigrant marches on May 1, 2006 not only failed to achieve reforms including a path to citizenship, but exacerbated anti-immigrant sentiment, or at least such was the perception among the Latino community.[23] The mobilization of thousands of people behind a discourse proclaiming their humanity and their claim to be included in the political community resulted in more rejection than a silent acquiescence would have done.

The outburst of violence and death in Mexico in the opening months of 2009, produced by drugs gangs putting pressure on the government, provoked dramatic policy responses from the US Department of Homeland Security. Fearful of a war which killed over 6,000 Mexicans during 2008 and in which organized criminal gangs parallel the power of the Mexican state, President Obama's Secretary for Homeland Security, Janet Napolitano announced the deployment of an additional 360 agents, the doubling of specialist security forces from 95 to 190 and a further 100 new customs officers to the US's southwest border.[24] The Bureau of Alcohol, Tobacco, Firearms and Explosives deployed an additional 100 agents of its own to the same location.

This intensification of the American State's efforts to keep the Mexican "wars" in Mexico continued in 2010 and 2011 and confirms the Mexico-US border as the frontier to be defended. The federal government has funded a wall along the US-Mexican border. It has expanded and upgraded the powers of US borders and customs officers, moving this agency into the Department of Homeland Security created in the wake of the 9/11 terrorist attacks on New York City and the Pentagon. High profile armed work raids have been conducted in which *illegals* are found and detained to be returned to their country of origin, with the responsible employers fined. Since 2003, the US Immigration and Customs Enforcement agency (ICE) has pursued a rigorous National Fugitive Operations Program with a budget of no

---

23. Mark Hugo Lopez and Susan Minushkin, "2008 National Survey of Latinos. Hispanics See their Situation in the U.S Deteriorating; Oppose Key Immigration Enforcement Measures," in *Pew Hispanic Center Report No. 93*. (Washington, DC: Pew Hispanic Center, 2008). Available at http:// pewhispanic.org/files/reports/93.pdf, accessed 09/14/2010.
24. Daniel Dombey and Adam Thomson, "Crackdown reflects US anxiety on Mexico," *Financial Times* 25 March, 2009.

less than $218 million in 2008.[25] Finally, state and local police have entered the struggle against *illegality* through agreements of cooperation with immigration authorities.[26]

The Internal War, Peoplehood, and Democracy

The importance of the transformation in the fight against *illegal* immigration exceeds the hard facts reflected in the resources and manpower devoted to it. Our interest in this process turns on what it can say about the political process in which reified and exclusionary identities are utilized by the state to justify the drawing of a frontier that symbolically marks a certain group as external to the polity, and thus unable to engage in political contestation. In other words, the branding of an enemy and the militarization of the state's struggle to stem illegals underlie processes of exclusion that both feed and are fed by narratives of national identity (or peoplehood) and in so doing intervene in the process of re-drawing the political boundaries of the *demos*.

To the extent that political struggle over immigration is one of the ways in which democracies contest the legitimate constitution of the *we*, it is important to investigate how these struggles are conducted.[27] Electoral processes and naturalization laws affect the way in which immigrants are included gradually – or not at all – in the *demos*.[28] However, laws and administration produce difference, and states can – and do – intervene in other ways, by shaping social definitions of difference.[29]

It is in this spirit that the examination of the increasing criminalization of the immigrant population in the United States is significant. Moreover, it is a neces-

---

25. Margot Mendelson, Shayna Strom, and Michael Wishnie, "Collateral Damage: An Examination of ICE's Fugitive Operation Program," *MPI Report* (2009). Available at http://www.migrationpolicy.org/pubs/NFOP_Feb09.pdf, accessed 03/12/2011, 9.

26. ACLU North Carolina and Immigration & Human Rights Policy Clinic, "The Policies and Politics of Local Immigration Enforcement Laws: 287(g) Program in North Carolina," in *UNC Chapel Hill School of Law*, February (2009). Available at http://www.law.unc.edu /documents/clinicalprograms /287gpolicyreview.pdf, accessed 09/14/2010; and American Immigration Lawyers Association, Mexican American Legal Defense and Educational Fund, National Council of La Raza, National Immigration Forum, and National Immigration Law Center, *State and Local Police Enforcement of Federal Immigration Laws: A Tool Kit for Advocates* (Washington, DC: National Council of La Raza, 2006). Available at http:// www.immigrationforum.org/images/uploads/ Localenforcementtoolkit.pdf, accessed 09/14/2010.

27. Sofia Näsström "The Legitimacy of the People," *Political Theory* 35 (2007): 624-658, 646.

28. Francisco E. Gonzalez, "Same Dreams, Different Fates: Latinos' Inclusion/Exclusion and U.S. Democratization," in *Democratization in America*, ed. Desmond King, Robert C. Lieberman, Gretchen Ritter, and Laurence Whitehead (Baltimore: Johns Hopkins University Press, 2009), 96-97.

29. Clarisa Rile Hayward, "The Difference States Make: Democracy, Identity, and the American City," *American Political Science Review* 97 (2003): 501-514, 501.

sarily critical task because – as we show below – documented and undocumented immigrants have been gradually and increasingly identified as an illegitimate subject in democratic America, one that is fuzzily identified with a shadow economy of poverty, gang violence, drug activity, and national security threats. Once such a group is identified and its character of threat assessed, it becomes an enemy that is worth fighting against. The criminalization and legal disenfranchisement that took place in the last two decades exceeds previous historical instances in which the state focused exclusively on *illegals*.[30] Today, the American state is invested in making all immigrants potentially deportable and their claim to political inclusion an illegitimate one. The state has mobilized ideological and material resources to back up this claim, prime among them has been the conflation of immigration on the one hand, and terrorism and national security threats on the other, which has resulted in a double strategy of sealing the border and raiding the interior for deportable *aliens*. In practice this policy renders Hispanic immigrants *and* Hispanic-Americans the main victims of the institutional expansion of the state's detention, deportation, and surveillance capacities that took place in the last two decades.

The gradual removal of rights and the erosion of access to basic welfare for immigrants has been a state goal on its own, but also a consequence of the advance of the state against other "enemies," such as drugs, welfare-dependent individuals, and, of course, terrorism. In this sense, we cannot see immigration as simply expressing the preferences of citizens towards the regulation of foreigners. Alternatively, we contend that the turn toward fortification and militarization in the realm of immigration needs to be evaluated as one component of a broader trend of exclusionary and punitive practices that the American state engages in, to the detriment of the quality of its democracy.

Finally, it must also be noted that the institutional dimension of these developments has narrowed spaces of democratic contestation, isolating the administration of immigration law from democratic processes by coupling it with national security, therefore making it more difficult for active civil society groups as well as the affected immigrants to engage. In contrast, right wing anti-immigrant groups and rhetoric have become part of the mainstream and hate crimes directed against immigrants have increased steadily, all evidence of the widespread rejection of pro-immigrants' rights claims. The transformation of immigration enforcement into a war, then, has hindered democracy not just by bringing to a halt amnesties and naturalizations, but also by hiding their process of decision-making behind the increased executive powers that characterized the era of the war on terrorism.

---

30. Mae M. Ngai, *Impossible Subjects* (Princeton: Princeton University Press, 2004), chapter 2.

The Seven Stage War on *Illegals* after 1986

We identify seven stages in the struggle over *illegal* immigration since the landmark legislation reform in 1986. This struggle has escalated into a conflict on the scale and with the trappings of a war. Features that we find today, such as employers' sanctions, increased border control, and the criminalization of immigrants, are all aspects of measures prefigured and gradually enacted in Congressional and executive policies from 1986 into the 1990s (see Table 1).

■ Stage I: Between a Path to Citizenship and Sanctions

On November 6, 1986, President Reagan signed the Immigration Reform and Control Act (IRCA). The content of this law was debated for more than a decade, often in the midst of nativist, anti-immigrant sentiment.[31] The law provided immediate amnesty for undocumented workers residing in the country, a path to legalization for certain eligible individuals, a special path to legal residency for seasonal agricultural workers, employer sanctions, and increased resources allocated to the Border Patrol.[32] The system of sanctions depended on employers' participation, as they had to request designated paperwork but were not required to verify the validity of the documents presented by the worker.[33] Compliance was attained if the documents examined appeared "on their face to be genuine,"[34] thus making employer compliance potentially inconsistent with the intended effect of the law, namely, to reduce the hiring of unauthorized workers. The most enduring effect of this legislation was paradoxically the amnesty and paths to legalization it provided, through which approximately three million undocumented immigrants achieved legal status.[35] It was also the last instance in which significant steps to include *illegal* immigrants would be pursued.

During the Clinton Administration, the US Congress investigated and enacted further recommendations for immigration policy-making. The Gallegly Task Force on Immigration, appointed by Speaker Newt Gingrich, and the Jordan Commission established by the 1990 Immigration Act became forums for restrictionists whose

---

31. Kitty Calavita, "The Contradictions of Immigration Lawmaking: The Immigration Reform and Control Act of 1986," *Law and Policy* 11 (1989): 17-47, 36. Robin Dale Jacobson, *The New Nativism* (Minneapolis: University of Minnesota Press, 2008).
32. Calavita, "The Contradictions," 21; Julie A. Phillips and Douglas S. Massey, "The New Labor Market: Immigrants and Wages after IRCA," *Demography* 36 (1999): 233-46, 233.
33. Calavita "The Contradictions," 28.
34. US Public Law 99-603 1986.
35. Jeffrey M. Togman, *The Ramparts of Nations* (Westport: Greenwood Publishing, 2002), 68.

Table 1

Ruling	Y	Origin of Rule	Main Target of Ruling	Effect over Immigrants	Stage
Stage 1: Between a Path to Citizenship and Sanctions					
IRCA	**1986**	**L**	**Immigration**	Regularization Farm Labor Program Employment Sanctions	1
Operation Alliance	**1986**	**E**	*Narcotics*	Border Militarization Inter-Agency Cooperation	1
Immigration Act	**1990**	**L**	**Immigration**	Deportation Visa Tightening (disease, crime, public charge, security) Compensation for States	1
Stage 2: Militarizing the Border					
National Strategy for Border Patrol	**1993-94**	**E**	**Immigration** *Narcotics*	Fencing Border Militarization Alien Tracking	2
Crime Bill	**1994**	**L**	*Crime*	Border Militarization Deportation Alien Tracking Punitive Immigration Measures	2
Operation Hard Line	**1995**	**E**	*Narcotics*	Border Militarization	2
Stage 3: From the Border to the Domestic Terrain					
Abscondee Removal Teams	**1995**	**E**	**Immigration**	Domestic Enforcement	3
Illegal Immigration Reform and Immigrant Responsibility Act	**1996**	**L**	**Immigration**	Border Militarization Welfare Curtailment (for *legal* immigrants) Domestic Enforcement (on hold by DoJ) Inter-Agency Cooperation (idem)	3
Anti-terrorism and Effective Death Penalty Act	**1996**	**L**	*(Domestic) Terrorism*	Alien Tracking Deportation (for *legal* immigrants too)	3
Personal Responsibility and Work Opportunity Reconciliation Act	**1996**	**L**	*Welfare*	Welfare Rights Curtailment (for *legal* and *long term* residents too)	3
Stage 4: The 9/11 Dynamic					
Patriot Act	**2001**	**L**	*Terrorism*	Detention (for *legal* immigrants too) Deportation	4
"Absconder Apprehension Initiative" (later "National Fugitive Operations")	**2002**	**E**	*Terrorism* **Immigration**	Domestic Enforcement Inter-Agency Cooperation	4
Reversal of restriction of enforcement by state and local police/sheriff, etc.	**2002**	**E**	**Immigration**	Domestic Enforcement Inter-Agency Cooperation	4
Homeland Security Act	**2002**	**L**	*Terrorism* **Immigration**	Bureaucratic expansion	4
SC Ruling 01-1491	**2003**	**J**	**Immigration**	Detention (indefinite no bail, for *legal* immigrants too)	4
Identity Theft Penalty Enhancement Act	**2004**	**L**	*Identity Theft*	Deportation Detention	4

Ruling	Y	Origin of Rule	Main Target of Ruling	Effect over Immigrants	Stage
Stage 5: The Secure Border Initiative					
Secure Border Initiative	2005	L	Terrorism Narcotics **Immigration**	Border Militarization Fencing	5
Stage 6: The Expansion of the Wall					
Secure Fencing Act	2006	L	Terrorism Narcotics **Immigration**	Fencing Border Militarization	6
Stage 7: Failed Legislation and Backlash/Intensification of the War at Home					
Clear Law Enforcement for Criminal Alien Removal (CLEAR) Act (never passed)	2003	-	**Immigration**	Domestic Enforcement Mandate	7
Border Protection, Antiterrorism, and "illegal" Immigration Control Act (never passed the Senate)	2005	-	Terrorism **Immigration**	Border Militarization Border Fencing (feasibility study of northern fence) Alien Tracking Detention/Deportation (including immigration violations) Criminalization of action directed to aid re-entry. Affirms Domestic Enforcement Authority Bars Sanctuary Provisions Reduces reach of immigration judges Further strips deportation form procedural rights	7
Operation Streamline	2005	E	**Immigration**	Channels into criminal prosecution all border crossers detained by the Border Patrol	7
Secure Communities, DHS	2008	E	**Immigration**	Detention (immigration checks at local/state jails)	7
Guidelines to Avoid Deporting US Citizens, ICE	2008	E	**Civil Rights**		7
No-Appeal Decision, Office of the Attorney	2009	E	**Immigration**	Procedural Rights	7

– Sources: B. Drummond Ayres Jr., "Border War Against Drugs is Stepped Up," *The New York Times* February 26 (1995); ACLU and National Immigration Forum, "Operation Streamline Fact Sheet" July 21 (2009); Julia Gelatt, "President signs DHS Appropriations and Secure Fence Act, New Detainee Bill has Repercussions for Noncitizens," *MPI Policy Beat* (2006); Linda Greenhouse "THE SUPREME COURT: SUPREME COURT ROUNDUP; Justices Permit Immigrants To Challenge Deportations," *The New York Times* June 26 (2001); Bill Ong Hing, *Defining America through Immigration Policy* (Philadelphia: Temple University Press, 2004); Susanne Jonas and Catherine Tactaquin, "Latino Immigrant Rights in the Shadow of the National Security State: Responses to Domestic Preemptive Strikes," *Social Justice* 31 (2004): 1-2, 67-91; Susanne Jonas, "Reflections on the Great Immigration Battle of 2006 and the Future of the Americas," *Social Justice* 33, no. 1 (2006): 6-20; Margot Mendelson, Shayna Strom, and Michael Wishnie, "Collateral Damage: An Examination of ICE's Fugitive Operation Program," *MPI Report* (2009); Midwest Coalition for Human Rights, "State and Local Enforcement – 287(g) Program," November 14 (2007); Midwest Coalition for Human Rights, "Report Cites Problems In Immigration Program That Uses the Local Police," March 4 (2009); Jose Palafox, "Militarizing the Border," *CovertAction Quarterly* (Spring 1996); Christian Parenti, *Lockdown America: Police and Prisons in the Age of Crisis* (London: Verso, 2000); John Schwartz, "Supreme Court Rules Against Government in Identity-Theft Case," *The New York Times* May 4 (2009a); John Schwartz "Ruling Says Deportation Cases May Not Be Appealed Over Lawyer Errors," *The New York Times* January 8 (2009b); US Citizenship and Immigration Services, "Legislation from 1981 to 1996." *Historical Immigration and Naturalization Legislation* (n/d); US Customs and Border Protection, "SBI Timeline," *Secure Border Initiative/About* (2009); US Department of Justice, "Follow up Report on Border Patrol's Efforts to Improve Border Security (Redacted Version)," *DOJ Report* No.I-2002-004 (2002); US Immigration and Customs Enforcement, *ICE Fiscal Year 2008 Annual Report. Protecting National Security and Upholding Public Safety* (2009).

political salience and stridency had grown. The change in mood was stark. Only five years after legislation had expanded the number of annual visas and created the lottery system, these commissions recommended reducing authorized immigration and devising punitive measures for unauthorized immigrants.[36]

■ Stage 2: Militarizing the Border

In 1993 and 1994, following an initiative by El Paso Border Patrol chief Silvestre Reyes to heighten border enforcement, the Clinton administration launched a new border strategy. It consisted of twin operations focused on urban areas along the border.[37] Border states could draw from a growing largesse of Federal allocations for enforcement intended to physically reinforce the Southwest border through augmented armed manpower, expanded surveillance technology, and the building of physical barriers starting at the Pacific Ocean Coast.[38] Operations included *Gatekeeper* in California, *Hold-the-Line* in Greater El Paso, Texas (originally called 'Blockade' but renamed after complaints by the Mexican government),[39] *Rio Grande* in Brownsville, Texas, and *Safeguard* in Arizona.[40]

This new strategy of "prevention through deterrence" included multiple and complementary means to deter *illegal* crossings, thus avoiding having to apprehend *illegals* after the fact.[41] Among the strategies were efforts to concentrate enforcement resources in each major entry corridor, including increased fencing, surveillance equipment, harsher penalties, and the expansion of law enforcement.[42] California had parallel fences permitting a patrol strip in the middle, and accompanied by klieg (stadium) lighting and surveillance cameras; its southern side was built with surplus US military landing mats, some of them dating back to Vietnam.[43]

Success was measured by a reduction in the number of crossings (and apprehensions). The implementation of these policies was supposed to make it more difficult

36. US Public Law 101-649 1996; Joseph Nevins, "Searching for Security:Boundary and Immigration Enforcement in an Age of Intensifying Globalization," *Social Justice* 28 (2001): 132-148; Daniel Tichenor, *Dividing Lines* (Princeton: Princeton University Press, 2002).

37. Peter Andreas, *Border Games: Policing the US-Mexico Divide* (Ithaca: Cornell University Pres, 2001), 92.

38. Bill Ong Hing, *Defining America through Immigration Policy* (Philadelphia: Temple University Press, 2004), 187.

39. Joseph Nevins, *Operation Gatekeeper: the rise of the 'illegal alien' and the making of the US-Mexico boundary* (New York: Routledge, 2001), 90; Andreas *Border Games*, 4.

40. Hing, *Defining America*, 187.

41. Andreas, *Border Games*, 92.

42. Andreas, *Border Games*, 92; Hing, *Defining America*, 187.

43. Tim Gaynor, *Midnight on the Line: The Secret Life of the US Mexico Border* (New York: Thomas Dunne Books, 2009), 97; and see Edward Alden, *The Closing of the American Border* (New York: Harpercollins 2008).

for immigrants to cross near urban areas, thus shifting them toward deserted spaces that the Border Patrol could control more easily.[44]

Congress supported these initiatives. Between 1993 and1997, the enforcement budget of the INS increased by 100 %, as well as the staffing and budget approved for the Border Patrol (see Graph 2).[45] While part of the border was already fenced, particularly in the area starting at the Pacific Ocean and extending eastward, the fencing increased from 19 to 52 miles between the beginning of these operations and late 1999.[46] Moreover, in 1996, President Clinton authorized the deployment of "up to 350 Marine Corps, Army, and National Guard soldiers to conduct aerial and ground surveillance along the US-Mexico border."[47] This showed some continuity with the inter-agency collaboration between the Border Patrol and the military that became common in the 1980s, after the former assumed subsidiary functions in the "war on drugs."[48] In May 1997, Esequiel Hernández Jr., an American citizen, was shot dead by a US Marine Corporal deployed in Redford, Texas, as part of the Joint Task Force Six,[49] an inter-branch command unit providing operational and intelligence support from the Pentagon to federal, regional, state, and local counter-drug efforts.[50] This death was the first one inflicted by armed forces on an American civilian since the 1970 Kent State University massacre, and the first since the troops were stationed on the border in the late 1980s.[51]

---

44. Palafox, Jose, "Introduction to "Gatekeeper's State: Immigration and Boundary Policing in an Era of Globalization," *Social Justice* 28, no. 2 (2001):132-148.
45. Hing, *Defining America*, 187.
46. Ibid.
47. Palafox, "Introduction," 3.
48. Timothy J. Dunn, "Border Militarization Via Drug and Immigration Enforcement: Human Rights Implications," *Social Justice* 28 (2001): 7-30, 8.
49. Now re-named Joint Task Force North, and described on its site as a "joint service command comprised of active duty and reserve component Soldiers, Sailors, Airmen, Marines, Department of Defense civilian employees, and contracted support personnel." Joint Task Force North, "Mission," *Joint Task Force North Website* (n/d). Available at http://www.jtfn.northcom.mil/subpages/mission.html, accessed 03/12/2011.
50. Joseph Nevins, "Death as a Way of Life," *counterpunch* Weekend Edition, July 26-27 2008. Available at http://www.counterpunch.org/nevins07262008.html; and Sam Howe Verhovek, "After a Marine on Patrol Kills a Teen-ager, a Village Wonders Why," *The New York Times*, June 29, 1997. Available at http://www.nytimes.com/1997/06/29/us/after-marine-on-patrol-kills-a-teen-ager-a-texas-border-village-wonders-why.html?scp=5&sq=esequiel%20hernadez&st=cse, accessed 03/29/2011.
51. Verhovek, "After a Marine"; and Monte Paulson, "Soldiers on US Borders: What Could Go Wrong? Start with the killing of Esequiel Hernández Jr.," *The Tyee* May 18, 2006. Available at http://thetyee.ca/News/2006/05/18/Soldiers/, accessed 03/12/2011.

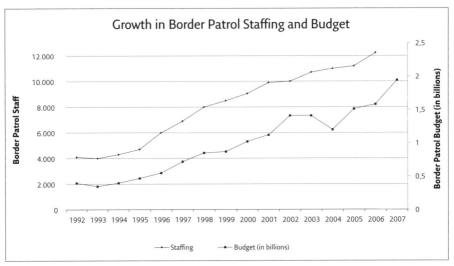

△ **Graph 2**

Source: Joe Shoulak, "Stopping Illegal Immigration at the Border." *The San Francisco Chronicle*, March 12 (2007). Available at http://www.sfgate.com/cgi-bin/object/article?f=/c/a/2007/03/12/MNGEUOJLNF1.DTL&o=0, accessed 03/12/2011.

■ Stage 3: From the border to the domestic terrain

Mirroring the militarization of the border, in stage three of the war on *illegals* the fight against immigration became a struggle that was not only waged at the borders, but also domestically.[52] The 1996 immigration laws, Illegal Immigration Reform and Immigrant Responsibility Act (IIRIRA), and the Antiterrorism and Effective Death Penalty Act (AEDPA) enacted important changes in the crimes and misdemeanors that made documented aliens deportable, and made these rules retroactive.[53] The laws automatically created a new pool of deportable criminal aliens, the target of internal operations, detention, and eventual deportation.

The enactment of the 1996 Illegal Immigration Reform and Immigrant Responsibility Act (IIRIRA) enhanced and legitimated inter-agency cooperation both horizontally at the federal level and vertically between the local, state, and federal authorities. This law included section 287(g) which authorized agreements between the federal level and the state and local level, permitting the latter to collaborate in the enforcement of federal immigration law.[54]

---

52. Christian Parenti, *Lockdown America* (London: Verso, 2000), 141.
53. Susanne Jonas, "Reflections on the Great Immigration Battle of 2006 and the Future of the Americas," *Social Justice* 33 (1996): 6-20, 8-9.
54. The initial application of this section was obstructed by an opinion of the Office of Legal Counsel from the Department of Justice, which denied this authority; the decision was reversed in 2002. American Immigration Lawyers Association et al., *State and Local Police Enforcement of Federal Immigration Laws*.

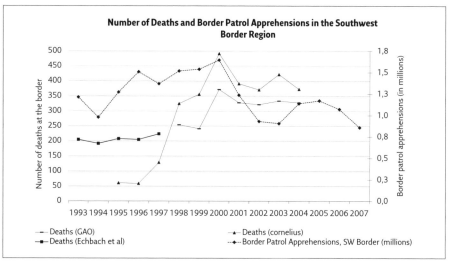

△ **Graph 3**

Source: Department of Homeland Security, *2007 Yearbook of Immigration Statistics* (2008), table 35; US Government Accountability Office, "Illegal Immigration. Border-Crossing Deaths Have Doubled since 1995; Border Patrol's Efforts to Prevent Deaths Have Not Been Fully Evaluated," *GAO Report GAO-06-770* (2006). Available at http://www.gao.gov/new. items/d06770.pdf, accessed 03/29/2011; Wayne Cornelius, "Controlling 'Unwanted' Immigration: Lessons from the United States, 1993-2004," *Journal of Ethnic and Migration Studies* (2005): 775-794, 784; and Karl Eschbach, Jacqueline Hagan, and Nestor Rodriguez, "Causes and trends in migrants' deaths along the U.S.-Mexico border, 1985-1998," *Center for Immigration Research Working Paper I-IV* (2001).

By the close of the twentieth century, as stage three of the war on *illegal* immigrants unfolded, the strategies of border fortification and domestic enforcement consolidated. The main consequence of the increased border security was the re-channelling of the border crossings away from the urban areas targeted by the border initiatives and toward more remote areas. This geographic shift increased the physical risk and cost associated with illegal entry, as measured by the fees charged by *coyotes* (professional people-smugglers) and the number of deaths among hopeful migrants, as well as a higher rate of permanent settlement among undocumented immigrants in the United States (see Graph 3).[55]

An effect of the emphasis on internal (as opposed to border) enforcement was

---

55. Wayne Cornelius, "Death at the Border: Efficacy and Unintended Consequences of US Immigration Control Policy," *Population and Development Review* 27, no. 4 (2001): 661-687: 667-669; and "Impacts of Border Enforcement on Unauthorized Immigration to the United States," *Testimony on the House Judiciary Committee Field Hearing on Immigration*, San Diego, California, August 2, 2006, 1-2; and Border Network for Human Rights, Border Action Network, and U.S.-Mexico Border and Immigration Task Force, "U.S.-Mexico Border Policy Report," 2008. Available at http://www.utexas.edu/law/centers/humanrights/borderwall/communities/municipalities-US-Mexico-Border-Policy-Report.pdf, 13, accessed 03/29/2011.

the increased number of detained and deported immigrants. This trend was in turn facilitated by new laws which retrospectively criminalized the immigrant population, as well as by the *de facto* enforcement of immigration law by local and state police.

■ Stage 4: The 9/11 Dynamic

The terrorist attacks on the Twin Towers and the Pentagon on September 11, 2001 created the conditions for wide legal reforms contained in the Patriot Act which were passed shortly thereafter, affecting the rights of all American citizens. This law and other legislation also had important consequences on immigrants, particularly those residing in the country without papers. Nationally President Bush placed the US on a war footing, a condition which helped the enactment of tough anti-immigrant measures considered improbable only a few months earlier. Indeed, prior to the 9/11 attacks a political coalition positive toward immigration reform seemed on the brink of success; its proposals included the potential legalization of about 3 million undocumented migrants already in the country.[56]

Instead, the US Patriot Act contained draconian measures directed toward immigrants that, unlike other measures affecting American's civil liberties, were approved to be permanent. Measures contained in this act gave extensive and unchecked powers to detain (documented or undocumented) non-citizens suspected of having terrorist ties for up to seven days without charges or access to a lawyer. Undocumented immigrants could be summarily subjected to detention and deportation solely for immigration violations. The law authorized deportation hearings to be held in secret and without access to a lawyer.[57]

The most significant innovation in state building in the federal war on *illegal* immigrants was the creation of the Department of Homeland Security (DHS) by the 2002 Homeland Security Act, and the transfer of all immigration functions to this department a year later. This transfer solidified the identification of legal and illegal immigrants with national security threats. Within the DHS, service and enforcement activities were divided, the former assumed by the US Citizenship and Immigration Services (USCIS), and the latter assigned to the US Immigration and Customs Enforcement (ICE). ICE, which self-defines as the "largest investigative agency of the Department of Homeland Security," took over functions previously

---

56. Eric Schmitt, "No Agreement Yet with Mexico on Immigration Plan, U.S. Says," *The New York Times* September 1, 2001; and Linda Greenhouse, "THE SUPREME COURT: SUPREME COURT ROUNDUP; Justices Permit Immigrants To Challenge Deportations," *The New York Times* June 26, 2001.

57. Susanne Jonas and Catherine Tactaquin, "Latino Immigrant Rights in the Shadow of the National Security State: Responses to Domestic Preemptive Strikes," *Social Justice* 31(2004): 67-91, 73.

discharged by the US Customs Service (in the Treasury), Immigration and Naturalization Service (in the Department of Justice), and Federal Protective Service.[58] At DHS, the ICE has five operational divisions and is in charge of domestic enforcement and coordination with local and state law enforcement on immigration matters.

■ Stage 5: The Secure Border Initiative

In 2005, DHS Secretary Michael Chertoff launched the Secure Border Initiative (SBI). It collected many of the existing DHS anti-immigrant programs together with the border fence, a program "designed to consistently slow, delay and be an obstacle to illegal cross-border activity."[59] Concurrently, this program provided the political support for significantly stepped-up domestic enforcement programs, detention, and deportation of undocumented immigrants based on pre-existing legal tools.[60]

The relocation of immigration administration into DHS introduced military terminology and rhetoric into the management of immigration operations, with terms such as "surge," "deterrence," and "national security" showing up often in their reports and descriptions of their activities.[61] In a recent statement at the Subcommittee on Homeland Security, the ICE Assistant Secretary Julie L. Myers claimed that unauthorized workers employed at critical facilities constituted serious "homeland threats" for being "vulnerable to exploitation by terrorists and other criminals given their status."[62]

The emphasis on homeland protection and national security in the management of immigration issues is maintained despite the fact that national security-related ICE removals have usually constituted less than 0.01 % of yearly ICE removals (see Graphs 4 and 5).[63] Additionally, if one focuses on the charges that the DHS has

58. US Immigration and Customs Enforcement, "About." In *ICE Website / Mission* (2009). Available at http://www. ice.gov/pi/dro/index.htm, accessed 05/04/2009.

59. US Customs and Border Protection, "SBI Programs," November 10, 2008, at http://www.cbp.gov/xp/cgov/ border_security/sbi/about_sbi/sbi_programs.xml. Cited in Chad C. Haddal, "Border Security: The Role of the US Border Patrol," *Congressional Research Service* 7-5700, March 2, 2010. Available at http://www.dtic.mil/ cgi-bin/GetTRDoc?Location=U2&doc=GetTRDoc.pdf&AD=ADA521236, accessed 03/12/2011.

60. See Graphs 3-9 and discussion below.

61. See National Immigration Forum, "Southwest Border Security Operations," in *National Immigration Forum Backgrounder* (2010). Available at http://www.immigrationforum.org/images/uploads/SouthwestBorderSecurity-Operations.pdf, accessed 8/3/2011.

62. US Congress 2007, 14, cited in Doris Meissner and Donald Kerwin, *DHS and Immigration. Taking Stock and Correcting Course* (Washington, DC: Migration Policy Institute 2009). Available at http://www.migrationpolicy.org/ pubs/DHS_Feb09.pdf, accessed 03/12/2011, 36f.

63. With a peak in 1996 of 0.052 % and a 1997 figure of 0.26 %, US Department of Homeland Security, *2007 Yearbook of Immigration Statistics* (2008).

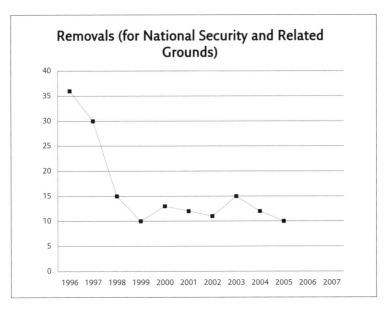

Removals (for National Security and Related Grounds)

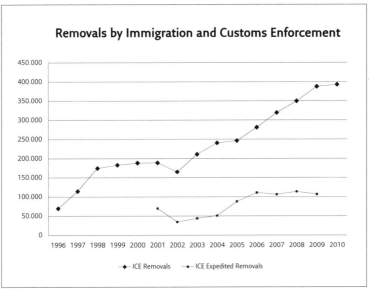

Removals by Immigration and Customs Enforcement

brought to immigration courts, only 12 of the 814,073 individuals ever charged by the DHS in immigration were connected to terrorist claims.[64]

Aiding the trend toward tougher domestic enforcement is the failure of all com-

64. Transactional Records Access Clearinghouse, "Immigration Enforcement: The Rhetoric, The Reality," *TRAC Report* 178 (2007). Available at http://trac.syr.edu/ immigration/reports/178/, accessed 03/12/2011.

prehensive reform attempts during the administration of George W. Bush. Enforcement is the prime tool of state intervention for the American government, enabling a quasi-military approach that operates within a blockaded country and in fact provides a free zone for enforcement officials at all levels to detain immigrants. Relying on the tools of criminalization enacted in 1996 and 2001 legislation, as well as on administrative directives supporting and increasing enforcement powers, the numbers for border apprehensions, worksite arrests, and deportations show a clear upward trend (see Graph 3, above, and Graph 4 for border apprehensions and removal numbers, respectively).

The average daily population of immigrants in detention increased from around 5,000 in 1994 to around 20,000 in 2001 and more than 30,000 in 2008 (see Graphs 7 and 8); deportations by the ICE grew from around 70,000 in 1996 to 190,000 in 2001 and more than 300,000 in 2009 (see Graph 6, above). It must be noted that criminal convictions can refer to immigration violations, such as "Re-entry of deported alien."[66] Moreover, since the establishment of "Operation Streamline" in 2005, even first time border crossers can be criminally prosecuted.[67] According to a recent report by the Transactional Records Access Clearing House at Syracuse University, the Department of Homeland Security refers the great majority of cases for immigration convictions.[68]

---

65. Graph 4 includes both expedited and total removals to convey approximately the amount of non-border, or "domestic" removals, given the lack of release of specific data by the DHS. Expedited removals are those that are done without referring an immigrant to an immigration judge and tend to be removals that follow border apprehensions. US Department of Homeland Security, "Definition of Terms," *Department of Homeland Security Website* September 10, 2009b. Available at http://www.dhs.gov/files/statistics/stdfdef.shtm#4, accessed 03/12/2011.

66. Transactional Records Access Clearinghouse, "Immigration Convictions for November 2010," in *TRAC Reports* February 16, 2011. Available at http://trac.syr.edu/tracreports/bulletins/ immigration/monthlynov10/gui/, accessed 03/12/2011.

67. ACLU and National Immigration Forum, "Operation Streamline Factsheet," in *National Immigration Forum Backgrounders* July 21, 2009. Available at http://www.immigrationforum.org/images/ uploads/OperationStreamlineFactsheet.pdf, accessed 03/12/2011.

68. Transactional Records Access Clearinghouse, "Immigration Convictions for November 2010," in *TRAC Reports* February 16, 2011. Available at http://trac.syr.edu/tracreports/bulletins/ immigration/monthlynov10/gui/,

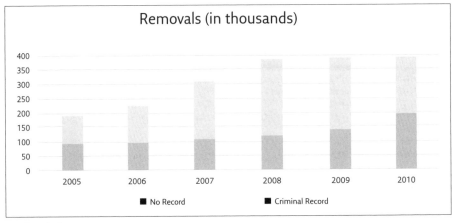

Removals (in thousands)

Legend: ■ No Record ■ Criminal Record

(Years: 2005, 2006, 2007, 2008, 2009, 2010; y-axis 0 to 400)

△ **Graph 6**

Source: Estimated based on: Ford Fessenden and Nina Bernstein, "Deportations, in thousands," *The New York Times* December 27, 2008. Available at http://www.nytimes.com/imagepages/2008/12/27/us/27detain_graph2.ready. html, accessed 03/12/2011. Julia Preston, "Deportations from U.S. Hit a Record High."

■ Stage 6: The Expansion of the Wall

In October 2006, President Bush signed into law the Secure Fence Act to establish operational control "over the entire international land and maritime borders of the United States" with such control understood to be "the prevention of all unlawful entries into the United States, including entries by terrorists, other unlawful aliens, instruments of terrorism, narcotics, and other contraband."[69] According to the SBI site, in September 2007 there were 154.7 miles of pedestrian fence built, with the plan to build an extra 300 miles of vehicle fence by the end of the 2008 fiscal year. The border fence requires contracts for maintenance, as well as complementary contractor services for the provision of surveillance technology, and even virtual border fences. The "construction" of the virtual border fence, named the SBI Network, has $2.5 billion of funding; its construction was allocated in 2006 to Boeing Co., and renewed in 2008.[70] The technologies utilized are adapted from those used in the battlefield, such as a camera-mounted drone that has been used by the Australian and Israeli armies, or various ground-based sensors that "have been used to thwart

---

accessed 03/12/2011. See also other TRAC monthly reports available at http://trac.syr.edu/tracreports/bulletins/annual_list.shtml, accessed 03/12/2011.

69. US Public Law 109-367.

70. Spencer S. Hsu and Griff Witt, "Plenty of Holes Seen In a 'Virtual Fence.' Border Sensors Not Enough, Experts Say," *The Washington Post* September 21, 2006, A03; Randall Mikkelsen "Boeing awarded contract on border fence: Chertoff," *Reuters* June 9, 2008. Available at http://www.reuters.com/article/domesticNews/ idUS-WAT00963120080609. Accessed 03/24/2009.

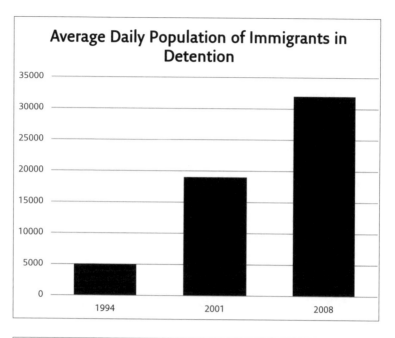

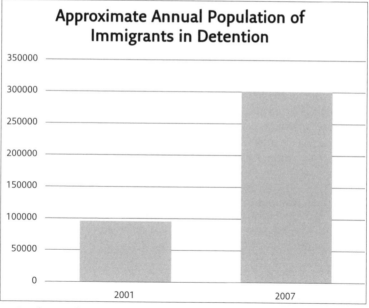

△ **Graphs 7 and 8**

Source: Detention Watch Network, "The History of Immigration Detention in the U.S. A Rapidly Expanding Immigration System," *Detention Watch Network* (2008). Available at http://www.detentionwatchnetwork.org/node/2381, accessed 3/6/2009.

insurgents in Iraq and Afghanistan."[71] The construction of the physical fence ignited complaints from environmental organizations, and was eventually granted waivers of several environmental and land management laws, covering 470 total miles, in the areas of California, Arizona, New Mexico, and Texas.[72]

Civil society organizations such as the Border Network for Human Rights have emphasized the human costs of the fencing, arguing that between the beginning of the construction of the fence, in 1994, and the end of 2008, approximately 4000 people have died trying to cross the border.[73] Numerical accounts of the deaths vary, but all agree in pointing out the increase in avoidable deaths resulting from the movement of crossing areas away from urban areas and toward the desert, in which physical effort and the extreme climate take their toll on migrants (see Graph 2, above). The concern with increased human deaths moved the Border Patrol to create the Border Safety Initiative (BSI), a program to prevent deaths and injuries among illegal crossers (USGAO 2006, 1). A recent report by the US General Accountability Office has established that the BSI's claims to have reduced deaths at the border is unsupported; the GAO also concluded that, compared with other sources measuring the number of fatalities amongst attempted immigrants, the BSI's statistics consistently underestimate the deaths they report.[74]

A different kind of civil organization has also been prominent in accompanying and complementing the growth in border security. Minutemen, or civilian border patrol groups, have grown out of anti-immigrant organizations, with the goal of patrolling the southwest border and engaging in other activities that seek to disrupt hiring sites for day laborers.[75] The most prominent of these groups, the Minuteman Project, was officially founded in April 2005 by retired California businessmen Jim Gilchrist and Chris Wincox.[76] As Roxanne Lynn Doty notes, private citizens

---

71. Hsu and Witt, "Plenty of Holes."

72. Randal C. Archibold, "Border Fence Work Raises Environmental Concerns," *The New York Times* November 21, 2007; US Customs and Border Protection, "SBI Timeline." In *Secure Border Initiative/About* (2009). Available at http://www.cbp.gov/xp/cgov/ border_security/sbi/about_sbi/sbi_timeline.xml, accessed 05/05/2009.

73. Border Network for Human Rights, Border Action Network, and U.S.-Mexico Border and Immigration Task Force, "U.S.-Mexico Border Policy Report. Effective Border Policy: Security, Responsibility and Human Rights at the U.S.-Mexico Border," *Report* (November 2008). Available at http://www.utexas.edu/law/centers/humanrights/ borderwall/ communities/municipalities-US-Mexico-Border-Policy-Report.pdf, accessed 03/12/2011, 12-13. See also Border Working Group, "Stop Border Deaths Now!" in *Maryknoll Office for Global Concerns* (2005). Available at http://www.maryknollogc.org/social/hilldrop060605.pdf, accessed 03/12/2011.

74. US Government Accountability Office, "Illegal Immigration. Border-Crossing Deaths Have Doubled since 1995; Border Patrol's Efforts to Prevent Deaths Have Not Been Fully Evaluated," in *GAO Report* GAO-06-770 (2006).

75. Roxanne Lynn Doty, "States of Exception on the Mexico-U.S. Border: Security, 'Decisions,' and Civilian Border Patrols," *International Political Sociology* 1 (2007): 113-137, 116; and Monica Varsanyi, "Immigration Policing Through the Backdoor: City Ordinances, the 'Right to the City,' and the Exclusion of the Undocumented Day Laborers," *Urban Geography* 29 (2007): 29-52, 37.

76. Doty, "States of Exception," 117.

have devoted themselves to protecting the Southwest border before: the Hanigans in Arizona in 1976; the KuKluxKlan Border Watch in San Ysidro, California, in 1977; and even an anti-communist paramilitary group acting on the Arizona area in 1986.[77] The growth in these groups and of the resources contributed to them are as much a feature of the post-9/11 period as the building of the border fence, and one that collaborates in creating the war-like atmosphere that has enveloped the American fight against immigration.

■ Stage 7: The Intensification of the War at Home

The militarization of the border has been accompanied by the increased militarization of domestic enforcement. The budget has accompanied these trends, with the allocations for the Fugitive Operation Program multiplying 23-fold in the 2003-2008 period, that of the Border patrol multiplying fivefold between 1993 and 2007, and its staffing swelling proportionally (see Graph 2 above).[78] As explained in the previous sections, the rise in detentions and deportations has been concomitantly stark. The operations that feed these numbers fall in one of three categories: the Fugitive Operations Program (FOP); the 287(g) agreements with state and local enforcement organizations, which authorize them to implement immigration law; and worksite raids. These three categories constitute the essence of stage seven of the war on *illegal* immigrants.

(a) The ICE-led Fugitive Operations Program was set up to locate and remove "dangerous fugitive aliens."[79] A legacy of a 1995 decision by Attorney General Janet Reno, the program acquired increased importance and resources in 2002, when it was re-named and then made part of the Office of Detention and Removal Operations (DRO) under ICE in the Department of Homeland Security, and later of the Secure Border Initiative, the scheme established by DHS Secretary Chertoff in 2005.[80] The main consequences of these transformations were the increased visibility and budget allocations of the program, as well as the explicit inter-agency collaboration built into the program since 2002, when the FBI and the US Marshals Service started cooperating formally with the INS (later ICE).[81] The cooperation between agencies was expanded by the creation in 2006 of the Fugitive Operation Support Center (FOSC), in charge of supporting the work of Fugitive Operations

---

77. Ibid.
78. Tyche Hendricks, "ON THE BORDER." *The San Francisco Gate* March 12, 2007. Availalble at http://articles.sfgate.com/2007-03-12/news/17234202_1_border-patrol-san-diego-sector-migrants, accessed 03/12/2011; and Mendelson et al., "Collateral Damage."
79. The discussion in this paragraph is based on the Migration Policy Institute: Mendelson et al., "Collateral Damage."
80. Ibid.
81. Ibid., 7.

Teams by investigating and coordinating partnerships with federal, state, and local enforcement agencies.[82] The character of the program allowed ICE officers to issue civil warrants, thus bypassing the approval of a judge, as well as the standards of review of evidence and probable cause that accompany this process.[83]

Contrary to the program's mandate, almost three-quarters of the detainees have "no criminal conviction."[84] The program faces multiple lawsuits for carrying out home raids without reasonable grounds, and conducting a campaign of intimidation, illegal search, and seizure. There is evidence that the imposition of a minimum quota of arrests indeed gave incentives for the fugitive teams to conduct searches in residential environments and to expand their searches to residences and passersby in areas where immigrants concentrate (see Graph 9).[85] The new Secretary of Homeland Security Janet Napolitano has ordered a review of the program.[86]

(b) A second high profile program of domestic enforcement is commonly known as 287(g), after the relevant section of the 1996 Law that regulated agreements between federal and state and local law enforcement agencies.[87] The main innovation of this regulation is to erase the line between civil and criminal immigration laws. While state and local police forces have always had the right the enforce the latter, the decision by the Department of Justice made it possible for the first time for these agencies to prosecute civil charges such as illegal entry, undocumented work, or visa overstays.[88]

Signing agreements of this type was encouraged by the Attorney General to make state and local authorities "assist with counter-terrorism efforts."[89] Regardless of the

---

82. US Department of Homeland Security, "Testimony of Secretary Napolitano before the Senate Committee on the Judiciary, 'Oversight of the Department of Homeland Security'," *Department of Homeland Security News* May 6, 2009a. Available at http://www.dhs.gov/ynews/testimony/testimony_1241706742872.shtm, accessed 03/12/2011.

83. Mendelson et al., "Collateral Damage," 9.

84. Ibid., 3.

85. Ibid., 20-21, and 25-26.

86. Nina Bernstein, "Target of Immigrant Raids Shifted," *The New York Times* February 3, 2009. Available at http://www.nytimes.com/2009/02/04/us/04raids.html, accessed 03/12/2011.

87. This authority was initially denied by the Department of Justice, a position that was reversed in 2002, when the "inherent authority" of state and local police to implement federal immigration law was recognized. American Immigration Lawyers Association, Mexican American Legal Defense and Educational Fund, National Council of La Raza, National Immigration Forum, and National Immigration Law Center, *State and Local Police Enforcement of Federal Immigration Laws.*

88. ACLU North Carolina and Immigration & Human Rights Policy Clinic, "The Policies and Politics of Local Immigration Enforcement Laws: 287(g) Program in North Carolina," in *UNC Chapel Hill School of Law* (February 2009), 18-19.

89. Nuñez-Neto, Blas, Michael J. Garcia, and Karma Ester. "Enforcing Immigration Law: The Role of State and Local Enforcement." *Congressional Research Service Report.* Washington, DC: Congressional Research Service, August 30, 2007, 17,.

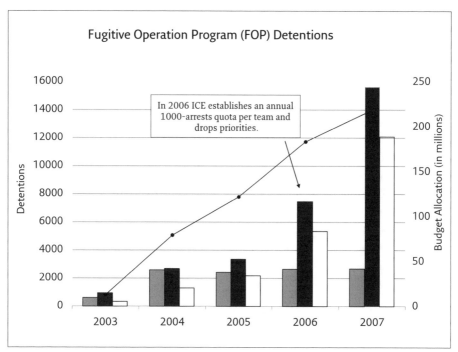

Fugitive Operation Program (FOP) Detentions

In 2006 ICE establishes an annual 1000-arrests quota per team and drops priorities.

△ **Graph 9**

Source: US Immigration and Customs Enforcement, *ICE Fiscal Year 2008 Annual Report. Protecting National Security and Upholding Public Safety* (2009). Available at https://www.ice.gov/doclib/news/library/reports/annual-report/2008annual-report.pdf, accessed 03/12/2011, 4. Mendelson et al., "Collateral Damage," 9-10 and 14.

fact that these programs target undocumented Hispanic immigrants, most defenses of these agreements rely on a rationale of national security.[90] The trend to channel measures supposed to prevent terrorism through the realm of immigration law is not unique to the United States; it has become widespread for developed countries to do so, mostly due to the reduced amount of due process and other legal obstacles to state action that characterizes this realm.[91]

The signature of these agreements, which currently number 67, coincided with local initiatives of immigration legislation in what was perceived as the local and state reaction to the inability of Congress to pass a comprehensive immigration reform.[92] These agreements and the complementary laws enabled local agencies to

90. US Congress 2009, 8.
91. Eminent Jurists Panel on Terrorism, Counter-terrorism, and Human Rights, "Assessing Damage, Urging Action," *International Commission of Jurists Report* (Geneva: International Commission of Jurists, 2009), chapter 5.
92. Serghetti, Lisa M., Karma Ester, and Michael J. Garcia. "Enforcing Immigration Law: The Role of State and Local Enforcement." *Congressional Research Service Report*. Washington, DC: Congressional Research Service, March 11, 2009.

implement immigration policy by checking immigration status at diverse instances, from traffic violations to the ending of criminal prison sentences.[93] Critics argue that these agreements generate fear among Hispanic communities, and make them reluctant to seek help from local authorities. Moreover, the implementation of immigration checks has been said to rely on racial profiling, thus violating discrimination provisions.[94]

Additional concerns about the implementation of these agreements have been raised by civil society, and are echoed in a recent report by the US General Accountability Office (GAO), which asserts that ICE lacks internal controls over the implementation of 287(g).

(c) A third component of the domestic enforcement of immigration laws are the worksite raids and arrests; these have grown in frequency and public profile in the second half of the 2000s. As Graph 10 shows, the growth in worksite arrests was not accompanied by a concomitant growth in sanctions toward employers, which were in clear decline until 2006, and then increased only slightly, settling at levels less than half of those of 2003. These arrests reflected an overall strategy of targeting immigrants rather than employers, smugglers, or other aspects of the infrastructure that supports and attracts undocumented migrants.[95] This strategy, however, is consonant with our argument about the marking of *illegal* immigrants as the war-enemy to be combated, increasing the numbers of detentions and deportations, as well as those labelled as criminal, without being consistently oriented to the achievement of results or the reduction of the war's "collateral damage."

Moreover, as numerous reports have argued, the sources for the investigation of employers' violations are still based on databases such as E-Verify or records by the Social Security administration, some of which are flawed and rely on directives that are potentially in violation of non-discrimination laws.[96]

A novel feature of worksite enforcement has been the criminalization of the detained workers by charging them with identity theft, thus moving the case from the civil to the criminal realm and getting access to the set of expediting legal tools

93. ACLU North Carolina & Immigration & Human Rights Policy Clinic, "The Policies and Politics of Local Immigration Enforcement Laws," 24; and Kennedy 2009.

94. Carrie L. Arnold, "Racial Profiling in Immigration Enforcement: State and Local Agreements to Enforce Immigration Law," *Arizona Law Review* 49 (2007): 113-142; ACLU and IHRPC, "The Policies," 25; Yolanne Almanzar, "Florida: Agency Faulted in Detention of Mother," *The New York Times* March 26, 2009. Available at http://www.nytimes.com/2009/03/26/ us/26brfs-AGENCYFAULTE_BRF.html, accessed 03/12/2011. Randal C. Archibold,"Lawmakers Want Look at Sheriff in Arizona," *The New York Times* February 13, 2009. Available at http://www.nytimes.com/2009/02/14/us/14sheriff.html, accessed 03/12/2011.

95. Meissner and Kerwin, *DHS and Immigration* 32.

96. Meissner and Kerwin, *DHS and Immigration*, 27-31; Calavita, "The Contradictions."

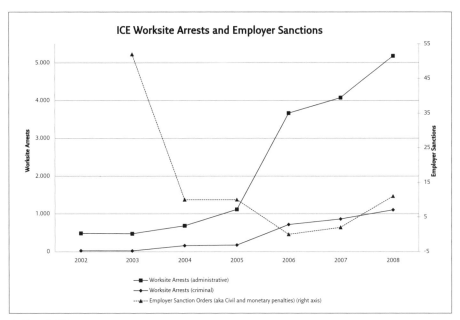

ICE Worksite Arrests and Employer Sanctions

- Worksite Arrests (administrative)
- Worksite Arrests (criminal)
- Employer Sanction Orders (aka Civil and monetary penalties) (right axis)

△ **Graph 10**

Source: US Immigration and Customs Enforcement, *ICE Fiscal Year 2008 Annual Report*; Andorra Bruno, "Immigration-related worksite enforcement: Performance measures," *Congressional Research Service* R40002 (2008). Available at http://fpc.state.gov/ documents/organization/115937.pdf, accessed 03/12/2011; and Meissner and Kerwin, *DHS and Immigration*.

established in the 1990s and 2000s (see "Worksite Arrests (criminal)" in Graph 10). These measures are sometimes complemented by having immigrants waive their right to the hearing that they otherwise have.[97] A particular instance of this general procedure was applied at the largest ICE raid in US history, in which 900 agents took part, directed at Agriprocessors Inc., a large kosher meat packing plant located near Postville, Iowa in May of 2008.[98]

The 983 undocumented immigrants apprehended were summarily tried and either deported or incarcerated for identity theft, to be deported thereafter.[99] The trials were conducted in secret, and the official strategy was to convince immigrants to plead guilty to identity theft in order to obtain shorter sentences. The prosecutors successfully converted civil violations (such as working without a permit) into felonies, thus facilitating deportation procedures. The use of these measures has

---

97. Midwest Coalition for Human Rights, "Report Cites Problems In Immigration Program That Uses the Local Police," March 4, 2009. Available at http://www.midwesthumanrights.org/government-report-cites-problems-immigration-enforcement-program, accessed 03/12/2011.

98. Erik Camayd-Freixas, "Interpreting after the Largest ICE Raid in US History: A Personal Account," *Latino Studies* 7, no. 1 (2009): 123-139.

99. Camayd-Freixas, "Interpreting," 133.

been consistently challenged in court, and was recently deemed inappropriate by unanimous decision of the US Supreme Court.[100]

In sum, the post-9/11 scenario of immigration enforcement has relied on the militarization of the border, aided and complemented by the criminalization of immigrants. While the former has relied on the construction of a physical and virtual border fence and has been advanced without concern of its human costs, the latter consists of a complex array of enforcement initiatives at the federal and local level. The prosecution of immigrants has relied on different and sometimes contradictory legal and administrative instruments, with the common goal of facilitating the expedited and unaccountable action of immigration officials. The relocation of immigration enforcement under the aegis of Homeland Security, the enactment of laws even more punitive than those approved in the 1990s, the non-legislative decisions targeting immigrants, and the rhetorical pairing of terrorism and immigration have further legitimized the *de facto* war against *illegal* immigrants, visible in the unprecedented violence at the border and armed operations in local communities.

President Bush left office in a style that was highly consonant with the orientation of his administration. On January 8, only 12 days before the inauguration of President Barack Obama, Attorney General Michael B. Mukasey ruled that immigrants do not have a "constitutional right to effective legal representation in deportation hearings," thus closing off one common avenue for appealing deportation decisions.[101]

An End to the War? President Obama, Democratization, and *Illegal* Immigrants

Initiatives to reform immigration policy faltered in the final years of the George W Bush administration and the issue has recurred to confront the Obama presidency. Facing an estimated population of 12 million undocumented immigrants, President Obama has little option but to address the problem (and the strong electoral support he received from Latino voters in 2008 also makes reform imperative to consolidate this support).

For those concerned about the war on *illegal* immigrants – its drift into greater violence, increased expenditure, and militarization of the US-Mexican border – the

---

100. Supreme Court of the United States, "Nken *v.* Holder"; and Adam Liptak and Julia Preston, "Justices Limit Use of Identity Theft Law in Immigration Cases," *The New York Times* May 4, 2009. Available at http://www.nytimes.com/2009/05/05/us/05immig.html, accessed 03/12/2011.

101. John Schwartz,"Ruling Says Deportation Cases May Not Be Appealed Over Lawyer Errors," *The New York Times* January 8, 2009. Available at http://www.nytimes.com/ 2009/01/09/us/09immig.html, accessed 03/12/2011.

hope is that President Obama will propose an expansive policy which connects immigration policy with the traditional language and practice of democratization.

Obama has instructed the Department of Homeland Security's immigration policing agencies to renew their focus on prosecuting employers who knowingly employ immigrants without legal papers, and to back away from the exclusive use of mass raids targeted on alleged illegal workers. This change signals a real switch towards targeting employers. President Obama accepts criticism about the limited efficacy of mass raids and the damage they inflicted on Latino communities, but he has not vowed to stop the detentions at worksites. Indeed, as the graphs above show, detention and deportation have reached record levels since President Obama took office.

Concurrently, President Obama is expected to announce an immigration policy with two familiar components: some sort of path to legal citizenship for *illegals* in the country combined with rigorous deterrence and exclusion of new illegal immigrants through enhanced border enforcement and further surveillance of employers hiring illegal immigrants. Thus as part of his proposed reform package the "war" as expressed by the border police and the US-Mexican Wall will continue. Furthermore, critics of the war on illegal immigrants are disappointed that President Obama's team have opted to expand the 287(g) program of national-local partnerships (though measures to improve supervision of the program have also been announced). Eleven new partnerships between local law enforcement agencies and Homeland Security signal the scheme's expansion, not its retrenchment; this expansion is not warmly supported by the local agencies, many of whom consider it a scheme which sits uncomfortably with community policing. Obama's team have also retained the Bush-era practice of requiring federal contractors and subcontractors to use E-Verify, a much-criticized electronic system that checks whether people are eligible to work.

However, a thorough democratization of immigration policy should involve more than just a path to citizenship for those residing in the United States. Rather, there should be a discussion and critique of the processes through which the war on immigrants was undertaken, including both the narratives of national security threat and the bureaucratic and physical transformations that they supported. These processes will have to come to terms with the militaristic features that we have identified in this chapter, and with the groups that support them inside the public bureaucracy, in civil society, and in the media.

The effects of the war on immigrants are society-wide, first by militarizing border communities, and later by taking the war to the domestic areas in which immigrants live and work. Moreover, this was accomplished by symbolically marking the whole Latino population, delegitimizing their claim to belonging, and devaluing their contributions to the American economy and society.

How do we deal with this kind of coercion? Democracies engage in coercion against citizens and non-citizens, but their democratic character imposes certain requirements to provide spaces of deliberation to revisit and rethink these instances of coercion. Our concern about the process of state building around the war on illegal immigrants derives from its negative effect on these spaces of contestation. While the lack of political rights makes immigrants a population ill-equipped to fight for their rights, they have increasingly done so. There has been a remarkable mobilization of immigrants, sanctuary parishes, and human rights advocates campaigning against the legislative transformations we describe. It is this mobilization that provides reasons for optimism about the continuing dialectic between immigration and democratization in American political development.

To date, the expansion of the war on *illegal* immigrants is proving a significant exercise in state building – not democratization. The beneficiaries of the resources predicated on national security needs are the US Department of Homeland Security's various sub units and bureaus, which are supposed to deal with the security risks posed by lax immigration and labor market imperatives. Consistent with the "war-like" strategy deployed by previous executives, considerable bureaucratic resources have been invested in creating enforcement teams, fortifying the border, and crafting federal, state, and local liaisons to identify, detain, and deport immigrants. Marking the end of the "war" on *illegal* immigrants will require quite deliberate policy statements from the White House and administration. Without purposeful action, scenes evoking the human tragedy captured in the conclusion of Thomas McCarthy's recent film *The Visitor* will endure.

Bibliography

Abizadeh, Arash. "Does Collective Identity Presuppose an Other? On the Alleged Incoherence of Global Solidarity." *American Political Science Review* 99, no. 1 (2005): 45-60.

ACLU North Carolina and Immigration & Human Rights Policy Clinic. "The Policies and Politics of Local Immigration Enforcement Laws: 287(g) Program in North Carolina," in *UNC Chapel Hill School of Law* (February 2009).

ACLU and National Immigration Forum. "Operation Streamline Fact Sheet." July 21, 2009.

Aizenman, Nurith C. "Report Cites Problems in ICE Training Program." *The Washington Post* March 4, 2009.

Alden, Edward. *The Closing of the American Border: Terrorism, Immigration and Security since 9/11.* New York: Harpercollins, 2008.

Almanzar, Yolanne. "Florida: Agency Faulted in Detention of Mother." *The New York Times* March 26, 2009.

American Immigration Lawyers Association, Mexican American Legal Defense and Educational Fund, National Council of La Raza, National Immigration Forum, and National Immigration Law Center.

State and Local Police Enforcement of Federal Immigration Laws: A Tool Kit for Advocates. Washington, DC: National Council of La Raza, 2006.

Andreas, Peter. *Border Games: Policing the US-Mexico Divide*. Ithaca: Cornell University Press, 2001.

Archibold, Randal C. "Border Fence Work Raises Environmental Concerns" *The New York Times* November 21, 2007.

Archibold, Randal C."Lawmakers Want Look at Sheriff in Arizona." *The New York Times* February 13, 2009.

Arnold, Carrie L. "Racial Profiling in Immigration Enforcement: State and Local Agreements to Enforce Immigration Law." *Arizona Law Review* 49 (2007): 113-142.

Ayres, B. Drummond Jr. "Border War Against Drugs is Stepped Up." *The New York Times* February 26, 1995.

Baldwin, Tom. "Immigrants barred by triple fences and double standards." *The Times* February 27, 2006.

Bartels, Larry. "Constituency Opinion and Congressional Policy Making: The Reagan Defense Buildup." *American Political Science Review* 85, no. 2 (1991): 457-74.

Beltrán, Cristina. "Going Public. Hannah Arendt, Immigrant Action, and the Space of Appearance." *Political Theory* 37, no. 5 (2009): 595-622.

Beltrán, Cristina. *The Trouble with Unity: Latino Politics and the Creation of Identity*. Oxford: Oxford University Press, 2010.

Bernstein, Nina. "Target of Immigrant Raids Shifted." *The New York Times* February 3, 2009.

Border Network for Human Rights, Border Action Network and US-Mexico Border and Immigration Task Force. "U.S.-Mexico Border Policy Report. Effective Border Policy: Security, Responsibility and Human Rights at the U.S.-Mexico Border." *Report* (November 2008).

Border Working Group. "Stop Border Deaths Now!" in *Maryknoll Office for Global Concerns* (2005).

Brownlee, W Elliot, ed. *Funding the modern American state 1941-1995*. Cambridge: Cambridge University Press, 1996.

Bruno, Andorra. "Immigration-related worksite enforcement: Performance measures," in *Washington, DC: Congressional Research Service* R40002 (2008).

Calavita, Kitty. "The Contradictions of Immigration Lawmaking: The Immigration Reform and Control Act of 1986." *Law and Policy* 11 (1989): 17-47.

Calavita, Kitty. "The New Politics of Immigration: 'Balanced-Budget Conservatism' and the Symbolism of Proposition 187." *Social Problems* 43, no. 3 (1996): 284-305.

Camayd-Freixas, Erik. "Interpreting after the Largest ICE Raid in US History: A Personal Account." *Latino Studies* 7, no. 1 (2009): 123-139.

Catanese, David. "Chris Simcox wants to dethrone McCain," in *Politico.com* (2009).

Parenti, Christian. *Lockdown America*. London: Verso, 2000.

Cornelius, Wayne. "Death at the Border: Efficacy and Unintended Consequences of US Immigration Control Policy." *Population and Development Review* 27, no. 4 (2001): 661-687.

Cornelius, Wayne. "Controlling 'Unwanted' Immigration: Lessons from the United States, 1993-2004," *Journal of Ethnic and Migration Studies* (2005): 775-794.

Cornelius, Wayne. "Impacts of Border Enforcement on Unauthorized Immigration to the United States." *Testimony on the House Judiciary Committee Field Hearing on Immigration*, San Diego, California, August 2, 2006.

Davila, Alberto, Jose A. Pagan, and Montserrat Viladrich Grau. "The Impact of IRCA on the Job Opportunities and Earnings of Mexican-Americans and Hispanic-American Workers." *International Migration Review* 32, no. 1 (1998): 79-95.

Detention Watch Network. "The History of Immigration Detention in the U.S. A Rapidly Expanding Immigration System." *Detention Watch Network* (2008).

Dombey, Daniel and Adam Thomson. "Crackdown reflects US anxiety on Mexico." *Financial Times* March 25, 2009.

Doty, Roxanne Lynn. "States of Exception on the Mexico-U.S. Border: Security, "Decisions," and Civilian Border Patrols." *International Political Sociology* 1 (2007): 113-137.

Doubler, Michael. *Civilian in Peace, Soldier in War*. Lawrence KS: University Press of Kansas 2003.

Dunn, Timothy J. "Border Militarization Via Drug and Immigration Enforcement: Human Rights Implications." *Social Justice* 28, no. 2 (2001): 7-30.

Eschbach, Karl, Jacqueline Hagan, and Nestor Rodriguez. "Causes and trends in migrants' deaths along the U.S.-Mexico border, 1985-1998." Center for Immigration Research Working Paper I-IV (2001).

Edwards, George C. *The Strategic President*. Princeton: Princeton University Press, 2009.

Eminent Jurists Panel on Terrorism, Counter-terrorism, and Human Rights. "Assessing Damage, Urging Action." *International Commission of Jurists Report*. Geneva: International Commission of Jurists, 2009.

Fessenden, Ford and Nina Bernstein. "Deportations, in thousands." *The New York Times* December 27, 2008.

Fitzgerald, Keith. *The Face of the Nation*. Stanford: Stanford University Press, 1996.

Fukuyama, Francis. "The Imperative of State-Building." *Journal of Democracy* 15, no. 2 (2004).

Gaynor, Tim. *Midnight on the Line: The Secret Life of the U.S. Mexico Border*. New York: Thomas Dunne Books, 2009.

Gelatt, Juli.a "President signs DHS Appropriations and Secure Fence Act, New Detainee Bill has Repercussions for Noncitizens." *MPI Policy Beat* (2006).

Gerstle, Gary. "The Resilient Power of the States across the Long Nineteenth Century: An Inquiry into a Pattern of American Governance," in *The Unsustainable American State*, edited by Lawrence Jacobs and Desmond King. New York: Oxford University Press, 2009.

Gonzalez, Francisco. "Same Dreams, Different Fates: Latinos' Inclusion/Exclusion and U.S. Democratization," in *Democratization in America*, edited by Desmond King, Robert C. Lieberman, Gretchen Ritter, and Laurence Whitehead. Baltimore: Johns Hopkins University Press, 2009.

Goyal, Vidhan K., Kenneth Lehn, and Stanco Racic. "Growth opportunities and corporate debt policy: the case of the US defense industry." *Journal of Financial Economics* 64, no. 1 (2002): 35-59.

Greenhouse, Linda. "THE SUPREME COURT: SUPREME COURT ROUNDUP; Justices Permit Immigrants To Challenge Deportations." *The New York Times* June 26, 2001.

Grossman, Andrew D. "Segregationist Liberalism: The NAACP and Resistance to Civil-Defense Planning in the Early Cold War, 1951-55." *International Journal of Politics, Culture and Society* 13 (2000).

Grossman, Andrew. *Neither Red Nor Dead*. New York: Routledge, 2001.

Guth, James L., Cleveland R. Fraser, John C. Green, Lyman A. Kellstedt and Corwin E. Smidt. "Religion and Foreign Policy Attitudes: The Case of Christian Zionism," in *Religion and the Culture Wars. Dispatches from the Front*, edited by John C. Green, James L. Guth, Corwin E. Smidt, and Lyman A. Kellstedt. Lanham: Rowman and Littlefield 1996.

Gzesch, Susan. "Central Americans and Asylum Policy in the Reagan Era," in *Migration Information Source*. Washington DC, 2006.

Haddal, Chad C. "Border Security: The Role of the US Border Patrol." *Congressional Research Service* RL32562, March 2, 2010.

Hamilton, Gary G. and John R. Sutton. "The problem of control in the weak state: Domination in the United States 1880-1920." *Theory and Society* 18 (1989): 1-46.

Hassouri, Parastou. "Clear Act Will Muddy Relationships Between Police and Immigrants." *American Civil Liberties Union of New Jersey* (2003).

Hattam, Victoria. *In the Shadow of Race*. Chicago: University of Chicago Press, 2007.

Hayward, Clarissa Rile. "The Difference States Make: Democracy, Identity, and the American City." *American Political Science Review* 97 (2003): 501-514.

Hendricks, Tyche. "ON THE BORDER." *The San Francisco Chronicle* March 12, 2007.

Higham, John. *Strangers in the Land. Patterns of American Nativism 1860-1925*. New Brunswick: Rutgers University Press, 1966.

Hing, Bill Ong. *Defining America through Immigration Policy*. Philadelphia: Temple University Press, 2004.

Hoefer, Michael, Nancy Rytna, and Bryan C. Baker. "Estimated on the Unauthorized Immigrant Population Residing in the United States: January 2010." *Population Estimates* (February 2011).

Honig, Bonnie. *Emergency Politics: Paradox, Law, Democracy*. Princeton: Princeton University Press, 2009.

Honig, Bonnie. "Between Decision and Deliberation: Political Paradox in Democratic Theory." *American Political Science Review* 101, no. 1 (2007): 1-17.

Hsu, Spencer S. and Griff Witte. "Plenty of Holes Seen in 'Virtual Fence.' Border Sensors Not Enough, Experts Say." *The Washington Post* September 21, 2009.

Huntington, Samuel. *Who are We? America's Great Debate*. New York, 2004.

Huspek, Michael. "Production of State, Capital, and Citizenry: The Case of Operation Gatekeeper" *Social Justice* 28, no. 2 (2001): 51-68.

Jacobson, Matthew Frye. *Whiteness of a Different Color*. Cambridge MA: Harvard University Press, 1998.

Jacobson, Robin Dale. *The New Nativism*. Minneapolis: University of Minnesota Press, 2008.

Joint Task Force North. "Mission." *Joint Task Force North Website* (n/d).

Jonas, Susanne and Catherine Tactaquin. "Latino Immigrant Rights in the Shadow of the National Security State: Responses to Domestic Preemptive Strikes." *Social Justice* 31, nos. 1-2 (2004): 67-91.

Jonas, Susanne. "Reflections on the Great Immigration Battle of 2006 and the Future of the Americas." *Social Justice* 33, no. 1 (2006): 6-20.

Kaminer, Ariel. "Becoming a Citizen the Naturalized Way." *The New York Times* July 2, 2010.

Katznelson, Ira, and Martin Shefter, eds. *Shaped by Trade and War*. Princeton: Princeton University Press, 2002.

Kenndy, Randy. "Texas Mayor Caught in Deportation Furor." *The New York Times* April 4, 2009.

Kennedy, David. *Over Here*. New York: Oxford University Press, 2004.

Kiely, Kathy, and David Jackson. "Chertoff chides left, rigth over bill: says opposition may hurt interests of both." *USA Today* (2007).

King, Desmond. "Mimicking War: How Presidents Coordinate the American State." *Working Paper No 74, Bremen TranState Working Papers Series* (2008).

King, Desmond and Robert C. Lieberman. "Ironies of State Building: A Comparative Perspective on the American State." *World Politics* 61 (2009): 547-588

King, Desmond S. and Rogers M. Smith. "Racial Orders in American Political Development." *American Political Science Review* 99 (2005): 75-92.

King, Desmond. *Making Americans: Immigration, Race and the Origins of the Diverse Democracy*. Cambridge MA: Harvard University Press, 2000.

King, Desmond. "State Making in the United States: How Mimicking War Coordinates the American State." *Working Paper No. 68-2, American University in Paris* (2008b).

Kryder, Daniel. *Divided Arsenal*. Cambridge: Cambridge University Press, 2000.

Lacey, Marc and Ginger Thompson. "As Clinton Visits Mexico, Strains Show in Relations." *The New York Times* March 24, 2009.

Lemann, Nicholas. *Redemption*. New York: Farrar, Straus and Giroux 2006.

Lichtblau, Eric. "Bush Commutes 2 Border Agents' Sentences." *The New York Times* January 19, 2009.

Lieberman, Robert C. "Rejoinder to Mearsheimer and Walt" *Perspectives on Politics* 7 (2009): 275-281.

Lieberman, Robert C. "The 'Israel Lobby' and American Politics." *Perspectives on Politics* 7 (2009): 235-257.

Lienesch, Michael. *Redeeming America. Piety and Politics in the New Christian Right*. Chapel Hill: The University of North Carolina Press, 1993. 211.

Light, Jennifer. *From Warfare to Welfare*. Baltimore: Johns Hopkins University Press, 2003.

Liptak, Adam and Julia Preston. "Justices Limit Use of Identity Theft Law in Immigration Cases." *The New York Times* May 4, 2009.

Lopez, Mark Hugo and Susan Minushkin. "2008 National Survey of Latinos. Hispanics See their Situation in the U.S Deteriorating; Oppose Key Immigration Enforcement Measures." *Pew Hispanic Center Report No. 93*. Washington, DC: Pew Hispanic Center, 2008.

Martin, William. "The Christian Right and American Foreign Policy." *Foreign Policy* 114 (1999): 66-80.

Martinez, Lisa M. "'Flowers From the Same Soil' Latino Solidarity in the Wake of the 2006 Immigrant Mobilizations." *American Behavioral Scientist* 52, no. 4 (2008): 557-9.

McKinley, James C. Jr. "U.S. is Arms Bazaar for Mexican Cartels." *New York Times*, February 25, 2009.

Mearsheimer, John J. and Stephen M. Walt. "The Blind Man and the Elephant in the Room: Robert Lieberman and the Israel Lobby." *Perspectives on Politics* 7 (2009): 259-272.

Meissner, Doris and Donald Kerwin. *DHS and Immigration. Taking Stock and Correcting Course*. Washington, DC: Migration Policy Institute, 2009.

Mendelson, Margot, Shayna Strom, and Michael Wishnie. "Collateral Damage: An Examination of ICE's Fugitive Operation Program," *MPI Report* (2009)..

Micklethwait, John and and Adrian Woolridge. *The Right Nation*. New York: Penguin, 2004.

Midwest Coalition for Human Rights. "State and Local Enforcement – 287(g) Program." *Midwest Coalition for Human Rights*, November 14, (2007).

Midwest Coalition for Human Rights. "Report Cites Problems In Immigration Program That Uses the Local Police," *Midwest Coalition for Human Rights*, March 4, (2009).

Mikkelsen, Randall "Boeing awarded contract on border fence: Chertoff." *Reuters*, June 9, 2008.

Narro, Victor, Kent Wong, and Janna Shadduck-Hernández. "The 2006 Immigrant Uprising: Origins and Future." *New Labor Forum* 16, no. 1 (2007): 49-56.

Näsström, Sofia. "The Legitimacy of the People." *Political Theory* 35 (2007): 624-658.

National Immigration Forum. "Southwest Border Security Operations," in *National Immigration Forum Backgrounder* (2010).

Nevins, Joseph. "Searching for Security: Boundary and Immigration Enforcement in an Age of Intensifying Globalization." *Social Justice* 28 (2001): 132-148.

Nevins, Joseph. *Operation Gatekeeper: the rise of the "illegal alien" and the making of the U.S.-Mexico boundary*. New York: Routledge, 2001a.

Nevins, Joseph. "Searching for Security: Boundary And Immigration Enforcement in an Age of Intensifying Globalization." *Social Justice* 28, no. 2 (2001): 132-148.

Nevins, Joseph. "Death as a Way of Life." *counterpunch* Weekend Edition, July 26-27, 2008.

Newton, Ina. *Illegal, Alien or Immigrant*. New York: New York University Press, 2008.

Ngai, Mae M. *Impossible Subjects: Illegal Aliens and the Making of Modern America*. Princeton: Princeton University Press, 2004.

Nuñez-Neto, Blas, Michael J. Garcia, and Karma Ester. "Enforcing Immigration Law: The Role of State and Local Enforcement." *Congressional Research Service Report*. Washington, DC: Congressional Research Service, August 30, 2007.

Palafox, Jose. "Militarizing the Border." *CovertAction Quarterly* (Spring 1996).

Palafox, Jose. "Introduction to 'Gatekeeper's State: Immigration and Boundary Policing in an Era of Globalization.'" *Social Justice* 28, no. 2 (2001): 132-148.

Parenti, Christian. *Lockdown America: Police and Prisons in the Age of Crisis*. London: Verso, 2000.

Paulson, Monte. "Soldiers on US Borders: What Could Go Wrong? Start with the killing of Esequiel Hernández Jr." *The Tyee* May 18, 2006.

Phillips, Julie A. and Douglas S Massey "The New Labor Market: Immigrants and Wages after IRCA" *Demography* 36 (1999), 233-46.

Phillips, Julie A. and Douglas S. Massey. "The New Labor Market: Immigrants and Wages after IRCA." *Demography* 36, no. 2 (1999): 233-246.

Preston, Julia. "Facing Deportation but Clinging to Life in U.S." *The New York Times* January 18, 2008.

Preston, Julia. "Students Spared Amid an Increase in Deportations." *The New York Times* August 8, 2010.

Julia Preston. "Deportations from US Hit a Record High." *The New York Times* October 6, 2010.

Reuters. "Chertoff says immigration bill 'bows to reality.'" *Latest News, Politics: Reuters* (2007).

Roediger, David R. *Working Toward Whiteness: How America's Immigrants Became White*. New York: Basic. 2005.

Rudolph, Christopher. "Security and the Political Economy of International Migration." *American Political Science Review* 97, no. 4 (2003): 603-20.

Sanchez, George J. *Becoming Mexican American*. New York: Oxford University Press, 1993.

Sassen, Saskia. "The Limits of Power and the Complexity of Powerlessness: The Case of Immigration." *Unbound* 3 (2007): 105-113.

Sawyer, Mark. "Commentary: On Black Leadership, Black Politics, and the US Immigration Debate." *Souls* 10, no. 1 (2008): 42-9.

Schmitt, Eric. "No Agreement Yet with Mexico on Immigration Plan, U.S. Says." *The New York Times* September 1, 2001.

Schwartz, John. "Supreme Court Rules Against Government in Identity-Theft Case." *The New York Times* May 4, 2009a.

Schwartz, John. "Ruling Says Deportation Cases May Not Be Appealed Over Lawyer Errors." *The New York Times* January 8, 2009b.

Serghetti, Lisa M., Karma Ester, and Michael J. Garcia. "Enforcing Immigration Law: The Role of State and Local Enforcement." *Congressional Research Service Report*. Washington, DC: Congressional Research Service, March 11, 2009.

Serrano, Alfonso. "Churches Providing Sanctuary to Immigrants." *CBS News* (2007).

Sheridan, Clare. "Contested Citizenship: National Identity and the Mexican Immigration Debates of the 1920s." *Journal of American Ethnic History* 21 (2003): 3-35.

Shoulak, Joe. "Stopping Illegal Immigration at the Border." *The San Francisco Chronicle* March 12, 2007.

Smith, Lamar. "ICE is Correct to Utilize 'Fugitive Operations Teams' to Target Fugitive Aliens." *New and Releases*. Washington DC: U.S. House of Representatives Committee on the Judiciary, Republicans, February 4, 2009.

Smith, Lamar. "SCOTUS Decision a Disservice to Americans." *New and Releases*. Washington, DC: U.S. House of Representatives Committee on the Judiciary, Republicans, April 22, 2009b.

Smith, Rogers M. *Civic Ideals*. New Haven: Yale University Press, 1997.

Smith, Rogers M. *Stories of Peoplehood: The Politics and Morals of Political Membership*. Cambridge: Cambridge University Press, 2003.

Southern Poverty Law Center. "Under Siege. Life for Low-Income Latinos in the South." A *Southern Poverty Law Center Report* (April 2009a).

Southern Poverty Law Center. "Intelligence Report. The Year in Hate." *Intelligence Report* 133 (2009b).

Supreme Court of the United States. "Nken *v*. Holder, Attorney General." *Ruling No.08-681* April 21, 2009a.

Supreme Court of the United States. "Flores-Figueroa *v*. United States." *Ruling No.08-108* May 4, 2009b.

Susanne Jonas. "Reflections on the Great Immigration Battle of 2006 and the Future of the Americas." *Social Justice* 33 (1996): 6-20.

The Pew Research Center and The Pew Forum on Religion & Public Life. *Religion in Campaign '08 Survey Report September 06*. Washington DC: The Pew Research Center, 2007.

The Pew Hispanic Center. "Trends in Unauthorized Migration: Undocumented Inflow Now Trails Legal Inflow." *Pew Hispanic Center Report* XCIV (2008).

Pew Hispanic Center. "Unauthorized Immigrant Population: National and State Trends." *Pew Hispanic Center Report* CXXXIII (2011).

Tichenor, Daniel J. "The Politics of Immigration Reform in the United States, 1981-1990." *Polity* 26, no. 3 (1994): 333-362.

Tichenor, Daniel. *Dividing Lines*. Princeton: Princeton University Press, 2002.

Tilly, Charles. *The Formation of National States in Western Europe*. Princeton: Princeton University Press, 1975.

Tilly, Charles. "War Making and State Making as Organized Crime," in *Bringing the State Back In*, edited by P. Evans, T. Skocpol, and D. Rueschemeyer. Cambridge: Cambridge University Press, 1985.

Togman, Jeffrey M. *The Ramparts of Nations Institutions and Immigration Policies in France and the United States*. Westport: Greenwood Publishing, 2002.

Transactional Records Access Clearinghouse. "Immigration Enforcement: The Rhetoric, The Reality." *TRAC Report* 178 (2007).

Transactional Records Access Clearinghouse. "Immigration Convictions for November 2010," in *TRAC Report* February 16, 2011.

US Citizenship and Immigration Services. "Legislation from 1981 to 1996," in *Historical Immigration and Naturalization Legislation* (n/d).

US Congress. "Statement of Julie L. Myers, Assistant Secretary, US Immigration and Customs Enforcement, Department of Homeland Security before House Appropriations Committee, Subcommittee on Homeland Security." In *110th Congress, First Session* March 27, 2007.

US Congress. "Statement of Kris W. Kobach, Professor at the University of Missouri (Kansas City) School of Law before House Committee on Judiciary Subcommittee on Constitution, Civil Rights, and Civil Liberties And Subcommittee on Immigration, Citizenship, Refugee, Border Security, and International Law." In *111th Congress* April 2, 2009.

US Customs and Border Protection. "SBI Timeline," in *Secure Border Initiative/About* (2009).

US Customs and Border Protection. "SBI Programs." November 10, 2008.

US Department of Homeland Security. *2007 Yearbook of Immigration Statistics*. (2008).

US Department of Homeland Security. "Testimony of Secretary Napolitano before the Senate Committee on the Judiciary, 'Oversight of the Department of Homeland Security'." *Department of Homeland Security News* May 6, 2009a.

US Department of Homeland Security. "Definition of Terms." *Department of Homeland Security Website* September 10, 2009b.

US Department of Homeland Security. "Immigration Enforcement Actions: 2009." *Annual Report* August, 2010.

US Department of Justice. "Follow up Report on Border Patrol's Efforts to Improver Border Security (Redacted Version)," in *DOJ Report* No.I-2002-004 (2002).

US Government Accountability Office. "Illegal Immigration. Border-Crossing Deaths Have Doubled since 1995; Border Patrol's Efforts to Prevent Deaths Have Not Been Fully Evaluated," in *GAO Report* GAO-06-770 (2006).

US Government Accountability Office. "Immigration Enforcement. Controls over Program Authorizing State and Local Enforcement of Federal Immigration Laws Should be Strengthened (Statement of Richard M. Stana, Director of Homeland Security and Justice)," in *GAO Report* GAO-09-381-T (2009).

US Immigration and Customs Enforcement. "Delegation of Immigration Authority Section 287(g) Immigration and Nationality Act," in *USICE Programs* (August 2008).

US Immigration and Customs Enforcement. *ICE Fiscal Year 2008 Annual Report. Protecting National Security and Upholding Public Safety* (2009).

US Public Law 101-649. "Immigration Act of 1990," in *Public Laws Amending the INA – US Citizenship and Immigration Services* (1990).

US Public Law 104-132. "Antiterrorism and Effective Death Penalty Act of 1996," in *Public Laws Amending the INA-US Citizenship and Immigration Services* (1996).

US Public Law 104-193. "Personal Responsibility and Work Opportunity Reconciliation Act of 1996," in *Laws & Policies-U.S. Department of Health and Human Services* (1996).

US Public Law 104-208. "Illegal Immigration Reform and Immigrant Responsibility Act of 1996," in *Public Laws Amending the INA-US Citizenship and Immigration Services* (1996).

US Public Law 107-296. "Homeland Security Act of 2002," in *Department of Homeland Security/About the Department* (2002).

US Public Law 109-367. "Secure Fence Act of 2006." (2006).

US Public Law 198-275. "Identity Theft Penalty Enhancement Act." (2004).

US Public Law 99-603. "Immigration Reform and Control Act of 1986," in *Public Laws Amending the INA – US Citizenship and Immigration Services* (1986).

Varsanyi, Monica. "Immigration Policing Through the Backdoor: City Ordinances, the 'Right to the City,' and the Exclusion of the Undocumented Day Laborers." *Urban Geography* 29, no. 1 (2007): 29-52.

Verhovek, Sam Howe. "After a Marine on Patrol Kills a Teenager, a Village Wonders Why." *The New York Times* June 29, 1997.

Weekly Compilation of Presidential Documents Vol. 40. Washington, DC: Government Printing Office.

Weekly Compilation of Presidential Documents Vol. 42. Washington, DC: Government Printing Office.

Westbrook, Robert B. *John Dewey and American Democracy*. Ithaca: Cornell University Press, 1991.

Winthrop, John. "A Defense of an Order of Court (1637)," in *The Puritans in America*, edited by Alan Heimert and Henry Delbanco. New York: Cambridge, 1985.

Wuthnow, Robert. *The Restructuring of American Religion. Society and Faith Since World War II*. Princeton: Princeton University Press, 1988.

Zelizer, Julian E. "The Uneasy Relationship: Democracy, Taxation and State Building since the New Deal," in *The Democratic Experiment*, edited by Meg Jacobs, William J. Novak, and Julian E. Zelizer. Princeton: Princeton University Press, 2003.

Zolberg, Aristide R. *A Nation by Design: Immigration Policy in the Fashioning of America*. Cambridge MA: Harvard University Press, 2006.

9 Narratives of Nation and Anti-Nation: The Media and the Construction of Latinos as a Threat to the United States

Leo R. Chavez

> *Identities are narratives, stories people tell themselves and others about who they are (and who they are not).*
> *Nira Yuval-Davis*[1]

The June 22, 1992 issue of the *National Review* magazine's cover featured the Statue of Liberty looking sternly at the reader and posed with her arm straight out and her hand up in the sign for "stop." Rather than her usual pose with her arm up holding the golden torch of welcome, this Statue of Liberty was now blocking the entry of immigrants, symbolically telling them that they were not welcome into the nation. The cover's text reinforced this message: "Tired? Poor? Huddled? Tempest-Tossed? Try Australia. Rethinking Immigration." Within the magazine, author Peter Brimelow warned of the dangers associated with continued high levels of immigration. He was particularly concerned with "Hispanics." "Symptomatic of the American Anti-Idea is the emergence of a strange anti-nation inside the U.S. - the so-called 'Hispanics.' The various groups of Spanish-speaking immigrants are now much less encouraged to assimilate to American culture."[2]

As Peter Brimelow and the *National Review* suggest, the United States of America, like many of the world's industrialized nations, is in the midst of a decades-long public debate over immigration and the place of immigrants in the nation. This chapter examines US public discourse about Latinos, or Hispanics, and their representation as a problem for the nation. Representing Latinos as a threat to the nation is problematic because its hyperbolic nature obscures more balanced characterizations of Latinos, and that makes arriving at a consensus on immigration reform difficult. For example, a key issue in the debate over comprehensive immigration reform is what to do with undocumented, or unauthorized, immigrants, most of whom are from Mexico and other Latin American countries. Should they be allowed

---

1. Nira Yuval-Davis, "Belonging and the politics of belonging," *Patterns of Prejudice* 40, no. 3 (2006):197-214.
2. Peter Brimelow, "Time to Rethink Immigration?," *The National Review*, June 22, 1992, 45.

Fig. 1: *National Review* Cover.

to become legal immigrants, that is, provided with a "path to citizenship"? Any discussion of a legalization program, however, is embedded in the often vitriolic rhetoric surrounding undocumented immigrants, and particularly the threat posed by Latinos, both immigrants and US-born.

The following questions frame this chapter: What do we mean by nation? How are Latinos represented as a threat to the nation? And how accurate are these representations of Latinos?

The United States as a Nation of Immigrants

Nation is used here to refer to "the people," as in the American people or the French people. Following Benedict Anderson's observations in his classic book *Imagined Communities*, the nation is imagined.[3] It is imagined because in all but the smallest societies, one cannot know all the members of the society, and yet "in the minds of each lives the image of their communion."[4] Anderson defines the nation as an imagined political community that is imagined as both inherently limited and sovereign. The nation is limited because no nation is imagined to consist of all humans alive at the time. Rather, the nation exists in contrast to other nations that lie just beyond its "finite, if elastic boundaries." Anderson highlights the relationship between the emergence of print media, especially novels and newspapers, and the development of the imagined community of the nation. "These forms provided the technical means for 're-presenting' the *kind* of imagined community that is the nation."[5] The visual images found on magazine covers, such as that of the *National Review* above, are merely an extension of this relationship since they too re-present the nation.

By examining public discourse, such as that found in national magazines, we can gain insights into the way the nation is imagined, especially who is and who is not included in that imagined nation. What emerges is a discourse of the nation. Stuart Hall has characterized the discourse of a national culture as "a way of constructing meanings which influences and organizes both our actions and our conception of ourselves. National cultures construct identities by producing meanings about 'the nation' with which we can identify; these are contained in the stories which are told about it, memories which connect its present with its past, and images which are constructed of it."[6]

---

3. Benedict Anderson, *Imagined Communities* (London: Verso, 1983).
4. Ibid., 15-16.
5. Ibid., 30.
6. Stuart Hall, "The Question of Cultural Identity," in *Modernity: An Introduction to Modern Societies*, ed. S. Hall, D. Held, D. Hubert, and K. Thompson (Cambridge, MA: Blackwell Publishers: 1996), 595-634, 613.

America was once viewed as a great "melting pot" that blended many immigrant strains into a single nationality. While we may now assert that ethnic identities and traditions are not so easily "lost" by immigrants, and that becoming American is not always a simple linear process, the melting pot continues to retain its narrative power as a metaphor for American society. The power of America to absorb immigrants is both marveled at and questioned, but continues to be an important story we tell about ourselves as a people and as a nation. That we can call ourselves "a nation of immigrants" depends on the power of this common narrative about our history.

During the latter decades of the twentieth century and into the first decade of the twenty-first century, the American public has been noticeably uneasy with both undocumented and legal immigration, and with the melting pot narrative, as the concerns expressed in the *National Review* indicate. Visible demographic changes, often talked of as changes to the "face of the nation," helped fuel the public's unease with immigration. Demographic projections presented the decline of "white" Americans in the US population, and the subsequent growth of Latinos and Asian Americans. Latinos, in particular, were projected to increase from 5 percent of the US population in 1970 to 25 percent in 2050. Whites, in turn, are projected to decrease from 83 percent of the population in 1970 to about half the population in 2050, or even earlier.

Tensions with such dramatic demographic projections revolve around the way we think of ourselves as a nation and as a people. As historian David Hollinger might put it, "the circle of we" is increasingly being debated and narrowed as immigrants, both legal and unauthorized, are targeted as belonging outside the "we."[7] The "rhetoric of exclusion" embedded in contemporary discourse on immigration runs the risk of arousing nativism.[8] In his classic book *Strangers in the Land*, John Higham defined nativism as "intense opposition to an internal minority on the ground of its foreign (i.e., "un-American") connections." Higham argued that nativism gets much of its energy from modern nationalism, and that "nativism translates broader cultural antipathies and ethnocentric judgments into a zeal to destroy the enemies of a distinctively American way of life."[9] Indeed, the proponents of restricting immigration often view today's immigrants as a threat to the "nation" that is conceived of as a singular, predominantly Euro-American, English-speaking culture. The "new" immigrants – the *transnationalists* – threaten this singular

---

7. David A. Hollinger, *Postethnic America: Beyond Multiculturalism* (New York: Basic Books, 1995).
8. Juan F Perea, ed., *Immigrants Out! The New Nativism and the Anti-Immigrant Impulse in the United States* (New York: New York University Press, 1997); Verena Stolcke, "Talking Culture: New Boundaries, New Rhetorics of Exclusion in Europe," *Current Anthropology* 36 (1995):1-24.
9. John Higham, *Strangers in the Land: Patterns of American Nativism, 1860-1925* (New Brunswick: Rutgers University Press, 2002 [1955]), 4.

vision of the "nation" because they allegedly bring "multiculturalism" and not assimilation.[10] From this perspective, the pot no longer has the capacity to melt.

Immigrants strain Anderson's conceptualization of an imagined nation. They are from outside the borders of the sovereign nation and yet live within the nation.[11] The extent to which the larger society "imagines" these liminal immigrants as part of the nation can vary historically.[12] In the contemporary period, the place of immigrants in the nation is subject to laws governing immigration and naturalization, attitudes towards immigrants, the criteria for and benefits of citizenship,[13] and perceptions of what constitutes the nation and its people.[14] None of these positions is fixed, immutable, and uniform; each is subject to a process of debate, a debate that has been played out, so to speak, in popular discourse.

---

10. See Leo R. Chavez, "Outside the Imagined Community: Undocumented Settlers and Experiences of Incorporation," *American Ethnologist* 18 (1991): 257-278; Samuel P. Huntington, *Who We Are: The Challenges to America's National Identity* (New York: Simon and Schuster, 2004); Arthur M. Schlesinger, Jr., *The Disuniting of America* (New York: W.W. Norton, 1992). Such views have their historical antecedents earlier in the twentieth century when eugenicists argued that continued immigration of southern and eastern Europeans posed the possibility of "race suicide" because they lacked the superior qualities of the "Nordic race," who were a people of "rulers, organizers, and aristocrats"; Dorothy Roberts, *Killing the Black Body: Race, Reproduction, and the Meaning of Liberty* (New York: Pantheon Books, 1997), 213. Moreover, immigrants reproduced faster than native Anglo-Saxon Americans and their children remained "foreign stock" (unacculturated) despite their birth on US soil (Roberts, *Killing the Black Body*, 212). As Francis A. Walker, superintendent of the census of 1870 and 1889 noted about the children of immigrants: "Although born among us, our general instinctive feeling testifies that they are not wholly of us. So separate has been their social life, due alike to their clannishness and to our reserve; so strong have been the ties of race and blood and religion with them; so acute has been the jealousy of their spiritual teachers to our institutions – that we think of them, and speak of them, as foreigners" (Quoted in Roberts, *Killing the Black Body*, 212).

11. Chavez, "Outside the Imagined Community"; Michael Kearney, "The Local and the Global: The Anthropology of Globalization and Transnationalism," *Annual Review of Anthropology* 24 (1995): 547-65.

12. For readings on various views of immigrants in American history see: John R. Kennedy, *A Nation of Immigrants* (New York: Harper and Row Publishers, 1986 [1958]); Daniel E. Segal, "Living Ancestors: Nationalism and the Past in Postcolonial Trinidad and Tobago," in *Remapping Memory: Politics of Time and Space*, ed. Jonathan Boyarin (Minneapolis: University of Minnesota Press, 1994); Stephen Steinberg, *The Ethnic Myth: Race, Ethnicity and Class in America* (Boston: Beacon Press, 1989); Perea, ed., *Immigrants Out!*; Rita J. Simon and Susan H. Alexander, *The Ambivalent Welcome: Print Media, Public Opinion and Immigration* (Westport, CT: Praerger Publishers, 1993).

13. Renata Rosaldo has argued for a "cultural citizenship" that respects cultural difference. "Cultural Citizenship in San Jose, California," *Polar* 17 (1994):57-63. Aihwa Ong expands on this concept, arguing that cultural citizenship is "a dual process of self-making and being-made within webs of power linked to the nation-state and civil society," in "Cultural Citizenship as Subject-Making: Immigrants Negotiate Racial and Cultural Boundaries in the United States," *Current Anthropology* 37, no. 5 (1996): 737-62.

14. Irene Bloemraad, *Becoming a Citizen: Incorporating Immigrants and Refugees in the United States and Canada* (Berkeley: University of California Press, 2006); Linda S. Bosniak, "Citizenship Denationalized," *Indiana Journal of Global Legal Studies* 7 (2000): 447-509; Michael Omi and Howard Winant, *Racial Formation in the United States: From the 1960s to the 1990s* (New York: Routledge, 1994).

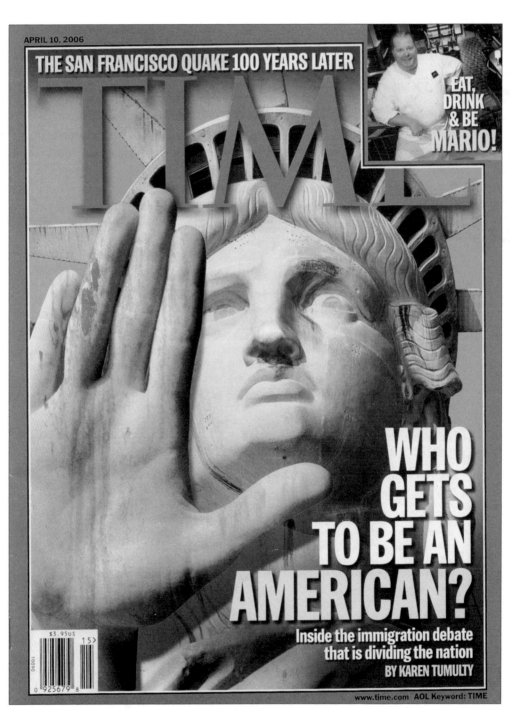

APRIL 10, 2006

THE SAN FRANCISCO QUAKE 100 YEARS LATER

TIME

EAT, DRINK & BE MARIO!

WHO GETS TO BE AN AMERICAN?

Inside the immigration debate that is dividing the nation

BY KAREN TUMULTY

$3.95US

15>

0 925679 8

www.time.com AOL Keyword: TIME

Fig. 2: *Time* Cover.

Immigrants are also problematic for the construction of national identity.[15] They are both celebrated in the origin myths of this identity and condemned as a threat to what is increasingly viewed as a fragile identity.[16] Representations of immigrants, as found in public discourse (e.g., on magazine covers), vacillate between the "we" in America's identity and the "Other," whose very presence is used to construct the "us."[17] As the morally questionable Other, the immigrant is often perceived as the "alien," "foreigner," "stranger," and "outsider" who is, as Michel Foucault put it, "at once interior and foreign, therefore to be excluded (so as to exorcise their interior danger)."[18] Although immigrants function as the "Other" in the construction of an American identity, the relationship cannot be reduced to a simple dichotomy between "us" and "them." The "us" were actually "them" in the not-too-distant past. It is perhaps this recognition of the self in the Other/immigrant that underlies the lack of a consistent societal position in regards to immigrants – the love-hate relationship that has been so characteristic of much of US history.[19]

Latinos as Threats to the Nation

Although immigrants may have been desired because of their labor, new waves of immigrants to the US were often viewed with suspicion and outright hostility.[20] Immigrants were said to lower wages, concentrate in ethnic neighborhoods, lack the ability or desire to assimilate, and bring disease. Public discourse attributes these same threats to today's Latinos. However, public discourse often characterizes Latinos as a threat to the nation in other important ways: their high levels of immigration and fertility rates are said to fuel an invasion and they, particularly those of Mexican origin, pose a potential threat of a take-over, or re-conquest, of

15. Susan Bibler Coutin and Phyllis Pease Chock, "Your Friend, The Illegal: Definition and Paradox in Newspaper Accounts of U.S. Immigration Reform," *Identities* 2 (1995): 123-48.
16. Kathryn Woodward, "Concepts of Identity and Difference," in *Identity and Difference*, ed. K. Woodward (Thousand Oaks: Sage Publications, 1997).
17. Edward Said, *Covering Islam: How the Media and the Experts Determine How We See the Rest of the World* (New York: Vintage Books, 1996).
18. Michel Foucault, *The Order of Things* (New York: Vintage Books, 1970), xxiv.
19. Leo Chavez, *Covering Immigration: Popular Images and the Politics of the Nation* (Berkeley: University of California Press, 2001); William S. Sax has argued that this is a basic feature of how cultures construct both themselves and the Other: "difference making involves a double movement, where the Other is simultaneously emulated and repudiated, admired and despised, and that the source of this ambivalence is the recognition of the Self in Other." William S. Sax, "The Hall of Mirrors: Orientalism, Anthropology, and the Other," *American Anthropologist* 100 (1998): 292-301.
20. Gary Gerstle, *American Crucible: Race and Nation in the Twentieth Century* (Princeton: Princeton University Press, 2001).

the Southwest United States. A few examples of the Latino threat will establish its prevalence as a pervasive narrative of the nation and anti-nation.[21]

In the 1970s, *U.S. News & World Report* began alerting the public that social, political and demographic trends in Mexico posed future problems for the United States. Their covers had headlines such as "Crisis Across the Borders: Meanings for the U.S." (December 13, 1976), "Border Crisis: Illegal Aliens out of Control" (April 25, 1977) and "ILLEGAL ALIENS: Invasion Out of Control?" (January 29, 1979). In all three cases, the subject was the growing flow of undocumented Mexican immigrants and their potential to take over the US Southwest and give it back to Mexico, and to over-use social services. *U.S. News & World Report*'s July 4, 1997 issue pointed to Mexican women's unchecked fertility as the problem that was fueling the flow of Mexicans to the United States.

The July 4, 1977, *U.S. News & World Report*'s cover reads: "TIME BOMB IN MEXICO: Why There'll be No End To the Invasion of 'Illegals.'" The image is of a group of men standing, most with their hands in the air or behind their heads. The scene is taking place at night, a strong light making the men visible. The men all have dark hair and appear Latino. A lone Border Patrol agent, barely visible in the background, helps to establish the scene's location: the US-Mexico border. Use of the word invasion conjures many images, none of them friendly or indicating mutual benefit. Friends do not invade; enemies invade. Invasion is an act of war, and puts the nation and its people at great risk. The war metaphor is enhanced by the prominence of the words "Time Bomb." The text conjures up an image of Mexico as a bomb which, when it explodes, will damage the United States. The damage, the message makes clear, will be the unstoppable flow of illegal immigrants to the United States.

The accompanying article cites predictions that Mexico's population, then at about 64 million, could grow to as many as 132 million by 1997 or so (predictions that did not prove accurate). The yearly population increase at the time was somewhere between 3.2 and 3.5 percent. In addition to population pressures, Mexico had to confront high levels of unemployment and underemployment (then affecting about 40 percent of the working age population), rapid urbanization which further strained a limited infrastructure, a level of agricultural production that failed to meet the needs of the country, growing inequality between the rich and poor, and political corruption at all levels of government. Added to these problems was the political consideration of America's interest in maintaining political stability in Mexico. In

---

21. Leo R. Chavez, *The Latino Threat: Constructing Immigrants, Citizens and the Nation* (Stanford: Stanford University Press, 2008). For analyses of media representations of Latinos, see Otto Santa Ana, *Brown Tide Rising* (Austin: University of Texas Press, 2002); Coutin and Chock, "Your Friend, the Illegal"; and Clara E. Rodriguez, *Latin Looks: Images of Latinas and Latinos in the U.S. Media* (Boulder, CO: Westview Press, 1997).

this sense, emigration is an "escape hatch" for Mexicans who might otherwise stay and foment political unrest. In short, all of these problems in the Mexican economy and society, combined with Mexico's attitude toward emigration, mean, according to *U.S. News & World Report*, that controlling the flow of undocumented migrant workers across the border would be difficult.

The 1980s witnessed continued alarmist discourse about Mexican immigration. *U.S. News & World Report*'s March 9, 1981 issue featured the headline "OUR TROUBLED NEIGHBORS – Dangers for U.S." The problem in Canada was the possible political turmoil resulting from the French-speaking Canadians' movement for political independence from English-speaking Canadians. On the Mexican side, continued immigration raises the possibility of Mexican demographic strength, which poses the probability of a separatist movement following the Quebec example.

Two years later, on March 7, 1983, *U.S. News & World Report* returned to the invasion theme. The cover's text announces: "Invasion From Mexico: It Just Keeps Growing." This cover is momentous in that the metaphor of war – invasion – is attached to a particular foreign country, Mexico. Mexico is now explicitly placed in the role of aggressor and the US is the nation whose sovereign territory is under attack by this hostile country and its people.

The image on the cover is a photograph of women being carried by men across a canal of water. The people in the picture are phenotypically Latino, or Mexican. In the accompanying articles we learn about the "flood of illegal aliens in unparalleled volume" which is no match for the understaffed and beleaguered US Border Patrol.[22] The "invaders," we learn, are desperate job seekers, willing to "risk all" to cross the border.[23] With an increase in the clandestine flow across the border came a rise in the number of deaths due to exposure to the elements in rugged hill country and open deserts. Deaths also occurred from accidents as migrants frantically crossed busy streets or attempted to jump onto freight trains moving further north.

A year later, *Newsweek*'s June 25, 1984 issue carried the headline: "Closing the Door? The Angry Debate Over Illegal Immigration. Crossing the Rio Grande." The cover's image relies on many of the same basic visual elements to tell its story as the *U.S. News and World Report* cover above. Once again we have a photographic image of a man carrying a woman across a shallow body of water. The woman is wearing a headscarf and a long shawl. The man carries the woman's handbag, which suggests she is traveling somewhere, moving with a purpose and for an extended amount of time. She holds a walking cane.

---

22. *U.S. News & World Report*, March 7, 1983, 37.
23. Ibid., 38.

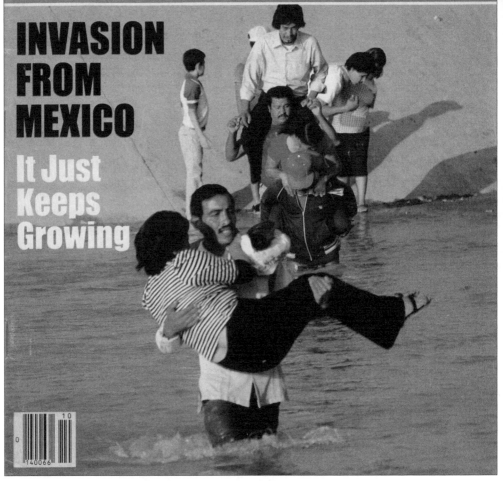

Fig. 3: *U.S. News & World Report* Cover.

Leaving aside the text on this and the previous cover for a moment, the images themselves do a lot to establish the theme and location of the events taking place. They do so through the use of stereotypical phenotypes, clothing, and "common sense" understandings of how Mexicans cross the border. In short, the images hit upon a number of touchstones related to undocumented Mexican immigration. For example, the water in the image could be anywhere, but the phenotypes, complexion (the color photographs clearly show their brown skin and black hair), and clothing suggest the people are Mexicans. In addition, the people – Mexicans – in conjunction with the activity they are engaged in – crossing water – situates otherwise nondescript water as "border water." This message derives from the American public's cultural understanding of the history of Mexican immigration to the United States. As Claire F. Fox has observed, "Generally speaking, the Rio Grande/Rio Bravo and the fence are the two primary contemporary icons used to establish the location of a narrative in the border region."[24] The cultural stereotype is that Mexican immigration occurs over water (water is also a basic metaphor for immigration). Mexicans in this immigration narrative arrive "wet" after having crossed the Rio Grande River to illegally enter the United States. The derogatory label "wetback," commonly applied to undocumented immigrants from Mexico, derives from this migration narrative. The images rely on this commonly held understanding of Mexican immigration to develop their narratives and to engage the reader's attention quickly.

There is also an important reference to women on the two covers. In both cases, it is a woman that is prominently featured as being carried across the water and into the United States. Since we are also warned that an "invasion" is occurring, the prominence of females in the images must be read as conveying an important message about the "invaders." Rather than an invading army, or even the stereotypical male migrant worker, the images suggest a more insidious invasion, one that includes the capacity of the invaders to reproduce. The women being carried into US territory carry with them the seeds of future generations. The images signal not simply a concern over undocumented workers, but a concern with immigrants who stay and form families and, by extension, communities in the United States. The images of the Mexican women being offered up, as it were, to American society bring to mind another image, that of the Trojan Horse. Indeed, a prominent feature of anti-immigrant discourse has been the fears of political unrest by the children of Mexican immigrants and a reconquest of US territory by reproduction. Moreover, reproduction of immigrant families not only raises issues of population growth, but their use of prenatal care and children's health services, education, and other social services. Importantly, the woman on *Newsweek*'s cover also carries a walking

---

24. Claire F. Fox, "The Fence and the River: Representations of the US-Mexico Border in Art and Video," *Discourse* 18, nos. 1, 2 (Fall, Winter 1995-96): 54-83.

stick, which subliminally raises the possibility that she is infirm and may require medical services in the United States.

U.S. News & World Report's August 19, 1985 cover escalated the invasion theme to a new level by suggesting that the US is losing cultural and political control over its territory. The text announces: "The Disappearing Border: Will the Mexican Migration Create a New Nation?" But it is the image that so artfully and so colorfully tells the story of Mexicans taking over the United States. The cover's image represents the relationship of the two nations through the strategic use of the colors in their respective national flags. The red and blue of the US flag are fading up into the sunset (of history?). Central to the image are the large block letters U and S; they are white. These letters sit in a field of green, and rest atop smaller red letters forming the word MEXICO (green and red being the principal colors in the Mexican flag). Placing the white US letters on a field of green suggests that the question of which flag the color belongs is irrelevant, since the US is embedded in – surrounded by – the green of Mexico. The US is already absorbed into Mexico's field.

Inside the magazine, immigration-related issues are addressed in no less than six articles. The first of these is titled "The Disappearing Border," and it sets up the magnitude of the changes wrought by Mexican immigration and profiles the immigrants' socioeconomic characteristics. The article begins by telling a story, a narrative of contemporary Mexican immigration that establishes a "reconquest" theme:

> Now sounds the march of new conquistadors in the American Southwest. The heirs of Cortés and Coronado are rising again in the land their forebears took from the Indians and lost to the Americans. By might of numbers and strength of culture, Hispanics are changing the politics, economy and language in the U.S. states that border Mexico.
>
> Their movement is, despite its quiet and largely peaceful nature, both an invasion and a revolt. At the vanguard are those born here, whose roots are generations deep, who long endured Anglo dominance and rule and who are ascending within the U.S. system to take power they consider their birthright. Behind them comes an unstoppable mass – their kin from below the border who also claim ancestral homelands in the Southwest, which was the northern half of Mexico until the U.S. took it away in the mid-1800s. Like conquistadors of centuries past, they come in quest of fabled cities of gold. America's riches are pulling people all along the continent's Hispanic horn on a great migration to the place they call *El Norte*. (p. 30)

Importantly, in *U.S. News & World Report*'s narrative of invasion and reconquest it is not just recent Mexican immigrants who pose a threat, but even those Americans descended from the first Spanish-speaking explorers of the Southwest. Not even four hundred years of living in the southwest, over a hundred and fifty years as US citizens, reduces the threat posed by Latinos (note the quotation's reference to

Good
Stocks
To Buy
Now

U.S.News
&WORLD REPORT
AUGUST 19, 1985 $1.95

Will the Mexican Migration Create a New Nation?

THE DISAPPEARING BORDER

Fig. 4: *U.S. News & World Report* Cover.

"Hispanics," not Mexican Americans) in the Southwest. Apparently, according to this argument, they have remained socially and linguistically separate, biding their time for a "revolt" and a takeover. In other words, the conspiracy for the reconquest of the Southwest has been in operation for generations and spans centuries. That so far-fetched and unsupported a scenario could be seriously presented in a national magazine attests to how deep the unquestioned assumptions about invasion and reconquest had, by this point, entered into public discourse. There is no critical perspective on the assumption of difference being put forward here, a difference so great and incommensurable that the people so designated are not even subject to the normal expectations of social and cultural change.[25] It is as if Mexican Americans and other Latinos exist in an ahistorical space apart from the life that takes place all around them. They are cast as "alien-citizens" with divided allegiances, perpetual foreigners despite being US citizens by birth, even after many generations.[26] Such notions have become an acceptable part of public discourse even among otherwise learned scholars.

In 1994, Patrick Buchanan, a nationally recognized conservative politician, expressed his deep concern that a Quebec-like threat loomed large in America's future. In an opinion article in the *Los Angeles Times*, Buchanan reasoned that sometime in the near future the majority of Americans would trace their roots not to Europe but to Africa, Asia, Latin America, the Middle East, and the Pacific islands.[27] He thus asked: What would it mean for "America" if, for example, South Texas and Southern California became almost exclusively Latino? He provided the following answer: "Each will have tens of millions of people whose linguistic, historic and cultural roots are in Mexico," and thus "like Eastern Ukraine, where 10 million Russian-speaking 'Ukrainians' now look impatiently to Moscow, not Kiev, as their cultural capital, America could see, in a decade, demands for Quebec-like status for Southern California." For Buchanan, Latino immigrants and their children pose the risk of a separatist movement, which would very likely seek to take over US territory and return it to Mexico's control. That some fifteen years later, the dire predictions of a demand for Quebec-like status by Latinos has not occurred has not given Buchanan pause, as his more recent writings (below) indicate.

The new century was greeted with more alarmist news about the threat posed by Mexicans and other Latinos in the United States. In 2000, writing in *The American Enterprise*, Samuel P. Huntington wrote:

---

25. Leo R. Chavez, "Cultural Change and Cultural Reproduction: Lessons from Research on Transnational Migration," in *Globalization and Change in Fifteen Cultures: Born in One World and Living in Another*, ed. J. Stockard and G. Spindler (Belmont, CA: Thomson-Wadsworth, 2006), 283-303.
26. Mae M. Ngai, *Impossible Subjects: Illegal Aliens and the Making of Modern America* (Princeton: Princeton University Press, 2004).
27. Patrick J. Buchanan, "What Will America Be in 2050?," *Los Angeles Times*, October 18, 1994, B7.

The invasion of over 1 million Mexican civilians is a comparable threat [to 1 million Mexican soldiers] to American societal security, and Americans should react against it with comparable vigor. Mexican immigration looms as a unique and disturbing challenge to our cultural integrity, our national identity, and potentially to our future as a country.[28]

BusinessWeek's March 15, 2004 issue also raised the possibility of an "Hispanic Nation" emerging within the United States. With a large and bold headline, its cover visibly shouts "HISPANIC NATION," followed by "Hispanics are an immigrant group like no other. Their huge numbers are changing old ideas about assimilation. Is America ready?" The cover's text represents the Latino population as unique in contrast to other immigrant groups, who did not form separate independent nations in the United States and for whom assimilation was, supposedly, a smooth and linear process. Assimilation for other immigrant groups, historically and today, is set up as the banner example of the "old ideas about assimilation." We can only assume that the Hispanics that are the subject of BusinessWeek's cover are changing these old ideas in ways that do not reflect assimilation but rather the social, cultural, and linguistic separatism that will result in a separate nation. In other words, BusinessWeek offers yet another rendition of the Quebec model.

Shortly thereafter, Pat Buchanan reiterated his dire predictions of the impact of Latinos on the nation. Speaking on MSNBC on 24 March 2009, he said: "Mexico is the greatest foreign policy crisis I think America faces in the next 20, 30 years. Who is going to care, 30 years from now whether a Sunni or a Shia is in Baghdad or who's ruling in Kabul? We're going to have 135 million Hispanics in the United States by 2050, heavily concentrated in the southwest. The question is whether we're going to survive as a country."[29]

Also in 2004, Samuel Huntington published *Who We Are: Challenges to America's National Identity*, which focused on the threat of Mexican immigration. He repeats the problems with Mexican immigration found in the quotations that began this chapter. He speaks of a Mexican "*reconquista*," a blurring of the border between Mexico and the United States, and the problem of a blending of cultures. This is happening, according to Huntington, because "Mexican immigrants and their progeny have not assimilated into American society as other immigrants did in the past and as many other immigrants are doing now.[30] Mexican immigrants and their children are not assimilating in use of English, educational attainment, occupa-

28. Samuel P. Huntington, "The Special Case of Mexican Immigration: Why Mexico is a Problem," in *The American Enterprise* 11, no. 8 (Dec. 2000): 20-22.
29. Buchanan's comment can be seen online: *MSNBC*, March 24 2009, accessed March 7, 2011, http://www.dailykostv.com/w/001046/.
30. Huntington, *Who Are We Now?*, 222.

tion and incomes, and intermarriage, he writes. "If this trend continues, it could produce a consolidation of the Mexican-dominant areas into an autonomous, culturally and linguistically distinct, economically self-reliant bloc within the United States."[31] In short, the "*reconquista*" leads to the formation of a separate nation, the Quebec model.[32]

Huntington was even more alarmist in his article in the March/April 2004 issue of *Foreign Policy*, in which he compared Latinos, especially Mexicans, to earlier waves of European immigrants, and found that "unlike past immigrant groups, Mexicans and other Latinos have not assimilated into mainstream U.S. culture, forming instead their own political and linguistic enclaves – from Los Angeles to Miami – and rejecting the Anglo-Protestant values that built the American dream."[33] He concluded that:

> In this new era, the single most immediate and most serious challenge to America's traditional identity comes from the immense and continuing immigration from Latin America, especially from Mexico, and the fertility rates of those immigrants compared to black and white American natives.[34]

Huntington's statements are all the more remarkable given the historical context in which they were made. At the time, the United States was waging war in Iraq, deeply involved in the war on terrorism in Afghanistan, and still searching for Bin Laden and al-Qaeda operatives worldwide. And yet amidst all these crises, Huntington singled out Latin American, particularly Mexican, immigration as America's most serious challenge.

Since the election of Barack Obama as President of the United States, there has been a growth in the number of militia groups. Government officials are worried by this trend, and an organization that tracks militias cites two reasons for this growth. The first is the poor economy and a liberal administration led by a black president. But the second reason has to do with "Conspiracy theories about a secret Mexican plan to reclaim the Southwest are also growing amid the public debate about illegal immigration."[35]

---

31. Ibid., 247.
32. Ibid., 230.
33. Samuel Huntington, "The Hispanic Challenge," *Foreign Policy* (March/April 2004).
34. Ibid., 32.
35. Eileen Sullivan, "Officials see rise in militia groups across US," *Associated Press*, August 12, 2009.

Is the Latino Threat Real?

The public discourse on Mexican and other Latin American immigration to the United States over the last forty years or so has characterized not only Latino immigrants as a threat to the nation but also their children, even going back for generations. This threat can be summarized as follows:

Latinos are unassimilable. Either they do not desire or do not have the ability to socially and culturally integrated into the nation.

Latinos do not learn English. They do not have a desire to participate with other members of the English-speaking nation.

Latinos live in their own social worlds. They do not desire to mix socially with members of the non-Latino community.

Latinos are immutable. They reproduce their own cultural world, which is made possible because they live apart from larger society, socially and linguistically.

Latinos are a reproductive threat. Their fertility levels are pathologically high and remain so because their cultural beliefs about womanhood and manhood value having many children. Adherence to the reproductive restrictions of Catholicism reinforces rampant fertility.

Because of these patterns of social and linguistic isolation, Latinos desire a reconquest of the US Southwest, or what has been called a Latino Quebec.

How accurate are these characterizations of Latinos?

To examine these characterizations of Latinos, we can analyze survey data collected in 2006 on 805 Latinos and 396 whites in Orange County.[36] Orange

---

36. The Orange County Survey was conducted in 2006 under the auspices of the Center for Research on Latinos in a Global Society (CRLGS), University of California, Irvine. The Interviewing Service of America conducted the telephone survey between January 4 and 31, 2006, using trained interviewers in both English and Spanish. The survey used random-digit dialing on a sample from a database that includes all US directory-published household numbers, both listed and unlisted, combined with a sample that had identified Hispanic markers. Both listed and unlisted numbers were included, avoiding potential bias due to exclusion of households with unlisted numbers (see SSI Survey Sampling Inc., *Statistical Analysis of Sample*). The cooperation rate was 70 percent. Interviews were in the interviewee's language of choice. Eligible participants were English- or Spanish-speaking men and women, 18 years of age or older, who were not institutionalized and who identified themselves as white (Anglo, Caucasian, non-Hispanic white) or Latino (Hispanic or more specific ethnic identifiers such as Mexican, Mexican American, Salvadoran, etc.).

County is the third most populous county in California, with an estimated 302,048 inhabitants in 2006.[37] It covers an area of 789 square miles, is largely urban, and contains 34 cities and numerous unincorporated communities. Latinos accounted for 32.5 percent of the county's population in 2005. Most Latinos are of Mexican heritage, but Latino immigrants from other nations in Latin America, particularly Central America, also live in the county. Latinos are found in greater concentrations in the northern half of the county, which includes Santa Ana, where about 4 out of 5 residents are Latino. The southern half of the county has been an area of rapid growth in new middle class, upper-middle class, and exclusive residential communities. Latino immigrants often work in south county communities but find less expensive housing in the many working class communities in the northern part of the county.

Of the 805 Latinos surveyed, most (84.7 percent) were Mexican immigrants or of Mexican origin. There were, however, Salvadoran and other Central American immigrants, some South Americans, and a few immigrants from the Caribbean. Of the Latinos surveyed, 573 (71.2 percent) were first generation, meaning that they were born in a foreign country and migrated to the United States.[38] Of these, 128 respondents, or 22.3 percent of the first generation Latino respondents, were in the 1.5 generation (foreign-born but migrated to the US under age 15). Most (105; 82 percent) of the 1.5 interviewees were born in Mexico, with the rest coming in smaller numbers from the same countries mentioned above. The second generation, those born in the United States with at least one foreign-born parent, accounted for 16.4 percent (N=131) of the Latinos sampled. Latinos of the third generation (or higher), born in the United States with both parents also US-born, accounted for 11.9 percent (N=95) of the sample.

Do Latinos learn English? If it were true that Latinos did not learn English, there would be little or no change across generations, let alone use of English among immigrants. Over time, however, Latinos in Orange County are more likely to speak all or mostly English at home. Even among the immigrant first generation, almost a quarter speak English, or are bilingual, at home. The considerable number of 1.5 generation immigrants, who grow up in the United States, helps explain why some of the first generation use English. The increasing use of English among the children of immigrants is not only found here but in other studies as well.[39]

---

37. US Census Bureau. "State and County Quickfacts: Orange County, California." Vol. 2007 (2007).

38. Of the 805 Latinos surveyed, 6 were missing values on this question. The percentages cited in the discussion here are based on the total of 799 who answered the question.

39. Kristin E. Espinosa and Douglas S. Massey, "Determinants of English Proficiency among Mexican Migrants to the United States," *International Migration Review* 31 (1997): 28-50; Alejeando Portes and Richard Schauffler, "Language Acquisition and Loss among Children of Immigrants," in *Origins and Destinies: Immigration, Race, and Ethnicity in America*, ed. S. Pedraza and R. Rumbaut (Belmont, CA: Wadsworth Publishing, 1996), 432-43.

Table 1: Language spoken by Latinos at home, by percentages of generations.

	1st Gen.	2nd Gen.	3rd+ Gen.
All or mostly Spanish	77.4	20.8	3.8
Bilingual	17.5	28.8	7.6
All or mostly English	5.6	50.4	88.6

Source: Center for Research on Latinos in a Global Society Orange County, California Survey, 2006.

If Latinos were truly socially isolated, we would expect that they would indicate few if any friends among members of the larger population. However, Latinos in Orange County said they had friends from many different ethnic groups. As Table 2 indicates, even first generation Latino immigrants have non-Latino friends. By the second generation, most Latinos have white friends and many have friends from other ethnic groups. Relatively low numbers of African Americans live in Orange County.

Table 2: Non-Latino friends of Latinos, by ethnicity and percentages of Latino generations.

	1st Gen	2nd Gen	3rd+ Gen
White friends	48.3	80.2	93.7
Asian American friends	26.4	53.4	65.3
Persian friends	9.8	25.2	29.5

Source: Center for Research on Latinos in a Global Society Orange County, California Survey, 2006.

Latinos also marry non-Latinos, which is another indicator of social integration (Table 3). By the second generation, almost a quarter of Latinos are married to non-Latinos. By the third-plus generations, about half of Latinos are married to non-Latinos. Among whites in the survey, 85.7 percent were married to other whites.

Table 3: Latino-Latino marriages by percentages of generation.

	1st Gen	2nd Gen	3rd+ Gen
Spouse Latina	98.4	76.9	51.8

Source: Center for Research on Latinos in a Global Society Orange County, California Survey, 2006.

One area where we might expect a strong adherence to cultural beliefs is religion. However, even here Latinos are not immutable, but do change in response to social influences. As Table 4 indicates, by the third generation, close to half of Latinos in our sample said they were no longer Catholics. They had taken up the beliefs of a different religion, typically a form of Protestantism and Evangelicalism. If changing religious beliefs can serve as a guide, Latinos do change in response to ideas with which they come into contact in the larger society. They do not live in a cultural bubble separate from the rest of society.

Table 4: Latinos and Religion in Orange County, percentages by Latino generations.

	1st Gen	2nd Gen	3rd+ Gen
Catholic	77.4	65.6	51.1
Protestant/ Christian	12.3	28	32.6
Other	3.7	1.6	8.7

Source: Center for Research on Latinos in a Global Society Orange County, California Survey, 2006.

Latina fertility has also been characterized as out of control. However, the data from Orange County suggests that here, too, the story is not so simple. Whites generally in the United States are an aging population compared to Latinas. Not surprisingly, Latinas in our sample were younger (mean age 42) than white women (mean age 58). The appropriate comparison, therefore, would be with women under 45 years of age for both groups. Table 5 indicates the number of children ever born for Latinas and white women of all ages and under 45 years of age in our sample. White women had the lowest number of children, but Latinas did not exhibit rampant fertility rates. First generation immigrant women of all ages had the most children, with 2.38 per woman. This is comparable to the current fertility rate in Mexico, which itself has seen a dramatic drop in the number of births per woman.[40] Indeed, some demographers are predicting that falling fertility rates in Mexico will mean a shortage of available young workers to migrate to the United States in the not too distant future.[41]

---

40. Population Reference Bureau, World Population Data Sheet, Total Births Per Woman, Mexico, vol. 2004 (2003); Elena Zuniga et al., "Cuadernos de salud reproductiva: Republica Mexicana," Mexico City: *Consejo Nacional de la Poblacion* (2000), accessed March 7, 2011, http://www.conapo.gob.mx/index.php?option=com_content&view=article&id=295&Itemid=15.

41. Philip Martin, "Mexico-US Migration," in *Nafta Revisited: Achievements and Challenges*, ed. G. Hufbauer and J. Schott (Washington, DC: Institute for International Economics, 2005), 441-86.

Table 5: Total children ever born, Latinas and White women in Orange County.				
	1st Gen	2nd Gen	3rd+ Gen	Whites
All ages	2.38	1.63	1.78	2.21
<45	1.91	1.28	1.27	1.16

Source: Center for Research on Latinos in a Global Society Orange County, California Survey, 2006.

Concluding Remarks

Nira Yuval-Davis has observed that: "The boundaries that the politics of belonging is concerned with are the boundaries of the political community of belonging, the boundaries that separate the world population into 'us' and 'them'."[42] US public discourse on the nation and immigration has focused on Latino immigrants, particularly Mexicans and their descendants, as a threat, as an anti-nation, and as an invading force. Academics and media pundits alike have made claims about the behavior and intentions of Latinos, which apparently include desires to remain apart from the larger society, to not learn English, to not assimilate culturally or socially into US society, and to form a fifth column – that is, an internal threat of those who will eventually take over territory and move to separate from the English speaking nation-state. High fertility levels among Latinos fuel the demographic reconquest. The fertility argument relies on the assumption that such rampant fertility increases Latino families only, since out-group marriage would undermine the threat of a demographic takeover.

Despite these often-repeated characterizations of Latinos, I find that Latinos are integrating into life in the United States. Latinos do learn English over time in the United States. The real problem is not that they retain Spanish forever; rather, it is the rapid loss of non-English languages among the children of immigrants. This constitutes the loss of an important linguistic resource in our contemporary globalized lives. Latinos also integrate socially, making friends among non-Latinos and marrying non-Latinos. Latinos are also not immutable. Their social relations among members of the larger society lead to cultural changes, even in an area as deeply personal as religious preferences. Latinas are also not immutable when it comes to fertility patterns. Women throughout the world are having fewer children, and Latinas are no exception to this trend. Latinas have an interest in fertility control and the benefits of having fewer children.

In the highly charged political debate over immigration and immigration reform, the perpetuation of such negative representations of Latinos in public discourse

---

42. Nira Yuval-Davis, "Belonging," 204.

does a disservice to the actual difficulties Latinos face as they try to make better lives for themselves and their children in the United States. It also does a disservice to the search for a rational solution to the nation's immigration problems. Blaming Latinos for imagined threats to the nation obscures their economic, social, and cultural contributions to the nation. Without a more balanced view of Latinos and their place in the nation, immigration reform will continue to be an elusive goal.

Bibliography

Anderson, Benedict. *Imagined Communities*. London: Verso, 1983.

Bloemraad, Irene. *Becoming a Citizen: Incorporating Immigrants and Refugees in the United States and Canada*. Berkeley: University of California Press, 2006.

Bosniak, Linda S. "Citizenship Denationalized." *Indiana Journal of Global Legal Studies* 7 (2000): 447-509.

Brimelow, Peter. "Time to Rethink Immigration?" *The National Review*, June 22, 1992, 30-46.

Buchanan, Patrick J. "What Will America Be In 2050?" *Los Angeles Times*, October 28, 1994, B7.

Chavez, Leo R. "Outside the Imagined Community: Undocumented Settlers and Experiences of Incorporation." *American Ethnologist* 18 (1991): 257-278.

Chavez, Leo R. "Immigration Reform and Nativism: The Nationalist Response to the Transnationalist Challenge," in *Immigrants Out! The New Nativism and the Anti-Immigrant Impulse in the United States*, edited by J.F. Perea., 61-77. New York: New York University Press, 1997.

Chavez, Leo R. *Covering Immigration: Popular Images and the Politics of the Nation*. Berkeley: University of California Press, 2001.

Chavez, Leo R. "Culture Change and Cultural Reproduction: Lessons from Research on Transnational Migration," in *Globalization and Change in Fifteen Cultures: Born in one World and Living in Another*, edited by J. Stockard and G. Spindler, 283-303. Belmont, CA: Thomson-Wadsworth, 2006.

Chavez, Leo R. *The Latino Threat: Constructing Immigrants, Citizens and the Nation*. Stanford: Stanford University Press, 2008.

Coutin, Susan Bibler, and Phyllis Pease Chock. "Your Friend, The Illegal: Definition and Paradox in Newspaper Accounts of U.S. Immigration Reform." *Identities* 2 (1995):123-148.

Espinosa, Kristin E., and Douglas S. Massey. "Determinants of English Proficiency among Mexican Migrants to the United States." *International Migration Review* 31 (1997): 28-50.

Foucault, Michel. *The Order of Things*: New York: Vintage Books, 1970.

Fox, Claire F. "The Fence and the River: Representations of the US-Mexico Border in Art and Video." *Discourse* 18, nos. 1, 2 (Fall,Winter 1995-96): 54-83.

Gerstle, Gary.*American Crucible: Race and Nation in the Twentieth Century*. Princeton: Princeton University Press, 2001.

Hall, Stuart. "The Question of Cultural Identity," in *Modernity: An Introduction to Modern Societies*, edited by S. Hall, D. Held, D. Hubert, and K. Thompson, 595-634. Cambridge, MA: Blackwell Publishers, 1996.

Higham, John. *Strangers in the Land: Patterns of American Nativism, 1860-1925*. New Brunswick: Rutgers University Press, 2002 [1955].

Hollinger, David A. *Postethnic America: Beyond Multiculturalism*. New York: Basic Books, 1995.

Huntington, Samuel P. "The Special Case of Mexican Immigration: Why Mexico is a Problem." *The American Enterprise* 11, no. 8 (Dec. 2000): 20-22.

Huntington, Samuel P. "The Hispanic Challenge." *Foreign Policy* (March/April 2004): 30-45.

Huntington, Samuel P. *Who We Are: The Challenges to America's National Identity*. New York: Simon & Schuster, 2004.

Kearney, Michael. "The Local and the Global: The Anthropology of Globalization and Transnationalism." *Annual Review of Anthropology* 24 (1995): 547-65.

Kennedy, John R. *A Nation of Immigrants*. New York: Harper & Row Publishers, 1986.

Martin, Philip. "Mexico-US Migration," in *Nafta Revisited: Achievements and Challenges*, edited by G. Hufbauer and J. Schott, 441-486. Washington, DC: Institute for International Economics, 2005.

Ngai, Mae M. *Impossible Subjects: Illegal Aliens and the Making of Modern America*. Princeton: Princeton University Press, 2004.

Omi, Michael, and Howard Winant. *Racial Formation in the United States: From the 1960s to the 1990s*. New York: Routledge, 1994.

Ong, Aihwa. "Cultural Citizenship as Subject-Making: Immigrants Negotiate Racial and Cultural Boundaries in the United States." *Current Anthropology* 37, no. 5 (1996): 737-762.

Perea, Juan F., ed. *Immigrants Out! The New Nativism and the Anti-Immigrant Impulse in the United States*. New York: New York University Press, 1997.

Portes, Alejandro, and Richard Schauffler. "Language Acquisition and Loss Among Children of Immigrants," in *Origins and Destinies: Immigration, Race, and Ethncity in America*, edited by S. Pedraza and R. Rumbaut, 432-443. Belmont, CA: Wadsworth Publishing Company, 1996.

Population Reference Bureau. World Population Data Sheet, Total Births Per Woman, Mexico, vol. 2004 (2003).

Roberts, Dorothy. *Killing the Black Body: Race, Reproduction, and the Meaning of Liberty*. New York: Pantheon Books, 1997.

Rodriguez, Clara E. *Latin Looks: Images of Latinas and Latinos in the U.S. Media*. Boulder, CO: Westview Press, 1997.

Rosaldo, Renato. "Cultural Citizenship in San Jose, California." *Polar* 17 (1994): 57-63.

Rumbaut, Rubén G., Douglas S. Massey, and Frank D. Bean. "Linguistic Life Expectancies: Immigrant Language Retention in Southern California." *Population and Development Review* 32, no. 3 (2006): 447-460.

Said, Edward W. *Orientalism*. New York: Random House, 1978.

Said, Edward W. *Covering Islam: How the Media and the Experts Determine How We See the Rest of the World*. New York: Vintage Books, 1996.

Santa Ana, Otto. *Brown Tide Rising*. Austin: University of Texas Press, 2002.

Sax, William S. "The Hall of Mirrors: Orientalism, Anthropology, and the Other." *American Anthropologist* 100 (1998): 292-301.

Schlesinger, Arthur M. Jr. *The Disuniting of America*. New York: W.W. Norton, 1992.

Segal, Daniel A. "Living Ancestors: Nationalism and the Past in Postcolonial Trinidad and Tobago," in *Remapping Memory: Politics of Time Space*, edited by Jonathan Boyarin. Minneapolis: University of Minnesota Press, 1994.

Simon, Rita J., and Susan H. Alexander. *The Ambivalent Welcome: Print Media, Public Opinion and Immigration*. Westport, CT: Praeger Publishers, 1993.

Steinberg, Stephen. *The ethnic myth: Race, ethnicity, and class in Amerca*. Boston: Beacon Press, 1989.

Stolcke, Verena. "Talking Culture: New Boundaries, New Rhetorics of Exclusion in Europe." *Current Anthropology* 36 (1995): 1-24.

Sullivan, Eileen. "Officials see rise in miliitias across US." *Associated Press*, August 12, 2009.

US Census Bureau. "State and County Quickfacts: Orange County, California." Vol. 2007 (2007).

Woodward, Kathryn. "Concepts of Identity and Difference," in *Identity and Difference*, edited by K. Woodward. Thousand Oaks: Sage Publications, 1997.

Yuval-Davis, Nira. "Belonging and the politics of belonging." *Patterns of Prejudice* 40, no. 3 (2006): 197-214.

Zuniga, Elena, Beatriz Zubieta, and Cristina Araya. "Cuadernos de salud reproductiva: Republica Mexicana." Mexico City: Consejo Nacional de la Poblacion (2000).

10 Immigration and the Intersection of Ethnic and National Narratives: The Case of Ethnic Mexicans in the United States

Tomás R. Jiménez

Several years ago, while still a graduate student, I took a trip to New York City where I visited Ellis Island, the primary entry point for 12 million European immigrants who came to the United States mostly between 1880 and 1920. Ellis Island no longer serves as a migrant screening station. It is now a United States National Park Service museum that contains a history of the Island, an ancestral research center in which visitors can search for immigrant ancestors who might have passed through the Island, and a Wall of Honor on which visitors can have the names of their immigrant ancestors inscribed for a fee. As a student of immigration to the United States, I was struck by how the museum extolled immigration as a central aspect of American national identity. In no uncertain terms, the Ellis Island museum embodies the United States' view of itself as a "nation of immigrants."

The symbolism of Ellis Island became clearer to me some years later when I moved to San Diego, California, for my first academic position. San Diego sits at the southwestern most point of the United States and shares an international border with Tijuana, Mexico. At the same time that European immigrants passed through Ellis Island, thousands of Mexican migrants crossed through San Diego on their way to destinations in the United States. Yet today the San Diego-Tijuana border crossing has no monuments, museums, or ancestral research center to commemorate this history. Instead, it is the busiest and one of the most fortified border crossings in the world. Thousands of people – workers, tourists, migrants, and smugglers – cross each day. Hundreds of cars line the highway leading through the main passage point, and US Immigration and Customs Enforcement Agents inspect vehicles for contraband and unauthorized migrants. Heavy metal fences and Border Patrol agents guard the area surrounding the main cross-border thoroughfare, and stretching east and west, a tall (and in some places multi-layered) fence separates the two countries. Along some portions of the border, large stadium lights illuminate patches of open space where migrants may attempt to cross. Border Patrol agents roam these areas in all-terrain vehicles searching for drugs, unauthorized crossers, and those who smuggle them. In more remote areas of the border east of San Diego, white wooden crosses memorialize individuals who have died attempting the trip north. It is also in these remote areas where organized "civil defense corps," like the Minutemen, monitor the border.

Comparing Ellis Island to the San Diego-Tijuana border crossing is a window into how immigration shapes both ethnic and national identities in the United States. The nostalgia found at Ellis Island is a function of the fact that the mostly European-origin wave of immigration that passed through the Island ended nearly 90 years ago. The descendants of these European immigrants – "white ethnics" – have become well integrated into US society, both socioeconomically and cultur-ally.[1] The fact that this wave of immigration ended so long ago, combined with the successful assimilation of the descendants of those immigrants, means that white-ethnic groups are not defined as foreigners, but as American ethnics who have fulfilled the American dream. The historical and psychological distance from the immigrant point of origin allows the individuals attached to these ethnic groups, and indeed the entire nation, to look upon that immigrant experience through a nostalgic lens.

As the scene at the San Diego-Tijuana border crossing suggests, neither people of Mexican descent, nor the nation as a whole, view Mexican immigration with the same nostalgia. Though Mexican immigrants came to the United States during the early part of the twentieth century, the later generation descendants of early Mexican immigrants – "Mexican Americans" – live in a US society in which immigration from their ethnic homeland has been continuous for nearly a century, but particularly heavy in the last 30 years. Ethnic Mexicans sit at center stage in ongoing debates about the "immigration crisis" in the United States. Foreign-born individuals make up nearly 40 % of the group, defining ethnic Mexicans demographically as well as in the national discourse on immigration. The degree and kind of assimilation expe-rienced by ethnic Mexicans remains an open question. Many scholars and pundits argue that ethnic Mexicans are not assimilating socioeconomically, displaying a negative form of cultural assimilation,[2] while others argue that their assimilation

1. Richard D. Alba, *Italian Americans: Into the Twilight of Ethnicity* (Englewood Cliffs, NJ: Prentice-Hall, 1985); *Ethnic Identity: The Transformation of White America* (New Haven: Yale University Press, 1990); Herbert J. Gans, "Symbolic Ethnicity: The Future of Ethnic Groups and Cultures in America," *Ethnic and Racial Studies* 2 (January 1979): 1-20; Mary C. Waters, *Ethnic Options: Choosing Identities in America* (Berkeley: University of California Press, 1990).

2. Samuel P. Huntington, *Who Are We? The Challenges to America's National Identity* (New York: Simon & Schuster, 2004); David E. López and Ricardo Stanton-Salazar, "Mexican Americans: A Second Generation at Risk," in *Ethnicities: Children of Immigrants in America*, ed. A. Portes and R. G. Rumbaut (Berkeley: University of California Press, 2001), 57-90; Alejandro Portes and Rubén. G. Rumbaut, *Immigrant America: A Portrait* (Berkeley, CA: University of California Press, 2006); Edward E. Telles and Vilma Ortiz, *Generations of Exclusion: Mexican Americans, Assimilation, and Race* (New York, NY: Russell Sage Foundation, 2008).

is progressing slowly and remains incomplete.[3] The popular perception is that ethnic Mexicans represent, at best, an American dream that remains unfulfilled, and at worst, an American dream gone bad.

I argue that there are numerous factors accounting for the difference between European-origin groups and ethnic Mexicans, including histories of colonization, race, and regional concentration. But no other factor contributes more to the difference in how these groups are defined in the popular imagination than immigration. The fact that European immigration stopped nearly 90 years ago has allowed for peoples once regarded as swarthy foreigners to become American ethnics. In contrast, the ongoing nature of emigration from Mexico to the United States means that ethnic Mexicans, including those whose generation roots extend deep into US history, continue to be defined as foreign ethnic group.

This chapter draws on in-depth interviews and observations with later-generation Mexican Americans to show how ongoing Mexican immigration shapes the ethnic identity of these descendants of early arriving Mexican immigrants. Interviews and observations show how immigration defines Mexican ethnicity – the Mexican ethnic "narrative" – in ways that prevent all people of Mexican descent from being written into an American national narrative rooted in *historical*, not contemporary or ongoing immigration. I argue that the "nation of immigrants" is an ideal. In reality, the role that immigration plays in America's national identity suggests an amended version of this narrative: the United States is a nation of *descendants of immigrants* who overcame the hardships of immigration and assimilation.

Ethnicity and Nationhood as Narratives

Ethnic identity is a subjective understanding of self and others based on a putative sense of ancestry, a shared history, and a set of symbols and practices that capture the epitome of that group.[4] Like ethnic identity, national identity revolves around claims of shared history and a set of symbols and practices that capture the essence of nationhood. National identity also involves claims to political unity and autonomy.

---

3. Frank D. Bean, Susan K. Brown, Mark A. Leach, and James Bachmeier, "Becoming U.S. Stakeholders: Legalization and Integration Among Mexican Immigrants and their Descendants" (Newport Beach, CA: Merage Foundation for the American Dream, 2007); Susan K. Brown, "Structural Assimilation Revisted: Mexican-Origin Nativity and Cross-Ethnic Primary Ties," *Social Forces* 85, no. 1 (2006): 75-92; Susan K. Brown, "Delayed Spatial Assimilation: Multigenerational Incorporation of the Mexican-Origin Population in Los Angeles," *City & Community* 6, no. 3 (2007): 193-209.

4. Stephen Cornell and Douglas Hartmann, *Ethnicity and Race: Making Identities in a Changing World*, 2nd ed. (Thousand Oaks, CA: Pine Forge Press, 2006).

At their core, ethnic and national identities are narratives – stories that groups of people tell about what it means to be "one of us" ("or one of them"). With regard to ethnic groups, Stephen Cornell explains that "ethnic categories are categories of collective life stories created through the selection, plotting, and interpretation of events that connect the experiences of a group of individuals.[5] Groups select events that may be big or small; episodic or quotidian; historical or ongoing. These events are plotted "in causal, sequential, associational, or other ways," and linked to a particular ethnic group.[6] Events are then interpreted, imbued with significance and subjected to claims about the extent to which the events themselves and the way they are plotted define the group. The result of this process is the construction of a narrative that "captures the central understanding of what it means to be a member of [a] group."[7] Put another way, an ethnic narrative is an account that group insiders (and outsiders) tell about who "we" (and "they") are.

Rogers Smith also draws on the idea of narratives – "stories of peoplehood" – as a basis for national identity.[8] According to Smith, national identities are institutionalized stories of a people based on economic, political, or ethically constitutive grounds. Political leaders can effectively draw on these stories to mobilize their followers so long as the followers regard these stories as a legitimate reflection of their own collective sense of political peoplehood: so long as they see the stories of the nation as *their* stories.

Conceptualizing ethnic and national identities as narratives requires close attention to the *events* that make up the narratives. In the United States, immigration is a central event that defines both the ethnic and American national narratives. American ethnic groups regularly celebrate their culture and history by acknowledging the homeland to which they trace their roots, and by celebrating the journey from that homeland and the subsequent integration in US society. Similarly, the United States, as a nation, celebrates immigration as a defining event in its larger national narrative. The common proclamation made by Americans and their leaders that the United States is a "nation of immigrants" captures the central role of immigration in the national myth of origins.[9] Indeed, one of the most recognizable symbols of national pride, the Statue of Liberty, is widely associated with the country's immigrant history.

In the US context, when an ethnic narrative includes immigration, it may seem

---

5. Stephan Cornell, "That's the Story of Our Life," in *Narrative and Multiplicity in Constructing Ethnic Identities*, ed. P.R. Spickard and W.J. Burroughs (Philadelphia, PA: Temple University Press, 2000), 45.
6. Ibid., 43.
7. Ibid., 42.
8. Rogers M. Smith, *Stories of Peoplehood: The Politics and Morals of Political Membership* (New York: Cambridge University Press, 2003).
9. Cf. John F. Kennedy, *A Nation of Immigrants* (New York, NY: Harper-Collins, 1964).

at first blush to create a perfect link between ethnic and national belonging. But the mere existence of immigration as a core event in an ethnic narrative does not allow all ethnic groups to link seamlessly their ethnic narrative to the American national one. As Cornell points out, the sequential plotting of events is key to how narratives unfold.[10] When immigration is plotted as a past event – one that can be looked upon with a large degree of nostalgia – in an ethnic narrative, the link between ethnic and national narratives is an easier fit. But when immigration is an event that is plotted closer to the present in an ethnic narrative, the folding of the ethnic into the national narrative is far more precarious because immigration does not carry with it the nostalgia that eases the melding of ethnic and national stories of peoplehood.

Ethnic Mexicans and Immigrant Replenishment

For ethnic Mexicans, the event of immigration has been virtually uninterrupted for a century, and can thus be plotted at almost any point in the Mexican ethnic narrative. The first significant presence of Mexicans in the United States dates to 1848, when the United States and Mexico signed the Treaty of Guadalupe Hidalgo, ending the US-Mexican War. The Treaty stipulated that Mexico cede what is today the southwestern United States for $18 million. The Treaty also granted ethnic Mexicans who lived in the southwestern territory – likely no more than 50,000[11] – American citizenship. But the first significant wave of Mexican migrants did not begin entering the United States until shortly after the turn of the twentieth century. The Mexican Revolution, combined with a growing demand for labor in the expanding agriculture industry in the United States, American labor shortages during World War I, and diminished numbers of Chinese and Japanese immigrant laborers "pulled" Mexicans northward in search of work.[12] In Mexico, agrarian reform induced mobility among Mexican peasants, while an expanding rail system linked Mexico and the United States, easing the movement of migrants northward.[13]

10. Cornell, "That's the Story.".
11. A.J. Jaffe, Ruth. M. Cullen, and Thomas D. Boswell, *The Changing Demography of Spanish Americans* (New York, NY: Academic Press, 1980); cited in Douglas S. Massey, Jorge Durand, and Nolan J. Malone, *Beyond Smoke and Mirrors: Mexican Immigration in an Era of Free Trade* (New York: Russell Sage Foundation, 2002), 25.
12. In 1882, Congress passed the Chinese Exclusion Act, effectively ending the flow of Chinese workers to the United States. When Japanese immigrant laborers took their place, similar nativist sentiment took hold, and the US and Japanese governments signed the "Gentlemen's Agreement" in 1907, whereby Japan agreed to stop issuing passports to Japanese citizens who wished to emigrate to the United States.
13. Lawrence A. Cardoso, *Mexican Emigration to the United States, 1897-1931* (Tucson, AZ: University of Arizona Press, 1980).

The US Congress passed a set of restrictive immigration laws in the 1910s and 1020s, culminating with the 1924 National Origins Quota act. But these laws were primarily designed to reduce immigration from southern and eastern Europe, and left the legal pathway open for Mexican immigration. Lawmakers and rank-and-file Americans saw Mexicans as a preferred source of labor since it was widely believed that they would eventually return to Mexico rather than permanently settle. But the onslaught of the Great Depression cast Mexican immigrants as low-wage replacements for American workers, souring perceptions of Mexican immigrant labor. In response, the US government sponsored mass repatriations of Mexican immigrants during the 1930s, the only decade during which Mexican immigration declined.[14]

World War II and a growing agricultural industry in the western United States created renewed demand for Mexican immigrant labor. Beginning in 1942, the United States and Mexico entered into a bi-lateral guest worker program, known as the Emergency Farm Labor Program, but more popularly called the "Bracero Program." For more than two decades, until 1964, the Bracero Program supplied low-wage labor to American agriculture primarily in the Southwest.[15] A year after the program concluded, Congress passed sweeping immigration reform that allocated visas more equitably across countries and regions of the world. The reform included a cap on nations in the Western Hemisphere, including Mexico, and represented the first formal limit on Mexican immigration.[16]

The post-Bracero Program era touched off a period of unauthorized Mexican immigration that continues to the present. Former braceros who stayed in the United States anchored social networks that reduced the cost of migration for subsequent Mexican migrants.[17] More recent economic and policy forces, combined with economic insecurity in Mexico, have perpetuated the rise in unauthorized Mexican immigration. The most notable was the passage of the 1986 Immigration Reform and Control Act (IRCA), which provided amnesty to more than two million unauthorized Mexican immigrants, added border security, and introduced fines for employers who knowingly hired unauthorized immigrants. Each of these provisions, combined with the militarization of the US-Mexico border in the 1990s, had the

---

14. According to Massey, Durand, and Malone, 458,000 Mexicans were deported from 1929-1937; see *Beyond Smoke and Mirrors*, 34.

15. Kitty Calavita, *Inside the State: The Bracero Program, Immigration and the I.N.S.* (New York: Routledge, 1992).

16. The 1965 immigration act placed 20,000-person per year quota on all Eastern Hemispheric nations, and a total cap was set at 170,000 for the entire Eastern Hemisphere. The 1965 law also capped visas for Western Hemispheric countries at 120,000 per year, without stipulating a per-country limit preference. In 1976, Congress imposed a 20,000 per country, per year visa limit on Western Hemisphere countries (excluding family reunification), including Mexico.

17. Massey, Durand, and Malone, *Beyond Smoke and Mirrors*, 42.

unintended consequence of perpetuating unauthorized Mexican immigration.[18] Additionally, the North American Free Trade Agreement (NAFTA), a tri-lateral trade accord between Canada, the United States, and Mexico that took effect in 1994, further integrated the US and Mexican economies, creating the conditions that initiate and perpetuate migration.[19] Meanwhile, periods of economic instability in Mexico during the last three decades have widened the wage differentials that make northward migration attractive to Mexican migrants.

Today, Mexico is the largest source of immigration to the United States. Mexican immigrants make up 30 % of the roughly 38 million foreign-born individuals in the United States[20] A large proportion of the Mexican immigrant population is unauthorized. Passel and Cohn estimate that 56 % of all Mexican immigrants are in the United States without authorization.[21]

Mexican migration to the United States is distinct from other immigrant groups in many respects, including its size, proximity of the sending country, and prevalence of unauthorized entry. But the long history of Mexican immigration makes it especially distinctive.

Figure 1 compares the number of foreign-born individuals from Mexico and several prominent European sending countries with deep histories of immigration.[22] Unlike the immigrant groups commonly invoked as part of the United States' history of migration, immigration from Mexico continued even after emigration from these European countries declined. Indeed, Mexico is the only prominent source of migration to span every period of modern United States immigration:[23] the classic period (1880-1920), the hiatus (1920-1965), and the contemporary period (1965-present).[24]

---

18. Wayne A. Cornelius, "Controlling 'Unwanted' Immigration: Lessons from the United States, 1993-2004," *Journal of Ethnic and Migration Studies* 31, no.4 (2005): 775-794.
19. Douglas S. Massey, "Why Does Immigration Occur?: A Theoretical Synthesis," *The Handbook of International Migration: The American Experience*, ed. C. Hirschman, P. Kasinitz, and J. DeWind (New York, NY: Russell Sage Foundation, 1999).
20. Migration Policy Institute. 2011. "2009 American Community Survey and Census Data on the Foreign Born by State." Washington, DC. http://www.migrationinformation.org/DataHub/acscensus.cfm accessed March 7, 2011.
21. Jeffrey S. Passel and D'Vera Cohn."Trends in Unauthorized Immigration: Undocumented Inflow Now Trails Legal Inflow" (Washington, DC: Pew Hispanic Center, 2008).
22. Other countries not listed in Figure 1 have long immigration histories in the United States. However, I compare Mexican immigration to European immigration because the sociological literature on later generation individuals is largely based on descendants from the latter.
23. Douglas S. Massey, "The New Immigration and Ethnicity in the United States," *Population and Development Review* 21, no.3 (1995): 631-652.
24. The immigrant character of the Mexican-origin population was persistent throughout the twentieth century. As González-Baker et al. show, foreign-born Mexicans made up at least 32.1 % (and as much as 65.7 %) of the

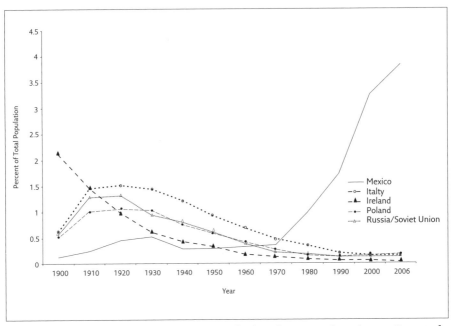

Figure 1. Number of Foreign-born from Mexico and Selected European Countries as a Percent of US Total Population, 1900-2006

In stark contrast to the white ethnics, Mexican Americans who trace their roots in the United States to the earliest waves of Mexican immigration live in a US society in which their co-ethnic immigration population continually adds to their numbers and informs the dominant narrative of ethnic Mexicans as a foreign group.

Studying the Mexican Ethnic Narrative on the Ground Floor

In order to understand how the ethnic Mexican narrative forms, I studied the every-day ways in which Mexican Americans experience ethnicity. My analysis is based on 123 in-depth interviews with later-generation Mexican Americans in Garden City,

---

total Mexican-origin population throughout the twentieth century, except in 1970, when they constituted only 16.7 % of the Mexican-origin population. Susan González-Baker et al., "The Growing Importance of Migration from Mexico," in *Crossings: Mexican Immigration in Interdisciplinary Perspectives*, ed. Mercelo M,. Suarez-Orozco (Cambridge, MA: Harvard University Press, 1998), 79-105. Although the recent and heavy influx of Mexican immigration represents an unprecedented upsurge in absolute terms, the foreign-born Mexican population does not constitute an unusually large proportion of the total Mexican-origin population relative to previous time periods (38 % in 2000). See González-Baker et al., "The Growing Importance."

Kansas, and Santa Maria, California. I also took nearly a hundred pages of typed observational notes and conducted roughly 20 interviews with informants, such as police officers, teachers, city officials, and employers. These data formed the basis for a larger project on the effect that ongoing immigration has on the assimilation and ethnic-identity formation of later generation Mexican Americans.[25]

Garden City is a small beef-packing town located in the southwestern corner of Kansas. The 2000 US Census reports that of the town's 28,451 residents, 9,865, or 34.7 % are of Mexican origin. Roughly half of the Mexican-origin population is foreign-born. The history of Mexican immigration to Garden City is best described as interrupted. Between roughly 1900 and 1930, Mexican immigrants came to the area to build the railroads and work the sugar beet fields.[26] But Mexican immigrant settlement shifted away from Kansas to other states in the middle of the twentieth century, and there was a nearly 40-year hiatus in Mexican immigration to the state.[27] In 1980, beef-packing plants opened in Garden City, and in combination with changes in federal immigration laws in 1986 that spurred a Mexican immigrant diaspora,[28] Garden City saw a resurgence of Mexican immigration.[29]

Santa Maria is an agricultural city located on the central coast of California. According to the 2000 US Census, 40,719, or 52.3 % of Santa Maria's 77,423 inhabitants are of Mexican origin. Like Garden City, roughly half of the Mexican-origin population is foreign-born. Unlike Garden City however, Mexican immigration to Santa Maria was constant throughout the twentieth century. While there was a hiatus in immigration in Kansas, California became an increasingly popular destination for Mexican immigrants in the middle of the twentieth century.[30] Agricultural work has always attracted Mexican immigrants to Santa Maria, but advances in agriculture in recent years have created a year-round demand for the inexpensive labor that Mexican immigrants provide.[31] Mexican immigrants are practically the only source of agricultural labor in the fields around the city.

25. Tomás R. Jiménez, "Weighing the Costs and Benefits of Mexican Immigration: The Mexican-American Perspective," *Social Science Quarterly* 88, no. 3 (2007): 599-618; "Mexican-Immigrant Replenishment and the Continuing Significance of Ethnicity and Race," *American Journal of Sociology* 113, no. 6 (2008): 1527-1567; *Replenished Ethnicity: Mexican Americans, Immigration, and Identity* (Berkeley, CA: University of California Press, 2010).
26. Henry J. Avila, "Immigration and Integration: The Mexican American Community in Garden City, Kansas, 1900-1950," *Kansas History* 20, no. 1 (1997): 22-37.
27. Jorge Durand, Douglas S. Massey, and Fernando Charvet, "The Changing Geography of Mexican Immigration to the United States: 1910-1996," *Social Science Quarterly* 81, no. 1 (2000): 1-15.
28. Ibid.
29. Donald D. Stull, "'I come to the Garden': Changing Ethnic Relations in Garden City, Kansas," *Urban Anthropology* 19, no. 4 (1990): 303-320.
30. Durand, Massey, and Charvet, "The Changing Geography."
31. Juan-Vicente Palerm, "Immigrant and Migrant Farm Workers in the Santa Maria Valley, California," Center for Chicano Studies Working Paper Series (Santa Barbara, CA: University of California, 2006); Juan-Vicente Palerm,

I chose Garden City and Santa Maria because both cities are geographically and demographically small in size, thus maximizing interactions between Mexican immigrants and Mexican Americans. Mexican Americans in Garden City and Santa Maria are not representative of Mexican Americans nationwide. Both of these communities are semi-rural, and Mexican Americans are predominantly an urban and suburban population. Nevertheless, the overall experiences of Mexican Americans in Garden City and Santa Maria are consonant with research conducted on later generation Mexican Americans in more urban settings.[32] Much like Mexican Americans in other parts of the United States, the respondents have experienced steady, if slow, upward socioeconomic mobility from one generation to the next.[33]

I interviewed people between the ages of 15 and 98 who were from an array of occupational and educational backgrounds in order to access a broad cross section of Mexican Americans in each city. I obtained respondents using the snowball sampling technique. I minimized sample-selection bias by utilizing several different networks of individuals. I analyzed interviews using ATLASti, a software package that allows users to attach coding categories to relevant parts of transcripts in order to compare similarly coded portions of text across interviews.

"The Expansion of California Agriculture and the Rise of Peasant-Worker Communities" (paper presented at *Del pasado al futuro: nueva dimensiones de la intergración México-Estado Unidos*, Mexico City, 1997)

32. Thomas Macias, "The Changing Structure of Structural Assimilation: White-Collar Mexican Ethnicity and the Significance of Ethnic Identity Professional Organizations," *Social Science Quarterly* 84, no. 4 (2003): 946-957; Thomas Macias, "Imaginandose Mexicano: The Symbolic Context of Mexican American Ethnicity Beyond the Second Generation," *Qualitative Sociology* 27, no. 3 (2004): 299-315; Thomas Macias, *Mestizo in America: Generations of Mexican Ethnicity in the Suburban Southwest* (Tucson, AZ: University of Arizona Press, 2006); Gilda Ochoa, "Mexican Americans' Attitudes Toward and Interactions with Mexican Immigrants: A Qualitative Analysis of Conflict and Cooperation," *Social Science Quarterly* 81, no. 1 (2000): 84-105; Gilda Ochoa, *Becoming Neighbors in a Mexican American Community: Power, Conflict and Solidarity* (Austin, TX: University of Texas Press, 2004).

33. Richard Alba, "Mexican Americans and the American Dream," *Perspectives on Politics* 4, no. 2 (2006): 289-296; Richard Alba, Dalia Abdel-Hady, Tariquel Islam, and Karen Marotz, "Downward Assimilation and Mexican Americans: An Examination of Intergenerational Advance and Stagnation in Educational Attainment," in *New Dimensions of Diversity: The Children of Immigrants in North America and Western Europe*, ed. M.C. Waters and R. Alba (Cambridge, MA: Unpublished manuscript, 2008); Deborah Reed, Laura E. Hill, Christopher Jepsen, and Hans P. Johnson, "Educational Progress Across Immigrant Generations in California" (San Francisco: Public Policy Institute of California, 2005); James P. Smith, "Assimilation Across the Latino Generations," *American Economic Review* 93, no. 2 (2003): 315-319; James P. Smith, "Immigrants and the Labor Market," *Journal of Labor Economics* 24, no. 2 (2006): 203-233; Edward E. Telles and Vilma Ortiz, *Generations of Exclusion: Mexican Americans, Assimilation, and Race* (New York, NY: Russell Sage Foundation, 2008).

Mexican Immigrant Replenishment and the Ethnic Narrative in Daily Life

My interviews and observations allowed me to capture the ways in which the continuousness of Mexican immigration is a prominent event in a Mexican ethnic narrative that plays out in the daily lives of my respondents. My data show that the presence of a large Mexican immigrant population dramatically shapes the way that Mexican Americans experience an ethnic identity, as well as affecting how others perceive them and how they perceive themselves as members of the nation. For Mexican Americans, ethnicity is a double-edged sword that produces both exclusion from and limited inclusion in the story of American peoplehood.

■ Ethnicity as a Source of Exclusion

Though Mexican Americans exhibit significant socioeconomic, residential, and marital assimilation,[34] ethnicity is not a purely optional and inconsequential aspect of identity as it is for white ethnics.[35] Instead, Mexican Americans regularly experience instances in which their ethnicity becomes a source of exclusion from an American mainstream. This exclusion cannot be explained using only the "usual suspect" independent variables – race, class, and a history of colonialism – in analyses of ethnic Mexicans. Instead, nativism – "an intense opposition to an internal minority on the ground of its foreign (i.e., 'un-American') connections" – interacts with race, class, and a history of colonialism to affect later-generation Mexican Americans' ethnic identity.[36]

The category "Mexican" in Garden City and Santa Maria is synonymous with "immigrant," and even "illegal immigrant." In both Garden City and Santa Maria, Mexican immigrants are the most visible among people of Mexican descent, and they are the most visible among immigrants in general.[37] Thus, Mexican immigrants

---

34. Susan K. Brown, "Delayed Spatial Assimilation: Multigenerational Incorporation of the Mexican-Origin Population in Los Angeles," *City & Community* 6, no. 3 (2007): 193-209; Deborah Reed, Laura E. Hill, Christopher Jepsen, and Hans P. Johnson, "Educational Progress"; Michael J. Rosenfeld, "Measure of Assimilation in the Marriage Market: Mexican Americans 1970-1990," *Journal of Marriage and the Family* 64 (February, 2002): 152-162; James P. Smith, "Assimilation Across the Latino Generations".
35. Richard D. Alba, *Ethnic Identity*; Mary C. Waters, *Ethnic Options*.
36. John Higham, *Strangers in the Land: Patterns of American Nativism, 1860-1925* (New York, NY: Atheneum, 1963), 4.
37. Although there is a sizable foreign-born population from other countries, Mexicans have come to represent all immigrants in these cities primarily because the number of foreign-born Mexicans dwarfs that of any other immigrant population in each city. According to the 2000 US Census, Mexicans make up 84 % of all foreign-born individuals in Santa Maria and 76 % of the total foreign-born population in Garden City. Filipinos are the second largest immigrant group in Santa Maria, comprising only 7 % (or 1,794) of the total foreign-born population. In

are the primary targets of nativism. But nativist expressions aimed at Mexican immigrants still have a profound effect on Mexican Americans, who become aware of anti-Mexican nativism in interpersonal encounters, when they hear publically made pronouncements, and, more directly, when they are mistaken for immigrants. Even respondents for whom ethnicity is minimally important in most realms of life reported feeling especially tied to their ethnic background when they bump up against nativism in daily life. Marcela Muñoz, a 19-year-old junior college student in Garden City, works at a local retail store as a customer-service agent in Garden City. Early in our interview, Marcela acknowledged the nativism that her ancestors faced upon coming to the United States and said she has witnessed similar forms of nativism in her job. She relayed the following experience in which a white customer expressed anger because of the Spanish phone menu on the customer-service line.

> We have a Spanish recording. And a guest called and she was asking about American flags. [I said] like, "No Ma'am. We're not scheduled to get any more until July. We're sorry for the inconvenience" [...] But she just opened her mouth and she was like, "Oh and by the way, what is up with that Mexican crap?" Like that. So I of course was like, "Ma'am over half of our community understands Spanish." And she started going off on me. I was like, "Ma'am I'm Mexican American." And she didn't know what to say! She just hung up.

Virtually every Mexican American I interviewed shared a similar experience of hearing friends, colleagues, peers, and strangers express anti-Mexican nativist sentiments.

Nativism is particularly visible when delivered in public forums. Infamous among the public denouncements of immigrants in Santa Maria were statements made by its then mayor, George Hobbs, in 1990. A leader with a reputation for being brash and outspoken, Hobbs pointed to Mexican immigrants as the source of what he perceived to be growing blight in the city. Speaking to a local civic organization, he proclaimed:

> At this time in Santa Maria, we have a Mexican problem. We have a difficulty with scads of illegal aliens that have come across the border, and they've made our neighborhoods look not like Santa Maria neighborhoods. In certain streets people (are) gathered around drinking beer, smoking cigarettes. It's a formidable experience for a lot of the older people who have been here for a long time...That's not speaking, of course, of our Santa Maria Mexicans that have been here forever. Those people came here with the idea of becoming Americans.[38]

Garden City, Vietnamese are the second largest immigrant group, also making up only 7 % (or 451) of the total foreign-born population there.

38. Jeanne Sparks, "Hobbs: Illegal Alien Situation Out of Hand," *Santa Maria Times*, July 17, 1990.

The mayor's comments gained infamy in Santa Maria when they made headlines in the *Santa Maria Times*, a local newspaper with wide distribution in the city, and remained in the news for days. Despite Hobbs' qualifier that he was not speaking about long-time Santa Maria residents of Mexican descent (i.e., later generation Mexican Americans), his declaration that Santa Maria has "a Mexican problem" etched a lasting memory in the minds of Santa Maria's Mexican American population. Following his statements, scores of residents, including some Mexican Americans, protested and called for his resignation. I was not in Santa Maria to observe directly the impact of his comments, but it was evident that his words reverberated years later. Several Santa Maria respondents recalled the comments during interviews. Gigi Bartolome, a 61-year-old retired retail clerk, reflected, "It kind of made me mad because he was talking about Mexicans. What he actually was talking about was illegals. But he said Mexicans, so every Mexican in town took it as them." Hobbs' statement ignited such a strong reaction among Mexican Americans, like Gigi, partly because he racialized his nativist worries. Using the term "Mexican problem," he tied poverty, crime, and overcrowding to Mexicans and in so doing, the statements reflected not just concerns about these issues but also a general animosity toward all people of Mexican descent.

There is a range of public forums in which residents of each city express anti-Mexican nativism, but the opinion and comment sections for print and online stories published by the local newspapers are popular pulpits for nativists, especially when issues surrounding immigration turn up in the local or national news. For instance, during the 2002 campaign for the Kansas State Board of Education, won by a candidate who ran on an anti-immigrant platform, the local newspaper sponsored an online chat room where individuals could share their views on education and unauthorized immigration. The chat room quickly filled with opinions about immigration, Mexicans, and related issues. Several people posted messages supporting the winning candidate's platform, including the following:

> I agree with the person that stated it's not fair for our children to have to learn the Mexican language just so the Mexicans can survive in this community, whether it be an adult or a child. If they want to live in OUR country... LEARN THE LANGUAGE FIRST!!! You wouldn't catch me going to a foreign country without knowing their language. Mexicans can at least learn our language before they come over here, well enough [so] you don't have to keep asking them what they are saying. I don't feel that illegal or legal Mexicans should go to any of our schools, like the other person said, it puts a damper on OUR society! And further more [sic], [no one], and I mean [no one], is going to tell me that this community belongs to the Mexicans now and that America belongs to them, as did one gentleman in a college course I was taking did. It's like we're being taken over by aliens![39]

---

39. Posted 9/9/2002.

There is no shortage of anti-Mexican nativism piping through talk radio and cable news channels, and the more locally produced nativist voices only sharpen categorization of ethnic Mexicans as a foreign group.

The foreignness of Mexican ethnicity becomes particularly apparent to Mexican Americans when they are mistaken as foreigners, despite the fact that their roots in United States extend back several generations. Mexican Americans who have dark skin were particularly likely to report that, at one time or another, they have been mistaken for an immigrant or had to prove their American nationality to those who assume that they are foreigners, or even unauthorized foreigners. The fact that more than half of all Mexican immigrants are unauthorized,[40] together with the political attention given to the US-Mexico border, support the conflation of race, ancestry, nativity, and legal status. Since both cities have industries that employ large numbers of unauthorized workers,[41] non-Mexicans sometimes assume that people of Mexican origin are not only foreign, but also *unauthorized* foreigners. Pedro Ramirez, a 52-year-old, third generation high school teacher in Santa Maria, recalled the especially troubling experience of being pulled over by the US immigration enforcement officer while traveling in his pick-up truck after doing yard work at a rental property he owns:

> It's this guy with a Smokey the Bear hat and wrap around glasses. It's *la migra*. It's the INS, the border patrol! So I get out [of my car] and the guy says "*ivete aquí!*" ("come here") I go oh no, and I'm laughing. I come over and say, "May I help you?" He says, "Do you speak English?" I said, "What the hell do you think I just said?" He says, "Do you have some ID?" I go, "What the hell do you want to know if I have ID for? I wasn't going past the speed limit. Besides you're not a cop. You're the Border Patrol. All right, I'll play your game." He said, "Do you have some ID?" So I pull out my driver's license and show him my wallet. "Do you have anything else?" I said, "Yeah." And I showed him my social security card. He wanted to reach for it and I go, "You ain't getting this. Forget that!" He goes, "You have anything else?" I go, "Sure I do." So I pull out my American Express card. And it's green. I said, "Don't leave home without it. This is harassment!" Guilt by association: Mexican needing a haircut and a shave on a Friday afternoon with bandana around his neck, with an old pickup truck loaded with mowers and edgers and stuff like that.

Pedro's experience represents the worst possible case of "mistaken (national) identity," but the dark-skinned respondents I interviewed report experiences that are

---

40. Jeffrey S. Passel and D'Vera Cohn, "Trends in Unauthorized Immigration."

41. While it is difficult to estimate the size of the unauthorized immigrant population in either city, a high ranking law enforcement official estimates that around 15,000 unauthorized immigrants live in Santa Maria (or roughly 61% of the total Mexican immigrant population). A labor contractor reported to me that he believes about 80% of the workers he hires are unauthorized. Nationally, Passel (2004) estimates that 54% of the total Mexican immigrant population is unauthorized.

similar in kind, even if generally less severe. Mexican Americans can never assume that others will see them as American nationals because in a context of heavy Mexican immigration being "Mexican" does not merely signal ethnic ancestry, but also nativity and even legal status.

The experiences that Mexican Americans reported of witnessing and directly experiencing anti-Mexican nativism demonstrate how "Mexicanness" and "foreignness" are connected in everyday life. In reflecting on these experiences, the Mexican Americans I interviewed give the immigrant experience primacy in the ethnic Mexican narrative. They invoked their families' immigrant history to show how the event of immigration can be plotted at virtually any point in the Mexican ethnic narrative. Mike Fernandez's comments illustrate this point. Mike is a 19-year-old junior college student in Santa Maria. He lives in an upper-middleclass neighborhood and attended a private high school. He described his family as "a white family who is Mexican" because his ethnic background plays only a small role in his family's life. But his ethnic background became important to him when he heard nativist comments about Mexican immigrants:

> When somebody will say something about Mexicans or, something like that, and it's not said towards me, it's not directed towards me. But at that point, I'll feel myself discriminated against. I'll put the discrimination on myself, feeling that even though they're not directing it toward me, I can't help but feel that it's degrading towards me in some way, when in fact I know it's not meant directly towards me; it's a general comment. But it just kind of makes me uncomfortable.

The reasoning that Mike offered for feeling uncomfortable reflects his attachment to a larger ethnic narrative centered on the immigrant experience:

> [T]hey're speaking about a Mexican family or a Mexican person and I know that, though my family is not in that position, somewhere along down before me, somebody in my family, I'm sure, has been in that position. And although I'm not in it, and probably never will be in that position, I just think that back when my ancestors were in that position and people were the same way towards them.

Although Mike may have had only a vague idea about his family's immigrant history, Mexican immigrants are a real-life representation of this history. My exchange with Lucia Pacheco, a 19-year-old college student in Santa Maria, reveals similar sentiments:

> [T]here's total discrimination against Hispanic people. And then they may not be sending it directly towards me, but I feel it too because the negativity, because of who I am and who my family is [...] There's times when you'll be in the mall or something and people will walk

by and people make really rude comments about who they are. And I just try to shut it off, but it gets to me.

TRJ: What about it gets to you?

R: The fact that people can be so mean and negative towards somebody. They can't help who they are or what they are [...] It's usually people that are from Mexico that you know that they're from Mexico because they don't speak English or something. Or they make fun of people because of the way they dress. And they're Mexican and they call them like gangster or *vato* or something like that.

TRJ: You said that bothers you because that's who you are and who your family is. What do you mean by that?

R: It's who I am. It's what I am actually. I am Hispanic. My family is Hispanic. I shouldn't feel bad about being Hispanic and people shouldn't really talk bad about us because we're just as human as they are. We have feelings and emotions.

Mexican Americans like Mike and Lucia feel a connection to Mexican immigrants vis-à-vis their own immigrant ancestors that leads them to internalize the nativism so fervently hurled in the direction of their immigrant co-ethnics. In identifying with the Mexican immigrant experience, respondents affirm the importance of immigration to the Mexican ethnic narrative.

■ Ethnicity as a Source of Inclusion

Although the continuous influx of Mexican immigration leads ethnic Mexicans to be written out of a larger national narrative, it can also make their ethnicity a tool for inclusion in politics, certain occupations, and popular culture. There is little doubt that societal and host contexts of reception are tilted negatively against Mexican immigrants,[42] as embodied in a widely articulated narrative of this group as a threat to the nation.[43] But the contexts of reception are not entirely bent in a negative direction. In contemporary US society, multiculturalism, which celebrates ethnic difference, guides politics, the policies of firms and organizations, and popular culture.[44] As Alba and Nee point out, federal legislation passed in the 1960s imposing stiff penalties for racial and ethnic discrimination has forced firms and

---

42. Portes and Rumbaut, *Immigrant America*.
43. Leo R. Chavez, *The Latino Threat: Constructing Immigrants, Citizens, and the Nation* (Stanford, CA: Stanford University Press, 2008).
44. Marcelo M. Suárez-Orozco, "Everything You Want to Know about Assimilation but Were Afraid to Ask," *Daedalus* 129, no. 4 (2000): 1-30.

organizations to adopt strategies to demonstrate compliance.[45] The responses to these legal changes have created "an institutionalized consensus on the value of diversity" that pervades,[46] even if superficially, in contemporary US society. The immigrant-driven growth of the Mexican origin population thus makes ethnicity a more valuable source of identity for the Mexican Americans I interviewed.

In recent years, politicians have been clamoring to win the "Latino vote" and Mexican American politicians like Los Angeles, CA Mayor, Antonio Villaraigosa, and New Mexico Governor and former Presidential Candidate, Bill Richardson, along with a growing number locally elected officials illustrate the growing importance of Mexican Americans in politics. As Mexican American respondents saw it, the immigrant-driven growth of the Mexican-origin population has contributed to Mexican American political ascendancy. According to Hank Pacheco, a 27-year-old law enforcement officer in Santa Maria:

> Actually now we're starting to take a lot larger role. Like you know, our former [Mexican American] mayor now is in the state legislature [...] But like our city council has a lot more Hispanics or Mexicans now [...] I think part of it is the increase in Mexican population. That's definitely one of them. [...] And actually knowing what [Mexican American politicians are] talking about and getting enough people to listen and then by doing that, it makes other groups of people in the area kind of open their eyes and take notice a little bit. I think it's been a really positive thing.

In an age when ethnicity is seen an important dimension of democratic representation, Mexican immigration may give Mexican Americans a leg up in some respects.

The growth of the ethnic Mexican population spurred by immigration also creates a demand for "Mexican" representation in business and commerce from which later generation Mexican Americans benefit. Since Mexican immigrants make up such a large proportion of the population in each city, businesses that discriminate or exclude them stand to lose a substantial source of potential revenue. Mexican Americans, especially those who speak Spanish, are among the primary beneficiaries of the strategy that firms utilize to attract and accommodate immigrant customers. Mexican Americans are often seen as highly valuable employees because they have a keen familiarity with American institutions and culture, *and* an ability to communicate effectively with Spanish-speaking clientele. Consider the case of Aaron Briseño, a 17-year old high school student whose grandfather taught him to speak Spanish. Aaron believed his ability to communicate with Spanish-speaking customers made him desirable as an employee at a local grocery store:

---

45. Richard Alba and Victor Nee, *Remaking the American Mainstream: Assimilation and Contemporary Immigration* (Cambridge, MA: Harvard University Press, 2003).
46. Ibid., 57.

If somebody asks me, "Do you know Spanish?" And I'll tell them if I can speak it. Yeah, I do. That's one of the reasons I got a job at [the grocery store]. A lot of Hispanic people live on that side of town and they tend to shop at that store. And I put on my application that I was a good translator and sometimes people back in pharmacy or grocery department need me to translate for them and I do that.

Several respondents also noted that their employer provides additional pay to workers who speak Spanish, a reward for bilingualism that only exists because of the large Mexican immigrant population.[47] Others recognized that the immigrant-driven growth of the Mexican-origin population may yield benefits in an era of multiculturalism because later generation Mexican Americans are most likely to "get the call" when firms and organizations need "Mexican" representation.

Culture is a means through which Mexican immigration has brought greater prominence to all people of Mexican descent, regardless of generational status. As corporate America recognizes the immense profit to be made by catering to Latino immigrants, they have launched targeted marketing campaigns aimed at attracting this population's spending.[48] This "market-driven multiculturalism" gives the Mexican-origin population growing prominence in popular culture as television, film, print media, and music increasingly reflect and celebrate people of Mexican origin.[49] As Mexican Americans see it, the rising number of ethnic Mexicans resulting from immigration gives them greater prominence in US popular culture. According to Mark Santos, a 29-year-old social worker in Garden City,

I see a lot of positives. Our culture has a lot of great things to offer. Of course our music is now mainstream, it's big time. Our festivities are growing in every city. Everyone is picking it up and doing those things and celebrating what we celebrate and what we stand for. I think it's great.

The Mexican Americans I interviewed, especially the youngest respondents, believed that they are part of a group that is defining the demographic and cultural futures of the respective cities in which they live, and the United States as a whole. The growing prominence of Mexican culture in US popular culture thus gives them a sense that they are connected to a group that is culturally ascendant.

But the ascendancy that ethnicity provides may come at a price. The sense

---

47. In a study of 119 municipal governments in the United States, Linton and Jiménez found that 41 % provided additional pay to bilingual employees. See April Linton and Tomás R. Jiménez, "Contexts for Bilingualism Among U.S.-Born Latinos," *Ethnic and Racial Studies* 32, no. 6 (2009): 967-95.
48. Arlene Dávila, *Latinos, Inc.: The Marketing and Making of a People* (Berkeley, CA: University of California Press, 2001); Arlene Dávila, *Latino Spin: Public Image and the Whitewashing of Race* (New York, NY: New York University Press, 2008).
49. Aristide R. Zolberg and Litt Woon Long, "Why Islam is Like Spanish: Cultural Incorporation in Europe and the United States," *Politics and Society* 27, no. 1 (1999): 26.

of inclusion that comes from the political, commercial, and cultural response to demographic and ideological changes may depend on a characterization of the Mexican-origin population that ultimately excludes them from being written into an American national narrative. The prominence of ethnic Mexicans depends on the preservation of their difference as a political constituency, members of the labor force, and consumers. Later generation Mexican Americans benefit from these trends only to the extent that they are willing to comply with representations of them as culturally different from the mainstream. As Arlene Dávila points out, efforts by politicians and marketers to paint Latinos as "just like us" glosses over the realities of race in the lives of Latinos.[50] But the inclusion of ethnic Mexicans as "Mexicans" in politics, commerce, and culture also rests on the premise that ethnic Mexicans (and all Latinos for that matter) are different in a way that requires giving them special attention. While Mexican Americans may recognize this attention as positive, all of the attention may come at the price of their full inclusion in popular ideas about what it means to be "American."

Conclusion

The United State is a self-described "nation of immigrants." But upon closer inspection, the centrality of immigration in the American national narrative does not mean that any group with immigrant origins can lay claim to belonging in the national story of peoplehood. The construction of ethnic and national narratives depends on the sequencing of particular events that, when put together, form a cohesive story about what it means to be a member of the ethnic group or nation.

Immigration is certainly central to the narratives that have formed about various American ethnic groups, and immigration allows some ethnic groups, particularly those from Europe, to tether an ethnic narrative to the larger national narrative. Richard Alba concludes from his study of later generation white ethnics that "From every group, one hears essentially the same story of people who came poor, suffered from discrimination and other early burdens, but worked hard and eventually made their way in the new land."[51] For later generation white ethnics, the fact that immigration is a *past* event – one that took place well *before* the later generation descendants of immigrants experienced significant assimilation – situates immigration as a bridging event between the American national narrative and the smaller ethnic narrative that it encompasses. Today, as Alba points out, white ethnics

---

50. Arlene Dávila, *Latino Spin: Public Image and the Whitewashing of Race* (New York, NY: New York University Press, 2008).
51. Alba, *Ethnic Identity*, 313-314.

recognize a larger shared narrative centered on having risen above the struggles of the immigrant generation such that the groups to which they trace their ethnic origins are no longer defined by their foreignness.

The Mexican ethnic narrative is not indistinguishably woven into the larger American narrative because of the prominent and present-day role of immigration as a defining event. Other events play a role in this narrative: colonization, the struggle for civil rights, the Chicano Movement, and the ascendancy of Mexican Americans in politics. But nothing defines the Mexican ethnic narrative today more than immigration. Because Mexican immigration is an ongoing event, people of Mexican descent living in the United States cannot be nostalgic about the immigrant experience, even if their ancestors came to the United States near the time of the mass European migration. Such nostalgia requires a psychological and historical distance from the immigrant experience that later generation Mexican Americans lack; it requires that immigration be situated as a past event in the ethnic Mexican narrative. As the interviews with Mexican Americans in Garden City and Santa Maria show, the importance of immigration to the Mexican ethnic narrative shows up in their everyday lives.

Mexican Americans assert a narrative that departs from the one that predominates in American society, pushing back against the dominant image of the Mexican-origin population as a foreign group. They may claim themselves to be "hyphenated Americans" just like other later generation descendants of immigrants. But immigration elongates the hyphen between "Mexican" and "American" in the eyes of many non-Mexicans. Even if others "exit" the group by not identifying as a person of Mexican origin at all,[52] a pattern that intermarriage precipitates, ongoing Mexican immigration lends credence to the dominant narrative of the Mexican-origin population as an unmeltable foreign group.

It is important to note that narratives are not fixed. They are continually written and re-written in response to new events and the struggles about the dominant story that should be told about who "we" are and who "they" are. Looking ahead, immigration will continue to be an event around which the American national narrative revolves and evolves. Ethnic Mexicans may yet be central players in the evolution of the national narrative. Although a large number of ethnic Mexicans are struggling to integrate in US society, particularly those who are foreign-born and lack authorization,[53] there is also a significant number of ethnic Mexicans who are experiencing significant upward mobility.[54] Many hold prominent posi-

---

52. Richard D. Alba, Dalia Abdel-Hady, Tariquel Islam, and Karen Marotz, "Downward Assimilation."
53. Frank D. Bean, Susan K. Brown, Mark A. Leach, and James Bachmeier, "Becoming U.S. Stakeholders."
54. Jody Agius and Jennifer Lee, "Brown Picket Fences: The Immigrant Narrative and Patterns of Giving Back among the Mexican Origin Middle-Class in Los Angeles," *Ethnicities* 9, no. 1 (2009): 5-31; James P. Smith, "Assimilation Across the Latino Generations."

tions in commerce and politics, and as Gregory Rodríguez points out, the death of Jim Crow and the passing of post-Civil Rights identity politics has allowed today's Mexican American leadership a sense of comfort with their ethnic identity that their predecessors lacked.[55] The increasing class, generational, and legal status diversity within the Mexican-origin population means that ethnic Mexicans and the United States as a whole will have to rethink the Mexican ethnic narrative and its place in the patchwork of ethnic narratives that make up the larger American story. If and when Mexican Americans gain greater political and economic voice, the American narrative that is written in the future may very well find a place for the San Diego-Tijuana border crossing alongside Ellis Island in the national myth of origins.

Bibliography

Agius, Jody and Jennifer Lee. "Brown Picket Fences: The Immigrant Narrative and Patterns of Giving Back among the Mexican Origin Middle-Class in Los Angeles." *Ethnicities* 9, no. 1 (2009): 5-31.

Alba, Richard D. *Italian Americans: Into the Twilight of Ethnicity.* Englewood Cliffs, NJ: Prentice-Hall, 1985.

Alba, Richard D. *Ethnic Identity: The Transformation of White America.* New Haven: Yale University Press, 1990.

Alba, Richard D. "Mexican Americans and the American Dream." *Perspectives on Politics* 4, no. 2 (2006): 289-296.

Alba, Richard, Dalia Abdel-Hady, Tariquel Islam, and Karen Marotz. "Downward Assimilation and Mexican Americans: An Examination of Intergenerational Advance and Stagnation in Educational Attainment." In *New Dimensions of Diversity: The Children of Immigrants in North America and Western Europe*, edited by M.C. Waters and R. Alba. Cambridge, MA: Unpublished manuscript, 2008.

Alba, Richard and Victor Nee. *Remaking the American Mainstream: Assimilation and Contemporary Immigration.* Cambridge, MA: Harvard University Press, 2003.

Avila, Henry J. "Immigration and Integration: The Mexican Americans Community in Garden City, Kansas, 1900-1950." *Kansas History* 20, no. 1 (1997): 22-37.

Bean, Frank D., Susan K. Brown, Mark A. Leach, and James Bachmeier. "Becoming U.S. Stakeholders: Legalization and Integration Among Mexican Immigrants and their Descendents." Newport Beach, CA: Merage Foundation for the American Dream, 2007.

Brown, Susan K. "Structural Assimilation Revisted: Mexican-Origin Nativity and Cross-Ethnic Primary Ties." *Social Forces* 85, no. 1 (2006): 75-92.

Brown, Susan K. "Delayed Spatial Assimilation: Multigenerational Incorporation of the Mexican-Origin Population in Los Angeles." *City & Community* 6, no. 3 (2007): 193-209.

Calavita, Kitty. *Inside the State: The Bracero Program, Immigration and the I.N.S.* New York: Routledge, 1992.

Cardoso, Lawrence A. *Mexican Emigration to the United States, 1897-1931.* Tucson, AZ: University of Arizona Press, 1980.

---

55. Gregory Rodriguez, *Mongrels, Bastards, Orphans and Vagabonds: Mexican Immigration and the Future of Race in America* (New York, NY: Pantheon, 2007).

Chavez, Leo R. *The Latino Threat: Constructing Immigrants, Citizens, and the Nation*. Stanford, CA: Stanford University Press, 2008.

Cornelius, Wayne A. "Controlling 'Unwanted' Immigration: Lessons from the United States, 1993-2004." *Journal of Ethnic and Migration Studies* 31, no. 4 (2005): 775-794.

Cornell, Stephan. "That's the Story of Our Life." In *Narrative and Multiplicity in Constructing Ethnic Identities*, edited by P.R. Spickard and W. J. Burroughs, 41-53. Philadelphia, PA: Temple University Press, 2000.

Cornell, Stephen and Douglas Hartmann. *Ethnicity and Race: Making Identities in a Changing World*. 2nd ed. Thousand Oaks, CA: Pine Forge Press, 2006.

Dávila, Arlene. *Latinos, Inc.: The Marketing and Making of a People*. Berkeley, CA: University of California Press, 2001.

Dávila, Arlene. *Latino Spin: Public Image and the Whitewashing of Race*. New York, NY: New York University Press, 2008.

Durand, Jorge, Douglas S. Massey, and Fernando Charvet. "The Changing Geography of Mexican Immigration to the United States: 1910-1996." *Social Science Quarterly* 81, no. 1 (2000): 1-15.

Gans, Herbert J. "Symbolic Ethnicity: The Future of Ethnic Groups and Cultures in America." *Ethnic and Racial Studies* 2 (January 1979): 1-20.

Higham, John. *Strangers in the Land: Patterns of American Nativism, 1860-1925*. New York, NY: Atheneum, 1963.

Huntington, Samuel P. *Who Are We? The Challenges to America's National Identity*. New York: Simon & Schuster, 2004.

Institute, Migration Policy. "2007 American Community Survey and Census Data on the Foreign Born by State." Accessed May 5, 2009. http://www.migrationinformation.org/DataHub/state.cfm?ID=US.

Jaffe, A.J., Ruth. M. Cullen, and Thomas D. Boswell. *The Changing Demography of Spanish Americans*. New York, NY: Academic Press, 1980.

Jiménez, Tomás R. "Weighing the Costs and Benefits of Mexican Immigration: The Mexican-American Perspective." *Social Science Quarterly* 88, no. 3 (2007): 599-618.

Jiménez, Tomás R. "Mexican-Immigrant Replenishment and the Continuing Significance of Ethnicity and Race." *American Journal of Sociology* 113, no. 6 (2008): 1527-1567.

Jiménez, Tomás R. *Replenished Ethnicity: Mexican Americans, Immigration, and Identity*. Berkeley, CA: University of California Press, 2010.

Kennedy, John F. *A Nation of Immigrants*. New York, NY: Harper-Collins, 1964.

Linton, April and Tomás R. Jiménez. "Contexts for Bilingualism Among U.S.-Born Latinos." *Ethnic and Racial Studies* 32, no. 6 (2009): 967-95.

López, David E. and Ricardo Stanton-Salazar. "Mexican Americans: A Second Generation at Risk." In *Ethnicities: Children of Immigrants in America*, edited by R.G. Rumbaut and A. Portes, 57-90. Berkeley: University of California Press, 2001.

Macias, Thomas. "The Changing Structure of Structural Assimilation: White-Collar Mexican Ethnicity and the Significance of Ethnic Identity Professional Organizations." *Social Science Quarterly* 84, no. 4 (2003): 946-957.

Macias, Thomas. "Imaginandose Mexicano: The Symbolic Context of Mexican American Ethnicity Beyond the Second Generation." *Qualitative Sociology* 27, no. 3 (2004): 299-315.

Macias, Thomas. *Mestizo in America: Generations of Mexican Ethnicity in the Suburban Southwest*. Tucson, AZ: University of Arizona Press, 2006.

Massey, Douglas. "The New Immigration and Ethnicity in the United States." *Population and Development Review* 21, no. 3 (1995): 631-652.

Massey, Douglas S. "Why Does Immigration Occur?: A Theoretical Synthesis." In *The Handbook of International Migration: The American Experience*, edited by C. Hirschman, P. Kasinitz, and J. DeWind, 34-52. New York, NY: Russell Sage Foundation, 1999.

Massey, Douglas S., Jorge Durand, and Nolan J. Malone. *Beyond Smoke and Mirrors: Mexican Immigration in an Era of Free Trade*. New York: Russell Sage Foundation, 2002.

Ochoa, Gilda. "Mexican Americans' Attitudes Toward and Interactions with Mexican Immigrants: A Qualitative Analysis of Conflict and Cooperation." *Social Science Quarterly* 81, no. 1 (2000): 84-105.

Ochoa, Gilda. *Becoming Neighbors in a Mexican American Community: Power, Conflict and Solidarity*. Austin, TX: University of Texas Press, 2004.

Palerm, Juan-Vicente. "Immigrant and Migrant Farm Workers in the Santa Maria Valley, California." Center for Chicano Studies Working Paper Series. Santa Barbara, CA: University of California, 1994.

Palerm, Juan-Vicente. "The Expansion of California Agriculture and the Rise of Peasant-Worker Communities." Paper presented at *Del pasado al futuro: nueva dimensiones de la intergración México-Estado Unidos*. Mexico City, 1997.

Passel, Jeffrey S. and D'Vera Cohn. "Trends in Unauthorized Immigration: Undocumented Inflow Now Trails Legal Inflow." Washington, DC: Pew Hispanic Center, 2008.

Portes, Alejandro and Rubén G. Rumbaut. *Legacies: The Story of the Immigrant Second Generation*. Berkeley and New York: University of California Press; Russell Sage Foundation, 2001.

Portes, Alejandro and Rubén G. Rumbaut. *Immigrant America: A Portrait*. University of California Press, 2006.

Reed, Deborah, Laura E. Hill, Christopher Jepsen, and Hans P. Johnson. "Educational Progress Across Immigrant Generations in California." San Francisco, CA: Public Policy Institute of California, 2005.

Rodriguez, Gregory. *Mongrels, Bastards, Orphans and Vagabonds: Mexican Immigration and the Future of Race in America*. New York, NY: Pantheon, 2007.

Rosenfeld, Michael J. "Measure of Assimilation in the Marriage Market: Mexican Americans 1970-1990." *Journal of Marriage and the Family* 64 (February 2002): 152-162.

Smith, James P. "Assimilation Across the Latino Generations." *American Economic Review* 93, no. 2 (2003): 315-319.

Smith, James P. "Immigrants and the Labor Market." *Journal of Labor Economics* 24, no. 2 (2006): 203-233.

Smith, Rogers M. *Stories of Peoplehood: The Politics and Morals of Political Membership*. New York: Cambridge University Press, 2003.

Sparks, Jeanne. "Hobbs: Illegal Alien Situation Out of Hand." *Santa Maria Times*, July 17, 1990, A5.

Stull, Donald D. "'I come to the Garden': Changing Ethnic Relations in Garden City, Kansas." *Urban Anthropology* 19, no. 4 (1990): 303-320.

Suárez-Orozco, Marcelo M. "Everything You Want to Know about Assimilation but Where Afraid to Ask." *Daedalus* 129, no. 4 (2000): 1-30.

Telles, Edward E. and Vilma Ortiz. *Generations of Exclusion: Mexican Americans, Assimilation, and Race*. New York, NY: Russell Sage Foundation, 2008.

Waters, Mary C. *Ethnic Options: Choosing Identities in America*. Berkeley: University of California Press, 1990.

Zolberg, Aristide R. and Litt Woon Long. "Why Islam is Like Spanish: Cultural Incorporation in Europe and the United States." *Politics and Society* 27, no. 1 (1999): 5-38.

11 The Writing of History and National Identity: the Danish Case

Claus Møller Jørgensen

The intimate relation between historical writing and forms of identification is a truism in contemporary historical scholarship. In particular, the relationship between the genre of national history and national identification has received much scholarly attention in the last decade or so. There is, therefore, no need discuss this; it will be taken for granted that historical writing serves identity purposes.

The aim of this article is twofold. First, I provide an introduction to the specific case of Danish historical writing. Second, I look for new ways of writing national history. This double task is thus both descriptive and normative. With respect to the latter aspect, let me state from the outset that I think that the future of national historical writing lies in getting beyond nationalized history. There are two methods that will allow us to get beyond nationalized history. First it is necessary to put the history of Denmark into context. I will refer to this necessary contextualization of the history of Denmark as the application of a transnational perspective, even though I am fully aware that the term is not applicable to all periods of Danish history. The second way to get beyond nationalized history is to call into question the traditional idea of Danish national identity as uniform and homogeneous. Neither of these strategies, I would like to emphasize, are absent from Danish historical writing, past or present. But as I see it, they need to be elaborated and drawn into Danish historical writing in a more conscious and systematic way.

With respect to describing the Danish case, I survey recent literature on Danish history which has the potential of bringing new perspectives to the formation of national identification in Denmark. I have tried to trace transnational perspectives on Danish history and the ways in which historians have dealt with the question of national identity in recent Danish historical writing (mainly from this century). Before turning to these questions, I will provide a very brief introduction to traditional Danish historical writing by way of introduction to the Danish case.

Traditional national narratives

Based on cultural templates prevalent in educated European circles in the early nineteenth century, various conceptions of the history of the Danish nation were formed in the decades after the end of the Napoleonic wars. In the academic community two models were developed. Both understood the nation as *Volk* or *people* as an organic whole, which reflects the fact that both conceptions were inspired by German idealist philosophy. Both viewed historical knowledge as a prerequisite for political and national identity formation. They differed, however, in their attitudes towards Europe, that is, the relation between the Danish nation and European civilization. The first conception can be attributed to the historian C. F. Allen (1811-1871) although it must be said that his view of the Danish past was quite common among the early nineteenth century intelligentsia in Copenhagen to which he belonged. The idea of a Norse peasant society based on freedom and equality was especially widespread in academic and educated circles.[1]

In brief, Allen's conception of Danish history, published for the first time in 1840, can be understood as a great curve formed by the development from an ancient golden age, followed by centuries of decline which reached an all-time low during absolutism, from which it rose towards a new golden age in the nineteenth century. On the brink of historic times, Allen maintained, the Danish people was a national unity comprised by free and freeholding peasants. It was a democracy, since problems were solved on the thingstead, a gathering of representatives of the people, most importantly the election of the king. This national and democratic unity was lost in the following centuries. First, internal class division led to the creation of a closed and selfish nobility. This nobility developed because of privileges based on their status as the king's warriors. During the late Middle Ages, this warrior caste became alienated from the common people because it acquired foreign customs and language. The second cause of decay was the foreign Catholic church, which preached in Latin without any concern for or relation to the people of which the peasants were the backbone. The third source of decay was the repression of the ordinary peasant, who lost his freedom, his rights, and his social standing, and who was ultimately enslaved in the first half of the eighteenth century. The decay of peasant freedom continued until the late eighteenth century, but was reversed by a series of reforms made by the Danish king, who liberated the peasants in 1788. This was the first crucial step towards a new golden age. The next step was the reunion of elite and mass culture with the romantic elite's rediscovery of the *Folk* and folk culture and language. Finally, the introduction of the Assemblies of the Estates in

---

1. Helge Paludan, "Vor danske Montesquieu," *Historie* 13 (1980): 1-32.

1831 represented a move towards the re-establishment of the original democracy. Allen's outline of Danish history generally perceives foreign influences as damaging influences. There are exceptions to this rule; according to Allen, the Reformation was a positive development, since it meant the nationalization of Christianity and the beginning of a positive relationship between people and Church. Nationality and national language were preserved by the peasantry, which Allen saw as the core of the Danish people outside the reach of foreign influence. The Fatherland mainly developed by virtue of its own internal qualities and the patriotism of at least some kings and cultural personalities.[2]

While Allen's book was immensely popular and influential throughout the nineteenth century, the second conception of Danish history that I want to introduce is more an example of a trend than an influential piece of historical writing. The model is based on the writings of J. N. Madvig (1804-1886), who was strictly speaking not a historian, but a classical philologist. Like many of his contemporaries, he was inspired by Hegel. His conception of Danish history is thus based on the idea of progress, and a particular conception of the relationship between the nation and European civilization. For Madvig, nations have been the organizing principle of societies throughout history. The Greek and Roman nations differed from all later nations because they laid the foundation of European civilization. After the Middle Ages, a period in which things did not really develop, we enter the period of modern nations in which the progressive development of European civilization was carried on the shoulders of the British, the French, and the Germans. They carried the torch of the progressive European *Geist* or civilization. Denmark and the Danish nation were situated at the periphery of Europe and were not drawn into the process of civilization until the end of the Middle Ages. From this time on, Denmark and Danish national culture were developed through impulses from Europe. The progress of the Danish nation would be unthinkable without its connection to European civilization.[3]

The histories of both Allen and Madvig were histories of the Danish people. The concept of the Danish people gave structure to their understanding of history, which was confined to what they perceived as the real Denmark: the Kingdom of Denmark. The reason that I mention them both in the context of this article is that they can be seen as representatives of the main trends in Danish historical writing from the nineteenth century until about 1960. Disregarding the tensions both within and between the two approaches, and disregarding the different developments and changes they underwent from the 1830s to the 1960s, I think that it is justified

---

2. C.F. Allen, *Haandbog i Fædrelandets Historie med stadigt Henblik paa Folkets og Statens indre Udvikling* (Copenhagen: C.A. Reitzel, 1840).

3. Claus Møller Jørgensen, "Civilisation og nation i dansk dannelsestænkning i det 19. århundrede," in *Fremmed og moderne*, ed. Peter Bang (Aarhus: Aarhus University Press, 2005), 97-112.

to claim that Danish historical writing was characterized by two perspectives, one European and one more purely Danish, until about fifty years ago. The important thing to notice is that both historical narratives were perspectives on national history; national history was the dominant theme among academic historians. But the view of Europe and foreign impulses was different. While a national conservative historian like Professor Johannes Steenstrup emphasized the self-developing character of the Danish nation and Danish history in around 1900,[4] the so-called social liberal interpretation of Danish history emphasized the European preconditions of the progress of Denmark. The idea of Denmark as a country in the European periphery developing through cultural impulses and commercial interaction with European centers was central to the social liberal account.[5]

It is clear that what Miroslav Hroch calls "ethnicisation" has also taken place in the construction of Danish national history. Hroch uses this term to refer to the fact that in former centuries members of national communities came to be defined on an ethnic basis. This meant that ethnic minorities were excluded from national histories.[6] In the Danish case, the idea of the real Denmark excluded other nationalities – Norwegian, Inuit, German – in the centuries during which they were part of the Danish Empire. This is still very much the case, as I will show below. A curious example can be found in the first volume of Erik Arup's *History of Denmark* from 1925. Erik Arup is a famous proponent of the social liberal interpretation of history. Inspired by racial theories and German archaeology and anthropology of the *Völkisch* type, he concluded that the Danes had always lived in Denmark. While the Danes adapted and accommodated European cultural impulses, they had nonetheless always been the same race and breed as present-day Danes, built in the same way and by implication thinking in the same way. Arup went further than most historians, theorizing that the origin of the white race was to be found in Denmark and its neighboring areas. However, his work is still a clear and illustrative example of the consequence of the social liberal interpretation: from the outset Denmark has been separated from the rest of the world by ethnicity or race, and at the same time Denmark has interacted with Europe and especially been influenced by it.[7]

---

4. E.g. Johannes Steenstrup, "Oldtiden og den tidlige Middelalder," in *Danmarks Riges Historie*, vol. 1 (Copenhagen: Det Nordiske Forlag, 1897-1904).

5. E.g. Kristian Erslev, *Valdemarernes Storhedstid* (Copenhagen: Universitetsforlaget i København 1972 [1898]); Thyge Svenstrup, "Erik Arup og Brooks Adams. Et bidrag til Arups historie- og metodesyn," *Historisk Tidsskrift* 95 (1995): 1-23. It should be noted that to the social liberals Denmark did deviate from European developments in some respects. According to Erslev, for example, Denmark never became feudalized as other European countries did.

6. Miroslav Hroch and Jitk Malečkova, "Historical Heritage: Continuity and Discontinuity in the Construction of National Histories," *Studia Historica* 53 (2000): 15-36, 33.

7. Kurt Villads Jensen, "Den hvide race og den danske jord," *Historie* (1998): 91-103, 94f.

One last point I would like to make about traditional national narratives is to do with the view of society they promote. Again one finds two paradigms. The first is organicist in the sense that the Danish people are perceived as an organism. The individual forms a part of the whole; the individual can be seen as the expression of the people. Internal divisions and antagonisms are not a prevalent feature in this conception of society, which perceives the people mainly as a harmonious unity. Both the historical perspectives discussed above combine this conception of society with a more class-based one. As I have already shown, Allen worked with both a concept of nation and a concept of estates or classes. The tension between people and class can also be found in the social liberal interpretation of Danish history. The history of society, with its emphasis on class and conflict, and the history of the Danish people coexisted in national historical writing in Denmark until about 1970. Since 1970 the people as an ethnic and organic category has played a more marginal role in academic historical writing in general and in histories of Denmark in particular. At the same time the history of society and class has become the central approach to Danish history.

Denmark in context

Some twenty years ago, the Danish historian Uffe Østergård criticized his contemporaries for the anachronistic and ahistorical error of projecting the nation-state created in the nineteenth century back into historical periods in which it made no sense. The history of Denmark was, consciously or unconsciously, defined by the borders of the post-1864 nation-state. But until 1864 Denmark was an empire consisting of Skåne, Halland, and Blekinge (parts of present-day Sweden), Norway (until 1814), and Slesvig and Holstein (now part of Germany with the exception of northern Slesvig, which has been Danish since 1920). Thus, the prevalent conception of Danish history gave an incorrect picture of Denmark by neglecting to contextualize it as a part of the multinational Danish Empire. Interpretations were nationalized; this nationalization lent an ahistorical continuity to the history of Denmark, and it built a teleological structure pointing towards the Danish nation-state into the nationalized narratives. This criticism was not of nineteenth century historical writing, to which it would obviously apply, but of contemporary scholarly works including the latest history of Denmark written for an academic audience, Gyldendal's *Danmarks Historie*, which was published between 1977 and 1992.[8]

---

8. Uffe Østergård, "Det danske rige – statshistorie eller nationalistisk historie," *Europas Ansigter* (Copenhagen: Rosinante, 1992): 29-50, 35ff.

To this neglect of the Danish Empire, one could add a more recent perspective. In recent years, transnational history has been presented as an approach to national history that should be seen not as post-national, but as a new and more accurate way of writing national histories. As Thomas Bender has phrased it, "The scholarly naturalization of the nation as the exclusive form of significant human solidarity has obscured the multiscaled experience of history that is clearer to us today."[9] The concept of transnationality refers to exchange, transfer, and interaction across borders. A transnational perspective on history emphasizes interconnectivity, exchange, imitation, and borrowing, focusing on processes of national adaptation and the appropriation of international or cross-national trends and processes. This appropriation can take place on many different levels, including political models and institutions; it can be cultural, and it can be practical and organizational. While the concept of transnational history ties the perspectives of interconnectivity to the nation-state, I see no problem in applying this perspective to pre-nation-state periods. I also take the term "transnational" to refer to interconnectivities and exchanges between continents, regions, and localities as well as nations. Denmark is (or was) no island; it is not and has never been a world apart, a self-sustained entity developed in relative isolation.[10] Seen in relation to my earlier remarks, this approach is no novelty with respect to one of the main trends in traditional Danish academic historiography, and as it will be apparent later, it is not entirely absent today.

I would like to begin by addressing two questions. First, how has recent Danish historical writing dealt with the nationalization of history, including the study of the Danish Empire? Second, can transnational or global tendencies be traced in the writing of Danish national history? As far as I can see, the historiography can be roughly divided into three periods defined by the years 1500 and 1900 to give the most precise answer to the questions posed. These divisions emerge from the observation that historical writing dealing with different periods has witnessed different impulses and undergone different developments in recent years.

Danish historical writing dealing with the Middle Ages can be described by the term "Europeanization." Europeanization has been a central concept in medieval

---

9. Thomas Bender, "The Boundaries and Constituencies of History," *American Literary History* 18, no. 2 (2006): 267-282, 271.

10. David Thelen, "The Nation and Beyond: Transnational Perspectives on United States History," *The Journal of American History* 86, no. 3 (1999): 965-975; Akira Iriye, "Transnational History," *Contemporary European History* 13, no. 2 (2004): 211-222; Sebastian Conrad and Jürgen Osterhammel, "Einleitung," in *Das Kaiserreich transnational: Deutschland in der Welt 1871-1914*, ed. Sebastian Conrad and Jürgen Osterhammel (Göttingen: Vandehoeck und Ruprecht, 2004), 7-27, 11ff.; Patricia Clavin, "Defining Transnationalism," *Contemporary European History* 14, no. 4 (2005): 421-439; Pernilla Jonsson and Silke Neunsinger, "Comparison and Transfer – A Fruitful Approach to National History?," *Scandinavian Journal of History* 32, no. 3 (2004): 258-280; C.A. Bayly, *The Birth of the Modern World, 1780-1914* (Oxford: Blackwell, 2004), 3, 10f. Bayly does not use the term transnational but speaks of internationalization, for example on p. 41.

research in general as well as in the Nordic countries and Denmark for several years. The concept refers to the transfer of cultural patterns, ranging from military tactics to forms of art, from European centers to the Nordic periphery, and to the growing interaction between states and economic regions.[11] Helge Paludan's book *Familia and Family* from 1995 can serve as an example of this trend. In this book, Paludan sets out to analyze modern family structure in Denmark as a result of European ideological influences communicated by the Catholic Church and social changes within a kinship society.[12] A more recent example is Kurt Villads Jensen's contribution to the *History of the Danish Empire* on the period up until the Reformation. With respect to the earliest periods, his interpretation of the history and development of the Danish Empire is firmly embedded in global processes and developments. Although longer sections of the narrative are well-known outlines of political events, they are contextualized in a European and sometimes global setting. Archaeological findings are used to show interaction and exchange, which supports the idea of political power as well as ideological and cultural transfer. Explicit warnings against projecting national concepts and expectations onto the ancient Danish Empire guide the reader into an analytical and reflexive narrative.[13] The books of both Paludan and Villads Jensen have revisionist aims. They aim to transgress formerly self-explanatory national traditions on the basis of their empirical inadequacies and overcome the assumption of the nation-state as the natural unit for historical studies. The European perspective is pursued systematically and the dissemination of cultural goods on a European scale is seen as central to cultural change in the Danish context.

The period after 1500 has not witnessed such attempts to pursue European or global perspectives on national history. In his three-volume outline of *Danish Cultural Politics* from 1750 to 1900, former professor of history Jens Engberg does not incorporate transnational perspectives at all. The explanatory framework used focuses on culture as a representation of prestige and power within Danish society, often connected to a desire to influence the worldview of the population of the Danish kingdom. Furthermore, culture is seen in the light of Danish class structure and class antagonisms, mainly as an expression of the dominant group or class.[14] There is no attempt to understand Danish cultural politics in the light of European cultural

11. Gunner Lind, "Europæiseringer i middelalderen og nyere tid. En komparativ analyse med Norden i fokus," *Historisk Tidsskrift* 103 (2003): 1-52, 1f.

12. Helge Paludan, *Familia og familie. To europæiske kulturelementers møde i højmiddelalderens Danmark* (Aarhus: Aarhus University Press, 1995); Claus Møller Jørgensen, "Århushistorier: Historisk Institut 1967-2002," in *Historiefaget 75 år*, ed. Nina Kofoed (Aarhus: Aarhus University Press, 2004), 77-327, 169ff.

13. Michael Bregnsbo and Kurt Villads Jensen, *Det danske imperium. Storhed og fald* (Viborg: Aschehoug, 2004), e.g. 14, 42.

14. Jens Engberg, *Magten og Kulturen*, vol. 1 (Copenhagen: Gads Forlag, 2005), 23.

currents. When, for example, Engberg deals with mid-eighteenth-century absolutist cultural policy, which drew heavily on French thinking about aesthetics and good taste, he is content with a narrative that centers on the fact that the leading political and cultural individuals were not Danish. Political leadership was not Danish and did not speak the language, even though Danish citizens provided the vast majority of the revenue with which the king financed his cultural extravagance.[15] Cultural institutions of great importance were introduced, Engberg states,[16] but the actual cultural content of these institutions – the opera, the royal theatre, the academy of art – is not explained with the introduction of their transnational preconditions, but lost behind the primary narrative on national and social antagonisms within Denmark.

Engberg's narrative is in many ways a very rich and comprehensive outline of Danish cultural politics in the broadest sense. It is not restricted to institutions of high culture. State sponsored institutions such as primary and secondary schools and civil society initiatives such as folk high schools, working class culture, and the women's movement are also integrated into the narrative. But there is no room for those international currents and trends to which these institutions and initiatives were more or less related. Now, Engberg is not alone in his methodological nationalism,[17] that is, his perception of Danish processes as processes best understood in a purely Danish context. In fact this strategy dominates broader works or outlines of Danish history after 1500.[18] Let me, therefore, very briefly mention another example which will form a bridge to the question of the Danish Empire or the Danish conglomerate state.

With the obvious exception of economic interaction, which would be impossible to confine to the Danish kingdom, Knud Jespersen does not pay much attention to cultural or political transfer or interaction in his recent book *A History of Denmark*,[19] which covers the period from 1500 to today. In this book, the particular

---

15. Ibid., 68.
16. Ibid., 241.
17. Andreas Wimmer and Nina Glick Schiller "are designating as *methodological nationalism* the assumption that the nation/state/society is the natural social and political form of the modern world." Methodological nationalism is the naturalization of the nation-state. National discourses, loyalties and histories are taken for granted and nationally bounded societies are taken to be the naturally given entities for study. While losing sight of trans-border connections, territorialization of the scholarly imaginary reduces the analytical focus to the boundaries of the nation-state. Andreas Wimmer and Nina Glick Schiller, "Methodological nationalism and beyond: nation-state building, migration and the social sciences," *Global Networks* 2, no. 4 (2002): 301-334, 304, 307, 327; quotation 302.
18. It should be noted that transnational elements are incorporated in outlines such as Claus Bjørn, *Fra Reaktion til Grundlov. Danmarkshistorien 1800-1850* (Copenhagen: Gyldendal & Politiken, 2003); Ove Korsgaard, *Kampen om Lyset* (Copenhagen: Gyldendal, 1997); this is especially true with respect to Ove Korsgaard, *Kampen om folket. Et dannelsesperspektiv på dansk historie gennem 500 år* (Copenhagen: Gyldendal, 2004).
19. Knud J. V. Jespersen, *A History of Denmark* (Houndmills: Palgrave Macmillan, 2004).

characteristics of the Danes are due to internal processes which have affected Danish self-perception and the formation of state institutions as well as civil society. Late in the narrative, very limited space is devoted to the Danish Empire, which is compared to the British Empire. The conclusion drawn from this comparison is that the collapse of the empire in both cases meant the re-emergence of older identities; that is, the re-emergence of national identities.

> The region we call Denmark today [...] was actually part of a large multi-national state up until 1864, called the Oldenborg Monarchy, the dual monarchy or the Union, in which each part had its own linguistic, cultural and national identity. The only element which actually united this complicated and diverse state was the common monarchy, which attempted to overcome regional differences and become the overall object of identification for all subjects [...] not dissimilar from that of promoting the concept of 'Britishness.'[20]

These remarks by Jespersen fit in very neatly with the characterization of Danish history writing made by Uffe Østergård in 1992: Denmark is defined and confined by the idea of the actual or real Denmark, that is, by the post-1864 nation-state. The developments in the centuries before 1864 are directly linked to the realization of this nation-state, in which the developing nation formed continuity with "its own linguistic, cultural and national identity." Thus, the Danish Empire is treated as a historical anomaly living on borrowed time rather than a historical reality. This brings me to the second question to be addressed in this section: How far has the study of the Danish Empire developed?

To put it quite bluntly, the history of the Danish conglomerate state is still to be written. By history here I mean an integration of both the state and societies of the Danish conglomerate state into one single narrative which shows how they developed and interacted economically, politically, and culturally. This lack may come as a surprise, but it is nonetheless the case. The conglomerate state of the Danish king existed from 1396 to 1864, but no one has written its history in its entirety. In 1997-98, a four-volume history of Denmark-Norway appeared. Even though it is only a partial history of the Danish conglomerate state, this work can be seen as a first central step in the history of the Danish Empire, especially with respect to political developments and the state. The idea behind the project was to get beyond nationalized history:

> The idea of writing a collaborative Danish-Norwegian work on the history of Denmark-Norway in the period under common rule feels so self-evidently right that one almost cannot believe that it has not been written long time ago. But in the tradition of national historical writing the histories of the two countries have been told separately within the boundaries of

---

20. Ibid., 193f.

the two nation-states. Today we find it natural to do collaborative research in and to write about the common inheritance, political, cultural and social.[21]

At the center of the project is the question of how the common state influenced Danish and Norwegian society during the period of common rule. Thus political history is treated as the most important topic, though all four volumes contain more than this, including analyses of social structures, commerce, culture, and religion. The ways in which the outside world and the remaining territories of the conglomerate state, Slesvig and Holstein, are dealt with differs from volume to volume. While the first volume, which is concerned with the Middle Ages, does place some emphasis on the importance of European developments and the two duchies for the understanding of the conglomerate state, the following two volumes do not devote much space to either issue.[22]

The final volume, on the period from 1720 to 1814, was written by Ole Feldbæk. It differs substantially from the previous volumes by virtue of the presence of both an explicit European perspective on cultural and political developments and a narrative that deals with all the components of the conglomerate state as the realm of absolutist politics. As an echo of the traditional European perspective on Danish history, Feldbæk emphasizes that

> [g]eographically the Oldenborg composite state was situated in the European periphery. However, economically, politically, and culturally this state had long since been integrated into world commerce, and therefore into the larger world of which Europe was a part. Thus, the conglomerate state can only be depicted and understood against the background of external economic and demographic forces, political challenges and cultural currents which neither knew nor respected state borders, and which the political leaders and groups of society in the various parts of the state meet, confronted and reacted upon [My translation].[23]

---

21. Knut Mykland, "Preface," in Esben Albrechtsen, "Fælleskabet bliver til, 1380-1536," *Danmark-Norge 1380-1814*, vol. 1(Oslo: Universitetsforlaget 1997), 5f.

22. Ole Feldbæk, "Nærhed og adskillelse 1720-1814," *Danmark-Norge 1380-1814*, vol. 4 (Oslo: Universitetsforlaget, 1998),138ff., 337; Øystein Rian, "Den aristokratiske fyrstestaten 1536-1648," *Danmark-Norge 1380-1814*, vol. 2 (Oslo: Universitetsforlaget, 1997), 351 does state that changes within the Oldenborg regime were related to European developments, but nevertheless European perspectives are sparse. The surrounding world appears with respect to international politics, commerce, and the Reformation. Through a comparative approach, Rian shows the differences and similarities between Denmark and Norway, for example that resistance to the Reformation was much more outspoken in Norway than in Denmark (p. 154), but Slesvig and Holstein are not draw into comparison and do not receive much attention at all. Ståle Dyrvik, "Truede tvillingriker 1648-1720," *Danmark-Norge 1380-1814*, vol. 3 (Oslo: Universitetsforlaget, 1998) concentrates on political history and the power struggles between king and council, foreign policy, and war. State finances and bureaucracy receive close attention while social structure and culture are mentioned briefly. The perspective is of Denmark-Norway's political history defined almost as narrowly as possible.

23. Ole Feldbæk, "Nærhed og adskillelse 1720-1814," *Danmark-Norge 1380-1814*, vol. 4 (Oslo: Universitetsforlaget, 1998), 19.

Feldbæk is true to this perspective in the following outline,[24] even though the dominant theme is the formation of national identities and the problems this created for the state and official state patriotism, which are treated as an expression of dynamics internal to the conglomerate state, though their European preconditions are underlined.[25] With respect to the relation between the state and the realm, Feldbæk underlines time and again that the state acted on an overall policy that had one aim: a strong state, internally and externally. Policies were adopted to capitalize on the different growth potentials of each part of the state without creating opposition from major power blocs within the four regions of the state. No part of the conglomerate state was treated with special favor; all had to contribute as much as possible to the development of the state.[26]

In Feldbæk's volume of the *History of Denmark-Norway 1380-1814*, which deals with the period from 1720 until the loss of Norway to Sweden after the Napoleonic Wars, we find the first modern contribution to the history of the Danish conglomerate state written by a historian. Feldbæk's integration of European perspectives into his narrative is extensive. On a more general level, the political scientist Tim Knudsen has written on Danish state formation in a European perspective; because state formation is embedded in war and competition with other states, it is a phenomenon which can only be seen in relation to other European states.[27] The state perspective on the Danish conglomerate state is also adopted in the first real attempt made by Danish historians to deal with the conglomerate state as such, the aforementioned history of the Danish Empire written by Kurt Villads Jensen and Michael Bregnsbo. The aim is to get beyond the nationalized interpretation of history, and the means is to choose another framework for description. They want to write the history of Denmark in its entirety, which means placing the conglomerate state in its European context. To them, the Empire is a historical phenomenon to be taken seriously. How did it work? What made the regions and lands into a unity? What did the different regions and lands contribute to the state economically and culturally?[28]

The second part of the book deals with the period after the Reformation of 1536. The analytical object is primarily the empire of the Danish king, the relations of the constituent parts to the state and the competitive relation of the state

---

24. Ibid., e.g. cultural diffusion, 20, religion 242ff., political ideology 175f.
25. Ibid., 161. See the review by Dan Ch. Christensen, "Ole Fældbæk: Nærhed og adskillelse 1720-1814," *Historie* 2 (1999): 355-364, 360ff.
26. Ole Feldbæk, "Nærhed og adskillelse," 24, 103, 379.
27. Tim Knudsen, *Dansk Statsbygning* (Copenhagen: Jurist og Økonomforbundets Forlag, 1995), 13: "Modern states do not exist alone. They developed in a cluster in Europe. Therefore it makes more sense to begin the history of Danish state formation in Europe rather than with Gorm the Old in Jelling."
28. Bregnsbo and Villads Jensen, *Det danske imperium*, 9f.

to other states. On the basis of this analysis, it seems clear that the king was king of an empire whose constituent territories were taxed, drafted, and in other ways treated in the same way as much as possible. Between 1720 and 1814, the state developed in the direction of a unitary state. By this, the authors mean a state in which all territories had the same political and administrative relations to the state.[29] While some sorts of national identifications surfaced in the latter part of the eighteenth century, according to Villads and Bregnsbo, none of these seemed to question the Empire as such. The national identities developed after 1830 (and as a political movement after 1840) in parallel movements in Copenhagen and Kiel questioned the Empire most fundamentally. These were the driving forces behind the eventual break-up of the Danish Empire in the Slesvig wars of 1848 and 1864, which led to the creation of a Danish nation-state "with one common culture, one common language and one common history."[30] Thus, the realization of the Danish nation-state is not to be seen as predetermined, but rather as the result of historical developments within the Danish conglomerate state.

Let me conclude this discussion with a few comments on Danish historiography which is concerned with the twentieth century. To judge on the basis of the newest edition of the multi-volume *History of Denmark* published between 2003 and 2005, the picture is somewhat fuzzy. The late Tage Kaarsted's narrative on the period 1925-1950 focuses quite strictly on political history, and there are surprisingly few elements of border-crossing transfer from the outside world to Denmark.[31] In Niels Finn Christiansen's volume on the period from the turn of the century to 1925, it is stated from the outset that national history was part of a larger, mainly European context: "Many people, also Danes, perceived Denmark as peripheral in relation to European cultural currents. But these currents did actually reach Denmark relatively fast, influencing domestic public debate."[32] Accordingly there are many observations of the way in which Danish society, culture, and politics were influenced by and accommodated American factory systems, German technologies, international ultranationalism, the international peace movement, and new forms in arts and literature, to mention only a few. Industrialists wanting to copy American ways of production and marketing were accompanied by syndicalists inspired by American radicals, while the Russian Revolution made its impact on the Danish left in general.[33]

29. Ibid., 148.
30. Ibid., 200.
31. Tage Kaarsted, "Krise og krig 1925-1950," *Danmarkshistorie*, vol. 13 (Copenhagen: Gyldendal & Politiken, 2004). There are some remarks concerning adaption and inspiration from abroad in arts and literature (63, 275f., 282f.), political movements (76, 86, 121f.), political ideology (119, 138, 182), and population policy (105f.).
32. Niels Finn Christiansen, "Klassesamfundet organiseres 1900-1925," *Danmarkshistorie*, vol. 12 (Copenhagen: Gyldendal & Politiken, 2004), 25.
33. Ibid., 114, 123f., 128f., 132, 153ff., 168, 173, 189ff., 195f., 228, 250ff., 311ff.

When we turn to contemporary history, this transnationalization of national history is pronounced. Besides urbanization, Henrik Nissen views internationalization as the main trend in the history of Denmark during the decades after the Second World War: "material and cultural influences from abroad made their impact faster and in a more forceful way and made the everyday life of the Danes more and more dependent on the surrounding world."[34] This is shown in numerous instances throughout the following narrative, mainly from the perspective of adaption to international circumstances, economically as well as politically,[35] and adaptation of new cultural trends from abroad, from McCarthyism to existentialism, jeans, movies, and the Youth Movement.[36] In the last two volumes of the *History of Denmark*, internationalization is described as a pervasive influence on Denmark which is continually increasing.[37] The European Union, migration, and popular culture inspired by or directly imported from the United States and Britain are seen as just as important as outlines on domestic politics, which, in accordance with tradition, still plays a key role in any outline of the history of Denmark.[38]

Danish identity

In 1997, Bernard Eric Jensen published an analysis of histories of Denmark from Allen's Handbook, which is described above, until the mid-1990s. His conclusion was that the genre had been emptied of its traditional content. Traditional narratives have been structured by the concept of the Danish people, and this was still the case with respect to Politiken's sixteen-volume *History of Denmark* from the 1960s. But in the following decades professional historians became more doubtful about the concept of the Danish people as the pivot around which Danish history should turn. This did not mean that professional historians turned their back on national history, but it did mean a break with the traditional national framework. Traditionally, writing Danish history had been synonymous with writing the history of the Danish people and Danishness. In the last couple of decades historians

---

34. Henrik Nissen, "Landet blev by 1950-1970," *Danmarkshistorie*, vol. 14 (Copenhagen: Gyldendal & Politiken, 2004), 11.
35. Ibid., 125f., 235, 262. International politics and economy play an important role in Nissen's book; e.g. western economy and the Marshall plan (69ff., 80), Cold War and international politics (111-125, 128f., 145ff. 154, 228ff., 251ff.), and foreign aid (343ff.).
36. McCarthyism (126f.), political movements (156, 212, 350ff., 359ff.), arts and literature (166f., 174f., 178, 180, 182f.), popular culture (192ff.).
37. Poul Villaume, "Lavvækst og Frontdannelser 1970-1985," *Danmarkshistorie*, vol. 15 (Copenhagen: Gyldendal & Politiken, 2005), 13.
38. Søren Hein Rasmussen, "Grænserne forsvinder 1985-2000," *Danmarkshistorie*, vol. 16 (Copenhagen: Gyldendal & Politiken, 2004).

have become more and more aware of the fact that Danish history and the history of Danishness are not two sides of the same coin.[39]

The iconic representative of this break was Søren Mørch's *The last history of Denmark* from 1996. For Mørch, it is meaningful to talk about Danish history in the national sense in the period in which Denmark was a nation-state: according to him, this period stretched from 1830 to the late 1960s. Between 1830 and 1855, ideas about Danishness, about Danish nature, and about Danish language and nationality were created by Danish civil servants and academics in Copenhagen. They did this by importing German thought and applying it to the Danish case, thereby laying the foundation of a national feeling which celebrates the mediocre.[40] It does not take a Hayden White to see that this story is written in the ironic trope. Furthermore, Mørch doubted whether it was possible to write Danish history at all, because "there are Danes of so many kinds that one might consider whether it is in fact possible to write their history. There are so many different kinds of histories of Denmark that it is, after all, only possible to write your own."[41] Accordingly Mørch is very present in the subsequent narrative, at the beginning and end of which he incorporates personal memories and reflections: Danish national sovereignty manifests itself in the fact that you have to drive 20 km/h slower on the Danish freeway than on German freeways. The nation-state is a thing of the past, and it is disintegrating quickly and independently.[42]

Mørch's modernistic and ironic account of the history of Denmark between 1830 and 1960s could be seen as the end of an older way of writing national history in Denmark. For academic historians the category of the Danish people is no longer tenable and has been pushed from the center to the margins of national narratives, if used at all. For Bernard Eric Jensen, this raises a problem, since a new core concept has not been introduced. Renewal of Danish history as a genre has not taken place, even though the concept of the people is no longer the organizing principle of Danish historiography. According to Jensen, this meant that multi-volume outlines of the history of Denmark, such as those published by Politiken and Gyldendal in the early 1990s, lacked inner coherence and a unifying perspective.[43]

For the most part, I agree with this analysis, and I will take it as my point of departure for the treatment of my next question about national identity in the Danish

39. Bernard Eric Jensen, "Danmarkshistorie – en genre i opløsning?," in *Danmarkshistorier – en erindringspolitisk slagmark*, ed. Bernard Eric Jensen, Carsten Tage Nielsen, Søren Schou, and Anne Birgitte Richard (Copenhagen: Samfundslitteratur, 1997), 17-199, 143.
40. Søren Mørch, *Den sidste Danmarkshistorie* (Copenhagen: Gyldendal, 1996), 85ff.
41. Ibid., 53; B.E. Jensen, "Danmarkshistorie," 166.
42. Søren Mørch, *Den sidste Danmarkshistorie*, 552f.
43. B.E. Jensen, "Danmarkshistorie," 174.

case: How is Danish national identity analyzed in recent broader works on Danish history? These works can be grouped in the following way:

Table 1			
	Primordialism	**Modernist**	
Cumulative harmonic uniform Danish national identity	Knud J. V. Jespersen: *A history of Denmark* (2004)		
Ongoing discursive struggle – epochal hegemonic identities – 'class' perspective		Ove Korsgaard: *The struggle for the people* (2004)	
Ongoing class struggle – 'class' perspective – middle class dominance over cultural institutions produce dominant middle class national identity		Jens Engberg: *Power and culture* I-III. (2005)	
– 'class' perspective			Niels F. Christiansen: *The organization of Class Society* 1900-25. (1991, 2004)

As this table shows, the perennialist conceptions of the nation which dominated traditional history writing do not have a place in modern Danish historical scholarship, though they continue to outside the profession. Søren Krarup, member of the Danish parliament for the Danish People's Party, believes that "Denmark has a more than thousand year history, based on the Danish people's ongoing battle to exist in spite of unfavorable geographic and strategic circumstances [My translation]."[44] For real historians, national identity is the outcome of historical processes of various lengths, but the nation is not to be seen as a natural community outside time. Thus, history cannot be written with an idea of a Danish people as a transhistorical entity. The existence of a Danish nation is not a predetermined or natural entity, but something to be explained historically. The main trend among Danish historians is modernist and constructivist, and the view of Danish society is based on class and struggle; but, as Knud J. V. Jespersen's *A History of Denmark* exemplifies, primordialist conceptions of a harmonious national identity exist as well.[45]

---

44. Søren Krarup, *Kristendom og danskhed. Prædikener og foredrag* (Aarhus: Hovedland, 2001), 65.
45. A spatial conception of Danishness connecting national identity formation to landscapes and bodily activities and recollections of nature, which places Denmark in a Nordic context of peasant idealization – the peasant as competent, independent, and just – as the integrating core of popular self-understanding is proposed by Niels Kayser Nielsen, but has not yet been applied to a broader outline on Danish history. Therefore, I will not consider

This is the first narrative of Danish history I want to introduce. Professor Jespersen's *A History of Denmark* was published in 2004. It sets out to find the historical roots of modern Danishness, a historical explanation for the habits and mentality of the modern Dane.[46] In this respect the title of the Danish version from 2008, *The History of the Danes*, is more apt than the title of the English volume. Although the passage cited earlier from Jespersen's book might seem to imply that Jespersen views Danishness as a very old form of identity, which would be a perennialist way of perceiving the problem, the predominant story in his book is how the Danish people came to perceive itself as Danish after 1500. His work is not perennialist, then, but rather primordialist, with an emphasis on the pre-modern conditions of the modern nation – in the Danish case the old village collectives with origins in the mists of the Middle Ages.[47]

According to Jespersen, modern Danishness consists of three major elements which sedimented into the Danish mentality at different points in time. The first element is the Danes' friendly view of the state and state intervention in society, which is explained as an effect of the *Danish Law* of 1683: "The fundamental attitude of modern Danes, that the state is a friend and ally, not an adversary, a protector and not an enemy, is very much an unconscious result of the fact that for generations, the Danes have been accustomed to a state of law fashioned by the *Danish Law*."[48]

The second element of modern Danishness is religious. Jespersen writes that there is a "religious nerve which exists in most Danes, however well hidden." The "view that Denmark is very secular and a long way away from the preceding Christian society is actually superficial. Christian values and evangelical Lutheran attitudes can, on closer examination, be seen to have permeated the Danish mentality and are actually the ethical foundation of the modern Danish welfare state."[49] The beauty of it all is that the religious element underpins the state's legitimacy: "The unshakable conviction that the state truly has the interests of its citizens at heart is deeply anchored in Lutheran Protestantism [...]"[50]

The third and most important element is Grundtvigianism and the concept of *folkelighed*. N. F. S. Grundtvig (1783-1872) is the most important person in modern Danish history, "whose initiative and philosophy have left an indelible stamp [...] on the whole way in which Danes perceive themselves and their ideas of what being a Danish citizen means." In addition to this, Grundtvigianism, the move-

this position in this context. See Niels Kayser Nielsen, *Steder i Europa* (Aarhus: Aarhus University Press, 2005), 198-218, 219-239.

46. Jespersen, *A History of Denmark*, 4.
47. Ibid., 209f.
48. Ibid., 47.
49. Ibid., 84f.
50. Ibid., 96.

ment he inspired, has "probably affected Denmark far more than other European political or ideological movement."[51] The core of Grundtvig's philosophy and the Danishness that stems from it is *folkelighed*. *Folkelighed* is tolerance, openness and liberalmindedness; the means to achieve *folkelighed* is enlightenment and committed dialogue aiming at consensus. The universal concept of solidarity underpinning the Danish welfare state "can well be seen as the concrete manifestation of Grundtvig's concept of *folkelighed*."[52] It is based on a voluntary concept of the nation. Belonging to a nation was a matter of free choice, but joining the nation meant mutual obligation and the desire to share it actively with others who wished to join. Again it is underpinned by Protestantism, to the extent that it would be "inconceivable without the Lutheran Christian foundation on which it firmly rests."[53]

The explanation Jespersen offers is premised on the existence of a pervasive *folkelighed* in the twentieth century, which is a modernization of the older, pre-modern village culture, the raising of village culture to a national level. "In short, the Denmark of the nineteenth century could be reasonably accurately described as a gigantic village, where uniformity predominated and social distances were modest."[54] "Grundtvig [...] transformed the old rules of conduct and norms of behavior from the old agrarian society into a coherent national utopia [...] the values of the ancient peasant society were promoted to common Danish values, and thus to an important element of the identity – further developed by politicians, artists and writers from the era of Romanticism onwards – which pointed the way forward to the modern welfare society."[55]

Friendliness towards the state and *folkelighed* form the mental backbone of the Danish nation, which is described as a tribe characterized sociologically by homogeneity, no – or very small – economic, social, or cultural differences, and a political culture based on solidarity, dialogue, and consensus. This was Denmark until recently. Over the last twenty-five years or so, the Danish model has come under a pressure that amounts to crisis, both from immigration, especially from Third World and Muslim societies, and the EU. For the Danish welfare system to function, according to Jespersen, it is necessary

> [...] that the citizens of the country are fairly homogenous in economic circumstances and culture, that the social divides are narrow, and that the population as a whole shares inherent feelings of solidarity and ideals of equality which are the real foundation of the whole welfare

---

51. Ibid., 103; "The impact of Grundtvig was so great during his life and after that his name and the eponymous movement he began have earned an almost religious status in the Danish consciousness" (ibid., 107).
52. Ibid., 110.
53. Ibid., 112.
54. Ibid., 111.
55. Ibid., 213.

system. These conditions largely prevailed in the middle of the twentieth century, when the system was seriously implemented. However, the large-scale immigration of recent decades, including the influx of refugees from the Third World, has radically changed the situation. These new citizens in principle have the right to the same welfare services as native Danes, but they also bring with them their experience and traditions which are inevitably not the same as those on which the Danish system is based. Many of them are also alien to the entire political consensus and tradition of agreement which is an essential historical condition for the welfare system to function. As a result of this immigration, the Danish population is slowly becoming multi-cultural and multi-ethnic, and the Danish tax-financed, universal welfare system is not designed to accommodate this diversity. So a new, unforeseen factor has become a part of Danish political life.[56]

Jespersen's approach differs considerably from the one presented by Professor Ove Korsgaard in his *The Struggle for the People,* published in 2004, the same year as Jespersen's *A History of Denmark.* The time frame of the two narratives is the same, but unlike Jespersen, Korsgaard is a modernist who draws a clear distinction between pre-modern religious and patriotic concepts and modern concepts of nationalism. Korsgaard's approach is that of conceptual history, and the struggle to which the title of the book refers is the struggle to define the concept of the Danish people. The period between the Reformation and today can be divided into four minor periods in which a dominant conceptual framework defined the boundaries within which the question of the Danish people could be answered. Between the Reformation and 1776, the answer was given within a religious framework, between 1776 and 1830 in patriotic terms, and between 1864 and 1972 within a national framework. Between 1776 and 1864 we find the transition from a Christian state to a nation-state; before 1776 it makes no sense to talk about national identity, since Danish society was permeated by Lutheran Protestantism, and national thinking only gradually replaced eighteenth-century patriotism in the first half of the nineteenth century.[57] Another difference from Jespersen's book concerns the role class plays in Korsgaard's narrative; different concepts of the Danish people are linked to different groups and classes. It should be noted, though, that this link is not a product of economy or social structure, but of socialization and schooling, the ways in which culture is transmitted and received by the individual.[58]

Korsgaard's explanation is not cumulative like Jespersen's, and it does not result in a stable, harmonious national identity. The core idea is struggle, and the concept of the Danish people is characterized by changing and disputed meanings. This does not mean, though, that Danishness is in a constant flux. Historical periods

---

56. Ibid., 79f.
57. Ove Korsgaard, *Kampen om folket,* 60, 101.
58. Ibid., 21f.

are characterized by a dominant or hegemonic concept of the nation, which is the concept of the politically dominant group or class or a compromise with which groups and classes can identify. The first period of the democratic Danish nation-state after 1848 was characterized by the civil servants, after the turn of the century it was defined by the Danish peasants with their base in the folk high school, and from the end of the 1920s the Social Democrats took on the role. What we learn is that Danishness is temporal and open for negotiation. The most important and influential concept of the Danish people in the period of the nation-state between 1864 and 1972 was Grundtvigianism. On this point, there is a measure of agreement between Jespersen and Korsgaard. But Korsgaard's focus on the coexistence of different conceptions of the people gives the argument a different emphasis. Furthermore, Korsgaard's Grundtvigianism is not a series of positive internalized mental attributes, but first and foremost the ideas that common people should participate in democracy, and that self-organization should exist outside the reach of the state. It was, thus, a way to mobilize Danish peasants to democratic participation in a given period.

Like Jespersen, Korsgaard takes his analysis up to the present. The last period is defined by Denmark's joining the EU in 1972. This period differs in fundamental ways from the epoch of the nation-state. The epoch of the nation-state was characterized by groups and classes which contributed to the development of Danish national democracy at different points in time; civil servants, peasants, and workers in turn made their mark and contribution. After 1972, Korsgaard is not able to find a group or class to take over: "it seems as if the motor of the epoch of the people has stopped [...There is] no new class able to influence the development of society in the same way as civil servants, the peasants, and the workers have done in the past."[59] What has happened is that traditional concepts of the Danish people have come under pressure from the EU, globalization, Islam, immigration, and human rights. Since 1972 EU, globalization and individualization have challenged the idea of the Danish people. The national concept of the people is no longer self-evident, but is rather at the center of heated debates.

While Korsgaard's main focus is on discourse, a more straightforward class perspective is applied by Jens Engberg in his book *Danish Cultural Policy 1750-1900*. To Engberg, cultural policy reflects class struggle. The main class actors in the period were successively the aristocracy, the middle class, the agrarian middle class, and the working class, and there were social and cultural distances between them. Engberg is, like Korsgaard, a modernist, underlining the non-national character of eighteenth-century patriotism and stressing that nationalism became a dominant

---

59. Ibid., 476.

middle-class ideology only after 1830. Starting in the middle of the eighteenth century, the cosmopolitan aristocracy headed the state and the culture. But the same period witnessed the rise of the middle class. After 1830 the middle classes, especially the educated part, took over one cultural institution after the other, and gave them a national content and character. Middle-class culture between 1830 and 1860 is described as a culture of the relatively few and as an exclusively metropolitan phenomenon; outside Copenhagen there were neither cultural institutions of any importance nor any educated middle class to bear and maintain them. The result was the creation of a national middle-class culture which was originally opposed to aristocratic cosmopolitanism, but which later gained dominance over the cultural institutions that democratic Denmark inherited from absolutism. Engberg presents this middle-class national culture in a kaleidoscopic fashion in relation to various cultural institutions, from the Royal Theatre, the Arts Academy, and the National Museum to primary and secondary schools. While the working class developed cultural practices of its own, in general it adopted middle-class culture. The agrarian middle class developed its own cultural institutions and practices, to some extent in opposition to urban middle-class culture, but "both parties were more or less equally enthusiastic in their Danishness even though there were some differences between pompous middle class Danishness and the peasants' folk high school-based conception of Danishness."[60]

The last group of narratives chosen for this survey does not really make use of the concept of the Danish people. Bernard Eric Jensen observed in 1997 that the concept of the Danish people had been replaced by concepts of class and class society described in terms of antagonisms and divides in cultural and social circumstances.[61]This group includes the majority of the works on Danish history included in this survey. One of many expressions of this can be taken from Niels Finn Christiansen's outline of early twentieth-century Danish history. "Socially, politically and culturally, the picture of Denmark at the turn of the century was full of contrasts," Christiansen finds, and the fact that political compromise has characterized the political process throughout the twentieth century does not alter this. Compromise was not to be seen as an expression of a consensus society or Danish mentality, but as the way in which democracy functions when governments are never majority governments.

> Through this a peculiar counterbalancing of class and group interests has been brought about, which, at least on the surface, has given the political development in Denmark a more harmonious character than in most other countries. Foreign observers have pointed

---

60. Engberg, *Magten og Kulturen*, cf. vol. 3, 506, vol. 2, 15, 129, 274f., 457, 479ff.; Jeppe Nevers, "Klassernes kulturkamp. Om Jens Engberg: Magten og kulturen: Dansk kulturpolitik 1750-1900," *Historie* (2006): 420-426.
61. B.E. Jensen, "Danmarkshistorie," 138f.

to this as a peculiarity of Denmark. This idealized picture covers the fact that beneath the cultivated political surface severe struggle between classes, social groups and organizations has taken place.[62]

Henrik Nissen emphasizes a cultural gap as characteristic of the decades after the Second World War.[63] When Nissen does, occasionally, use the concept of the Danish people, it is not in order to underline its cultural or mental uniformity:

> The Youth Movement at the end of the 1960s and the reactions it provoked demonstrated some of the cultural distances in the Danish people. A few years earlier the debate about the cultural gap had done the same. Compared to other nations, social and cultural differences were not big in Denmark; but now it seemed as if the gap of understanding was insurmountable.[64]

Discussion, critique, and conclusions

I started this article with the opinion that national history could be renewed by being denationalized. Nationalized history puts too much emphasis on external difference and on internal uniformity. The solution is to transnationalize national history and to avoid reductive concepts of national identity.

Let me start with the latter. What is wrong with the traditional organicist conception of the people is that it evades cultural and social differences. The traditional conception of the people claims that society is homogeneous and uniform at the level of identity, and that this homogeneity and uniformity was constituted in prehistoric times, with the consequence that national identity is essentialized and stabilized. According to this traditional conception, the Danish people is seen either as a historical constant outside time or an entity with the peculiar quality of being able to change in order to remain the same.[65]

Even though Danish historians have given up the idea of "the people" in the traditional sense, it seems to me that some of these assumptions have reappeared in recent interpretations. This is especially apparent in Jespersen's narrative, in which all social and cultural differences disappear and the Danes are perceived as a tribe with special Danish values and inward solidarity and consensus, while the

---

62. Niels Finn Christiansen, *Klassesamfundet organiseres*, 25, 77.
63. Nissen, *Landet blev by*, 270ff.
64. Ibid., 365.
65. Dorthe Gert Simonsen, "Historiens bedrift og folkeejendommelighedens mytologi," in *Historiske analyser – nye teorier og metoder*, ed. Claus Møller Jørgensen and Carsten Tage Nielsen (Frederiksberg: Roskilde Universitetsforlag, 2001), 212-240, 231ff.

outside is relatively excluded.[66] In this way, national identity is essentialized and stabilized. My objection to this is that it appears to run counter to empirical findings.

Denmark is not – alas – a country without social and cultural differences. Even in Denmark, these differences reveal themselves in the fact that there is no agreement with respect to what Danishness is. On the level of discourse, you find struggle, as Korsgaard and others have shown.[67] This does not preclude the existence of uniform national identity on the level of mentality, the level of the collective unconscious. But as far as I can see, no one has produced a satisfying explanation of how this uniform mentality could have been brought about. The most common explanation is the schools, especially the Grundtvigian folk high schools and free schools.[68] But in Denmark as in all other countries school systems have produced and reproduced social and cultural differences.[69] Furthermore, the notion of mentality seems to assume that ideas are transferred to passive subjects, not actively interpreting individuals. But why, then, does the school system produce a national mentality of relatively uniform character while, at the same time, it does not produce political uniformity? The answer, I think, is that what is actually produced is not a series of values that are taken over by the recipient, but a way of thinking. To put it in a provocative manner: Danishness is a common sense fact, but what it actually means to be Danish is open to politically and socially conditioned subjective interpretation.

On the symbolic level, the existence of Danishness is attested both on the official and the private and banal level; but as we now know concepts of Danishness are both temporal and context-bound. National identification seems compatible with other forms of identification such as political, class, gender, and regional identifications, which may colour national identifications. Therefore, this discussion about Danishness has been taking place since the idea of nationality made its entrance in Denmark after 1800, and it will continue to do so until the idea of the nation

---

66. Jespersen, *A History of Denmark*, 211.
67. E.g. Leif Lazlo Haaning, "Kampen om det nationale – nationsbegrebet og dets anvendelse i Danmark 1885-1915," *Den jyske Historiker* 96 (2002); Lasse Koefoed, *Glokale nationalismer. Globalisering, hverdagsliv og fortællinger om dansk identitet* (Roskilde Universitet: Institut for Geografi og International Udviklingsstudier, 2006). On the contentious nature of concepts of the nation see also Robert J. C. Young, *The Idea of English Ethnicity* (Oxford: Blackwell, 2007); Timothy Baycroft and Mark Hewitson, *What is a Nation? Europe 1789-1914* (Oxford: Oxford University Press, 2006).
68. One variant of the Grundtvigianism thesis is provided by Uffe Østergård. Østergård builds his argument on the basis of certain personal sensibilities and a Gramscian approach which allows him to draw the conclusion that because the Danish peasants were the economically dominant class, their Grundtvigian ideology (i.e. introverted, self-centered, self-aggrandizing, and suspicious of foreigners) became the dominant ideology which in turn was internalized by the Danish population becoming a national identity. Uffe Østergård, "Peasants and Danes – The Danish National Identity and Political Culture," *Comparative Studies in Society and History* 34, no. 1 (1992): 3-17.
69. Detlef K. Müller, Fritz Ringer, and Brian Simon, *The Rise of Modern Educational Systems* (Cambridge: Cambridge University Press, 1986), xiif.

ceases to exercise its interpretive function. And this must be the point of departure for the history of Danish national identity. In the process of nation building and in traditional historical writing, national stereotyping has been the order of the day. I do not see this as the purpose of contemporary historical scholarship. Danishness seems to be something that is the object of struggle and disagreement, rather than an essence. Narratives that purport to convey Danishness as an essence are either highly reductionist or characterized by a need to explain away the influence of competing interpretations of Danishness. Any interpretation of Danishness as a series of positive mental characteristics runs the risk of essentializing and stabilizing what is, in fact, context-bound, temporal, and the object of continuous discursive struggle and disagreement.

I shall not pretend to have refuted the idea of national identity on the level of a shared unconscious mentality, only to have indicated the extent to which I find it unsatisfactory as a historical explanation. On the level of identity politics I find it unsatisfactory because of its exclusive character and its inability to handle plurality. Generally I do think that the force of the democratic nation-state has been its ability to deal with plurality and disagreement. I do not really see the need to conceal this under an idealization of consensus and uniform identity.

On the one hand this leads me to the conclusion that national historical writing in Denmark has been renewed with respect to the problem of national identity. This is not to say that the final narrative of Danish history has been written, or that the question has been settled on an interpretive or theoretical level. But I do think that the focus on discursive struggle and on social and cultural differences point to new ways in which historical writing can qualify the ongoing discussions about past, present, and future Denmark and Danishness.

On the other hand, with respect to the question of transnational perspectives, renewal is harder to find in recent Danish historical writing.[70] Feldbæk, Bregnsbo, and Villads Jensen go some way towards it. What is important in their work is that their analyses are not defined by or confined to the post-1864 Danish nation-state. Their histories are not written in a teleological fashion that points always towards the realization of the nation-state. The Danish conglomerate state is not seen as a historical anomaly, but as a functioning state. The different territories had different

---

70. This does not seem to be a peculiarity of the Danish. A recent evaluation of Norwegian historical scholarship reached the conclusion that methodological nationalism was a prevailing feature. Bo Stråth et. al, *Evaluering af norsk historiefaglig forskning* (Oslo: Norges Forskningsråd, 2008), 26. With respect to British, German, Italian, and French historiography, none of these has moved substantially beyond the national agenda, even though this agenda has become far more contested and controversial, especially from the 1960s onward. This according to Stefan Berger, "A Return to the National Paradigm? National History Writing in Germany, Italy, France, and Britain from 1945 to the Present," *The Journal of Modern History* 77 (2005): 629-678, 673. This conclusion seems to cover the Danish case as well.

economic and cultural characteristics, but the point is that the Empire did function with linguistic, ethnic, and judicial diversity. The Empire expressed economic and geopolitical rationalities, and mirrored the prestige and power of the Danish king.[71] This is an important departure from a nationalized history,[72] which paints a richer and more accurate picture of the Danish past. In my survey of recent Danish scholarship on modern history, I have found no counterpart to Feldbæk's or Villads Jensen and Bregnsbo's books. The approach to modern history is mainly national.[73]

Knut Mykland notes in his preface to the history of Denmark-Norway that the national separation of Danish and Norwegian history runs the risk of causing substantial and systematic errors of interpretation.[74] I think that this conclusion should be expanded to include not only the Danish Empire in its entirety, but to a more systematic integration of transnational and transregional perspectives into national histories. In this respect, Feldbæk's narrative of the Danish conglomerate state points forward, and in comparison with Engberg's history of Danish cultural policy it comes out on top. Most of the topics Engberg deals with could and should have been related to extra-national developments and circulations. Neither

---

71. Bregnsbo and Villads Jensen, *Det danske imperium*, 228ff.

72. Steen Bo Frandsen has approached the history of the Danish empire from a regional angle in two very important books that I have excluded from this survey. His overall aim seems to be to show that the Danish Empire was a functioning historical-political unit which was not, as the national interpretation of the Danish conglomerate state always claims, doomed to fall apart sooner or later. The conglomerate state was a state of regions, and as such it formed a functioning, although not always well-functioning, unit. It was united by a king whose overall ambition was to integrate the regions as much as possible under his rule, and to have the state penetrate as far into civil society as possible. In this doctoral thesis from 1996, the argument is that is it was not given from the outset that Northern Jutland should form a part of the Danish nation-state; in the early nineteenth century this region was economically oriented southwards towards Altona and Hamburg, and it had no significant cultural ties to Copenhagen. But it did not have any regional political or cultural elite which could propagate a regional identity, and was, therefore, integrated into the Copenhagen- based economy, in a process of politicization, nationalization, and centralization after the mid-1820s. Steen Bo Frandsen, *Opdagelsen af Jylland* (Aarhus: Aarhus University Press, 1996). In his new book *Holsten i Helstaten* Frandsen offers the most comprehensive account of the history of Holstein in Danish. Holstein was influenced by its long connection to Denmark, but it was never culturally integrated into the conglomerate state. Contrary to Northern Jutland it had potential to develop a regionalism with Kiel and its university as the political center after 1830. The attempt by the Danish king to "Danicize" Holstein after 1806 backfired with the development of a Slesvig-Holsteinian regionalism which was neither Danish nor German, and the development of a regional liberal public in the beginning of the 1830s. Only during the 1840s and the processes of nationalization and politicization did the position of Slesvig-Holstein regionalism become more and more difficult to sustain until the radicalization of the 1848 revolutions finally made it impossible. Steen Bo Frandsen, *Holsten i Helstaten* (Copenhagen: Museum Tusculanum, 2008).

73. In part some elements of the history of the Danish conglomerate state can be found in Leon Jespersen et al., eds., *Dansk Forvaltningshistorie*, vol. 1 (Copenhagen: Jurist og økonomforbundets forlag, 2000). But the outline builds on the idea that the administration can be delimited to "*det egentlige Danmark*," Denmark proper, that is, the Danish Kingdom. Thus the narrative can concentrate on the precursor for the Danish nation-state leaving the other parts of the Empire aside, and after 1814 neglecting them all together. See review by Claus Møller Jørgensen, "Rigets rygrad," *Historie* 2 (2002): 160-176, 166, 175.

74. Mykland, "Preface," 14.

eighteenth-century patriotism nor nineteenth-century nationalism were Danish inventions, but European phenomena. The same is the case with respect to music, educational thought, literary forms, religious debates,[75] and so on.

The point is that no nation is an island; Denmark "ist keine Insel, keine scharf umgrenzte und auf sich selbst bezogene Welt."[76] Modern history is not characterized by insular cultures or societies but by interconnectivity, exchange, interaction, and adaptation. The nationalization of culture has overshadowed this fact. Among historians, this has to a large degree resulted in a widespread methodological nationalism. The most remarkable result of this has been that the comprehensive multi-volume account of the history of the Danish Empire has not yet been written, though the first important steps have been taken towards such a work. Danish historians know very well that Danish history is embedded in the larger world and that cultural, political, economic, and technological transfer has happened throughout history. As Engberg notes, most cultural impulses came to Denmark from Europe, but habit and convenience and the need to limit the workload makes the national frame convenient and thus methodological nationalism is predominant.[77] I have tried to show that transnational perspectives are not absent from Danish historical scholarship, but it must be concluded that no systematic effort to incorporate transnational transfer, exchange, and interaction has taken place with respect to the broader works on Danish history. In medieval and twentieth-century history the situation is best, but in the intermediate period transnational perspectives are almost absent.

In relation to identity politics, this gives the false impression of nations as developed by and for themselves, and accordingly suggests that national cultures are best preserved as static and insular. The wrong conclusion is that, if national cultures should develop at all, they should do so only from the inside; that the outside world is a threat against national identity. National developments have more often than not had transnational preconditions; nationalism, democracy, human rights, and technological, scientific, and economical development are transnational phenomena and have been so for a very long time. Thomas Bender has proposed

75. Maurizio Viroli, *For Love and Country: an Essay on Patriotism and Nationalism* (Oxford: Oxford University Press, 1997; online ed. 2003), 63ff.; Juliane Engelhardt, "Patriotism, nationalism and modernity: the patriotic societies in the Danish conglomerate state, 1969-1814," *Nations and Nationalism* 13, no. 2, (2007): 205-223, 208; Joep Leersen, *National Thought in Europe. A Cultural History* (Amsterdam: Amsterdam University Press, 2006), 19, 169; Jens Henrik Koudal, "Musikken. På sporet af 'originale nationaltoner'," in *Veje til Danskheden*, ed. Palle Ove Christiansen (Copenhagen: C.A. Reitzel, 2005), 95-124; Claus Møller Jørgensen, *Humanistisk dannelse og videnskab i Danmark i det 19. århundrede I-II. Reform, nationalisering, professionalisering* (Aarhus: Begrebshistorisk Netværk, 2000); Franco Moretti, *Atlas of the European Novel 1800-1900* (London: Verso, 1998), 171ff.; Ole Feldbæk, "Nærhed og adskillelse," 242ff.
76. Conrad and Osterhammel, "Einleitung," 7.
77. Engberg, *Magten og Kulturen*, 35.

that transnationalizing national history is to widen the "circle of we". Transnationalizing history is being attentive to the fact that a national history was part of a larger history, a province of a larger global human community and history: "Such a history can and still ought to have a strong national narrative with which the citizen can identify, but they could and should identify themselves as rooted cosmopolitans, not nationalists."[78] The lesson of transnational national history is to my mind a kind of trustful cosmopolitanism resting on the acknowledgement that the development of Danish culture and society is and has always been related to interaction with the surrounding world.

History as a scholarly discipline has to keep up with "the times," developments in "the surrounding society" or the "surrounding world," or whatever more or less illuminating metaphor one might choose to describe the need for continuing adaption between processes of knowledge production and the context of knowledge production. For a short period, it seemed a viable conclusion that the nation-state was to diminish and eventually wither away as a political and cultural entity in a globalizing world. Today this analysis of the present seems less plausible. Globalization and the nation-state seem to be part of the same process; that is, modern nation-states were formed in the period of globalization that started around 1750. The conclusion is, therefore, that the nation-state is an entity to be taken into account, and with it national cultures and national politics, etc. But as a research paradigm, and the idea of the nation did in many ways start its long and effective career as a research paradigm, the old idea of the nation as a container of self-sustained culture, politics, and economy seems to have reached its limits. The interconnectivity of the present requires us to re-address the question of the nation to provide a fuller understanding of the nation in the broader context in which it is and always has been situated. Re-contextualizing national history in a European or global setting presents different perspective on national history and shows how artificial the decontextualization of national history can be.[79] The problem with old and new efforts to spell out the essence of the nation, the attributes of national identity, or the elements of national character is that they all end up as decontextualized stereotypes which are neither historically correct nor helpful as a means of orientation in the world we live in today.

---

78. Bender, "The Boundaries and Constituencies of History," 277f.
79. See Ute Frevert, "Europeanizing Germany's Twentieth Century," *History and Memory* 17 (2005): 87-116.

Bibliography

Allen, C.F. *Haandbog i Fædrelandets Historie med stadigt Henblik paa Folkets og Statens indre Udvikling.* Copenhagen: C.A. Reitzel, 1840.

Baycroft, Timothy and Mark Hewitson. *What is a Nation? Europe 1789-1914.* Oxford: Oxford University Press, 2006.

Berger, Stefan. "A Return to the National Paradigm? National History Writing in Germany, Italy, France, and Britain from 1945 to the Present." *The Journal of Modern History* 77 (2005): 629-67.

Bayly, C.A. *The Birth of the Modern World, 1780-1914.* Oxford: Blackwell, 2004.

Bender, Thomas. "The Boundaries and Constituencies of History." *American Literary History* 18, no. 2 (2006): 267-282.

Bjørn, Claus. *Fra Reaktion til Grundlov. Danmarkshistorien 1800-1850.* Copenhagen: Gyldendal & Politiken, 2003.

Bregnsbo, Michael and Kurt Villads Jensen. *Det danske imperium. Storhed og fald.* Viborg: Aschehoug, 2004.

Christensen, Dan Ch. "Ole Fældbæk: Nærhed og adskillelse 1720-1814." *Historie* 2 (1999): 355-364.

Christiansen, Niels Finn. "Klassesamfundet organiseres 1900-1925." *Danmarkshistorie*, vol. 12. Copenhagen: Gyldendal & Politiken, 2004.

Clavin, Patricia. "Defining Transnationalism." *Contemporary European History* 14, no. 4 (2005): 421-439.

Conrad, Sebastian and Jürgen Osterhammel. "Einleitung," *Das Kaiserreich transnational. Deutschland in der Welt 1871-1914*, 7-27. Göttingen: Vandehoeck und Ruprecht, 2004.

Dyrvik, Ståle. "Truede tvillingriker 1648-1720." *Danmark-Norge 1380-1814*, vol. 3. Oslo: Universitetsforlaget, 1998.

Engberg, Jens. *Magten og Kulturen*, vols. 1-3. Copenhagen: Gads Forlag, 2005.

Engelhardt, Juliane. "Patriotism, nationalism and modernity: the patriotic societies in the Danish conglomerate state, 1969-1814." *Nations and Nationalism* 13, no. 2, (2007): 205-223.

Erslev, Kristian. *Valdemarernes Storhedstid.* Copenhagen: Universitetsforlaget i København 1972 [1898].

Feldbæk, Ole. "Nærhed og adskillelse 1720-1814." *Danmark-Norge 1380-1814*, vol. 4. Oslo: Universitetsforlaget, 1998.

Frandsen, Steen Bo. *Opdagelsen af Jylland.* Aarhus: Aarhus University Press, 1996.

Frandsen, Steen Bo. *Holsten i Helstaten.* Copenhagen: Museum Tusculanum, 2008.

Frevert, Ute. "Europeanizing Germany's Twentieth Century." *History and Memory* 17 (2005): 87-116.

Haaning, Leif Lazlo. "Kampen om det nationale – nationsbegrebet og dets anvendelse i Danmark 1885-1915." *Den jyske Historiker* 96 (2002).

Hein Rasmussen, Søren. "Grænserne forsvinder 1985-2000." *Danmarkshistorie*, vol. 16. Copenhagen: Gyldendal & Politiken, 2004.

Hroch, Miroslav & Jitk Malečkova. "Historical Heritage: Continuity and Discontinuity in the Construction of National Histories." *Studia Historica* 53 (2000): 15-36.

Iriye, Akira. "Transnational History." *Contemporary European History* 13, no. 2 (2004): 211-222.

Jensen, Bernard Eric. "Danmarkshistorie – en genre i opløsning?" In *Danmarkshistorier – en erindringspolitisk slagmark*, edited by Bernard Eric Jensen, Carsten Tage Nielsen, Søren Schou, and Anne Birgitte Richard, 17-199. Copenhagen: Samfundslitteratur, 1997.

Jensen, Kurt Villads. "Den hvide race og den danske jord." *Historie* (1998): 91-103.

Jespersen, Knud J. V. *A History of Denmark.* Houndmills: Palgrave Macmillan, 2004.

Jespersen, Leon et al., eds. *Dansk Forvaltningshistorie*, vol. 1. Copenhagen: Jurist og økonomforbundets forlag, 2000.

Jonsson, Pernilla and Silke Neunsinger. "Comparison and Transfer – A Fruitful Approach to National History?" *Scandinavian Journal of History* 32, no. 3 (2004): 258-280.

Kaarsted, Tage. "Krise og krig 1925-1950." *Danmarkshistorie*, vol. 13. Copenhagen: Gyldendal & Politiken, 2004.

Kayser Nielsen, Niels. *Steder i Europa*. Aarhus: Aarhus University Press, 2005.

Knudsen, Tim. *Dansk Statsbygning*. Copenhagen: Jurist og Økonomforbundets Forlag, 1995.

Koefoed, Lasse. *Glokale nationalismer. Globalisering, hverdagsliv og fortællinger om dansk identitet*. Roskilde Universitet: Institut for Geografi og International Udviklingsstudier, 2006.

Korsgaard, Ove. *Kampen om Lyset*. Copenhagen: Gyldendal, 1997.

Korsgaard, Ove. *Kampen om folket. Et dannelsesperspektiv på dansk historie gennem 500 år*. Copenhagen: Gyldendal, 2004.

Koudal, Jens Henrik. "Musikken. På sporet af 'originale nationaltoner'," in *Veje til Danskheden*, edited by Palle Ove Christiansen, 95-124. Copenhagen: C.A. Reitzel, 2005.

Krarup, Søren. *Kristendom og danskhed. Prædikener og foredrag*. Aarhus: Hovedland, 2001.

Lind, Gunner. "Europæiseringer i middelalderen og nyere tid. En komparativ analyse med Norden i fokus." *Historisk Tidsskift* 103 (2003): 1-52.

Leersen, Joep. *National Thought in Europe. A Cultural History*. Amsterdam: Amsterdam University Press, 2006.

Moretti, Franco. *Atlas of the European Novel 1800-1900*. London: Verso, 1998.

Müller, Detlef K., Fritz Ringer, and Brian Simon. *The Rise of Modern Educational Systems*. Cambridge: Cambridge University Press, 1986.

Mykland, Knut. "Preface." In Esben Albrechtsen, "Fælleskabet bliver til, 1380-1536," *Danmark-Norge 1380-1814*, vol. 1, 5-7. Oslo: Universitetsforlaget, 1997.

Møller Jørgensen, Claus. *Humanistisk dannelse og videnskab i Danmark i det 19. århundrede I-II. Reform, nationalisering, professionalisering*. Aarhus: Begrebshistorisk Netværk, 2000.

Møller Jørgensen, Claus. "Rigets rygrad." *Historie* 2 (2002): 160-176.

Møller Jørgensen, Claus. "Århushistorier: Historisk Institut 1967-2002," in *Historiefaget 75 år*, edited by Nina Kofoed, 77-327. Aarhus: Aarhus University Press, 2004.

Møller Jørgensen, Claus. "Civilisation og nation i dansk dannelsestænkning i det 19. århundrede," in *Fremmed og moderne*, edited by Peter Bang, 97-112. Aarhus: Aarhus University Press, 2005.

Mørch, Søren. *Den sidste Danmarkshistorie*. Copenhagen: Gyldendal, 1996.

Nevers, Jeppe. "Klassernes kulturkamp. Om Jens Engberg: Magten og kulturen: Dansk kulturpolitik 1750-1900." *Historie* (2006): 420-426.

Nissen, Henrik. "Landet blev by 1950-1970." *Danmarkshistorie*, vol. 14. Copenhagen: Gyldendal & Politiken, 2004.

Paludan, Helge. "Vor danske Montesquieu." *Historie* 13 (1980): 1-32.

Paludan, Helge. *Familia og familie. To europæiske kulturelementers møde i højmiddelalderens Danmark*. Aarhus: Aarhus University Press, 1995.

Simonsen, Dorthe Gert. "Historiens bedrift og folkeejendommelighedens mytologi," in *Historiske analyser – nye teorier og metoder*, edited by Claus Møller Jørgensen and Carsten Tage Nielsen. Frederiksberg: Roskilde Universitetsforlag, 2001.

Steenstrup, Johannes. "Oldtiden og den tidlige Middelalder." *Danmarks Riges Historie*, vol. 1. Copenhagen: Det Nordiske Forlag, 1897-1904.

Stråth, Bo et al. *Evaluering af norsk historiefaglig forskning*. Oslo: Norges Forskningsråd, 2008.

Svenstrup, Thyge. "Erik Arup og Brooks Adams. Et bidrag til Arups historie- og metodesyn." *Historisk Tidsskrift* 95 (1995): 1-23.

Thelen, David. "The Nation and Beyond: Transnational Perspectives on United States History." *The Journal of American History* 86, no. 3 (1999): 965-975.

Villaume, Poul. "Lavvækst og Frontdannelser 1970-1985." *Danmarkshistorie*, vol. 15. Copenhagen: Gyldendal & Politiken, 2005.

Wimmer, Andreas and Nina Glick Schiller. "Methodological nationalism and beyond: nation-state building, migration and the social sciences." *Global Networks* 2, no. 4 (2002): 301-334.

Viroli, Maurizio. *For Love and Country: an Essay on Patriotism and Nationalism*. Oxford: Oxford University Press, 1997; online ed. 2003.

Young, Robert J.C. *The Idea of English Ethnicity*. Oxford: Blackwell, 2007.

Østergård, Uffe. "Det danske rige – statshistorie eller nationalistisk historie," in *Europas Ansigter*, 29-50. Copenhagen: Rosinante, 1992.

Østergård, Uffe. "Peasants and Danes – The Danish National Identity and Political Culture." *Comparative Studies in Society and History* 34, no. 1 (1992): 3-17.

12 Grand Narratives in Danish History: From Functional Identity to Problematic Identity

Ove Korsgaard

"We the People of the United States": these famous words are the first of the US Constitution. Similarly, the French Declaration of the Rights of Man and of the Citizen begins: "The representatives of the French people." Furthermore, the Basic Law of the Federal Republic of Germany is alleged to be adopted by the German people.[1] But what is meant by "the people"? Who constitute "a people"? According to the American democratic theorist Robert A. Dahl, no problem within political philosophy is so difficult to deal with as these innocent questions.[2]

The meaning of the term "the people" is often taken for granted in discussions about democracy. It is an implicit assumption that the people existed before the emergence of democracy, indeed, that the people have existed from time immemorial. However, history shows that constantly changing conceptions of the notion are at work; "people" is a dynamic concept.

To be sure, the notion "the people" was in use before the invention of democracy and modern nation states. However, it was not associated with a sovereign people and a sovereign nation but rather with *household* and *family*. During most of the period of absolute monarchy in Denmark the words "people" and "folk" were used particularly as designations for a social category; a distinction was drawn between "upstairs" and "downstairs," and the term was used when referring to the lower levels of society, i.e. servants and subjects. In this sense, "the people" were always part of a hierarchical structure determined by the relation between a master and a people. The notion of "the people," understood as subjects, was applied in relation to the father of the house, the king of the country, and the Lord God. As part of the struggle for democracy, then, the term "the people" had to gain a new meaning, namely that of the people as sovereign. Democracy presupposes a sovereign people: without the people, there is no rule by the people.[3]

---

1. Roger M. Smith, *Stories of Peoplehood. The Politics and Morals of Political Membership* (Cambridge: Cambridge University Press, 2003), 13.
2. Robert A. Dahl, *Demokratiet og dets antagonister* (Stockholm: Ordfront, 1999), 132.
3. Ove Korsgaard, *The Struggle for the People. Five Hundred years of Danish History in Short* (Copenhagen: Danish School of Education Press, 2008), 13ff.

According to the Italian philosopher Giorgio Agamben: "Every interpretation of the political meaning of the term *people* must begin with the singular fact that in modern European languages, *people* also always indicates the poor, the disinherited, and the excluded. One term thus names both the constitutive political subject and the class that is, *de facto* if not *de jure*, excluded from politics."[4] In common speech as in political parlance, the Italien *popolo*, the French *peuple*, the Spanish *pueblo*, the English *people*, the German *Volk*, and the Danish *folk*, designate both the complex of citizens as a unitary political body and the members of the lower class. What we called *people* is in reality not a unitary subject but, according to Agamben, an oscillation between two poles.

However, instead of two poles, I prefer a model with four elements: people as household (*oikos*), people as a political entity (*demos*), people as a cultural entity (*ethnos*), and people as a social entity (*pléthos*).

Oikos means "household" or "family". In ancient Greek, *oikos* was the basic unit of the polis, and it included the head of the house and his people, his household. That people belong to a house constitutes a common understanding in the history of Europe from Aristotle, through Cicero, to Luther. In the history of ideas the change and transformation from *oikos* to *demos*, *ethnos*, and *pléthos* can be traced back to thinkers such as Rousseau, Herder, and Marx and Engels. Rousseau was the first to formulate the groundbreaking idea that the people hold the political power. The impulse to regard the people as the ultimate sovereign with a new kind of political and governmental structure came from Rousseau. Herder also formulated an important principle, namely that the people hold the cultural power. With Herder the notion "people" also came to denote specific peoples, independent of political systems. At the core of Herder's cultural interpretation of the notion "people" is an understanding of collective identity as a deep-seated reality shaped by language and culture; the understanding of people as ethnic groups. Karl Marx and Engels also broke with people as *oikos*. However, they did not, like Rousseau, associate people with *demos* or like Herder with *ethnos*: they associated people with *pléthos*. In *the Communist Manifesto* they claimed that the proletariat had no fatherland and therefore they had to conquer the nation. "Because the proletariat first has to conquer the political power, lift themselves to a national class, constitute themselves as a nation, it is therefore itself national, although with a whole different meaning than the bourgeois."[5] According to Marx and Engels, the working class had to achieve sovereignty by conquering the nation.

Rousseau, Herder, and Marx all broke with the old notion of the people as sub-

---

4.   Giorgio Agamben, *Homo Sacer: Sovereign Power and Bare Life* (Stanford: Stanford University Press, 1995), 176.

5.   K. Marx and F. Engels, *Udvalgte skrifter* (Copenhagen: Rhodos, 1974), 44.

jects; however, they put forth three separate versions of the people as sovereign. While Rousseau linked the concept of sovereignty to people who establish a social contract, Herder linked his concept to people with a common language and culture, and Marx to people belonging to the same social class, namely the working class.

Democracy in Denmark

The process of democratization in Denmark is an exceptional illustration of the growing tension between different understandings of the concepts "people" and "nation" in the late eighteenth century, and can be described as a tension between *oikos*, *demos*, *ethnos*, and *pléthos*.

When the democratic wave reached Denmark in 1848, the United Monarchy was still a multinational and multilingual composite of the Kingdom of Denmark and the duchies Slesvig, Holstein, and Lauenburg; the North Atlantic isles Iceland, Greenland, and the Faroe Islands, as well as a few minor colonies around the world. When the demand for democracy was raised, the following question became urgent: How in one process introduce democracy and keep the multinational and multilingual state together? Democracy requires a *demos*, that is to say a people. But who were the people of the United Monarchy? Did "people" correspond to population? Or were there several peoples within the state? The answer to this question depended upon the understanding of the notion of "people." Was it to be understood as a political, a cultural, or a social category?

The different interpretations of the concept of "people" were a hindrance to the transformation of the United Monarchy into a democratic state. The fundamental issue was whether democracy actually required a new state system, or whether the new political system could be incorporated into the old state system. In other words, does democracy require a state with only one dominating *ethnos*, or could there be one *demos* in a state consisting of competing *ethnos*? The advocates of democracy proposed at least three different answers, and as they could not cohere in one *demos*, civil war broke out. It was not a war between the proponents of the old and the new political systems, but primarily a war among the various proponents of democracy. Imposing democracy in Denmark was not the peaceful process we learned about in school; on the contrary, it led to a radical destabilization – in fact a complete breakdown of the existing multinational and multilingual state.

The civil war did not provide an answer to the pivotal question of whether the Danish and the German speaking populations could unite in one *demos*. From 1848 to 1864, the United Monarchy was weakened by the strong nationalistic opinions that were formulated primarily by the National Liberals on both sides of the linguistic boundary. The different attempts to find a common solution to the constitutional issue did not bring the parties any closer; quite the contrary. In 1863, with the so-called November constitution (*Novemberforfatningen*), the National Liberals in the Kingdom of Denmark decided to put all their eggs into one basket; they gave up the United Monarchy and declared the sovereignty of the Ejder-state. When they realized how enormous the political consequences of this decision would be, it was too late. A war with Prussia and Austria broke out and led to the loss of the duchies.[6]

A turning point

1864 played an extremely important role in the formation of a Danish identity. With the loss of Slesvig, Holstein, and Lauenburg, the old multinational and multilingual state was finally destroyed. Out of this collapse a new Danish nation-state emerged. After the defeat, Denmark came close to fulfilling the ideal requirements for a nation-state, i.e. the complete overlap of state, nation, language, and ethnicity.

The war was also a turning point in German history. Under the leadership of Bismarck, German initiated its policies of expansionism, attacking Denmark in 1864, Austria in 1866, and France in 1870-71. These three wars completely altered the geopolitical situation in Europe, and Denmark thus confronted the following dilemma: was the country to be defended to the last man, or should Denmark surrender the moment the nation was attacked by a major power? Or was there a third possibility?

The defeat in 1864 brought about a groundbreaking change in political thinking, as expressed in Danish culture through literature and art, in historiography, and in the Enlightenment in general. The Danes' perception of themselves and the rest of the world was entirely altered. After the war, new stories and tales of what it had been like to be Danish in times past were developed, and Denmark's past as a multinational and multilingual state was soon forgotten. Such a manoeuvre required an active and conscious effort in the politics of remembrance. Danish historians began to tell the tale of the Danish nation as a historical power that had existed since the dawn of time. In order to establish and maintain such a way of recollecting history, it was necessary for historians to partake in "forgetting" and "suppressing" certain events and processes related to the creation of the nation state. For the Danes, it was about "forgetting" the bloody transition to the political system of democracy and to the state system of the nation-state.

Until recently, young Danes were taught in school that the transformation from

---

6. Ove Korsgaard, *Medborgerskab, identitet og demokratisk dannelse* (Aarhus: Aarhus University Press, 2005), 134-40.

absolute monarchy to democracy was a smooth and successful process; only one peaceful demonstration took place, in Copenhagen on March 21, 1848 – and we got democracy. While this transition was peaceful in Denmark, it was quite the opposite further south in Europe. Of course, we were also taught about a war taking place at the same time in the southern part of Denmark, but it was not construed as a civil war: we were given the impression that it was a war between the "good" Danes and the "bad" Germans, and that, fortunately, the Danes won the war. However, in 1864 the Germans came back and Denmark lost not only the German speaking duchies, Holstein and Lauenburg, but also Slesvig, half of whose population spoke Danish.

The story of the peaceful process towards democracy in Denmark has been so strong because the ethnically homogeneous nation state has been considered the obvious framework for democracy, and the question of whether a functional democracy could have been established within the framework of the United Monarchy has therefore hardly been raised.

From commoners to people

What did we learn in school? What stories was told? Until recently, we learnt two main stories about the Danish people, one about the peasants and another about the workers: how the peasants became part of the Danish people, and how the workers later on became part of the same people. These stories about the peasants and the workers became two "grand narratives" which have shaped our understanding of modern Danish history.

The narrative about the Danish peasants often begins with the following slogan: What is outwardly lost should be inwardly gained! This slogan has been repeated again and again since 1864. We lost Slesvig and Holstein, but gained other things instead, things with both a material and a cultural dimension.

The material dimension is primarily connected to E. M. Dalgas (1826-1894), the leading figure in the cultivation of the moors of Jutland. He was co-founder and the first director of the Danish Heath Society, which from 1866 gradually turned infertile moorland into fertile agricultural land. Dalgas' story is also a story about the peasant movement in Denmark, which came to play a role that is unique in a European context.

The cultural dimension of the slogan is primarily connected to N.F.S. Grundtvig (1783-1872) and his followers, the Grundtvigians, who might be regarded as the peasantry's cultural vanguard. Since the 1830s Grundtvig had called for a new type of high school, a People's High School that would offer further education to ordinary people. The first People's High School was founded 1844 in the village of Rødding in the northern part of Slesvig. However, the major breakthrough of the People's High School movement did not occur until after "the great accident." From 1865 to 1872 about 50 new high schools were established for young adults. The curriculum at these People's High Schools did not emphasize skill training; rather, they mostly concerned themselves with civic education and empowerment. They created a vision for young farmers by differentiating between the two concepts "commoners" and "people," which had been more or less synonymous terms. The young farmers were taught not to regard themselves as commoners but rather as equal members of the Danish people. "From commoners to people" became a motto of the people's enlightenment at the folk high schools. "People" is thus not an empirical but a normative and reflexive category. "The people" does not exist in itself: a people requires self-awareness as a people.

The Grundtvigian Cultural Revolution not only had a tremendous impact on the growth of civil society; it also affected the Danish capitalist market economy. The internationalization of the 1870s – the first step toward globalization – meant radically increased agricultural competition. Cheap grain, predominantly from the United States, gained a foothold in European markets. New railroads and steamboats were the technological precondition that gradually made it possible to transport American grain to Europe while still keeping prices competitive. The growing crisis in Danish farming brought a demand for the excision of regulations; but the call for protectionist policies never really caught on, and instead the agricultural industry responded to the crisis by shifting from grain to livestock production. This shift called for research and reforms of the current agricultural training, the establishment of a new agribusiness, the processing industry, with dairies and slaughterhouses and a new distributing network. A key concern was whether "agribusinesses" were to be governed by the laws of capitalism, as the urban industries had been, or whether they were to be based on ideas of co-operation. The Danish farmers' prevailing choice was to organize dairies and slaughterhouses as co-operative companies. The emphasis on empowerment in the folk high schools has often been regarded as a great influence on the Danish farmer's choice of the co-operative model.

The People's High Schools and the co-operative movement gained international renown in the twentieth century, inspiring a series of reform movements in Eastern Europe in the inter-war period and in the Third World in the decades succeeding World War II.

The cultivation of the moors of Jutland, the establishment of the People's High Schools, and the way out of the agricultural crisis together formed a "grand narrative" in Danish written history. At the core of this narrative is the concept of the "popular," which became almost synonymous with what was outside the state. And in this manner, in Denmark, the notion "popular" came to be equivalent with the liberal notion of voluntariness. Neither the state nor the free market could guarantee national solidarity; that depended on whether "popular" and "civil" society constituted the moral groundwork of society in general. In contrast to the old interpretation of the term "people," the new one was based on a combination of *demos* and *ethnos* as the core of the collective identity.[7]

From workers to people

Marx and Engels' vision of workers united across national borders raised the question of how a socialist should relate to the question of nationality and democracy. First of all, was it possible to implement socialism within the framework of liberal democracy? For the Social Democrats, the relations between socialism, democracy, and the nation-state were in general an unresolved ideological issue up until World War I.

However, after World War I, the social democratic strategy in Denmark as well in the rest of Scandinavia was formed in order to create socialism on a national and democratic foundation; the democratic nation-state was now seen as the main framework for building a welfare state. When the Social Democrats came to power in 1929, they worked to ground socialism on national soil. Under the leadership of Thorvald Stauning (1873-1942) the ideological motto became "Denmark for the people," which was used as the title of a new party manifesto in 1934. By translating the class concept into popular terms, the Social Democracy Party established itself as the large party of the people.

The struggle between different interpretations of the concept "people" was intensified when the Nazis assumed power in Germany in 1933. In *Mein Kampf* Hitler made race the constituting principle of a people in Germany, and in some sense in all of Europe. It is the task of the nation-state to protect people, but while for Herder and Grundtvig that meant the protection of a language community, for Hitler the aim was the protection of a biological organism. According to Hitler, the nation-state should secure the future of the race, "in relation to which the individual's desire and egoism should not matter the least and whose only duty is to yield."[8] The race ideology of National Socialism was extreme, but it was nurtured by thoughts that were already widespread both before and after World War I. In Germany especially, the internal struggle within the concept of "people" turned into a nightmare, when the German *Volk,* representative *par excellence* of the "people" as a whole body, sought to eliminate the Jews forever.[9]

---

7. Korsgaard, *Medborgerskab*, 146f.
8. Adolf Hitler, *Min kamp* (Copenhagen: Gyldendal, 1966), 27.
9. Agamben, *Homo Sacer*, 179.

Stauning's greatest political achievement was the so-called Kanslergade settlement, whereby the leading parties entered into a historic settlement on a series of social reforms intended to counter the social consequences of the Great Depression. The settlement's importance was thrown into further relief by the fact that it was signed on 30 January 1933, the very day that Hitler was appointed Reich Chancellor in Berlin. In contrast to the racist interpretation of the term "people" adopted primarily by National Socialism, the Social Democracy Party developed a popular concept based on a social and democratic interpretation; *pléthos* and *demos* became connected. In order to strengthen the feeling of democratic co-citizenship, citizens were ensured a number of economic and social rights.

Because of the Depression in the 1930s and the occupation of Denmark 1940-45, however, the welfare state had its breakthrough only after World War II.[10] The welfare state can be construed as the materialization of the view that a democratic state should have a "social" form. At its core lies the idea that the state must counter the asymmetry generated by the market and establish a state of symmetry among its citizens. Social rights must be extended to rectify the inequalities brought about by the market. The welfare state is to secure the basic social and economic safety of every citizen, provide everybody with decent housing and access to health care as well as to education; and replace poverty relief with the right to receive support. Further, democratic citizenship was to be based on certain rights that would be valid for everyone, regardless of social and economic status. As the later Social Democratic Party Prime Minister, Jens Otto Krag (1914-1978), argued in 1956 with reference to the law on public pensions, it was important to experience "the feeling of being a citizen with rights." He added: "Democratic freedom now has a social content."[11] The underlying political idea was that social rights ensure equality of status in relation to the state and independence from the market. In contrast to the old interpretation of the term "people," the new one was based on a combination of *demos* and *pléthos* as the core of the collective identity.

Two narratives become one

Looking back on the progression since 1864, the development of Danish identity has been propelled by stories of two different "classes." The peasants and the Grundtvigian "popular" movement regarded civil society, not the state, as the complement of the people; "popular," in the Danish context, became almost synonymous with what is external to the state in the liberal tradition. After World War I, the labour

---

10. *The Danish Democracy Canon* (Copenhagen: Ministry of Education, 2008), 66 f.
11. Ibid., 59.

movement and the Social Democrats regarded the nation-state as the basis for the realization of democracy and socialism. The link between democracy and sociality gained a core position for the future of the concept of the nation. A key element in the social democratic model is the concept of the "friendly state," which stands in contrast to the fundamental Grundtvigian state-scepticism. But, during and following World War II, a number of Grundtvigians such as Hal Koch (1904-1963) began to approach the social democratic perspective on the state. The establishment of the welfare state did not lead to a complete abandonment of liberal ideas, however. Unlike a totalitarian system, the welfare state was ultimately based on a liberal view of the state.[12]

During World War II, the two grand narratives became more integrated, and after the war, the establishment of the Danish welfare state became a more or less common narrative. It was Hal Koch who made the greatest contribution to formulating a national compromise uniting the liberal and the social-democratic conceptions of the state, nation, people, and democracy. This compromise became the foundation for the creation in the post-war period of the welfare state, governed by socialistic as well as liberal ideas. The welfare state, however, was founded not only in a social-political, but also in an identity-political program. Welfare and Danishness became one and the same. To be Danish was (and still is) to identify oneself with the Danish welfare project.[13]

Problematic Identity

To a large extent, the Danish identity is still rooted in these two grand narratives about the peasant movement and the labour movement. Both narratives have "people" as a core concept. However, these narratives are no longer functional to the same extent as before, primarily because they do not include a European or a multicultural perspective. The key question seems to be, if - or how - it is possible to maintain a democratic community without the well-known close connection between *demos* and *ethnos*?

The Europeanization process has raised the question of whether it is possible or desirable for Danes to belong to a European "people." And what is meant by a European "people" today? After the Maastricht Treaty in 1992, Danes not only got legal access to the single market, they also became citizens of the Union, which has been described as an important symbolic step, postulating the existence of a common popular sovereignty to complement - or to rival - the common sovereignty

12. Ove K. Pedersen, *Demokratiets lette tilstand* (Copenhagen: Spektrum, 1994), 125.
13. Christian Albrekt Larsen, *Danskernes nationale forestillinger* (Aalborg: Ålborg Universitetsforlag, 2008), 40f.

of the nation-state. However, the introduction of the citizenship of the Union was brought about by a deep sense of malaise and public disaffection with the European construction. In Denmark the majority voted against the Maastricht Treaty, but a year later, the majority voted "yes" – with four exceptions to the terms. If the EU represents a form of "polity," it must accordingly have a relationship to the "people" who are its "members." Is such a transnational membership possible? Or can we only talk of "people" in relation to a nation-state? According to Jürgen Habermas, it is necessary to focus on the development of a postnational democracy within the framework of the European Union. This does not imply, however, that the national democracies and nation-states are to be dissolved. A European *demos* is not meant to replace the national *demos*; it is intended to supplement it. In principle, there are two solutions to the problem of the EU's lack of a *demos*. One is to create a European *demos* applying the same methods used more or less successfully by a number of nation-states to create national demos – via schooling, compulsory use of a common language, the use of symbols, the writing of history, mass media, etc. Habermas rejects this solution. Instead, he advocates an alternative solution, which is based on a clear distinction between the political and cultural levels. At the cultural level, no attempt should be made to create a single European people; rather, this should be done at political level. The community of rights must be raised to supranational level. In other words, the aim is to create a European *demos*, but not a European *ethnos*.[14] Though it is possible to identify a number of weaknesses in Habermas' analyses, they raise a number of questions where the answers will exert a decisive influence on the future development of democracy in Europe. At this juncture, there is every reason to ask whether democracy has found its final form, with the nation-states serving as a framework. Or is it possible to develop a European social order based on post-national, democratic principles?

While for centuries migration has been from Europe towards other continents, the flow is now reversed. Denmark is thus distancing itself from the ideal of coinciding state, people, language, and culture. The migration process has raised another difficult question: Is it possible or desirable for immigrants to belong to a Danish people? And what does it mean to belong to a Danish people today? Does it imply belonging not only to a Danish *demos*, but also a Danish *ethnos*? Some argue that we should get rid of the term "people" and replace the stories of a Danish people with stories of multiculturalism. Too many evils have been committed in its name, and too many struggles have wasted lives for ideals that have often been proclaimed but never more than very imperfectly realized. But will stories of multiculturalism create the necessary sense of shared citizenship? Is it possible to sustain a stable

---

14. Jürgen Habermas, "Citizenship and National Identity. Some Reflections on the Future of Europe," in *Citizenship. Critical Concepts*, ed. Brian S. Turner and Peter Hamilton (London: Routledge, 1994).

and well-functioning society whose citizens are increasingly culturally, religiously, and ethnically diverse? The defenders of multiculturalism do not seem to put forward convincing answers to questions about stability in the kind of society they wish to bring into being, preferring to talk about the need to celebrate diversity, resist ethnic oppression, and abjure coercive assimilation. Cultural diversity seems to be a gift to every society – *if* it can be bound together by stories of peoplehood. Democracy is not necessarily dependent on the same *ethnos*; however, it is highly dependent on a sense of belonging to the same *demos*. If there is no *demos*, there can be no democracy.

The changes brought about by Europeanisation and migration have made it necessary for Danes to re-imagine what is meant by, and who constitute, a people. According to Benedict Anderson, this is not possible without narratives.[15] Narratives are necessary because they inspire in ways unequalled by plain facts about predatory welfare, self-serving elites, and downtrodden or resistant masses. Because history and narratives have much in common, the teaching of national history will be an especially important area in a more culturally, ethnically, and religiously diverse society. Historiography and the teaching of history can bring into focus the fact that the concept of "people" has undergone vast changes over time and has been understood in different ways. Today, new narratives may draw on elements in Danish history from both before and after 1864. In order to develop new functional narratives it might be useful to look at historical events that have been "forgotten" and "suppressed" – for example how, for hundreds of years, Denmark was a multinational and multilingual state, and the fact that the implementation of democracy in Denmark was a very bloody affair. In many ways, Europe is facing the same challenges as those faced by the United Monarchy in 1848, when the main issue was whether or not it was possible to institute a free and common constitution within the existing multinational monarchy. Denmark, as we know, did not succeed, and whether Europe will remains an open question.

History is a construction of the past, written to enable an appropriate learning process. Today it is necessary to find the references in the past in which we can mirror ourselves most beneficially. The way we create the past is crucial for the future. The future is dependent on a creative design of the past, on a rewriting of history that can unleash the forces locked up in outdated explanations of the same reality.

---

15. Benedict Anderson, *Imagined Communities. Reflections on the Origin and Spread of Nationalism* (London: Verso, 1983).

Bibliography

Agamben, Giorgio. *Homo Sacer: Sovereign Power and Bare Life*. Stanford: Stanford University Press, 1995.

Anderson, Benedict. *Imagined Communities. Reflections on the Origin and Spread of Nationalism*. London: Verso, 1983.

Dahl, Robert A. *Demokratiet og dets antagonister*. Stockholm: Ordfront, 1999.

The Danish Democracy Canon. Copenhagen: Ministry of Education, 2008.

Habermas, Jürgen. "Citizenship and National Identity. Some Reflections on the Future of Europe," in *Citizenship. Critical Concepts*, edited by Brian S. Turner and Peter Hamilton. Routledge: London, 1994.

Hitler, Adolf. *Min kamp*. Copenhagen: Gyldendal, 1966.

Korsgaard, Ove. *Medborgerskab, identitet og demokratisk dannelse*. Aarhus: Aarhus University Press, 2005.

Korsgaard, Ove. "The Danish Way to establish the Nation in the Hearts of the People," in *National Identity and the Varieties of Capitalism. The Danish Experience*, edited by John L. Campbell, John A. Hall, and Ove K. Pedersen. Montreal: McGill-Queen's University Press, 2006.

Korsgaard, Ove. *The Struggle for the People. Five Hundred years of Danish History in Short*. Aarhus: Aarhus University Press, 2008.

Larsen, Christian Albrekt. *Danskernes nationale forestillinger*. Aalborg: Ålborg Universitetsforlag, 2008.

K. Marx and F. Engels. *Udvalgte skrifter*. Copenhagen: Rhodos, 1974.

Pedersen, Ove K. *Demokratiets lette tilstand*. Copenhagen: Spektrum, 1994.

Smith, Roger M. *Stories of Peoplehood. The Politics and Morals of Political Membership*. Cambridge: Cambridge University Press, 2003.

13 Who Are We Now? A Multicultural Canada in the Twenty-First Century

J.L. Granatstein

Let me begin with some personal history. I was born in Toronto, Ontario, Canada in 1939. My father was born in Lodz, Poland and came to Toronto at age 14 in 1922, speaking only Yiddish. My mother, whose parents came from Minsk in Czarist Russia, was born in Toronto a few years after their immigration. She too had Yiddish as a first language. Neither went beyond Grade 5 in school, but both spoke English well by the time I was born, though neither could write it adequately. They were Canadian citizens, they voted (usually for the social democratic party), and they adapted in generally harmonious ways to the Anglo-Canadian world in which they lived. Neither was very religious, but they had a real concern that being Jewish hurt them within the broader community. They were of the lower middle class by the time I was in my teens, and they quietly encouraged their children in their schooling. Their two sons ended up with PhDs, mine in history, my brother's in engineering. Both of us assimilated into Canadian society completely, abandoned our religion by choice as soon as we could and married outside it.

To me, this is a Canadian assimilationist success story, a North American success story, very common among Jews, but also similar to those of countless European immigrants of the pre-Second World War era. Whether it would be seen as a success today by those who are Multiculturalists, intent on preserving many cultures in Canada, is less clear. A hundred years ago, the first generation struggled and made a home from which their offspring assimilated and often moved into the professions even though there were no concessions from the school system, and no human rights legislation to protect them from discrimination. If my family story was one of success, of course, there were unquestionably many others who were not helped or even harmed by the Canadian state's relative indifference to those who managed to join it.[1]

---

1. Some recent scholarship, heavily ideological in a self-professed "left feminist anti-racist" fashion, sees the Canadian state and its agents relentlessly forcing immigrants toward Anglo-Canadian middle class assimilation during the Cold War, something totally at odds with my perceptions of that or previous eras. See Franca Iacovetta, *Gatekeepers: Reshaping Immigrant Lives in Cold War Canada* (Toronto: Between The Lines, 2006). For the last thirty-plus years, by contrast many Canadian critics of Multiculturalism have complained that the state has tried to prevent immigrants from assimilating.

The Canada into which I was born had a population of some 11.5 million (1941 Census figures) which was made up of those of British and French origin (50 percent and 30 percent respectively), and others (20 percent). The others were of German, Ukrainian, Scandinavian, and Dutch origin in the main, with a scattering of other ethnicities. There were few Blacks, Chinese, or South Asians; the Canadian population was overwhelmingly white. The corporate, cultural, and political leaders in Canada were nearly all drawn from among those of British origin, and French-speaking Quebec for the most part was pulled along (such as Canada joining in British wars) with more or less resistance depending on circumstances.

It is certainly fair to say that nation building in the symbolic and cultural sense was oriented toward the replication of a British type of society in Canada. Culturally, this was reflected in Canada's political, economic, and social institutions. All Canadians were defined as British subjects until the passage of the *Canadian Citizenship Act* in 1947, and a variety of cultural symbols ranging from the monarchy to the names of army regiments legitimized the British underpinnings of English-speaking Canada.[2] By and large, government considered racial and ethnic differences as detrimental to Canada's character and integrity. There were almost no national leaders from amongst the "others," though "padrones," brokers who dealt with the Anglo elite, were to be found in every ethnic group. The restaurants, a few in Montreal aside, were almost uniformly dreadful.

Canada – and especially Toronto, where I still live – is very different today. In the 2006 Census (the most recent), the "other" category in Canada, now with some two hundred ethnicities, constituted 50 percent of the 31 million population (although the statistics are difficult to interpret because one in three Canadians refused to offer their ethnic origin and preferred to say they were "Canadian"). For example, there were reported to be 1.35 million Chinese, 962,000 East Indians, and 436,000 Filipinos (and 200,035 Canadians of Danish origin), and one in six Canadian residents was from a "VisMin," a visible minority.[3] In Greater Toronto, 46 percent of the 5.1 million population were immigrants, an increase of 27 percent in five years, and more than four in ten, or 43 percent of the population, were

---

2. According to Grazia Scoppio, "Diversity Best Practices in Military Organizations in Canada, Australia, the United Kingdom, and the United States," *Canadian Military Journal* 9, no. 3 (2009), 17ff., the Canadian Forces have been and remain resistant to Multiculturalism.

3. Statistics Canada, "Ethnocultural Portrait of Canada Highlight Tables, 2006 Census," accessed 3 January 2008, www12.statcan/english/census06/data/highlights/ethnic/SelectGeo.cfm?Lang=E.... In 1901, Canada had 1 percent VisMins; in 1991, 9 percent; in 2006, 16 percent. An interactive map of the 2006 population distribution is available online: www.cbc.ca/news/interactives/map-visibleminorities/, accessed 6 January 2008.

visible minorities, primarily Chinese, South Asian, or Black.[4] India and China now provide most of the immigrants to Canada and Toronto, and in an ordinary year at least a quarter of a million new immigrants come to the country, more than forty percent of them heading to Toronto. At the time I was born and for my first fifteen years, by contrast, the British Isles were the main source of immigrants to Canada.

So Canada has changed, and certainly much for the better. There are Members of Parliament in turbans, the Chief of Defence Staff is of Ukrainian ethnicity, and the Governor General is a female Haitian immigrant who succeeded a female Chinese immigrant. Jews hold three of the nine seats on the Supreme Court; a Chinese-Canadian multimillionaire made a huge donation to the Royal Ontario Museum and a group of Italian-Canadian millionaires matched that with equally grand gifts to the Art Gallery of Ontario; the public service is as multi-hued as the nation;[5] and Toronto's public schools declare themselves the most multicultural in the world – Thorncliffe Park Public School in Toronto's east end has 1,913 students speaking 54 languages –[6]and based on anecdotal evidence, many of the inner city schools are almost color-blind (or so my granddaughter, one-quarter Fijian, tells me). Mixed-race marriages are increasingly common in the larger cities, and adoptions abroad have created multiracial families all across the country. The Chinese food in Toronto's five Chinatowns is the best in North America, the Indian close behind, and there is an extraordinary variety of ethnic cuisines available, ranging from Ethiopian to Thai to aboriginal Canadian.

Multiculturalism in the eyes of many is perhaps the most recognized and celebrated characteristic of Canadian citizenship. The Aga Khan, for one, has proclaimed that Canada has done a superlative job in bringing peoples of disparate race, ethnicity, and religion together.[7] Urban thinker Richard Florida pronounced Canada's "mosaic principle [...] one of the core enduring principles of our economy and society," and newspaper columnist John Ibbitson called the country's "robust multicultural identity" the key to "preventing the emergence of a race-based underclass" like that in the United States and Western Europe.[8] Canadian diplomats

4. Ibid., "Immigration in Canada: A Portrait of the Foreign-born Population, 2006 Census: Portraits of Major Metropolitan Centres," accessed 9 January 2008, 22212.statcan.ca/english/census06/analysis/immcit/toronto.cfm. The percentage of immigrants in Toronto in 2009 is probably more than fifty.

5. *Ottawa Citizen*, March 24, 2009.

6. "Pupils of the World," *National Post*, February 14, 2009.

7. Charles Enman, "Why the World Needs more Canada," *Ottawa Citizen*, July 12, 2008. But see the article reporting 2009 Angus Reid poll results, John Geddes, "What Canadians Think of Sikhs, Jews, Christians, Muslims...," *Maclean's*, May 4, 2009, 20ff. Canadian tolerance appears somewhat more limited than most appear to believe.

8. Richard Florida, "Toronto's 'mosaic principle' a golden example for American cities," *Globe and Mail* (Toronto), May 2, 2009; John Ibbitson, "Welcome to Americanada," *Globe and Mail* (Toronto), May 2, 2009. See the paean of

say the same: "When I would speak at the United Nations on anything that had to do with human rights or human security," said one, "I got a very respectful hearing. [...] in terms of welcoming others and integrating them into society, nobody does it better than we do [...] and we get a lot of credit for that in the international community."[9] Certainly Canadians are proudly polite and relatively uncomplaining, making Canada perhaps the best nation in which to make Multiculturalism work.[10] But the food and the multiracialism of Toronto, Vancouver, and Montreal apart, why are so few Canadians cheering?

The answer can be found in the Canadian debate over multiculturalism. What is Canadian multiculturalism and where did it come from?

The major political and cultural issues of the 1960s in Canada centered on French-Canadian/English-Canadian relations, and the growing *nationaliste/indépendantiste* sentiment in Quebec led to the establishment of a Royal Commission on Bilingualism and Biculturalism in 1963. The Commission produced a host of recommendations, some of which were adopted, but an unintended consequence was that other ethnicities, notably Ukrainian-Canadians,[11] began to fear that they were being left out, as the two "founding peoples" tried to deal with their historic differences. Much pressure led the Royal Commission to consider the contribution of other ethnic groups to the cultural enrichment of Canada. The Commission recommended the "integration" (not assimilation) into Canadian society of ethnic groups with full citizenship rights and equal participation in Canada's institutional structure.[12] These recommendations led to a policy on Multiculturalism, announced in October 1971. Its main aims were to assist cultural groups to retain and foster their identity and to overcome barriers to their full participation in Canadian society while maintaining their right to identify with select elements of their cultural past if they so chose. In effect, the Multiculturalism policy aimed to integrate immigrants (and second and third generations) by offering equal rights and opportunities; in return, they were expected to conform to certain societal norms. If successful, as Canadian philosopher Will Kymlicka said, the policy would lead immigrants to "integrate into an existing societal culture and come to view their life chances as

praise in Michael Adams, *Unlikely Utopia: The Surprising Triumph of Canadian Multiculturalism* (Toronto: Penguin, 2007).

9. M. Valpy, "A beacon of fairness," *Globe and Mail* (Toronto), July 1, 2008.

10. "In the Olympics of self-admiration," historian Desmond Morton wryly told a Quebec City meeting on September 29, 2005, "Canadians would compete eagerly – for their traditional bronze medal." Desmond Morton, "The Canadian Connection" (paper presented at the 22nd International Churchill Conference, Quebec City, September 29, 2005).

11. See M.R. Lupul, *The Politics of Multiculturalism: A Ukrainian-Canadian Memoir* (Toronto: CIUS Press, 2005).

12. *Report of the Royal Commission on Bilingualism and Biculturalism*, vol. 4 (Ottawa: Queen's Printer, 1969).

tied up with participation in the range of social institutions, based on a common language, which define that societal culture."[13] A Ministry of Multiculturalism was duly created and a variety of programmes established.

The architects of the 1971 policy had perceived barriers to social adaptation and economic success largely in linguistic or cultural terms. But as immigration patterns shifted and more visible minorities came to Canada, new concerns such as obtaining employment, housing, and education, and fighting discrimination forced a shift in policy thinking. Equality through the removal of racially discriminatory barriers became the main focus of Multicultural programs, and race relations policies and programs were put in place to combat racial discrimination. In 1982, Canada changed its constitution and embedded the *Canadian Charter of Rights and Freedoms in it*. Section 27 of the Charter stated that "This Charter shall be interpreted in a manner consistent with the preservation and enhancement of the multicultural heritage of Canadians." Multiculturalism, therefore, was as permanent as the Constitution, and the Constitution's rules for amendment were so difficult as to make change almost impossible. Assimilation now was explicitly not a Canadian goal. At the same time, the Charter also declared (Section 15(1)) that "Every individual is equal before and under the law and has the right to equal protection and equal benefit of the law without discrimination and, in particular, without discrimination based on race, national or ethnic origin, color, religion, sex, age, or mental or physical disability." The courts have subsequently made their decisions in accordance with the Charter.

The Charter and the recognition of the continuing changes in the composition of the population led in 1988 to the passage of the *Multiculturalism Act* by Parliament. The Act acknowledged Multiculturalism as a fundamental characteristic of Canadian society that was to assist in the preservation of culture and language, to reduce discrimination, to enhance cultural awareness and understanding, and to promote culturally sensitive institutional change at the federal level. Thus the Act sought to preserve, enhance, and incorporate cultural differences into the functioning of Canadian society, while ensuring equal access and full participation for all in the social, political, and economic spheres.

The Act recognized the need to increase minority participation in Canada's major institutions by bringing diversity into them as a natural, normal, and positive component of decision-making, resource allocation, and the setting of priorities. All government agencies, departments, and Crown corporations – not just the ministry responsible for Multiculturalism – were expected to provide leadership in advancing Canada's multicultural mix and to take part in the design and implementation of

---

13. Will Kymlicka, *Finding Our Way: Rethinking Ethnocultural Relations in Canada* (Don Mills, ON: Oxford University Press, 1998), 28.

plans, programs, procedures, and decision-making strategies to enhance the participation of minorities within institutional structures. What this meant in practice was the establishment of *de facto* quotas, preferences in hiring, and active recruitment schemes. This took place at the same time as women received preferential treatment in hiring and, in the federal government, after years of preferential hiring for francophones. It is fair to say there was and is substantial resentment in the segments of the population that felt themselves newly discriminated against by government.

Since 1988, there have been many organizational changes in Ottawa and the policy has shifted as governments lost and gained power. The current Conservative government and its minister of Citizenship, Immigration and Multiculturalism seems to be interested in altering past practice. Announcing the end of the nation's heritage languages programme, Hon. Jason Kenney told a journalist that "I think it's neat that a fifth-generation Ukrainian Canadian can speak Ukrainian – but pay for it yourself." A Liberal Member of Parliament, Boris Wrzesnewskyj, responded by accusing Kenny of "fundamentally disagree[ing] with the intent of the [Multiculturalism] legislation that supports his portfolio."[14] In other words, as columnist Andrew Cohen put it, "Championing a more integrated country is often called intolerant, even racist, as if the conversation were taboo."[15] Nonetheless there seems little doubt that capital-M Multiculturalism remains a major policy to which the Canadian government is committed. Lower-case-m multiculturalism is a fact of life, visible at once in Canada's big cities, and accepted by and large by the majority of Canadians. The policy, Capital-M Multiculturalism, has many defenders[16] but is overall much less favorably viewed.[17]

Why? The answers are many and various, but let me treat only five areas. First, there is the sense that Multiculturalism was an imposed myth, "that Canada was a mosaic of many cultures and national identities of which the Quebecois were but one and English Canadians another. The effect of this," wrote political sociologist J.F. Conway, "was to deny the essential bi-national, bi-cultural reality of Canada, while effectively masking the continuing hegemony of English Canada. Official [M]ulticulturalism ignored the sociological reality that immigrants have largely

---

14. *National Post*, March 28, 2009. The *Globe and Mail*, Canada's national newspaper, agreed with the government's new approach. *Globe and Mail* (Toronto), April 17, 2009. For Minister Kenney's views, see his interview in *Maclean's*, May 4, 2009, 16-18.

15. "Kenney's Canada," *Ottawa Citizen*, March 31, 2009. See also Lawrence Martin, "Enough of multiculturalism – bring on the melting pot," *Globe and Mail* (Toronto), March 31, 2009.

16. The best case is advanced by Will Kymlicka, *Finding Our Way*.

17. Among the most articulate critics is columnist Robert Sibley who has written at length on the "dark side" of Multiculturalism in the *Ottawa Citizen*, e.g., September 10, 2006; May 17-19, 2008.

joined – and often uniquely and dramatically influenced – one or the other of the English-Canadian or Quebecois nations through a sort of functional integration (while resisting assimilation)."[18] That belief, widespread if not usually so forcefully put, fed into the view that government is not only not watching as the nation is changing but that it is favoring newcomers over the old with its preferences and policies. White Canada, both English- and French-speaking, sees Canada's demographics altering with great speed and worries for the future of its way of life. Will the new immigrants from Guangdong and Manila, from Jamaica and the Punjab, integrate into Canadian life? Will those who choose to settle in Quebec learn French? Will new immigrants accept or even understand the democratic norms that shape Canada's political life?[19] How much will Canadians need to adapt to the newly-arrived? That such questions can still be asked suggests doubt about the goals laid down in 1971 and 1988.

Change is always difficult, and the fear of change is understandable; it will, of course, become even more difficult for Canadians to deal with and accept if the economic recession of 2009 is long-lasting.

The fear of societal change seems especially strong in Quebec, the French-speaking province that since the 1960s has sought increasing autonomy within Canada and twice has held referenda on separating from it. In 2007, the village of Hérouxville became notorious when its town council passed a resolution laying down a code of behavior for immigrants (no polygamy, no honor killings, no sex discrimination), something particularly notable because there were almost none in this rural municipality. But Hérouxville sparked a crisis over "reasonable accommodation," over just how far Quebec had to go in accommodating itself to the demands of Orthodox Jews not to see scantily clad women jogging, for example, or the rights of Muslim women to keep their faces covered for their driving licence photographs or in court proceedings.[20]

The upshot was a major provincial government commission that studied the issue and, in October 2008, a government declaration that, beginning in January, 2009, prospective immigrants had to sign a statement promising to accept the

18. J.F. Conway, "Reflections on Canada in the Year 1994," *Journal of Canadian Studies* (Fall, 1994).

19. See, e.g., Jack Jedwab, "The 'Roots' of Immigrant and Ethnic Voter Participation in Canada," *Electoral Insight* (December, 2006). There is a substantial literature on citizenship education. See esp. the bibliography in Alan Sears and A. Hughes, "Citizenship: Education or Indoctrination?," *Citizenship Teaching and Learning* (July, 2006), and Will Kymlicka's many writings, notably *Politics in the Vernacular: Nationalism, Multiculturalism and Citizenship* (New York: Oxford University Press, 2001).

20. Québécois tolerance for minorities and religious groups was much lower than the Canadian averages, according to an Angus Reid poll, reported in John Geddes' article in *Maclean's*, May 4, 2009. The concern about minorities is not limited only to Quebec, however. See "Mosque fights for rights, but slurs Jews and West," *Toronto Star*, November 12, 2008. The 2007 honor killing of a young Muslim woman by her father in a Toronto suburb stirred enormous controversy. See Mary Rogan, "Girl, Interrupted," *Toronto Life* (December, 2008), 53ff.

"shared values" of Québécois. Quebec declared itself a pluralist, liberal-democratic society where French is the official language, the sexes are equal and, though all can follow their own faith, church and state are separate, while secular law takes precedence over religious law. Immigration, the province's responsible minister said, "is a privilege, not a right."[21] There were objections to this declaration, but its issuance resolved the political nature of the problem, at least for the immediate future (which included an election won by the Liberal government that had issued the declaration). Immigrants would know in advance what kind of society they proposed to join and, if it offended them, they could go elsewhere. Quebec's declaration has not yet been replicated elsewhere in Canada, though the Conservative federal government is talking in very similar terms about its nearly-completed review of Canada's immigration and citizenship policies.[22]

Secondly, there is the widespread sense that many immigrants only come to Canada for economic opportunity, to become citizens (after only three years of residence), to get a passport, and often to return "home" with a Canadian bolthole available to them and their children for the rest of their lives, but without adopting many of the values Canadians preach. During the troubles in the Former Yugoslavia, for example, Canadian Serbs and Croats fought in the streets of Toronto and many returned "home" to fight in the civil wars. One Croat-Canadian became the first Defense minister of Croatia and fired the opening shot in the civil war against Serbia. Had he not died, he likely would have faced an international war crimes trial. Other Canadians in Former Yugoslavia took up arms against members of the Canadian Forces trying to keep the peace; one Serb-Canadian left Edmonton, Alberta to "fight Muslims" and in the course of that goal kidnapped a Canadian Forces officer and held him hostage tied to a pole to deter NATO airstrikes. (He was eventually given a jail term by a Canadian court.[23]) There are similar accounts of Canadian citizens acting in much the same way in Somalia and Sri Lanka,[24] and there are Canadian

---

21. "Herouxville Wins," *National Post*, October 31, 2008; ibid., October 30, 2008. See also Amy Nugent, "Demography, National Myths, and Political Origins: Perceiving Official Multiculturalism in Quebec," *Canadian Ethnic Studies* (2006), 21ff. There are many who argue that the concept of "shared values" is a chimera. See Joseph Heath, *The Myth of Shared Values in Canada*, The 2003 John L. Manion Lecture (Ottawa: Canadian Centre for Management Development, 2003).

22. *National Post*, April 15, 2009.

23. Ibid., June 14, 2008.

24. Sri Lankan Tamils, many of whom are supporters of the vicious terrorist group, the Tamil Tigers, live in huge numbers in Toronto (estimates are close to 200,000). Their mass demonstrations in Ottawa in April 2009 aimed at forcing Canadian political intervention in the Sri Lankan civil war and led *Globe and Mail* columnist Margaret Wente to note that even second and third generation Tamils are "reaffirming their ethnic identity," something sociologists believe is increasingly common among "vis min" Canadians. In other words, she noted, they feel less, not more, Canadian, and thus more transnational. "How will Canada evolve when so many people have multiple allegiances, to homeland and host land?," she asked. Margaret Wente, *Globe and Mail* (Toronto), April 23, 2009.

Muslims who actively fought against NATO and American forces in Afghanistan and participated in or supported terrorist activities in Canada, the United States, and Britain.[25] The problem is compounded by an immigration and refugee system that can best be described as porous and completely unable to screen even a portion of those who seek entry to Canada.[26]

Then there were the actions of dual citizens. The Israeli-Hezbollah conflict of 2006 stunned Canadians by revealing that more than forty thousand of their fellow citizens lived in Lebanon and claimed to be eligible for evacuation from the war zone by Canada. (Some 15,000 were evacuated – and half returned to Lebanon within six weeks.) Many of these putative citizens had lived in Lebanon for decades, their only link to this country being their passport. Consider Rasha Solti who wrote in the Toronto *Globe and Mail* that "I hold a Canadian passport, I was born in Toronto when my parents were students there. I have never gone back. I left at age 2."[27] Ms Solti clearly retained her passport only to let her come to Canada if she ever needed to do so. Did Canada owe her anything? Had dual citizenship (or triple or quadruple) made Canadian citizenship, Canadian Multi-culturalism, farcical? Such questions are not trivial; indeed, they go to the heart of national identity. Does Canadian citizenship mean something or is it a citizenship

25. See J.L. Granatstein, "Multiculturalism and Canadian Foreign Policy," in *The World in Canada*, ed. D. Carment and D. Bercuson (Montreal: McGill-Queen's University Press, 2008). For a sharp critique, see Rema Berns-McGown, "Asking the Right and Wrong Questions," *Literary Review of Canada* (April, 2008): 24-5. An Environ-ics poll (February 13, 2008) found 12 percent of Canadian Muslims believed that a terrorist plot to blow up Parliament and behead the Prime Minister was "justified." Licia Corbella, in *Calgary Sun*, February 19, 2007. A positive statement of immigrant integration is Michael Valpy, "Our part-time home and *native* land," *Globe and Mail* (Toronto), June 28, 2008.

26. According to James Bissett, former executive director of the Canadian Immigration Service, Canada took in 700,000 asylum seekers in the last 25 years. There are 40,000 outstanding warrants for those whose where-abouts are unknown and a backlog of 62,000 claims. In addition, since 1996, Canada has absorbed 140,000 Pakistani immigrants, 75,000 Iranians, and 33,000 Algerians. As Bissett said, "None [...] may be terrorists but the reality is that only about 10 per cent [...] are checked for security." This lax policy leads to US concerns that result in the thickening of the Canada-US border. James Bissett, "Americans are right to worry," *Ottawa Citizen*, April 27, 2009. There have been reports that Hezbollah and Hamas supporters had been appointed by the Liberal government (in office to early 2006) to positions on the Immigration and Refugee Board. The Liberals, heavily dependent in Ontario on ethnic voters, were also unwilling to label the Tamil Tigers a terrorist group, something the Conservatives did very soon after taking power. UN data for 2008 suggested that Canada had 36,900 refugee claims, compared to 49,000 in the ten times larger US. Canada accepted 42-46 percent of those who applied. The 30 percent increase in claims in 2008 led the responsible minister, Jason Kenney, to say it was "an abuse of Canada's generosity." *National Post*, March 24, 2009. See Martin Collacott, *Canada's Inadequate Response to Terrorism*, Fraser Institute Digital Publication (February 2006); A. Moens and M. Collacott, eds., *Immigration Policy and the Terrorist Threat in Canada and the United States* (Vancouver, 2008); and the devastating letter by Julie Taub, a former member of the Immigration and Refugee Board, in *National Post*, April 1, 2009. It is worth noting that Czechs and Mexicans are the most successful applicants for refugee status in Canada, not the genuinely persecuted.

27. *Globe and Mail* (Toronto), July 22, 2006.

of convenience? Is Canada just a first class hotel which people can check into when it suits them, as novelist Yann Martel famously put it, and check out when their own interests so require? Citizenship matters. It is in Canada's national interest that its people understand and accept that there are rights and obligations that come from being Canadian.[28]

Thirdly, unlike Australia which actually tries to enforce its regulations that require immigrants to be fluent in English before they arrive "Down Under,"[29] Canada has been lax in imposing any language controls on those who enter from abroad. Only one in five of the 260,000 immigrants who arrived in 2008, for example, had had their language skills assessed.[30] The linguistic test of either French or English comes only at the examination for citizenship, and even then the standards are a national joke, so much so that the present Minister of Citizenship, Immigration and Multiculturalism, Jason Kenney, said he had met many new citizens who could not speak either of Canada's official languages, no surprise as 40 percent of immigrants speak neither English nor French. This matters, Kenney said, declaring that henceforth citizenship would be denied to those without language skills because linguistic fluency is the key that opens the door to good jobs.[31] Canadian research demonstrates irrefutably that linguistic proficiency outstrips job experience, educational background, gender, and age as the factor that has the greatest impact on an immigrant's ability to make a new life in Canada.[32] The Opposition in Parliament predictably pronounced Kenney "intolerant."[33] Political sources report that Kenney now seems to be moving toward the Australian language model for immigration, a points system that demands proficiency in English or French.[34]

Canada's failure to live up to its own immigration and citizenship regulations has fuelled resentment among both native-born Canadians and immigrants. In the last decade, up to 40 percent of professional class male immigrants – after jumping through the hoops of Canada's difficult and slow immigration system – leave in

---

28. See J.L. Granatstein, "Canada's Dual Citizenship Problem," *Globe and Mail* (Toronto), July 31, 2006; and John Chant, "The Passport Package," C.D. Howe Institute *Backgrounder* (December 2006). The government booklet that is provided to those seeking citizenship, *A Look at Canada* (Ottawa, 2005), does talk briefly of rights and obligations, as well as giving a broadbrush overview of history, the political system, the environment, and peacekeeping – a curious mishmash, in other words. The booklet is now being re-written. For Minister Kenney's reaction to the booklet, see the interview with him in *Maclean's*, May 4, 2009, 16-18.

29. See Lesley Anne Hawthorne, "The Impact of Economic Selection Policy on Labour Market Outcomes for Degree-Qualified Migrants in Canada and Australia," Institute for Research on Public Policy *Choices* (May 2008).

30. Rudyard Griffiths, "Sticky Citizenship," *National Post*, April 29, 2009.

31. *Toronto Star*, March 21, 2009.

32. Rudyard Griffiths, "Immigrants must speak our languages," *National Post*, March 24, 2009. See also Griffiths' book, *Who We Are: A Citizen's Manifesto* (Vancouver: Douglas & McIntyre, 2009).

33. *National Post*, March 28, 2009.

34. *Calgary Herald*, March 27, 2009.

despair within a decade, in substantial part because, their foreign credentials usually not accepted, they cannot break into the "guilds" that control the professions. Others feel that they are being exploited, and educated immigrants earn barely half what Canadian-born workers are paid.[35] In 2006, one in three immigrants lived in poverty, an increase from one in four in the 1980s.[36] So much for Canada as the land of economic opportunity.

Meanwhile, the Canadian-born complain bitterly about dealing with people – from taxi drivers to doctors to public servants – whose English or French is all but incomprehensible and whose skills seem negligible. (On the other hand corporations are finding that bicultural immigrants can bring major benefits to their bottom line.[37])

Fourth, Multiculturalism has led many Canadians to fear to exercise the rights of free speech that are their historic legacy and also guaranteed under the Canadian Charter. The most important recent case occurred over the famous 2005 Danish cartoons that satirically portrayed Mohammed and led to riots, deaths, and threats around the world. For fear of upsetting Canada's 700,000-strong Muslim community, no Canadian newspaper or TV station dared to publish the (anodyne) cartoons; only a small-circulation Alberta magazine called *Western Report* reacted against the fear by devoting several pages to the drawings on the reasonable grounds that the cartoons were news. A local Calgary imam, after failing to get the police to intervene, hauled *Report*'s publisher, Ezra Levant, before the Alberta Human Rights Commission for hearings that lasted three years and cost Levant $100,000 before the Commission gave up the case in the face of Levant's relentless attacks. (The imam's costs, as the complainant, were covered by the Commission which may explain why the province of Alberta seems to have been the sole jurisdiction in the Western world that investigated a citizen for the "crime" of publishing the Danish cartoons.[38]) Levant's magazine ceased publication, but he wrote a book,

35. Griffiths, "Immigrants must..."; Jason Kirby, "Forget the '70s," *Maclean's*, April 20, 2009, 38. *The Toronto Star* on March 22, 2009 asked if immigration helped or hurt during a recession (and concluded that it helped), and on March 28, 2009 reported on an immigrant academic from India with a PhD in agricultural science who was working as a security guard in Toronto for $10 an hour. The difficulties well-educated immigrants face in getting good jobs increased between 1991 and 2006, according to Statistics Canada. *Globe and Mail* (Toronto), December 23, 2008; this mattered greatly because immigrants' children were among Canada's best educated. Ibid., October 9, 2008. If the parents leave, do the children stay?

36. Griffiths, "Sticky Citizenship."

37. "Biculturalism pays big dividends," *National Post*, November 10, 2008. See esp. "Report on Diversity," a special section in *Globe and Mail* (Toronto), January 26, 2009. But there are different success rates among different immigrants, Statistics Canada reported, with Chinese and South Asians doing vastly better than Blacks, Filipinos, or Latin Americans. See *Globe and Mail* (Toronto), October 6, 2008. Immigrants, according to one study, believe they must "Canadianize" to succeed. *National Post*, June 25, 2008.

38. Noted by Mark Steyn, "We have a winner!," *Steyn On-line*, April 30, 2009, accessed May 3, 2009, www.steynonline.com/content/blogsection/14/28.

Shakedown: How Our Government is Undermining Democracy in the Name of Human Rights, that quickly became a 2009 bestseller.[39]

A roughly similar case led the Canadian and international columnist Mark Steyn to be hauled before the Ontario and British Columbia Human Rights Commissions for publishing an excerpt from his book, *America Alone*,[40] in *Maclean's* magazine. Fortunately the magazine had deep pockets and a commitment to free speech, and Steyn, even better at generating mocking publicity than Levant, eventually prevailed. Levant and Steyn's articulate counterattacks brought the entire structure and processes of Canada's human rights commissions into disrepute and sparked political reviews.

Curiously, if expressing views that are not politically correct can be dangerous, this rule does not seem to apply to young immigrants, especially Muslims, Sikhs, and Hindus. Immigrant teenagers, according to a major survey, "Project Canada," run by University of Lethbridge sociologist Reginald Bibby, are more polite, honest, and hard-working than Canadian-born teens. They are also much less tolerant about issues such as gay marriage, abortion, or raising children out of wedlock, all subjects on which there is now fairly broad consensus in Canada – and so are their parents. As 42 percent of teenagers are now immigrants, this is likely to become politically important as immigration continues and these teenagers begin voting, unless the assimilationist pressures of Canadian society begin to alter views, as they might. There is already some indication that Canadian-born children of immigrants are somewhat more tolerant than their immigrant peers.[41]

The important point, one that both Steyn and Levant make, is that Multiculturalism tends to promote conformist speech on public and social questions. People are increasingly afraid to speak out lest they be labelled racist. Many Canadians seem to have forgotten that diversity of opinion is at least as important, indeed more important, to democracy as diversity of race, gender, and religion.

Finally, there is the question of Canadian identity and Multiculturalism. Pollster Michael Adams has suggested that Canada's lack of a strong national identity helps make Canada relatively free of prejudice, a place where newcomers can feel comfortable. Nations or communities with a stronger identity can be less tolerant, he says, and Adams points to Western Europe and parts of Quebec as examples.[42] This

39. Ezra Levant, *Shakedown: How Our Government is Undermining Democracy in the Name of Human Rights* (Toronto: McClelland & Stewart, 2009).

40. Mark Steyn, *America Alone* (Washington: Regnery Publishing Inc., 2006). See also M.R. Cohn, "An Unholy zeal for tolerance," *Toronto Star*, November 25, 2008.

41. Reginald Bibby, *The Emerging Millenials: How Canada's Newest Generation is Responding to Change* (Lethbridge, AB: Project Canada Books, 2009). See also Ken MacQueen, "Polite, Honest...Bigoted?," *Maclean's*, April 13, 2009, 42.

42. Michael Adams, *Unlikely Utopia: The Surprising Triumph of Canadian Pluralism* (Toronto: Viking Canada, 2007).

neglects the fact that Canada has long sought an identity strong enough to resist the magnetic pull of the United States, something that can hold its peoples together. For generations "not being American" was the touchstone of Canadianness, coupled with pro-British sentiment. But the decline of Britain in the twentieth century and the establishment of North American free trade in the latter part of that century have weakened those ideas, and only Multiculturalism was there to take their place. But Multiculturalism does not seem to have enough glue to hold the country together.

Instead, some have argued that immigrants choose Canada because it has its own history and its own institutions, its own record of fighting for democracy and freedom, its own history of hard-won tolerance. But when they arrive and send their children to school, they learn almost nothing of the new country. Unfortunately, Canadian history has largely been squeezed out of school curricula over the last four decades, replaced instead by social studies and civics, a curriculum that extracts useful lessons from the past to demonstrate how women have suffered, how immigrants and labor have been abused, and how Canada under the Charter of Rights and Freedoms is a better, multicultural nation than anything in the past dark ages. Perhaps it is, but snippet history teaches children nothing about the context in which Canada developed and, by making the past only a sugar-coated tale of oppression, grossly distorts history. This is important because the way the past is presented suggests to students, both native-born and immigrant, that Canada has no past worth the study. Why then assimilate or integrate into such a society? Why then not retain the old country's culture?

In fact, federal government policies that touched on history for the last twenty-five years have focused on apologies for past sins. Japanese-Canadians, Ukrainian-Canadians, Italian-Canadians, Jews, Sikhs, Chinese-Canadians, First Nations, and others have sought or received government apologies and sometimes cash compensation for historic grievances. The apology mania has only confirmed the "bad old days" version of the Canadian past.

The result of the killing of Canadian history, driven in substantial part by Canadian Multiculturalism, has been to leave all Canadians with little sense of where they have come from and, as a result, even less understanding of where they are now or where they might wish to go. The federal government has been forced to try to sell Canada to its citizens, trying to establish an identity which the public can buy into. The difficulty is that the Canadian identity itself has been fragmented by government policy.[43] Multiculturalism, in other words, by definition cannot be the national identity.

---

43. See J.L. Granatstein, *Who Killed Canadian History?*, rev. ed. (Toronto: Harper Collins, 2008) for an exposition of this viewpoint. On "Selling Canada to Canadians," see the article of this title by Emily West in *Critical Studies in Media Communication* (June 2002), 212ff.

The result is that Multiculturalism, something of which many Canadians claim to be inordinately proud and something that is taught in schools with near-religious fervor, is teetering on the knife edge of public disapproval. A survey in March 2002 by the Centre for Research and Information on Canada found that 92 percent of those polled agreed that Canadians had a responsibility to make sure that people of different races and cultures felt welcome. At the same time (August 2002), in an EKOS opinion survey, 49 percent agreed that Canada had a serious problem with domestic terrorist groups and 37 percent indicated that their feelings toward Muslims had altered negatively after 9/11.[44] Another poll by The Strategic Counsel in November 2002 found 44 percent favoring restrictions on Muslim immigration.[45] The terror attacks of 9/11 and the wars in Iraq and Afghanistan undoubtedly colored opinions in those polls. Nonetheless, whatever their acceptance of Multiculturalism, 70 percent in one poll and 69 percent in another, both taken in the second half of 2005, believed new immigrants should adapt to the Canadian way of life, compared to only 20 percent who felt they should be able to sustain their home country's culture.[46]

The polls can vary in their methodology and reliability, of course, but the conclusion seems reasonably clear: Multiculturalism is popular only if immigrants adapt to Canadian norms and act as other Canadians do. The government policy of Multiculturalism, however, encourages separateness and discourages adaptation. As one columnist put it, Multiculturalism is "a woolly minded notion that immigrants can come here, live distinct lives, retain old prejudices and remain essentially who they were."[47] The contradictions between the way Canadian governments for the past four decades have seen things and the way the public views them are clear and not readily resolved, but Canadian elites have generally been very successful in persuading themselves that they have succeeded in making Multiculturalism work. Nations in Europe have failed, they are wont to say, but not us. If only it were true.

Canada wants and needs immigrants, and very few want to close the door to newcomers on grounds of race or religion.[48] But Canada is a formed and democratic society with its own history, institutions, and mores. Those who immigrate to the nation today should know this and know, too, that they must adapt to what they find, as immigrants have done for centuries.

---

44. Cited in Samantha Arnold, "Securing Canada: Muslims and the Myth of Multiculturalism in the post-9/11 World" (paper presented at the meeting of the International Studies Association, Honolulu, 2005).

45. The poll was taken for the *Globe and Mail* and *Maclean's*.

46. The Strategic Counsel poll, August 2005; Innovative Research Group poll, November 15, 2005.

47. Andrew Cohen, *Ottawa Citizen*, March 31, 2009.

48. A Nanos poll in May 2008 found 72.6 percent of Canadians believed immigration important to the future of Canada. Nik Nanos, "Nation Building Through Immigration," *Policy Options* (June 2008), 30ff.

So, who are we now? Canada remains a nation unsure of its national identity but,[49] although the assimilationist pressures of North America continue to be important, it is impossible to doubt that Canadians are multicultural, increasingly so, and especially in the nation's three largest cities. But are they Multiculturalists? To a substantial extent they are, though very uneasily. Beyond Toronto and Vancouver, many English-speaking Canadians worry that Multiculturalism weakens their already shaky sense of nationality, and outside Montreal, French-speaking Canadians fear that it threatens their hard-won francophone language and culture. I believe that assimilation remains the goal for many, perhaps most, immigrants, just as it did in my family. But even those Canadians who worry about their national identity still want to believe that they can make Multiculturalism work as well as multiculturalism has.

Bibliography

Adams, Michael. *Unlikely Utopia: The Surprising Triumph of Canadian Multiculturalism*. Toronto: Penguin, 2007.

Bibby, Reginald *The Emerging Millenials: How Canada's Newest Generation is Responding to Change*. Lethbridge, AB: Project Canada Books, 2009.

Granatstein, J.L. *Who Killed Canadian History?*, rev. ed.. Toronto: Harper Collins, 2008.

Granatstein, J.L. "Multiculturalism and Canadian Foreign Policy," in *The World in Canada*, edited by D. Carment and D. Bercuson. Montreal: McGill-Queen's University Press, 2008.

Griffiths, Rudyard. *Who We Are: A Citizen's Manifesto*. Vancouver: Douglas & McIntyre, 2009.

Kelley, Ninette and Michael Trebilcock. *The Making of the Mosaic: A History of Canadian Immigration Policy*. Toronto: University of Toronto Press, 2010.

Kymlicka, Will. *Finding Our Way: Rethinking Ethnocultural Relations in Canada*. Don Mills, ON: Oxford University Press, 1998.

Kymlicka, Will. *Politics in the Vernacular: Nationalism, Multiculturalism and Citizenship*. New York: Oxford University Press, 2001.

Nugent, Amy. "Demography, National Myths, and Political Origins: Perceiving Official Multiculturalism in Quebec," *Canadian Ethnic Studies* (2006), 21ff.

Ryan, Phil. *Multicultiphobia*. Toronto: University of Toronto Press, 2010.

---

49. "Canada's current crisis of national identity seems to deepen daily," historian Bryan Palmer wrote in 2009, "and just what Canada is remains a vexing, seemingly unanswerable, project of interrogation. [...] all Canadians are pressured [...] to think that what they have seemingly lost, even if it never existed, is somehow to be cherished, whatever its history of undeniable costs, impossible contradictions, and ongoing uncertainties." Bryan Palmer, *Canada's 1960s: The Ironies of Identity in a Rebellious Era* (Toronto: University of Toronto Press, 2009), 430.

14 Canada's Story: The Urgency of History

Andrew Cohen

Canada *is* a plural society and it *has* a story of nationhood. The more pluralistic, or diverse, that Canada becomes, the greater the need to tell that story. Hence, the necessity, indeed the urgency, that the people celebrate their past.

Despite its size, age, experience, affluence, democracy, and diversity, Canada remains largely ignorant of its past. Canada has had enormous successes, to be sure, reflected in a society of peace, order, and good government. Its inclination for compromise and its celebration of diversity is the reason some call it the world's first postmodern nation. It is not a young country, as its untutored politicians like to tell its untutored citizens, but rather an old one; indeed, as a functioning federation its make-up and institutions look much as they did in 1867, the year it became independent from Britain. Canada has abundant natural resources – fossil fuels, minerals, oil, and water – an educated workforce, little violent crime, and generous social welfare.

But if it is the world's second largest county, it has the world's largest inferiority complex. It is shy about its achievements. Unlike other peoples, for whom boasting is natural, Canada is reluctant to speak its name. This has consequences in a nation of growing diversity and fragile unity.

Let me address this assertion first: that Canada simply doesn't know its own past. On the whole, history is unimportant to us. In some parts of the country we ignore it; in other parts, we diminish it. Equally harmful, we distort it, deny it, and dismiss it, largely by concentrating on the wrong ideas and the wrong themes. Our mistreatment of history is self-destructive. Says J.L. Granatstein, one of the country's leading historians: "Canada must be one of the few nations in the world, certainly one of the few Western industrialized states, that does not make an effort to teach its history positively and thoroughly to its young people. It must be of the few political entities to overlook its own cultural traditions – the European civilization on which our nation was founded – on the grounds that they would systematically discriminate against those who come from other cultures. The effects of these policies on a generation of students are all around us [...]."

Granatstein believes that we have "killed" Canadian history. For this we can blame politicians for failing to establish national standards; bureaucrats for failing to set rigid curricula and yielding to political correctness; historians for writing about the frivolous, the anxious, and the aggrieved; the media for trivializing history; and ethnic interest groups for whitewashing history. Who killed Canadian history? In a sense, we all did.

This is no small matter in a nation with an enduring secessionist movement. Fourteen years ago Quebec held a referendum and came within a half a percentage point of declaring sovereignty. The nation is fragile, and one reason is the lack of a history that would bind Canadians together. As Granatstein says, "it is not that we do not have such a history. It is simply that we have chosen not to remember it."

Some argue the reason for this is not political correctness or bureaucratic folly. They believe that history is irrelevant to most Canadians because they do not live "historical" lives. One historian argues that the collapse of history is part of the new socio-economic order that ignores the past, if not denies its value. The real problem? It's the zeitgeist, stupid.

The point remains that history is essential to our process of self-discovery as a people. The Unconscious Canadian is an ignorant Canadian. He has detached himself from his past, a touchstone of identity in a world of accelerating scientific advance and technological innovation and the movement of people and ideas.

History guides us, explains us, inspires us, roots us – even if we may not always agree on what happened, where, why, and to whom. It is what we are because it is what we were. In 1941, Samuel Bronfman, the founder of the House of Seagram, made this argument in his introduction to *Canada: The Foundations of its Future*, a volume the distillery commissioned from the celebrated historian, economist, and humorist, Stephen Leacock. "The history of Canada is the sum total of the biographies of all its citizens," he said. "In its unfolding, all have a share; from its narrative, all derive that pride that comes of participation. Written in national terms, it is yet, in so far as every Canadian is concerned, a deeply personal record; for here, fashioned into a composite picture are the activities, in peace and war, of industry and commerce, of labour and capital, of the great and the humble. Other departments of letters may perhaps have a special appeal; history belongs to all."

It belongs to all of us because history is us. We didn't just arrive here yesterday, in this empty land, *deus ex machina*. We came from somewhere. We did things together. We built, we struggled, we explored, we fought, we died. We survived. Astonishing as it may seem, though, we choose not to remember this, which has consequences for us as a people. As older Canadians die, taking their repository of memory with them, our collective sense of the past dims. It makes us an ahistorical people. We stumble about in a kind of poetic fog, with little idea of where we were and what we did. Because we do not know our past, we cannot teach it to our children or to our compatriots who come here from abroad. Behold, Canada, a nation of amnesiacs.

How little do Canadians know about their past? Let us count the ways. First, we have surveys. In 2006, pollsters commissioned by The Dominion Institute and Can-West Newspapers asked a broad sample of Canadians a series of questions about their country. The questions covered Canada's geography, its history, its arts and culture, its industry and commerce, and its role in the world. The questions tested a rudimentary knowledge of the country one would expect of an average citizen with a basic education. The answers were published on Canada Day in the *Ottawa Citizen* and other newspapers across the country.

On its birthday, barely two-thirds of those questioned knew Canada has ten provinces and three territories. Slightly fewer than that could name the three oceans bordering the country. Only 61 percent could name the five great lakes. Tested on their history, Canadians knew even less. Barely half could name Canada's first prime minister, Sir John A. Macdonald. Just a tenth knew the Charlottetown Conference, at which Canada was founded in 1867; less than a third could identify Mackenzie King, Canada's longest serving prime minister. Only 42 percent could name one of the wars (the War of Independence, the War of 1812) in which Canada was invaded by the United States; only 23 percent knew the United Empire Loyalists; only 46 percent could name the United Nations as the body Canadians helped create after the Second World War: only 43 percent could answer a similar question on Canada's role in creating NATO. It was an equally unhappy story in the number of respondents (21 percent) who could identify Canada's role in creating the Universal Declaration of Human Rights (which was drafted by John Humphrey, a Canadian lawyer); Canada's historic opposition to apartheid in South Africa (50 percent); and Canada's role in the creation of the International Criminal Court (10 percent).

Who is Canada's head of state? Only 8 percent knew that it is Queen Elizabeth. When was the patriation of the British North America Act? Only 15 percent knew it was 1982. What part of the Constitution guarantees "basic rights and freedoms?" Only 32 percent could associate "rights and freedoms" with the Charter of Rights and Freedoms. When it came to identifying events related to the two world wars, the response was also dismal. Only 33 percent knew why November 11 is called Remembrance Day (though 73 percent knew the significance of wearing a poppy). Asked about the disastrous Canadian raid on the North Atlantic coast in 1942, only 27 percent knew it was Dieppe. Some questions were particularly troublesome. Asked what great event ended in 1885 "with the hammering of the last spike," only 54 percent answered the Canadian Pacific Railway, meaning that most could not make the association between "spike" and "railway." But when asked which minority was removed from the west coast of Canada during the Second World War, however, 61 percent answered the Japanese, leading critics to suggest that when it comes to victimhood, we remember more clearly.

More reason to wonder. Only 28 percent knew what the conscription plebiscite in 1942 was about. Only 43 percent knew that the Korean War, in which Canadians fought and died, was the first armed conflict of the Cold War. Only 50 percent could identify *In Flanders Fields* as "Canada's most famous war poem." Just 46 percent knew Halifax was devastated by a great fire in 1917. Only 64 percent could identify Vimy Ridge as Canada's great battle of the Great War and only 44 percent knew our fondness for "peacekeeping" began in the Suez Crisis of 1956. This was particularly telling. Here was Canada's great victory and vocation, celebrated in our pantheon, but Canadians knew little of it. But don't despair. Almost all respondents (95 percent) knew that *O Canada* is the country's national anthem – even if only 68 percent could recite the first two lines. Fortunately, they were not asked about the subsequent lines.

Other polls at other times have also reflected a widespread ignorance in Canada. In February, 2006, Canadians also failed a quiz on three of Canada's most famous prime ministers. Only 47 percent knew that Sir John A. Macdonald was Canada's leading Father of Confederation; 44 percent knew that Pierre Elliott Trudeau invoked the War Measures Act; 18 percent knew that Sir Wilfrid Laurier was Canada's first francophone prime minister and had declared that the twentieth century belonged to Canada. These results were worse than those from a questionnaire in 2002.

Of course, these are just surveys. Some historians wonder what they prove. In a spirited exchange with Granatstein in a book called *Great Questions of Canada* published by The Dominion Institute in 2000, Michael Ignatieff argues that many Canadians knew very little about Canada even as they fought for it in the trenches of Europe in the Great War. If you believe that historical knowledge is the *sine qua non* of citizenship, he said, "we can all too easily conclude that the country is going to hell in a handcart. We can surrender to the kind of nostalgic pessimism that is apt to seize anyone over 50 who surveys the apparently appalling ignorance of the younger generation. Historical ignorance is unattractive [...] but it is a *folie de grandeur* to believe the country is done for if our citizenry can't repeat the names of all our prime ministers back to Confederation, the major battles since 1759 and the key provisions of the BNA Act." Ignatieff's point is that history is nice but not necessary for civic virtue.

Possibly Canadians know more about their country than they admit. But it is unlikely. Surveys may not tell the whole truth but they are a truth. They are one measure, however imperfect, of this country's amnesia.

How else do we recognize the Unconscious Canadian? We can examine the absence of history in the curricula of our schools. Or the deterioration of our historical sites. Or the content and presentation of our museums. Or the absence of biographies and memoirs about and by our leaders. Or the strange disappearance of Dominion Day, which was the name of our national holiday on July 1 from Confederation until the 1980s.

Let us begin with the teaching of history in our schools. Under the constitution, education is a provincial jurisdiction; schools are run by the provinces, not the federal government. Edmonton, Victoria, and Halifax set the curriculum, not Ottawa. The provinces decide what they will teach, when they will teach it, and what texts they will use. This is what happens when education is a provincial responsibility. Like so much else in this balkanized country, different practices apply in different places. In terms of history, the approach is inconsistent. On the whole, the truth is that most provinces do not teach Canadian history.

A decade ago, four provinces required just one Canadian history course – sometimes only one term long – to graduate from high school. Two provinces required two courses. Four had no Canadian history requirement at all. In its most recent survey published in June, 2009, the Dominion Institute found the situation in Canada remained "troubling."

It is sobering to survey the teaching of history in Canadian high schools. Province by province, the pickings are slim. In British Columbia, there is no separate course for Canadian history; a Grade 11 student of social studies will, however, have had some exposure to twentieth-century Canadian history. In Alberta, there is no separate history course, though, like BC, students have some twentieth-century Canadian history as part of social studies. In Saskatchewan, Grade 12 students must take a course in Canadian studies in which they can select history, native studies, or social studies. In Manitoba, Grade 11 students must take a general survey course that includes twentieth-century Canadian history. In Ontario, there is mandatory Canadian history course in Grade 10 that focuses on Canada after 1914. In Quebec, there is a mandatory course on the history of Quebec in Canada in Grade 10. In New Brunswick, there is a compulsory course in Grade 11 on world history and an optional course in Canadian history. In Nova Scotia, the compulsory course in Canadian history allows students to choose Canadian history, African history, or Gaelic, African-Canadian, or Mic'maq studies. In Prince Edward Island, graduating students must have taken a history course with some elements of Canadian history. In Newfoundland and Labrador, there is no mandatory course; students can study Canadian history or world history.

What to make of this crazy quilt? Collectively, it suggests a country with no compulsion to tell its story to its children. As we can see, in most provinces a student can receive a high school diploma – which may be all the formal education he or she receives in life – with little or no exposure to Canadian history in the upper grades. In New Brunswick, for example, it is fine to study the history of the world but not of Canada. In British Columbia, it is fine to take some history as part of something else. In Nova Scotia, other histories – that of blacks, Acadians, Africans, or aboriginals – are as important as Canada's. In Ontario, history is restricted to the twentieth century, and that seems to begin in 1914. A student can leave high school never knowing that Canada began in the nineteenth century, and although the twentieth century was to be Canada's, it is 14 years shorter than in other jurisdictions. Elsewhere, history is subsumed by "social studies," a euphemism for virtually anything.

In Quebec, it is no surprise that the history taught in secondary schools is the history of Quebec, or perhaps Quebec within Canada. This has meant that students learn the story of the tensions between French and English, often with the Québécois as victims. When the government of Jean Charest – perhaps the most federalist premier elected in the province since Jean Lesage in the 1960s – proposed changes to the curriculum in the spring of 2006, it caused an uproar. The purpose was to play down linguistic and ethnic tensions. "It represents a departure from the traditional framework of history structured around conflict between francophones and anglophones to offer a more unifying history," explained historian Jean-Francois Cardin, who advised the government on the changes. But politicians, commentators, and unionists protested that the new approach would gloss over the Conquest of 1763, the patriation of the constitution in 1982, and the collapse of the Meech Lake Accord in 1990. They called it an "ultra-federalist" view of the past that would represent Canada more than Quebec. They said it played down the sovereigntist movement, overlooking "essential elements of Quebec history."

Here is the argument over *whose* history. The debate in Quebec is a lesson – indeed an inspiration – to the rest of Canada. Quebeckers think more about their history than English Canadians do about theirs. "History has always had a special status in the province," writes Kevin Kee, a history teacher who moved to Quebec from Ontario. As he quickly learned, it is largely because "l'histoire est plus présente" – Quebeckers are surrounded by their past in song, verse, places, names. They have a rich past, going back to the early explorers of the sixteenth century, and they cherish it. It is true that English Canada is uncomfortable with "je me souviens" ("I remember"), the defiant slogan stamped on Quebec licence plates. Michael Ignatieff thinks that if it invites the Québécois to keep faith with old quarrels, injustices, hurts, and slights "I'd prefer my licence plate to read 'I've forgotten'." It's an example of history as controversy. When that declaration was originally adopted by the Parti Québécois in the 1970s, it suggested a sense of grievance. It may still, but not in the same way. What is important is that Quebeckers are *remembering*. It is the act itself, which reinforces their pride and self-awareness.

As cities the age of Quebec know well, a nation's history is not only found in classrooms and textbooks. History is written in the wood, stone, steel, tin, brick, and glass of houses, churches, legislatures, schools, libraries, statues, cemeteries, convents, bridges, factories, and other great public edifices. There is history in architecture. This is our physical history we are ignoring in our in our villages, towns and cities. Neglecting our past is as dangerous as denying it. As Joseph Howe said in 1871: "A wise nation preserves its records, gathers up its monuments, decorates the tombs of its illustrious dead, repairs its great public structures, and fosters national pride by perpetual reference to the sacrifices and glories of the past."

So serious is the assault on our historic sites that Sheila Fraser, the Auditor-General of Canada, devoted an entire chapter to it in her report to Parliament in 2004. Because she uncovered the improprieties of the sponsorship scandal in the same report, her warning was largely unnoticed. That was unfortunate. Fraser conducted what she called the first audit of cultural heritage anywhere in the world. She found that almost two-thirds of the historic properties administered by Parks Canada were in "poor to fair condition" and in need of work in two to five years, without which they could be lost. Many buildings and sites were falling into disrepair.

One of the worst was the Cave and Basin National Historic Site in Banff National Park – the first of Canada's national parks, established in 1885 – which draws thousands of visitors a year. Another is Fort Henry in Kingston, Ontario, an imposing stone redoubt that was built between 1832 and 1837. A third is the National Library of Canada, the repository of millions of books and documents, where 90 percent of the collection is housed in unacceptable conditions. "Once a piece of history is lost, it is lost forever," said Ms. Fraser.

Fraser's report has the dry, antiseptic tone of the accountant she is. This is an audit, written in the numbered paragraphs of a legal brief, innocent of anxiety or anger, as dry as ancient timbers. But it carefully catalogues our inventory of things historic, traces why we have allowed this to happen (budgetary cutbacks), and proposes how to respond (money and administrative change). In a nutshell, the Auditor General describes the challenge facing Canada in protecting and preserving its heritage. Ms. Fraser was telling us what historians, archivists, curators, and others who tend the garden of the past have been warning for years: that we are in danger of losing a part of ourselves.

Examples of a past at risk, in one part of the country or another, in one form or another, are everywhere. One is how we remember our prime ministers. By and large, we don't. What would normal in other parts of the world – not just America – is unusual in Canada, where few of our 20 leaders are remembered. We have an inconsistent approach to preserving and identifying their birthplaces, their residences, and their gravesites. We have an interest in some and not others.

It is the same with the posthumous recognition of the Fathers of Confederation. Most of the homes of the 17 founding fathers who lived in Ottawa after 1867 have disappeared. Only six of the 17 residences survive; the rest were destroyed by fire or demolished to make way for parking lots, office towers, and apartment blocks.

Generally speaking, Canada remembers its luminaries reluctantly. Few governors general, soldiers, doctors, writers, musicians, scholars, inventors, scientists, artists, and athletes are celebrated as persons of stature in Canada, as they would be in other societies. Writers are revered in Ireland. Artists are venerated in Italy. Musicians are celebrated in Germany. Everyone is a star in America. Not in Canada.

But the loss of our past goes beyond schools that don't teach national history and governments that ignore historic places. The same pattern is at work in national institutions in the national capital. They show how we present and interpret our history – or how we don't.

The Canadian Museum of Civilization reflects Canada, for example, but much of what it reflects is political correctness. You can see this in its exhibitions which do not address certain topics. The charges of political correctness apply not only to the Canadian Museum of Civilization. The same was largely true of the Canadian War Museum in 1998, which made no mention of the North Atlantic Treaty Organization for example, which Canada helped found after the Second World War. Now, fortunately, we do have a new Canadian War Museum, which opened in 2005.

The federal government had hoped to address lacunae in our knowledge of ourselves when it announced the creation of the Canada History Centre in Ottawa in 2003. After three terms, Jean Chrétien was in his last six months in office. The centre would be part of his legacy. It would promote, exhibit, and interpret the great events and the great people of our past, both on display and online. More telling, it would be created in the Government Conference Centre, the storied old railway station in the heart of the capital, the venue of so many historical constitutional conclaves, including the one that returned the British North America Act to Canada in 1982. "The Canada History Centre is being created to address a gap in the telling of our political and democratic history, which is often presented in a fragmented manner," said the government.

Given what was missing in the Canadian Museum of Civilization, given the ignorance of national history among young Canadians and new Canadians, given the promise of renewal of a magnificent historic building, this seemed to be the right idea in the right place. When a new government came in, though, it cancelled the museum.

We also wanted to create a national portrait gallery. The government of Jean Chrétien believed that Canada should have a place to display historical art like the galleries in London, Paris, Washington, and Australia, which recently opened one in Canberra. It was not a new idea; Vincent Massey proposed a portrait gallery in 1948. "Canada possesses no national portrait gallery where the likenesses of all the eminent figures in Canadian life could be found," he wrote in *On Being Canadian* some 60 years ago. "Such portraits should be acquired not because of any artistic merit they might possess but as documentary records in whatever form they are available. Suitably housed and catalogued, the collection would be of the greatest value to students of Canadian history and of genuine interest to the general public."

The Portrait Gallery of Canada was to be created in the former Embassy of the United States, a nineteenth-century jewel that sits on Wellington Street directly across from Parliament. The location is unique in the capital. Money was allocated; preparatory work began. The plan was to renovate the embassy and build an addition. All that stopped when the Conservatives came to office.

The purpose of the portrait gallery is less the art than the history, inviting Canadians to make the connection between their past and its faces, many of whom they do not know. It is an indispensable part of a nation's legacy. Sandy Nairne, the director of the National Portrait Gallery in London, wonders why there is even a debate on the question and says it would be "a tragedy" if the project didn't proceed. "How can you do without it?" he asks. "No great country can think of itself without thinking of those who made it a great country." The reason, he said, is that it creates a sense of nationhood. "Debates about nationality never finish. They carry on and everyone's part of it. Everybody engages, thinking about where they came from and how they've become who we are."

If there was any doubt about the need for a national portrait gallery or a national history museum, it was confirmed by *The Greatest Canadian*, a popular television series broadcast on the CBC in the autumn of 2004. Based on similar series in Great Britain and Germany, the show invited viewers to choose those Canadians who had made the greatest contribution to Canada. It was clear from many of the 100 original nominees that the audience knew almost nothing about their compatriots, living or dead, who had built this country. As we know, historians have long said that Canadians are appallingly ignorant of Canada. Now *The Greatest Canadian* proved it. Many of the 100 nominees were less about history than celebrity. They included singers, comedians, broadcasters, and even a mischievous broadcaster from Winnipeg who had asked his listeners to mount a write-in campaign with his name.

The pantheon of the top 20 Canadians is revealing. The gallery of greats included David Suzuki, the scientist and broadcaster known for his strong opinions on global warming and other environmental threats (5); Don Cherry, the sports broadcaster whose opinions are as loud and tasteless as his sport jackets (7); Alexander Graham Bell, the inventor of the telephone, a Scotsman who lived in the United States and vacationed in Canada (9); and Wayne Gretzky, the legendary hockey player (10). They are in company with more defensible choices: Tommy Douglas, the Prairie politician and father of Medicare (1), Terry Fox, the one-legged runner who died of cancer while running across Canada (2), Pierre Trudeau (3), Sir Frederick Banting, the discover of insulin (4), Lester Pearson (6), and Sir John A. Macdonald (8).

That Tommy Douglas was chosen "the Greatest Canadian" is predictably Canadian. A man of courage, tenacity, and acuity, Douglas was a former bantamweight boxer who was premier of Saskatchewan from 1947 to 1961. Against much opposition, he introduced universal healthcare and hospital insurance. When he entered national politics as leader of the newly formed New Democratic Party, Douglas joined Lester Pearson in creating universal healthcare for all Canadians. Today Medicare, like peacekeeping, has become a part of the Canadian iconography, a secular religion. We talk about it endlessly. It has psychological benefits for us, including making us different from the Americans, or allowing us to feel better than they are. So it was no surprise that Canadians chose Douglas; in a sense, he is us.

Another reason. It is a good bet that Canadians did not even consider John A. Macdonald for the top five because they knew little of him or his contemporaries. They remembered Pierre Trudeau and Lester Pearson, nation-builders both, and they knew of Banting. All would be legitimate candidates for the greatest Canadian, as were many others down the list, like Laurier and King. But that suggests a serious view of this exercise and that would be a mistake. Others did take it more seriously, though.

Three years before the CBC, the BBC asked their viewers to nominate their "great Britons." They responded enthusiastically. Their top ten: Elizabeth I, William Shakespeare, Oliver Cromwell, Horatio Nelson, Isambard Kingdom Brunel, Charles Darwin, Winston Churchill, John Lennon, Princess Diana. Keen to know if this list truly represented what Britons think, the BBC commissioned a poll of 2,000 respondents and found the results were almost exactly the same for eight of ten nominees. The striking thing about the British list is that beyond the top ten, it still reflects men and women of stature. There are some dubious picks – pop musician Boy George (46), actress Julie Andrews (59), and footballer Bobby Moore (69) – but there are few of them. These are a serious people, conversant with their past, making serious choices. As essayist Mark Harrison put it in *Great Britons: The Great Debate*: "The clearest image to emerge from this snapshot of public opinion is that the British are sustained and stirred more by greatness forged in the white heat of history than by greatness conferred by the bright light of celebrity." Or, put more simply, Britons know their past and cherish it. *The Greatest Briton* was a wonderful, educational exercise. *The Greatest Canadian* was entertainment, pure and simple.

It isn't just the schools, the museums, the government and the media that fail us. It is also the professional historians, their books and periodicals. Academic historians in Canada have stopped writing political and national history. They prefer to write about labour history, women's history, ethnic history, and regional history, among others, often freighted with a sense of grievance. This kind of history has its place, of course, but our history has become so specialized, so segmented, and so narrow that we are missing the national story in a country that has one and needs to hear it. Says Jeffrey Simpson of *The Globe and Mail*: "History departments now largely teach particularist histories of people defined by region, locality, gender or ethnicity. Political history is considered passé in many quarters, as is history on a grand scale. Micro-history has taken over, galvanizing some, boring most."

Does that mean that all historians have to write about the big picture? Hardly. There is always room for novelty, personality, and discovery in exploring our past. But it is also true there is *less* room than other countries. A country as understudied as Canada, which has so few books on so many important topics, can ill-afford this endless excursion into esoterica that seems to preoccupy so many of our professional historians. When critics lament the decline of political history or biography, as they do, they need only point to the paucity of fresh biographies on our greatest prime ministers, particularly those before 1950. Indeed, we hardly have any. At the same time, we have little autobiography. There isn't the same tradition of writing magisterial memoirs in Canada as in Britain or the United States, and our prime ministers have left few of them. Macdonald, Laurier, King, and St. Laurent did not write their memoirs, though King did leave his celebrated diary. Pearson and Diefenbaker each left memoirs. Trudeau did not, at least not in a diligent way, preferring to edit the transcripts of television interviews. (Since 2007, however, Brian Mulroney, Jean Chretien, and Paul Martin have written memoirs, though John Turner and Joe Clark have not).

On the whole, Canada knows more about its politicians today than it did two or three decades ago, but it is still not enough, and the situation is very different from that in America and Britain. Every autumn and spring, bookstores in the United States are full of new interpretations of George Washington, John Adams, Thomas Jefferson, Benjamin Franklin, Alexander Hamilton, Franklin Roosevelt, and Harry Truman. Just when one thinks there is nothing new to say about the Founding Fathers, David McCullough or Joseph Ellis come out with a new book. When Theodore Roosevelt seems old hat, Edmund Morris publishes a masterful two-volume biography. In America, even dead white males get a second act, and Americans love it. Doris Kearns Goodwin published a dazzling interpretation of the leadership of Abraham Lincoln in 2005 that returned to the bestseller list when Barack Obama let slip that he was reading it. The indefatigable Robert Caro is still turning out volumes on the life of Lyndon Johnson, which he has been writing since 1976. The Kennedys remain a cottage industry in the United States; so is the Civil War, the Second World War, and the civil rights movement.

The British are not dissimilar. In his retirement, Roy Jenkins, the erudite public man, turned out a splendid volume on Winston Churchill. Martin Gilbert, the great man's biographer, has made a career of chronicling Churchill's life, as well as other epochal events of the twentieth century. That's what good historians do: they rescue what would otherwise be forgotten and give it new life.

It isn't enough to argue, as the apologists do, that Canada is smaller than the United States or Britain, and that our past is not as interesting. Yes, we are, and yes, it is. But there is a long, vivid history out there, if only we would seek to discover it.

"History loves company," reads an advertisement for the Historical Hotels of Canada. It is catchy but misleading. Hotels may love company but history doesn't; not in Canada. The problems of history, as we have seen, go beyond the scholars who won't write what people will read; the curators of the museums who won't take risks; the civil servants in the education ministries that won't require history in the schools; the politicians who won't make something more of our historic sites; and the media that trivializes history. It is about taking ourselves seriously. We abuse our past in Canada. Or we deny it.

In 1982, for example, we did away with Dominion Day. Somebody in Parliament decided that it was bad idea, a colonial remnant, too British. It was put in a private member's bill and was passed one afternoon when almost no one was in the Commons. The Senate approved it. That Dominion is a lovely term, taken from the Bible, didn't matter. It was replaced with Canada Day, a term of such crushing insipidness that it could only come from a bureaucrat. Not Independence Day, mind you. Canada Day. As one commentator said, this was "identity theft."

If we do not deny history, we apologize for it. The latest apology for the sins of our ancestors involved the head tax on the Chinese. In June of 2006, Prime Minister Harper offered the nation's regrets for "the racist actions of our past." Wrapping himself in sackcloth and ashes, Harper apologized for a government that imposed the head tax between 1885 and 1923. He said that Canada's failure to acknowledge "these historical injustices has prevented many in the community from seeing themselves as fully Canadian." So he offered symbolic payments of $20,000 to a few remaining victims. The tax was racist and wrong; issuing apologies for the acts of others, as Brian Mulroney did for the Japanese interned in the Second World War, is a way of coming to terms with our past. The problem is there have been other injustices in our past, and the claimants – such as Jews, Italians, and Sikhs – no doubt have their grievances, too, and will soon be seeking their compensation.

Why does this matter? Why does a country which ignores its past imperil its future?

Let us return to the pluralistic society. History matters to Canada because it is a country which accepts some 250,000 immigrants a year, most of whom will become citizens within three years. Having been born elsewhere, these people do not know our history when they arrive here. They won't know our traditions and often they will import theirs, including prejudices.

The remarkable thing is that we have no compulsion to teach them our history. Indeed, until recently, the manual issued by the federal government to acquaint new Canadians with Canada had more pages on the environment – particularly the values of recycling – than it did on history. Fortunately, that's now changing.

But it is not just new Canadians. As we can see, older Canadians do not know our past. This has consequences. In December 2008, for example, Canada found itself in a constitutional crisis. The three opposition parties, angry with the Conservative government, decided to form a coalition in Parliament. We have not had coalition government in Canada since 1917, but it is perfectly legitimate. Still, the Conservatives, who dissolved Parliament rather than risk losing a vote of confidence, told Canadians that it was foreign, sinister, virtually a *coup d'etat*. The truth is that coalitions are rare, even extraordinary, but they are not unconstitutional. Because most Canadians believed the government, its popularity surged. Had they known more about our past, Canadians could have made wiser choices. The point: history matters.

But history matters, as well, because it tells all of us, in a diverse, fragmented country, divided by race, region, religion, and language, that this country has done things together. That it has a past. That it matters.

One of the misapprehensions in Canada is that Canadians do not know much about their history because they are not interested in it. Actually, that isn't so; when Canadians are given an opportunity to learn more about themselves, they respond with enthusiasm. We know this from the success of television documentaries and other forms of popular history.

Offer it and they'll embrace it. In other words, if the country were to teach its history, preserve its historic places, mark its anniversaries, remember its leaders, and create new museums, it would find an enthusiastic audience. The challenge isn't demand, it is supply. The demand for history isn't simply nostalgia or sentimentality; it is a deep desire, in a world that is changing, to understand some of the fundamentals. So whether we do it by creating new museums or new monuments, we write our biography every day. The alternative is a life of ignorance. We can choose that, too. If the happiest nations are those with no history, as someone once said, our cheerful, willful amnesia – for that is what it is – could bring us a lifetime of contentment. But, we ask, at what cost?

Bibliography

Adams, Michael. *Fire and Ice: The United States, Canada and the Myth of Converging Values*. Toronto: Penguin, 2003.

Conway, Jill Ker. *True North: A Memoir*. Toronto: Alfred A. Knopf Canada, 1994.

Cooper, John. *Great Britons: The Great Debate*. London: National Portrait Gallery Publications, 2002.

Kilborn, William. *Canada: A Guide to the Peaceable Kingdom*. Toronto: MacMillan Company of Canada, Ltd., 1970.

Granatstein, J.L. *Who Killed Canadian History?* Toronto: Harper-Collins Publishers Ltd., 2000.

Griffiths, Rudyard, ed. *Great Questions of Canada*. Toronto: Stoddart Publishing Co., 2000.

Leacock, Stephen. Canada: *The Foundations of its Future*. Montreal: Gazette Printing Co. Ltd., 1941.

Massey, Vincent. *On Being Canadian*. Toronto: J.M. Dent & Sons (Canada) Ltd., 1948.

Moore, Brian. *Canada*. New York: Time Life Books, 1963.

15 National Identity, American and Otherwise

Francis Fukuyama

Samuel P. Huntington's last book, *Who Are We? The Challenges to American National Identity*,[1] confronts directly an issue that many of his countrymen would prefer to ignore, namely, the nature of the cultural bonds that constitute the basis for national community in the United States. His assertion that American national identity was rooted in religion and the cultural traditions of a particular ethnic group – what he called "Anglo-Protestant" culture – was bound to cause controversy. Huntington suggested that American identity consisted in something more than lowest-common-denominator allegiance to American political institutions, and was not so entirely different from the blood-and-soil identities of Europe.

In my view, Huntington was absolutely correct in raising the question of what American national identity was and ought to be, even if his specific answer left something to be desired. National identity is not inevitably a force for exclusion and intolerance; it is in fact a necessary condition for a modern state and a workable society. No liberal democracy can exist without a sense of national identity, since the latter is what provides the matrix within which a shared political life can be lived.

The importance of national identity can be seen most clearly in societies that lack it. We are aware, of course, of the violent conflicts that have riven ethnically divided societies like the former Yugoslavia, Sudan, and Iraq. In these cases, allegiance to the central state is so low that it is in danger of fragmenting into smaller units. But these are in a sense the easy cases, since one could argue that separation could lead to a coherent nation within the borders of a successor state, be it a Kurdistan or Southern Sudan.

The more common problem of weak national identity occurs in countries where there are no separatist movements or highly concentrated minority enclaves, but where the nation simply does not constitute the primary source of allegiance for the majority of the country's population. No one in contemporary Kenya, for example, wants to create an independent Kikuyuland or Luoland; nonetheless, these ethnic

---

1. Samuel P. Huntington, *Who Are We? The Challenges to America's National Identity* (New York: Simon and Schuster, 2004).

identities serve to define Kenyans more clearly than their national identity. This has led to the depressing spectacle of an ethnic spoils politics being practiced over the decades, and occasionally breaking into outright violence as after the contested presidential election of 2007. Indeed, much of what Europeans or Americans describe as political corruption in developing countries is actually a byproduct of weak national identity: politicians are primarily interested in sending rents and resources back to their tribe, ethnic group, or region, and have no sense of a larger national purpose. They are not necessarily corrupt as individuals; rather, they are primarily loyal to a group other than the nation-state.

Identity and democracy

National identity – that is, "stories of nationhood" that explain to citizens who they are, where they came from, and what binds them together – is thus the necessary framework for collective action, dispute resolution, and political order more generally. It is a necessary component of a well-functioning democratic society. But it also exists in some tension with the underlying principles of modern democracy, since the latter do not provide guidance as to the boundaries of national community. Part of the reason that national identities are weak today in liberal democracies is due to a fear that strong assertions of identity will violate the principle of universal human equality.

In an article written in 1997, the French political theorist Pierre Manent made the following observation:

> The world of democratic nations was formed when the principle of consent was adopted by political bodies that had been constituted in accord with other principles, both political and religious. Now that the principle of consent has banished every other principle, it is not clear how a new body could form and then subject itself to the principle of consent that constituted the democratic nation. The political molds are broken, and democratic vigilance inhibits their reconstruction.[2]

Manent points to a fundamental problem that contemporary democratic polities have been reluctant to acknowledge or confront politically. Liberal democracies embed the principles of rule of law and popular sovereignty (or as Manent puts it, "consent"), themselves built on a foundation of universal and equal rights. But nowhere in democratic theory does one find a principle by which one can define the boundaries of any given democratic political community. Actual democracies

---

2. Pierre Manent, "Democracy without Nations?," *Journal of Democracy* 8 (1997: 92-102. See also his book *A World Beyond Politics? A Defense of the Nation-State* (Princeton, NJ: Princeton University Press, 2006).

came into being in nation-states that were constituted on dynastic, religious, or ethno-nationalist grounds. But violent nationalism rooted in ethnicity has, for good reasons, been rejected, in parallel with an earlier rejection of religion as a definer of community. As Manent suggests, having used the nation-state to come into being, democracy has pushed the nation away in favor of a more universalistic principle of justice.

The US Constitution begins with the phrase "We the People": a People who are the legitimating authority for everything that follows. But American democracy cannot reach back into its foundational principles to answer the question of who the "We" is in any clear-cut way. Why does American identity end at the Rio Grande river? It is just a matter of geography and historical accident, or is there something about the people living on the other side that excludes them from the American community?

The problem is even more severe in Europe. Postwar Europe has deliberately sought to suppress sovereignty, the nation-state, or any other form of religious or ethnic identity around which communities have historically defined themselves. But the European Union does not provide a strong alternative ground for a "post-national" identity. The problem begins with the fact that it is not clear what the EU is in the first place. It has gotten as far as it has through deliberate ambiguity as to whether it is simply a complex multilateral organization, or an incipient sovereign nation-state. But the failure to define the EU politically leaves Europeans facing a huge degree of confusion as to whether they are Europeans first, and Spaniards, Germans, or Dutch second, or else Catalans or Scots in preference to any of the above. And if they are Europeans, can that identity encompass a large, non-Christian country like Turkey?

Into the vacuum that exists in the heart of modern liberal democracy has rushed modern identity politics. Liberal democracy is based on the universal recognition of people as free and equal human beings. But people are not content with that; they want to be recognized for being members of a host of other smaller and more exclusive communities that provide a stronger sense of identity and bonding – as Ukrainians, or Muslims, or indigenous peoples, or gays, or African-Americans. In the absence of big, overarching national identities, modern politics provides us with a host of smaller, particularistic, and often ascriptive ones. So liberal democracy must deal with two questions of identity: How does the whole community define itself and its boundaries, and how does it deal with demands for recognition of groups and group rights on the part of its citizens?

The fact that modern liberal democracies do not demand strong identification with the national community, but rather encourage multiple, shifting, and overlapping ones, is something that is rightly celebrated by many. A citizen of a contemporary democracy can be simultaneously Anglican, gay, professional, and a fancier of Yorkshire terriers, and switch these allegiances voluntarily over time. Amartya Sen contrasts this aspect of modernity with the more traditional fixed identities of religion, ethnicity, and caste that have been the grounds for a great deal of violence both at present and historically.[3] Shifting voluntary identities are necessitated by modern market economies that encourage both a proliferation of social roles and social mobility, as well as by the *de facto* multicultural character of the contemporary globalized world.

Unfortunately, however, there are inherent limits to liberal cultural pluralism. The fact of the matter is that liberal democracy is not itself culturally neutral, but contains certain assumptions about human nature and human behavior that are not compatible with every cultural practice. Democratic political theory is based on the assumption that the original rights-bearers are individuals, and not families, sects, or other kinds of social groups. Modern liberalism is, moreover, founded on belief, born of Europe's own experience with politicized religion, that religious belief must be confined to a sphere of private belief, a view that is not compatible with all religious self-understandings. Basic conflicts of democratic principle have thus arisen in recent years when, for example, a democratic state is confronted with demands by minority groups to set rules with respect to family law that violate the rights of the individuals that make up that group, as when a woman wants to marry someone rejected by her family.

The emergence and evolution of identity politics

The very concept of identity and identity politics is a modern phenomenon. It is safe to say that in medieval Europe, virtually no one worried about questions related to identity. Identity, in the form of religion, social status, occupation, citizenship, and nationality, was almost completely ascribed by the surrounding society, and was not a matter of individual choice. Subjectively, it is unlikely that anyone pondered at great length the potential conflict between what one truly felt oneself to be on the inside, and the social roles that were imposed on individuals by their families, villages, priests, or sovereigns, since there was little choice in the matter.[4]

Modern notions of identity in the West begin in an important sense with the Protestant Reformation. Martin Luther argued that salvation could only be achieved through an inner state of faith, and attacked the Catholic emphasis on works –

---

3. See Amartya K. Sen, *Identity and Violence: The Illusion of Destiny* (New York: W.W. Norton, 2007).
4. This generalization of course applies to societies broadly speaking. Philosophers and other thinkers from Socrates to Augustine have of course contemplated the potential conflict between one's inner beliefs about the truth and the opinions demanded by the larger society.

that is, exterior conformity to a set of social rules established by the Church. The Reformation thus identified true faith as an individual's subjective state in direct relation to God, thereby dissociating inner identity from external social practice.

The Canadian philosopher Charles Taylor has written extensively about the subsequent historical development of identity politics.[5] Jean-Jacques Rousseau, in both the *Second Discourse* and the *Promenades*, argued that there was a critical disjuncture between our outward selves. Natural man was born happy and free; it was the accretion of social customs and habits over historical time, such as the invention of private property and the habit of comparing oneself to others, that enslaved him. This then established the ground for conflict between our social identity and our true inner natures. Happiness lay in the recovery of inner authenticity, "le sentiment de l'existence" that was masked by the passions generated by social dependence. In Taylor's words, "This is the powerful moral ideal that has come down to us. It accords moral importance to a kind of contact with myself, with my own inner nature, which it sees as in danger of being lost [...] through the pressures toward outward social conformity [...]."[6]

The disjuncture between one's inner and outer self comes not merely from the realm of ideas, but is something produced by the social reality of modern democratic societies with free-market economies. After the American and French revolutions, the ideal of a *carrière ouverte aux talents* was increasingly put into practice as traditional barriers to social mobility were removed. One's social status was achieved rather than ascribed, the product of one's natural talents, work, and effort rather than an accident of one's birth. One's life story was the search for fulfillment of an inner plan, rather than conformity to the expectations of one's parents, kin, village, or priest.

Thus the process of modernization itself pushed questions of identity to the forefront. Many of the famous dichotomies of classic modernization theory – Ferdinand Tönnies' transition from *Gemeinschaft* to *Gesellschaft*,[7] Henry Maine's distinction between status and contract,[8] or Durkheim's contrast between mechanical and organic solidarity[9] – reflected the experiences of individuals in European societies during the eighteenth and nineteenth centuries as they moved from small village

---

5. See Charles Taylor, *Multiculturalism: Examining the Politics of Recognition* (Princeton, NJ: Princeton University Press, 1994); and *Sources of the Self: The Making of the Modern Identity* (Cambridge, MA: Harvard University Press, 1989).

6. Taylor, *Multiculturalism*, 30.

7. Ferdinand Tonnies, Community and Association (Gemeinschaft und Gesellschaft) (London: Routledge and Kegan Paul, 1955).

8. Henry Maine, *Ancient Law: Its Connection with the Early History of Society and Its Relation to Modern Ideas* (Boston, MA: Beacon Press, 1963).

9. Emile Durkheim, *The Division of Labor in Society* (New York: Macmillan, 1933).

communities to modern industrial cities. The fixed and limited social roles offered by the former were replaced by the fluid and ever-changing division of labor required by an industrial order. Instead of being surrounded by a narrow circle of kin and neighbors, one was suddenly plunged into a far more diverse and pluralistic society which no longer defined one's social identity clearly. This increase in moral options was subjectively experienced by those who went through it both as a liberation, and as an acute crisis of identity that produced the phenomena of alienation and anomie.

There is a large and well-established literature explaining nationalism as a modern phenomenon that arose out of the transition from *Gemeinshaft* to *Gesellschaft*, and sought to deal precisely with the problem of the alienating character of modern industrial society.[10] The unity of the village was destroyed, and replaced by the unity of language and culture, which become the only shared characteristics of people encountering each other in a large, diverse urban setting.

The intellectual grounds for modern nationalism were laid by thinkers like Johann Gottfried von Herder, who argued that inner authenticity lay not just in individuals but in peoples, in the recovery of what we today call folk culture or national identity.[11] But as Ernest Gellner has argued, those national identities were not just lying around from time immemorial; they had to be deliberately constructed by elites as a means of binding populations to a new agenda.[12] All nationalists pretend that national identity is something ancient and sacred handed down to contemporary people through the generations, when it is in fact the nationalists themselves who have constructed it through the myths, stories, and heroes they celebrate. They are the purveyors of the modern idea of "culture," which acts as a kind of glue that seeks to rejoin the disrupted inner self to its new external social roles. And it is up to the purveyors of these myths to define the territorial boundaries of culture and national identity, whether it is *Grossdeutsch* or *Kleindeutsch*, based on a Slavic core or a cosmopolitan Russian empire.

In European history, the emergence of democracy is closely linked to the creation of national identity. The French Revolution mobilized a "nation in arms" not on the basis of a peasant's feudal obligations, but on the basis of their being Frenchmen with equal rights and duties. Thus, as Manent explains, European democracy, which today seeks to push aside nationalism as a basis for identity, was previously dependent on it for its success.

---

10. Ernest Gellner, *Nations and Nationalism* (Oxford: Blackwell, 1983); Fritz Stern, *The Politics of Cultural Despair: A Study in the Rise of German Ideology* (Berkeley: University of California Press, 1974).
11. Johann Gottfried von Herder, *Herder: Philosophical Writings*, ed. Michael N. Forster (Cambridge: Cambridge University Press, 2002).
12. See Ernest Gellner, "Nationalism and the Two Forms of Cohesion in Complex Societies," *Culture, Identity, and Politics* (Cambridge: Cambridge University Press, 1987).

Taylor points out that modern identity is inherently political, because it ultimately demands *recognition* in the Hegelian sense. One's inner self is not just a matter of inward contemplation; it must be intersubjectively recognized if it is to have value. The idea that modern politics is based on the principle of universal recognition comes from Hegel. But what we find increasingly is that universal recognition based on a shared humanness is not enough, particularly for groups that have been discriminated against in the past. Hence as we move closer to contemporary times, we find identity politics revolving around demands for recognition of group identities, that is, public affirmations of the equal dignity of formerly marginalized groups, from the Québécois to African-Americans to women to indigenous peoples to gays.

It is no accident that Charles Taylor is Canadian, since contemporary multiculturalism and identity politics was in many ways born in Canada with the demands of the Francophone community for recognition of their rights as a "distinct society." The latter's attempted codification of special rights for Quebec in the Meech Lake amendment to the Canadian Federal Charter would have violated the liberal principle of equal individual rights. French speakers enjoy linguistic rights not shared by English speakers: it is illegal, for example, for a Francophone or immigrant to send their children to an English-speaking school in Quebec, while a similar law protecting Anglophones would not be permitted in Alberta or British Columbia.[13]

Multiculturalism understood not just as tolerance of cultural diversity in *de facto* multicultural societies, but as the demand for legal recognition of the rights of ethnic, racial, religious, or cultural groups, has now become established in virtually all modern liberal democracies. American politics over the past generation has been consumed with controversies over affirmative action, bilingualism, and gay marriage, driven by formerly marginalized groups that demand recognition not just of their rights as individuals, but of their rights as members of groups. America's Lockean tradition of individual rights has meant that these efforts to assert group rights have been tremendously controversial.

American Identity

The contemporary debate over American national identity can be understood in terms of the polarity that exists between the views of two great political scientists, Seymour Martin Lipset and Samuel P. Huntington. Their differences can be described in terms of the relative priority they assigned to the state and the nation in

---

13. See the discussion in Taylor, *Multiculturalism*, 53.

defining American identity. Lipset believed that America was a state before it was a nation, while Huntington argued that the existence of a nation made possible the creation of the American state.

According to Lipset, American identity was always political in nature and arose out of the circumstances of the American founding, the fact that the country was created in a revolution against the authority of the British crown.[14] American identity is therefore based on the political creed that emerged from the founding, or what we might call "civic" America. It consisted of five basic values: equality, understood as equality of opportunity rather than outcome; liberty, in the sense of freedom from excessive state control; individualism, meaning that individuals could determine their own social station; populism; and laissez-faire in economic life. Because these qualities were both political and civic, they were in theory accessible to all Americans, and have remained remarkably durable over the American republic's history. Robert Bellah once described America as having a "civic religion," but it was a church that was open to newcomers to the country.[15]

The creed of Civic America was not written down in any formal documents; nonetheless, it was reflected in a host of institutions and historical practices. The separation of powers enshrined in the US Constitution reflected a deep distrust of concentrated executive power; the American government was weak by design and the presidency was a relatively powerless institution up through the early twentieth century. The American welfare state was late in developing when compared to Europe, due both to Americans' distrust of government and their belief that individuals ought to be responsible for their own lives and well-being. Americans have always cherished entrepreneurship and the private sector; when railroads were first introduced, they were built by private companies rather than state-owned ones as was the case in much of Europe. Americans like to take risks and defy authority to a greater extent than their counterparts in most other developed democracies; thus both the rate of entrepreneurship and stock ownership, as well as the rate of crime, tends to be higher in the US. American foreign policy has always embraced democracy promotion and at least paid lip service to the Wilsonian ideal of creating a world order based on democratic principles, precisely because democracy has been more central to American identity than in the case of other countries that had a national existence before they were democratic.

Huntington agreed fully that there was an American creed, and would probably not have disputed Lipset's characterization of it. He argued, however, that American national identity was not simply civic, but rooted in specific cultural practices of

---

14. Seymour Martin Lipset, *The First New Nation* (New York: Basic Books, 1963); *American Exceptionalism: A Double-Edged Sword* (New York: W.W. Norton, 1995).
15. Robert N. Bellah and Phillip Hammond, *Varieties of Civil Religion* (San Francisco: Harper and Row, 1980).

America's English settlers – what he calls "Anglo-Protestant" culture – that predated the founding of the American state.[16] Religion – specifically, sectarian Protestantism – was very important in defining that culture. In a famous line, he asserted:

> Would America be the America it is today if in the seventeenth and eighteenth centuries it had been settled not by British Protestants but by French, Spanish, or Portuguese Catholics? The answer is no. It would not be America; it would be Quebec, Mexico, or Brazil.[17]

These cultural givens were understood by the country's founders; as John Jay said in Federalist No. 2, "Providence has been pleased to give this one connected country to one united people – a people descended from the same ancestors, speaking the same language, professing the same religion, attached to the same principles."[18]

What were the cultural values that became part of American identity? The one that Huntington emphasizes centrally is the Protestant work ethic, which in his view differentiates Anglo-Protestants from other Europeans. He also points to the legacy of Tudor England, including traditions of common law, jury trials, reliance on local militias rather than a standing army, and the responsibility of legislators to their local communities, as distinguishing components. To this he could have added what Tocqueville identified as the American "art of association,"[19] that is, the proclivity of Anglo-Protestants to organize themselves in congregations at the grassroots level, a practice that soon spread beyond religious affairs in both England and North America to become a general habit.

While the civic and cultural views of American identity laid out by Lipset and Huntington have been an enduring polarity in American life, it is possible to overstate their degree of disagreement. Lipset was also of the view that the sectarian nature of American Protantism was critical to the shaping of American culture. It was, according to him, the source of the moralism that pervades American politics that is up until the present moment reflected in American foreign policy. And Huntington, for his part, sees the Anglo-Protestant cultural heritage in largely political terms, making it hard to distinguish which part of identity is derived from the political system and which from culture.

In the end, I believe that it is possible to reconcile the civic and cultural views of American identity, and to arrive at an understanding of Americanism that is more akin to Lipset's view than that of Huntington. Huntington is undoubtedly right that there are very specific features of American national identity that are rooted

16. Samuel P. Huntington, *Who Are We? The Challenges to America's National Identity* (New York: Simon and Schuster, 2004).
17. Huntington, *Who Are We?*, 59.
18. Alexander Hamilton, James Madison, and John Jay, *The Federalist Papers* (New York: New American Library, 1961).
19. Alexis de Tocqueville, *Democracy in America* (New York: HarperPerennial, 1988).

both in religion and in the specific habits of the English settlers who populated the colonies. Indeed, the historian David Hackett Fischer has shown that there were actually four distinct sub-cultures imported into the United States from different parts of England that account for features of American identity still visible today, for example in the still vigorous gun culture that traces its origin to the Scotch-Irish borderlands of northern England and Ireland.[20]

But these cultural habits have over time become deracinated from the specific ethnic groups that originally practiced them, becoming entirely creedal in nature. Take, for example, the famous Protestant work ethic. Poll data show, for example, that Americans not only work much harder than Europeans, but that they believe like Weber's early Protestants in the morally redeeming nature of work. But who in today's America works hard? It is not necessarily the descendants of the original white Anglo-Protestants, who exhibit a bimodal distribution both above and below the average socio-economic status of the country as a whole. An obsessive work ethic today is much more likely to be characteristic of the Russian cab driver, or Korean shopkeeper, or Mexican day-laborer, than a white Anglo-Saxon Protestant.

Thus what Huntington identifies as pre-political cultural components of identity are in fact broad virtues that can be adopted by any American, regardless of religious confession or ethnicity. He does not take the further step of observers like Patrick J. Buchanan who see the United States as an overtly "Christian country" or describe conditions of loyalty in essential tribal terms. Nor does he ground identity in one specific ethnicity or race, and therefore never takes shelter in a blood-and-soil concept of nation. In this I believe he is essentially correct, because one can accurately acknowledge America's specifically Christian roots without saying it is a Christian country, and point to its Anglo-Protestant heritage without saying that true Americans are Anglo-Protestants.

Indeed, Huntington is almost a century too late in trying to ground American identity in Anglo-Protestant culture. At the beginning of the twentieth century, there was still an identifiable Anglo-Protestant elite in the United States, one that strongly identified with Britain and believed in the joint duty of the "Anglo-Saxon races" to shape global order. But the cultural hegemony of this elite had already vanished by the middle of the century on both sides of the Atlantic – in America, due to the huge wave of Southern and Eastern Europeans who immigrated to the US at the turn of the century, and in Britain because of the experience of the two World Wars. Recovering a strong version of Anglo-Protestant culture is an uphill struggle in contemporary America.

---

20. David H. Fischer, *Albion's Seed: Four British Folkways in America* (New York: Oxford University Press, 1991).

Identity in the Twenty-First Century

If a strong Anglo-Protestant version of identity is not presently available, what general characteristics should Americans seek in defining their story of nationhood? Several general observations are in order.

First, modern democracies need a stronger sense of national identity in which to anchor citizenship than most currently have. Their problem is the proliferation of identities in a cacophony of demands for group recognition. Identity in the sense in which it is used today may be, as Pierre Manent suggests, a "passive and lifeless" concept; in contemporary politics it is often as not a source of conflict and division as identity groups argue for special recognition, compensation, and treatment, often at the expense of others. Liberal democracy is not a congerie of ships passing each other in the night, isolated and self-contained; it is a public space for debate and decision, based on a set of shared values. A multiculturalism that allows groups to set rules governing their own internal affairs on issues like education and women's rights is inherently problematic for a democracy.[21]

A second observation would seem to cut in the opposite direction. National identities have to bind people together, but they also have to be accessible to migrants and other outsiders to the cultural system in what is *de facto* an increasingly multicultural world. This means in practice that identity has to be rooted in political values rather than religious or ethnic ones. The debate over including reference to Europe's Christian heritage in the European constitution is understandable and merited if understood properly (i.e., that Europe's modern democratic values are historically rooted in Christianity). The practical impact of this kind of self-understanding, however, is likely to be negative for the integration of non-Christians into the political community.[22]

Finally, national identity needs to have some positive content beyond a spare, procedural vision of liberalism. National identity cannot be rooted in tolerance and nothing else. The modern liberal project was proposed in the early modern period by thinkers like Hobbes, Locke, and Montesquieu in response to the religious warfare

---

21. All modern democracies make exceptions for particular religious groups to pursue their traditions even when the latter run contrary to broadly accepted laws. In the United States, the Amish and certain orthodox Jews have been exempted from requirements for national service and education; in Europe, religious schools can receive public funding (even in France) and there are obviously established religions like the Anglican Church in Britain. In Italy, crucifixes are displayed in many public buildings. Generally Europeans have accepted these violations of the principle of the separation of Church and State because the overall force of religion was declining in the twentieth century. Assertions of religious rights by Muslims have been seen as more threatening today primarily because Muslims seem to take religion itself more seriously.

22. Despite the fact that Americans as individuals are much more religious than Europeans, it would be unthinkable for an American politician to have an explicit reference to Christianity inserted into the Constitution today. Overall, the separation of church and state is more rigorously followed in the US than in Europe.

of their time. Particularly after the Reformation, strong notions of what constituted the good life asserted themselves politically and led to endless bloody struggles. Modern liberalism deliberately sought to lower the bar and exclude contestation over ultimate ends from politics for the sake of social peace. The progressive exclusion of religion as the basis of national identity in the years since then did not mean, however, that substantive views of virtue and the good life were thereafter banished from societies' self-conceptions. Every country had its founders, heroes, and national myths that in some way defined the positive virtues around which their identities were fashioned.

I believe that the ultimate appeal of Huntington's culturalist vision of American national identity lies less in its historical accuracy than in the fact that it makes an appeal to virtue. In other words, it is not enough to say that we are Americans because we obey the law, respect the Constitution, and tolerate one another. We are Americans because we actively practice virtues like hard work, civic engagement, patriotism; we are risk-takers, entrepreneurial, skeptical of authority, and self-reliant. Stated in this form, American national identity is not an ascriptive set of characteristics one inherits by birth, whatever its roots in a particular religion and ethnic group. It defines a community from which one can be excluded only as a matter of individual choice. Understood in this sense, it is ultimately little different from Lipset's view of Civic America.

Bibliography

Bellah, Robert N.and Phillip Hammond. *Varieties of Civil Religion*. San Francisco: Harper and Row, 1980.

Durkheim, Emile. *The Division of Labor in Society* New York: Macmillan, 1933.

Fischer, David H *Albion's Seed: Four British Folkways in America*. New York: Oxford University Press, 1991.

Gellner, Ernest. *Nations and Nationalism*. Oxford: Blackwell, 1983.

Gellner, Ernest. "Nationalism and the Two Forms of Cohesion in Complex Societies," in *Culture, Identity, and Politics*. Cambridge: Cambridge University Press, 1987.

Hamilton, Alexander Hamilton, James Madison, and John Jay, *The Federalist Papers*. New York: New American Library, 1961.

Herder, Johann Gottfried von. *Philosophical Writings*, edited by Michael N. Forster. Cambridge: Cambridge University Press, 2002.

Huntington, Samuel P. *Who Are We? The Challenges to America's National Identity*. New York: Simon and Schuster, 2004.

Lipset,Seymour Martin. *The First New Nation*. New York: Basic Books, 1963. Lipset, Seymour Martin. *American Exceptionalism: A Double-Edged Sword*. New York: W.W. Norton, 1995.

Maine, Henry. *Ancient Law: Its Connection with the Early History of Society and Its Relation to Modern Ideas*. Boston, MA: Beacon Press, 1963.

Manent, Pierre. "Democracy without Nations?," *Journal of Democracy* 8 (1997): 2-102.

Manent, Pierre. *A World Beyond Politics? A Defense of the Nation-State* Princeton, NJ: Princeton University Press, 2006.

Sen, Amartya K. *Identity and Violence: The Illusion of Destiny*. New York: W.W. Norton, 2007.

Stern, Fritz. *The Politics of Cultural Despair: A Study in the Rise of German Ideology*. Berkeley: University of California Press, 1974.

Taylor, Charles. *Multiculturalism: Examining the Politics of Recognition* Princeton, NJ: Princeton University Press, 1994.

Taylor, Charles. *Sources of the Self: The Making of the Modern Identity*. Cambridge, MA: Harvard University Press,1989.

Tocqueville, Alexis de. *Democracy in America* New York: HarperPerennial, 1988.

Tönnies, Ferdinand. Community and Association. London: Routledge and Kegan Paul, 1955.

16 Narratives of Peoplehood, National History, and Imagined Nations amidst Diversity. A Conclusion

Michael Böss

On May 10, 1977, one of the fathers of Irish academic history, Theodore Moody, gave a presidential address to the Trinity College History Society on "Irish History and Irish Mythology" in which he made a distinction between national history and national myth. Moody, who was close to the end of a long and distinguished career, defined history as "the knowledge that the historian seeks to extract by the application of scientific methods to his evidence." Myth, in contrast, combined elements of fact and of fiction and was derived from "popular traditions, transmitted orally, in writing, and through institutions."[1]

Moody, who gave his address against the background of the bloody Troubles in Northern Ireland, reflected on the way interpretations of Irish history had been transformed into nationalist myths that had fed the fires of ethno-national conflict for more than a century. He sketched out two contrary myths: a separatist sectarian myth, which he associated with Ulster loyalism, and a unitary, nationalist myth, which he saw as the hallmark of southern republicanism. He went on to offer a number of examples of how, over the past couple of decades, the two myths had been undermined by historical research. He ended by concluding that historical revisions and the writing of "good" history might thus contribute to peace in Northern Ireland.

Moody did not deny that history and historians have social roles and ethical obligations towards their community. He granted that all polities and societies needed to have knowledge of their past in order to preserve their "corporate identity and distinctive patterns of living." Like individuals, nations needed self-knowledge, and one of the functions of history was to provide them with it. He also acknowledged that peoples need myths to sustain them in times of strain, crisis, or unresolved conflict. What was problematic, however, was when myths diverged from facts. In the Irish context, nationalist mythology had been "a way of refusing to face the

---

1. T.W. Moody, "Irish History and Irish Mythology," *Hermathena* 124 (1978): 7-24; in the following quoted from Ciaran Brady, ed., *Interpreting Irish History* (Dublin: Irish Academic Press, 1994), 71-86.

historical facts." Hence, it was the duty of historians to confront the public with those facts, however painful it might sometimes be.[2]

Moody's paper became a common point of reference in a rancorous debate, which raged well into the 1990s, between "revisionists" and "anti-revisionists," who represented arguments for and against Moody's claim that false ideas and narratives of Ireland's past had had a real effect on Irish society. I want to use some reflections on this debate as my point of departure for this concluding chapter in which I discuss how "stories of peoplehood" might be related to the way we – as historians, political scientists, and sociologists – understand and conceptualize "people," "nation," and national "master narratives." I conclude with some thoughts about the ethics of narrating peoplehood in plural societies.

Revising the national story

In Ireland, the term "revisionism" goes back to the arrival of New History at Irish universities in the mid-1930s when Moody and his colleague Robert Dudley Edwards, both graduates of the University of London's Institute of Historical Research, set out to revolutionize the aims, methods, and style of Irish historiography by founding, in 1936, the Ulster Society for Irish Historical Studies and the Irish Historical Society. In 1938, they launched *Irish Historical Studies*, an academic journal modelled on journals like *Historische Zeitschrift*, *Revue Historique*, and *English Historical Review*. The new journal only published articles based on primary sources. However, apart from presenting articles of the highest academic standard, the journal had a further purpose: educating the public and school teachers. It did so by including in each volume a special category of essays called "Historical Revisions." These articles were meant to refute received ideas and assumptions concerning historical events, persons, and processes by means of results from new empirical research. It is this category which caused later generations of critical historians to be nicknamed "revisionists" in the fiery debate on the social and political use of history that followed after Moody's address in 1977.

The debate engaged the Irish public because many ordinary citizens felt that revisionists whitewashed British imperialism, denied the historical injustices towards Ireland, and thus came close to questioning the whole cause of Irish anti-colonial emancipation. There were also historians of distinction who were skeptical of revisionism, not least the version of Oxford historian Roy Foster. At the end of the 1980s, Foster's monumental *Modern Ireland 1600-1972* (1988) became a common

---

2. Ibid., 71, 86.

point of reference for ant-revisionists.[3] As one of his critics wrote, it replaced nationalist historiography with an "Anglocentric view of Irish history."[4] Foster was also accused of writing out the "catastrophic" and "tragic" elements from Irish history. The often quoted example was the Great Famine, which was only given a page and half, and which was written in a style that appeared insensitive to the amount and degree of human suffering it had caused.[5]

The critique of anti-revisionists not only had an ethical dimension, but also one which concerned history as an academic discipline. Anti-revisionists were critical of the conviction shared by many adherents of "scientific history": that it is possible to give an empirically based objective account of the past. This also seems have been an idea which motivated Moody and Edwards in the 1930s. Undoubtedly, the "school" they founded did Irish historiography a great service in raising the level of academic history. But it also served the public in providing it with thoroughly researched books and articles that gave more nuanced and complex accounts of the history of the Anglo-Irish relationship than Irish school books were delivering in the 1950s and 1960s. In this way, revisionism helped pave the way for today's pluralist Ireland and new near-consensus that Ireland's past cannot be rendered as a simple "story," and that there are many "varieties of Irishness."[6] However, revisionist historiography was not devoid of its own political biases and theoretical shortcomings. Many revisionists were evidently anti-nationalists. In addition, they shared the preference of the Annales School for socio-economic explanations. They had little regard for the role of ideas as sources of "social power,"[7] and they leaned towards the modernist view of nationhood as a product of modernization. Hence, they rejected the idea that modern Irish nationalism was rooted in pre-modern Irish identities and political causes.

In a significant critique of the revisionist project, the Oxford medievalist Brendan Bradshaw emphasized that he did not wish to "question the validity of subjecting the received version of Irish history to critical scrutiny, much less to rehabilitate it, myths and all." What motivated him to intervene in the debate was to question the idea and utility of a "value-free" historiography as a means of approaching the past and understanding the Irish historical experience. Bradshaw argued that

---

3. Roy F. Foster, *Modern Ireland 1600-1972* (London: Allen Lane, 1988). For main documentation of the debate see Brady, *Interpreting Irish History*.

4. Kevin O'Neill, "Revisionist Milestone," in Brady, *Interpreting Irish History*, 217-21.

5. Desmond Fennell, "Against Revisionism," in Brady, *Interpreting Irish History*, 181-90; Brian Murphy, "The Canon of Irish Cultural History: Some Questions Concerning Roy Foster's Modern Ireland," ibid., 222-233; and Brendan Bradshaw, "Nationalism and Historical Scholarship in Modern Ireland," ibid., 191-216.

6. Roy Foster has traced the tradition of the story version of Irish history in *The Irish Story: Telling Tales and Making It Up in Ireland* (London: Allen Lane, 2001).

7. Cf. Michael Mann, *The Sources of Social Power*, 2 vols (Cambridge: Cambridge University Press, 1993).

revisionist historiography was far from value-free, and had not proved immune to its own interpretative distortions. Furthermore, the "corrosive cynicism" which characterized the style of revisionist historiography tended to trivialize the past and its significance for present generations. With its interpretative principles and tacit evasions, revisionism represented not only a denial of historical truth, but also the abdication of historians of social responsibility.[8]

The eminent Irish philosopher Richard Kearney was critical of the anti-nationalist bias of revisionists:

> In endeavouring to go beyond negative nationalism one must be wary [...] not to succumb to the opposite extreme of anti-nationalism. Those who identify all forms of nationalism with irredentist fanaticism habitually do so in the name of some neutral standpoint that masks their own ideological bias. To roundly condemn Irish nationalism, for instance, by refusing to distinguish between its constitutional and non-constitutional expressions and omitting reference to the historical injustices of British colonialism and unionism, amounts to a tacit *apologia* of the latter.[9]

In a number of articles in *The Crane Bag*, a journal Kearney co-founded in the late 1970s, he had delivered his own deconstructionist exposés of the myths of militant nationalism. But he was critical of the way revisionist historians naïvely conceived of the role of myth in society. National myths had not played only a sinister role in the past by, for instance, encouraging aggression towards "others." It had also played a pivotal role in mobilizing sentiments of national identity, and in serving legitimate interests of social emancipation and political resistance. Mythical narrative should be seen as a two-way street: It could lead to perversion in the form of bigotry, racism, and fascism. But it could equally be a liberating force in re-activating "a genuine social imaginary open universal horizons."[10] Hence, Kearney argued, with reference to Paul Ricoeur, that modern societies needed to both "demythologize" and "remythologize."[11] Historians should contribute to this process by discriminating between authentic and inauthentic uses of "myth," but they should not leave society without a story that could help citizens deal with present and future challenges:

> At best, myth invites us to reimagine our past in a way which challenges the present status quo and opens up alternative possibilities of thinking. At worst, it provides a community with a strait-jacket of fixed identity, drawing a *cordon sanitaire* around this identity which excludes dialogue with all that is other than itself.

---

8. Bradshaw, "Nationalism," 201, 207, 213.
9. Richard Kearney, *Postnationalist Ireland* (London and New York: Routledge, 1997), 58.
10. Ibid., 121.
11. Ibid.

> Without mythology, our memories are homeless; we capitulate to the mindless con-
> formism of fact. But if revered as ideological dogma, and divorced from the summons of
> reality, myth becomes another kind of conformism, another kind of death. That is why we
> must never cease to keep mythological images in dialogue with history. And that is why
> each society, each community, each nation, needs to go on telling stories, inventing and
> reinventing its mythic imaginary, until it brings history home to itself.

Kearney's normative reflections on myth and history may shed some light upon the subjects we have debated in this collection. What he concludes is that it is in each nation's own interest to be capable of telling stories about itself. Not stories unfounded in the past, however, but stories that "bring history home to itself," i.e. empowers it to define and enact its own purposes, aims, and values. Historians have an important role to play in this process. For stories of peoplehood not to be reduced to mere "ideology" or "memory," there is need for critical historians. But historians should not see themselves as being beyond society and historical processes in the belief that their studies are immune to the political and social agendas of their own age. And they should be aware that they mediate "stories of peoplehood" whether or not they agree on the very concepts of "nation" and "people."

Conceptualizing narratives of nation and people

The kind of narratives which this volume has been dealing with, stories of people-hood, are related to what is sometimes called "grand narratives" or "master narra-tives." The two terms originate in the writings of Jean-Francois Lyotard and Claude Lévi-Strauss, and were later to influence the postcolonial theory of Homi K. Bhabha.

For Lyotard, grand narratives – or *meta-récits* – were the great ideals of the En-lightenment which had legitimized the institutions of western modernity, but whose modes of "unification" and dreams of "totality" had also led to the totalitarianisms and terrors of the twentieth century. In post-industrial society and postmodern culture, he claimed, these grand narratives – and the idea of universal historical progression they represented – were losing credibility, whether in aesthetics or science or politics. Eventually, they would be replaced by dissenting and plural "small stories."[12] An earlier "postcolonial" take on the idea had been delivered by Lévi-Strauss, who, in his intellectual memoir *Tristes tropiques* (1955), described how Western "master narratives" had justified slavery and the subjugation of non-European peoples.[13] These two strands come together in the writings of Homi K. Bhabha. In his famous collection *Nation and Narration* (1990), Bhabha defined the

---

12. Francois Lyotard, *La Condition Postmoderne: Rapport sur le Savoir* (Paris: Les Éditions de Minuit, 1979).
13. Claude Lévi-Strauss, *Tristes tropiques* (Paris: Librairie Plon, 1955).

nation as "a form of narrative – textual strategies, metaphoric displacements, subtexts and figurative stratagems" which construct "a field of meanings and symbols" through which people understand their lives within the national society.[14]

The new ideas were widely disseminated in the academic world in the 1980s and 1990s, especially within literary and cultural studies. Historians were also affected by the "linguistic turn" they represented, in so far as some theorists rejected the idea of history as an empirical science and instead saw it as an ideologically fraught discipline reproducing socially, culturally, and politically hegemonic discourses. By critiquing the master stories of nation and state and by arguing for the need of "small," suppressed, and subaltern stories to be told, postmodern historians not only affirmed history as an interpretive discipline, but also contributed to the fragmentation of history, which had accelerated since the Annales school revolutionized professional history in the 1930s. However, historical departments were not equally affected. For long, the critique of national master narratives remained chiefly an Anglo-American phenomenon. In the United States the debate began when pleas for a revival of "coherence," "synthesis," and "narrative" in national historiography were met with postmodernist attacks on the very concepts of "nation" and "national history." Against Thomas Bender's call for a new notion of America based on the development of public culture,[15] his critics argued that such synthesizing represented processes of exclusion and homogenization, and served to confirm political legitimacy, social power, and cultural hegemony. Nell Irwin Painter, for example, saw Bender's plea as a return to the 1950s when historians had claimed that they spoke on behalf of all American people, whereas they were just writing the history of only a small segment, "white, male elites, presenting an illusion of synthesis that was no synthesis at all."[16]

The new critique of the very idea of "national history" now made it an object of research in its own right to identify and deconstruct national grand narratives. Inspired by Hayden White and French theory,[17] historians began to unravel national narratives identifying the literary modes, metaphors and genres on which they were allegedly constructed. Social and political history was submerged into "new cultural studies" as notions of, say, community and nation, were explained as no more than discursive strategies meant to obscure and cover up social differences,

---

14. Homi K. Bhabha, "Introduction," in *Nation and Narration*, ed. Homi K. Bhabha (London: Routledge: 1990), 2, 3.
15. Thomas Bender, "Wholes and Parts: The Need for Synthesis in American History," *Journal of American History* 73 (1986): 120-36.
16. Nell Irvin Painter, "Bias and Synthesis in History," *Journal of American History* 74 (1987):110-11.
17. Hayden White, *Metahistory: The Historical Imagination in Nineteenth-Century Europe* (Baltimore: Johns Hopkins University Press, 1973) and *Tropics of Discourse* (Baltimore: Johns Hopkins University Press, 1978).

conflicts, and struggles.[18] But even though there were those for whom material and social reality came near to being little more than construction, and even though notions of progress, modernization, and emancipation were relativized, the frontal attack of "postmodern history" proved only to be a passing phenomenon. At the end of the millennium, history had not only survived as an academic discipline, but had also regained new vitality and social relevance after the "acid bath" of postmodernist critique.

As Richard J. Evans argued, the postmodernist view of history as a form of literature and historians as creators of fictions had failed to convince. Still, post-modernism had had a positive effect: it emboldened historians "to come out from the barricades of scientific objectivity and project their own voice once more." Thus a cultural climate was created in which authorial identity and narrative could once again be adopted "without sacrificing history's claim to present sound views of the past."[19] Fundamentally, this was the position originally taken by E.H. Carr in 1961, when in *What Is History?* Carr had argued (in Evans' words) that historians were not "empty vessels through which the truth about the past was conveyed from the documents to the reader, but individuals who brought their own particular views and assumptions to their work."[20] All historians, Carr had claimed, had "bees in their bonnets," and if you could not hear the buzzing when you read their work, then there was something wrong. However, Carr had gone on, this buzzing was not only the product of the historian's idiosyncrasies, but also of the collective discourse of the community of historians at a particular time and in a given context. History would thus invariably reflect the time in which was written.

If we want to uphold the terms of "grand" or "master" narratives, I want to suggest, these observations should be kept in mind. The individual historian's text is a narrative in which there is a tension between the authorial voice and a number of wider social and professional narratives and discourses on the meanings of the past. In the "dialogues" between these interpretive narratives, certain "stories" will acquire predominance. Not just because they represent consensual – or hegemonic – social and political values, but also because they are "true": true in the sense of being convincing within the community of historians. Such narratives, I would argue, will be greatly influential for national identities and will shape the stories of peoplehood expressed in both popular and public culture. Hence, we need to explore the nature of master narratives and their relationship to stories of peoplehood a little further.

18. Cf. Lynn Hunt, ed., *The New Cultural History* (Berkeley: University of California Press, 1989).
19. Richard J. Evans, "Prologue: *What Is History?* – Now," in *What Is History Now?*, ed. David Cannadine (Basingstoke: Palgrave Macmillan, 2002).
20. Ibid., 15. Evans referring to E.H. Carr, *What is History?* (Basingstoke: Palgrave, 2001 [1961]).

The Dutch historian Krijn Thijs rightly argues that a "master narrative" ought not to be understood as an expression of "extreme, polarised social relations between rulers and ruled," nor as the narrative of a maestro, i.e. a single author. Instead it should be seen as a frame of understanding the past connected to a culture, a society, or a system of political rule. The power of master narratives is expressed in their ability to shape other narratives. He describes this dominance as similar to the way in which, in printing technology, a copy retains the structure of the master original:

> In this understanding, master narratives dictate their narrative framework to numerous partial stories, and therefore integrate them and lend them legitimacy. As a result we could understand the master narrative as an ideal typical "narrative frame" whose pattern is repeated, reproduced and confirmed by highly diverse historical practices.[21]

Master narratives are products of social dominance and socially and politically constructed communal identities. "Dominance," however, should not be understood merely in terms of the social power of its supporting groups, but also in terms of their influence on "local" narratives, i.e. partial histories covering a short time-scale (eras, dynasties, revolutions), limited spaces (regions, cities, state territories), specific groups, and

> other historical practices, such as museums, celebrations, anniversaries or monuments. Such "official" forms of historical practice are dependent on the master narrative, which is thus situated at the top of a *narrative hierarchy*. Its function as a source of meaning and of discipline, its tendency to legitimise "local" histories and its power to exclude differing narratives which do not copy its structure and meaning ensure that this hierarchy is both the product and a producer of social reality.[22]

Thijs's definition of master narratives has relevance for the conceptualization of "stories of peoplehood," for historical narratives produce notions of nation and people.

In my introduction to this book, I defined stories of peoplehood as narratives and memories of shared historical experience that contribute to national awareness and social values, motivate collective political action, and legitimize social and political institutions. "Stories of peoplehood" should, of course, be seen as an analytical concept rather than as something "out there" in a specific culture and an individual's or a collectivity's lifeworld. They are not a special kind of narrative genre, but rather patterns of images and values that inform social identities with reference to the past,

---

21. Krijn Thijs, "The Metaphor of the Master," in *The Contested Nation: Ethnicity, Religion and Gender in National Histories*, ed. Stefan Berger and Chris Lorenz (Basingstoke: Palgrave, 2008), 68.
22. Ibid., 69.

and which inform the continuous process of interpretation and re-appropriation of the past by historians, by the public, and by the state. They affect the way individuals understand their private and public lives, their sense of belonging, affiliation, and identity, their values and norms. They are central to what David Miller understands as the "public culture" dimension of national identity, and they are crucial for building coherent societies, as Rogers M. Smith argues.[23] To the extent that professional historians deal with the history of their people and state, they contribute to this continuous process of story and identity-making, which also takes place in museums, schools, acts of public commemoration, popular culture, public and social institutions, and political discourse and rhetoric. Stories of peoplehood create an ethical "we community," which is imagined as stretching back in time and continuing into the future. In times of crisis or external threat, they tend to cover up memories of historical disruption, social conflict, and political dissent.[24]

Conceptualizing stories of peoplehood in this way opens up the possibility of conducting comparative studies similar to the ones that Thijs suggests for historical master narratives. One may, for example, examine internal, structural similarities between "smaller" and "larger" stories, i.e. between local and national stories. Or one may make comparisons between national narratives on the basis of core narrative elements known from structural narratology. As Thijs suggests for master narratives, we should thus look at elements such as:

(1) The central actors of the story: Which historical figures represent the core of the nation? Who is identified as the nation's main agents?

(2) The central antagonists or enemies of the nation: Where do the threats of the nation come from? Have these forces been excluded or defeated?

(3) The progress of national history: How does the narrative account of the historical progress of the nation and the factors behind it?

(4) The periodization of national history: Where are the national origins of the nation located? Which events, wars, victories, defeats, and sufferings are seen as turning points in the past?

(5) The time economy: Does the narrative define a golden past, celebrate the present, or promise a glorious, utopian future? Are there periods which cannot be told and occur as blank spots?

---

23. David Miller, *On Nationality* (Oxford: Clarendon, 1995); Rogers M. Smith, *Stories of Peoplehood: The Politics and Morals of Political Membership* (Cambridge: Cambridge University Press, 2003).

24. Cf. Anne Rigney, *The Rhetoric of Historical Representation: Three Narrative Histories of the French Revolution* (Cambridge: Cambridge University Press, 1990); James Wertsch, *Voices of Collective Remembering* (Cambridge: Cambridge University Press, 2002); Alistair Thomson, *Anzac Memories: Living with the Legend* (Oxford and New York: Oxford University Press, 1994); and Paul Connerton, *How Societies Remember* (Cambridge: Cambridge University Press, 1989).

It goes without saying that such studies are only meaningful if stories of people-hood are not seen in isolation, but rather as results of transnational imports and exchanges. Narrative structures may be derived from broader "cultural narratives" that originate in religious tradition, for example. Furthermore, it is important to study how dominant narratives have at times been contested by counter-narratives de-legitimizing social and political structures.

As Thijs points, it is only "when the changes within the vision of history trans-gress the permitted range that the master narrative loses credibility and makes way for new narrative forms." In periods of relative historical calm, the master narrative embodies what is generally considered to be the most natural version of the past, and conveys general knowledge of a society and its history, which is echoed in the work of historians, political scientists, and journalists. However, the common nar-rative framework is nevertheless "subject to constant and subtle, though relatively limited, change."[25]

It is a commonly heard claim today that the European states need to abandon or revise their stories of peoplehood - and the historical master narratives that feed into them - because they are no longer "functional" (cf. Korsgaard in this volume). This claim assumes that because they are social constructs, they may easily be re-constructed. Historical experience does not support such political agendas, and the reason is probably that stories of peoplehood not only produce but also reflect collective identities and public cultures. However, since identities are dynamic, they will, of course, be affected by changing social, cultural, and political contexts.

Modernist historians also question the way notions of "nation" and "people" are used by "perennialist" or "primordialist" historians (cf. Claus Møller Jørgensen in this book). In the Nordic countries, this kind of critique has largely been a Danish phenomenon. Examples - as described by Møller Jørgensen - are the "counter-narratives" of Søren Mørch in "The Last History of Denmark" (1996) or Michael Bregnsbo and Kurt Villads Jensen in "The Danish Empire: Its Greatness and De-cline" (2004).[26] However, it is doubtful whether one may argue that there has truly been a collapse of the Danish master narrative. Instead one may say that the effect of the critique of Danish national history has been an increased awareness of social divisions, cultural plurality, marginal groups, and the transnational aspects of Danish history.[27] Typically, major popular and more or less official histories of Denmark, as for instance "Kjersgaard's Danish History" (1998) or Bo Lidegaard's *A Short History of Denmark in the Twentieth Century* (2009), draw on the established

---

25. Thijs, "The Metaphor," 72.
26. Søren Mørch, *Den sidste Danmarkshistorie* (Copenhagen: Gyldendal, 1996); Michael Bregnsbo and Kurt Villads Jensen, *Det danske imperium: Storhed og fald* (Copenhagen: Aschehoug, 2004).
27. Peter Aronsson et al., "Nordic National Histories," in Berger and Lorenz, *The Contested Nation*, 256-82.

hierarchy of narratives[28] – of which Knud J. V. Jespersen's *A History of Denmark* (2004) is an almost paradigmatic model.[29]And the tradition of identifying coherent patterns in a Danish history, beginning in the Stone Age and taking us up to the twenty-first century, is far from dead, as Bernard Eric Jensen predicted it would soon be in 1997.[30]

Leaving the political agendas of contemporary "counter-histories" aside, I want, therefore, to assess to what extent the notions of nation and people, which master narratives assume, are justified.

Conceptualizing peoplehood

Nationalism, Walker Connor, once put it, is at its most basic an expression of "homeland psychology,"[31] i.e. a feeling of attachment to kin and place. No doubt this attachment reflects transhistorical human nature that makes it natural to think in "primordial terms" about one's people, and also to think of social development in terms of patterns of continuity. However, as Jonathan Hearn points out, "social evolution is not so much one of progressing through stages, marching from one social form to the next, but rather one of the overlaying of older forms with newer ones, such that principles that were once dominant in governing human behaviour are not so much replaced as encysted within new and more complex forms."[32] So with each new layer, new patterns of community and social imaginaries have arisen, which should not be seen simply as adding to the collective identities of earlier forms. Seen from this perspective, there is no direct line from the prehistoric tribe based on kinship ties over the subjects of medieval kings to the citizens of modern nation-states.

Claus Møller Jørgensen is justified, of course, in rejecting ethno-national essentialism and the notion of a primordial Danish people that has existed from time immemorial. He is also right in wanting us to understand the process by which national consciousness has developed as a part of a larger, "transnational" history. But getting beyond "nationalized history" does not require us to conclude, as

---

28. Erik Kjersgaard, *Kjersgaards Danmarkshistorie* (Copenhagen: Aschehoug, 1998); Bo Lidegaard, *A Short History of Denmark in the Twentieth Century* (Copenhagen: Gyldendal, 2009).

29. Knud J.V. Jespersen, *A History of Denmark* (Basingstoke: Palgrave, 2004).

30. See, e.g., Benito Scocozza, *Politikens étbinds Danmarkshistorie* [Politiken's One-Volume Danish History] (Copenhagen: Politiken, 2007); Bernard Eric Jensen, "Danmarkshistorie: en genre i opløsning?," in Bernard Eric Jensen, *Danmarkshistorie: en erindringspolitisk slagmark* (Copenhagen: Roskilde University Press, 1997).

31. Cf. Walker Connor, "Homelands in a World of States," in *Understanding Nationalism*, ed. M. Guiberneau and J. Hutchinson (London: Polity Press, 2001).

32. Jonathan Hearn, *Rethinking Nationalism* (Basingstoke: Palgrave Macmillan, 2006), 64-65.

Jørgensen does, that the category of peoplehood may be thrown into the dustbin as no longer useful for historians. It only requires us to conceptualize nation and peoplehood within the framework of the gradual social and political development of the state since the Middle Ages: to see nation building as intertwined with the building of kingdoms, states, and empires, and also with the narrated experiences, memories, and identifications of cultural and territorial peoples that form collective identities whether or not they make up a political community (cf. Heisler in this volume).

The stories and symbols of peoplehood which nationalists drew on in the nineteenth century were no mere inventions. Of course, in the Middle Ages nations were cultural and linguistic and should generally not be understood as political communities.[33] Still, even in the Italian city-state and the medieval *Stände-stat*, one may observe the development of the notion of a people as a kind of corporate entity which may be represented politically.[34] But this did not mean that they could not be mobilized for the king's "political" projects in terms of wars against others. As Anthony D. Smith argues, ethnic communities (or cultural nations) – based on a common cultural and linguistic identity and "a sense of continuity on the part of successive generations of a given cultural unit of the population"[35] – were the cradles of modern political nations. And as Smith, Armstrong, Hastings, Kidd, Grosby, and I have argued, the Christian Bible delivered the primary ideas and narratives which, through ecclesiastical and monarchical chronicles and histories, informed the way medieval kings and political elites understood concepts like kingdom, people, justice, and the king's relationship to his lords and subjects.[36]

The rise of the modern European state is usually taken back to the first centralizing monarchical states, which were formed from the 1500s onwards in large kingdoms such as England, France, and Spain, but also in minor ones such as Portugal, Denmark, and Sweden, in the wake of increasing dynastic rivalries. As

---

33. Cf. Adrian Hastings, *The Construction of Nationhood: Ethnicity, Religion and Nationalism* (Cambridge: Cambridge University Press, 1997).

34. Joseph P. Canning, "Ideas of the State in Thirteenth and Fourteenth-Century Commentators on the Roman Law," *Transactions of the Royal Historical Society* 33 (1983): 1-27; *A History of Political Thought, 300-1450* (London: Routledge, 1996), 9-32.

35. Cf. Anthony D. Smith, *National Identity* (London: Penguin, 1991), 25.

36. Anthony D. Smith, *The Cultural Foundations of Nations* (Oxford: Blackwell, 2008) and *Chosen Peoples: Sacred Sources of National Identity* (Oxford: Oxford University Press, 2003); John Armstrong, *Nations before Nationalism* (Chapel Hill, NC: University of North Carolina Press, 1982); Colin Kidd, *British Identities before Nationalism* (Cambridge: Cambridge University Press, 1999); Adrian Hastings, *The Construction of Nationhood: Ethnicity, Religion and Nationalism* (Cambridge: Cambridge University Press, 1997); Steven Grosby, *Nationalism: A Very Short Introduction* (Oxford: Oxford University Press, 2005); Michael Böss, "Europas grundfortællinger" [Europe's Founding Narratives of Nationhood and State], in *Fra modernitet til pluralisme* [From Modernity to Pluralism], ed. Jens Holger Schjørring and Torkild Bak (Copenhagen: ANIS, 2008), 29-65.

Otto Hintze has argued, the development of the institutions of the modern state in this period should be understood against the background of these conflicts and the popular enmities they created.[37] The new kind of state, which supplanted the much more loosely organized and territorially fluid post-carolingian state,[38] was characterized by (1) royal control of a well-defined, coherent territory, (2) centralization, (3) independence of other kinds of social organization (as for instance the church), (4) monopoly over physical power, and (5) the expansion of the dominant urban centre into territorial and cultural peripheries.[39] State building was a process involving a number of interdependent factors of which war was by far the the most important since it had multiple social and political side effects. The monarch's ability to control his state depended on his ability to extricate it from the jurisdiction of a church which claimed universality and was therefore by defintion "anti-national." Another important factor was the development of early capitalism, which enabled the monarch to increase taxation. Taxes went to finance the king's wars, which, again, required him to secure internal social order within his realm, both through the expansion of his royal courts and the creation of militias that "policed" his territory. The small court of the medieval king thus expanded into bureaucracies of professional officers and servants, and the new institutions of control and administration gave the king's territory an increasingly higher degree of economic and juridical homogeneity. Parallel with this development ran a process of cultural homogenisation as a result of the standardization of dominant vernaculars, the invention of the printing press, confessional regimentation, and greater literacy. As a consequence, a population which had hitherto either been culturally diverse or united by language, myth, and memory gradually became the "king's people." Such a people saw themselves as members of a community united by their loyalty to their king and his territory, even in their cultural diversity.[40] This new collective identification was therefore greatly enhanced by the king's wars. His enemies became their own enemies. After the Reformation, enemies were not only neighboring rival powers, but also confessional "others."

Monarchs needed patriotic subjects to secure their rule at that time. Late Renaissance kings could no longer rely on professional armies to defend their territories, but depended on the loyalty and service of their subjects. However, nation building

---

37. Otto Hintze, *The Historical Essays of O. Hintze* (Oxford: Oxford University Press, 1975), 162.
38. Cf. Gianfranco Poggi, *The Development of the Modern State* (Stanford: Stanford University Press, 1978); and Hagen Schulze, *States, Nations and Nationalism* (Oxford: Blackwell, 1998).
39. Charles Tilly, ed., *The Formation of National States in Western Europe* (Princeton: Princeton University Press, 1975); Stein Rokkan, "Territories, Centres and Peripheries," in *Centre and Periphery: Spatial Variations in Politics*, ed. J. Gottman (London: Sage, 1980), 163-204.
40. Susan Reynold, "The Idea of the Nation as a Political Community," in *Power and the Nation in European History*, ed. Len Scales and Oliver Zimmer (Cambridge: Cambridge University Press, 2005).

was not only a top-down process. Conscious of the king's importance as defender their faith and material well-being, the king's subjects saw their own interests as being tied up with their rulers. However, to the extent that the kings abrogated what the lower aristocracy and the rising class of "burghers" regarded as their rights and "ancient liberties," they would increasingly hold the king accountable and see the relationship between king and people as contractual. This implied a re-imagining of the old story of nationhood according to which the king and his lords made up the nation.[41] This was first seen in England, but it was to lead to the political emancipation of the third estate, first in France and later in other parts of Europe. In all these cases, subjects re-appropriated the concept of nationhood and declared themselves a politically sovereign people with the right to govern its own state.

To sum up, then, the notions of nation and peoplehood originate in medieval ethnic and cultural narratives, mostly based on biblical tradition. These notions became intertwined with the development and consolidation of European states as individuals and groups increasingly identified not only with their homelands and kin, but also with their king, territory, and state. They began to imagine themselves as being part of a community of "equals" larger than that of kin, village, town, and land, and different in kind from their state's others. In general, therefore, national identity might be defined as an individual and collective awareness which follows from living in a territorial state, sharing collective experiences and memories, and internalizing the values of stories of peoplehood and other symbolizations which these experiences give rise to.

Although national identities have often served to unify societies and states, collective experiences and the new idea of political nationhood also led to the break-up of multiethnic states and empires from the end of the 1700s. In the following, I want to illustrate this by briefly discussing the experience that transformed English colonists in North America into Americans. The example also illustrates that, although a "people" or a "nation" are definitely a discursively and socially constructed phenomena, they draw on shared experiences and memories retained in narratives and expressed in social, cultural, and political practices, and are hence no less real than other social institutions.

The construction of Americans

At the dawn of the American Revolution, colonists of English or Scottish origin did not regard themselves as "Americans," but as British subjects living in North

---

41. Liah Greenfeld, *Nationalism: Five Roads to Modernity* (Cambridge, MA: Harvard University Press, 1991).

America. They were, as Benjamin Franklin put it, "British people."[42] The colonial elite shared the ideology of the English Whigs. They regarded themselves as the freest people on earth, and, in the tradition of Locke, they took their tradition of freedom back to the Germanic roots of their English heritage. Their devotion to the political ideal of freedom thus not only had a history, but also a story of people-hood. Paradoxically, however, it was this story – and the values associated which it – which motivated them to rebel against their king and parliament in London.

As is well known, the rebellion was motivated by the British government's decision to centralize and reform the financing of the Empire after its costly wars with France. During the war, which ended in 1763 with the incorporation of France's North American territories, the American colonists had enjoyed a high degree of self-government. It was this political freedom they now saw themselves deprived of when it was demanded that they cover the war expenses. Their argument was that, if this was to be the case, they were entitled to the right of political representation. Taxation without representation amounted to tyranny, they famously claimed. However, the British government answered that, as colonists, they had to subordinate themselves to the imperial household budget without expecting political rewards.

This response provoked the thirteen colonies, each with their distinct assembly, to draft a common Declaration of Independence in 1776. Here they declared that they were a "people" endowed with certain rights, and among these was the right to rebel against a tyrant. Thomas Jefferson, who drafted the declaration, later in his life said that it should not be seen as an expression of his own ideas, but that it reflected an American "awareness." And, truly enough, prior to the break with Britain, political leaders in colonies had begun describing the populations in the colonies as "nations."[43] When they later began to draft constitutions for each of the colonies, they did it from the assumption that what united each of these "nations" were the same principles and rights as had been guaranteed by the Bill of Rights, i.e. the charter of rights and freedoms that had received royal signature at the Glorious Revolution of 1688-89. The new constitutions represented an innovation in so far as the rights they encoded were pinned up on references to natural law. They also articulated the rights of the individual more liberally than the original charter. In this way, it was made clear that political separation from Britain would mean both "national" freedom and increased freedoms for the individual vis-à-vis the state.

The federation of the states in 1788 and the writing of a federal Constitution were to play an all-important role in the way Americans understood themselves as

---

42. Quoted in Gerald Stourzh, *Benjamin Franklin and American Foreign Policy* (Chicago: Chicago University Press, 1969), 81.
43. Edward Dumbauld, *The Constitution of the United States* (Norman: University of Oklahoma Press, 1964), 29-30.

a nation: Americans were a people made up of free individuals who needed to be protected from the state.[44] The American Revolution thus gave the colonists an American identity in which the British tradition of "freedom" was re-interpreted. But American identity was not only based on a legal document, the Constitution. It was also a product of the experiences that had led up to it – the events of the Revolutionary war – and the narratives it produced. Thus American identity developed as a new "narrative identity," which was no longer informed by the British Whig and the "stories" on which it had drawn, but was shaped by narrated experiences of revolution. As Samuel H. Beer puts it: "The colonists began as Englishmen demanding a greater degree of self-government and ended as Americans declaring their independence."[45]

Since the Founding Fathers saw their new creation, the United States of America, as a historically unique community, the old Puritan narrative of America as a "city upon a hill" was soon to acquire a new, secular meaning (as explained by Rogers M. Smith in this volume). Similarly, the secularized values and virtues of Puritanism were to become the building blocks of an American identity (as Francis Fukuyama describes it in his chapter). The American "we" that was coming into being was a people with both origins and a collective destiny. It was not a purely abstract people, but a people whose story and values bore the imprint of America's history of settlement. However, in the middle of the 1800s, this story of peoplehood came under pressure by westward expansion and the need to accommodate immigrants. As Eric Rauchway explains in his chapter, the new narrative was a result of regional political conflicts and therefore not uncontested. But in the long term, it turned out to be eminently functional for a culturally diverse polity, even though, once again, it appears to have come recently under strain as a result of the New Immigration from the end of the 1900s.

This leads me to discuss the final, normative issue we have been concerned with in this book: how to imagine – and re-imagine – nationhood amidst diversity.

Narrating peoplehood amidst diversity

In his contribution to this book, Bernard Eric Jensen suggests – with reference to Charles Taylor – that stories of nation and peoplehood should be seen as parts of larger "social imaginaries" as Taylor defines them, i.e. the "the ways people

---

44. Gertrude Himmelfarb, *The Roads to Modernity: The British, French, and American Enlightenments* (New York: Knopf, 2004).
45. Samuel H. Beer, *To Make a Nation: The Rediscovery of American Federalism* (Cambridge, MA: Harvard University Press, 1993), 134.

imagine their social existence, how they fit together with others, how things go on between them and their fellows, the expectations that are normally met, and the deeper normative notions and images that underlie these expectations."[46] Social imaginaries are not merely mental phenomena. They are institutionalized by being actively lived out in the meaningful actions and interactions of the members of a given society. What characterizes national imaginaries, as I see it, is that they add a historical dimension to the social imaginary: nations are societies and peoples imagined diachronically, so to speak. But notions of nation and people – both as intersubjective imaginings and as publicly symbolized and narrated – are subject to change: they are transformed by internal and external circumstances, including geopolitical contexts, changing demographies, and socio-cultural processes. Most western states have gone through periods during which national imaginaries have been transformed. It happened, as just indicated, at the onset of mass immigration in the middle of the 1800s when battles were fought over American identity in light of a changing demography. It also happened in Denmark, when the political failure in integrating the German-speaking duchies into a Danish nation-state led to the break-down of the conglomerate state in 1864 and made it necessary to re-imagine Danishness within a dramatically reduced territory. Since the early 1970s, Canada has been trying to re-imagine peoplehood amidst cultural diversity – with little success so far, according to Jack Granatstein's and Andrew Cohen's contributions to this volume. Australia has done the same, but so far more successfully, probably because governments – the public – have insisted that multiculturalism should be reconciled with the notion of an Australian people.

As I mentioned earlier, calls are made today for the old nation-states of Europe to "re-invent" their national identities in order to make room for immigrants within the nation. The debate on the place of Latinos in the American people, as documented in the three chapters by Leo Chavez, Tomás Jiménez, and Desmond King and Ines Valdez, should be seen from the same perspective.

Scholars of a modernist, postmodernist, or multiculturalist bent are sceptical of such calls and instead predict the death of the European nation-state proper as a result of European integration, globalisation, and cultural hybridization. They believe that the rise of various forms of supranational governance will diminish the need for states and national belonging.[47] In the 1990s, Yasemin Soysal argued that the intensification of transnational discourse and the introduction of supranational

---

46. Charles Taylor, *Modern Social Imaginaries* (Durham: Duke University Press, 2004), 23.
47. A classic example of the modernist approach to nationhood is, of course, Eric Hobsbawm's *Nations and Nationalism since 1780* (Cambridge: Cambridge University Press, 1990). Representative of later post-nationalist critique is Philip Spencer and Howard Wollman's *Nationalism: A Critical Introduction* (London: Sage, 2002).

legal instruments would end up disconnecting citizenship from nationhood.[48] But Sheila L. Croucher critiques the "post-nationalist" argument:

> [I]t is not always clear whether these postnationalist scholars are describing the supersession and destabilization of the nation or of the state. More problematic, however, is that neither the postnationalists nor the modernists who suggest the nation's demise can account adequately for the contemporary persistence, even resurgence, of nationhood as a form of belonging. And [...] the allure of nationhood persists not only among established nation-states, but also among new or newly transitional states – whether in the case of South Africa or in projects of regional integration like the EU.[49]

Croucher grants that nations are historically contextual formations which have been shaped by social and material conditions. But she goes on to argue that it is the very fact that they are by definition dynamic, malleable, and contextual that explains why and how nation-states persist, and why nations keep on being imagined and re-imagined. The experiences of the past decade appear to support her argument. Economic globalization has not diminished the need for states.[50] Neither has social globalization: welfare regimes, the integration of immigrants, the prevention of international crime, and national security issues require states to define who belong and who do not belong to the nation. In a globalized world, individuals also seem more than ever in need of national belonging and rooted identities, both as citizens and as human subjects. "Nationhood [...] continues to be a functional, familiar, and legitimate mechanism for belonging," Croucher rightly concludes.[51] And as the contributions by Jimenez, Chavez, and King and Valdez reflect, the arguments in favour of opening the American border to Mexican immigrants are not based on a wish to undo the American nation, but to give them a place within it.

National identities and the stories that inform them were not only functional when we lived in industrial societies. They are perhaps even more important in late-modern liberal, market-based, and culturally plural societies, as Francis Fukuyama argues. In liberal societies, many private economic interests compete and sometimes clash; they are therefore prone to fragmentation and social division. For such societies to cohere and function, citizens must feel they have obligations towards each other and the state. If not, they will, as individuals or as groups, seek to use each other and the state for their own benefit. A state which the citizens

---

48. Yasemin Soysal, *Limits to Citizenship* (Chicago: Chicago University Press, 1994) and "Citizenship and Identity: Living in Diasporas in Post-War Europe," *Ethnic and Racial Studies* 23, no. 1 (2000): 1-15.

49. Sheila L. Croucher, *Globalization and belonging: The Politics of Identity in a Changing World* (Lanham: Rowman and Littlefield, 2004), 99.

50. See, for example, Michael Böss, ed., *The Nation-State in Transformation: Economic Globalisation, Institutional Mediation and Political Values* (Aarhus: Aarhus University Press, 2010).

51. Ibid., 107.

regard as their own rather than as a common project that stretches from past into future generations (cf. Edmund Burke) is bound to be a weak state. In the long term, it risks losing the legitimacy on which its sovereignty is based and without which its laws, courts, and other executive institutions cannot function. A liberal society depends on the existence of an overarching national identity among the citizens, so that they may identify with each other and see the state as a project which represents an interest higher than that of their many private interests and that they may act as stewards of its institutional, cultural, and material resources. Besides, national identity is important for democracy. Not only because democracy often requires compromises to be made, but also for the very basic reason that it assumes the minority's willingness to accept electoral defeat instead of resorting to rebellion. As the Danish theorist of state and ethnologist Thomas Højrup puts it: "If people do not imagine themselves to be stakeholders in the practices of the state, the democratic state will not be able to exist."[52] Finally, increased immigration and cultural diversity make it urgent for societies to define and articulate common values, common points of identification and reference, and, therefore, shared stories of nationhood. The challenge today is to tell our stories in such a way that they include and unite rather than exclude and divide the citizens and residents of a country.

As Granatstein and Cohen argue, culturally diverse societies also need to tell stories about themselves, and for these stories to make sense, they must reflect historical events and experiences. Societies cannot be based on fictions, myths, and wishful thinking that cover up real social and cultural divisions and create a semblance of harmony and homogeneity. Citizens are entitled to be told both the stories and the histories of themselves as a people – in all their diversity – in order to be able to understand the forces, powers, and conflicts that have shaped their state and social values.

This involves an awareness of the past as a room of many voices and stories. Historical awareness of social plurality is a stepping stone towards understanding the values of pluralism in general, for example the need to tolerate and empathize with those who do not share the values and stories of one's own group. In light of contemporary immigration and increased cultural diversity, it is important to introduce immigrants to the cultural, structural, economic, political, spatial, and institutional heritage and conditions of the national collectivity. But the introduction should be "dialogical," as Martin Heisler puts it: migrants and members of the national collectivity should interact in interpreting and assessing the multiple stories and voices of the nation's past and re-imagine the nation together. Not in

---

52. Thomas Højrup, *Dannelsens dialektik* (Copenhagen: Museum Tusculanum, 2002), 295.

arbitrary ways, however, but with reference to empirical cases, i.e. by drawing on the knowledge and interpretations of historians. In order to welcome newcomers to the national society, it is thus important to engage in exchanges of stories and histories.

In his essay "Reflections on a New Ethos for Europe," Paul Ricoeur reflects on how an "ethic of hospitality" can provide room for the story of the other, the stranger, the victim, and the forgotten ones. What is needed, he argues, is "taking responsibility in imagination and in sympathy for the story of the other, through life narratives which concern the other."[53] Ricoeur shows how this calls for an "ethic of narrative flexibility." He explains this with reference to national memorials. Such memorials face the challenge of resisting the reification of a particular historical event, reducing it to fixed dogma and a closed interpretation of the past. Historians have taught us, however, that all historical events are told in different, if not quite contradictory, ways by succeeding generations and by different narrators. This does not relativize the past or open it up for arbitrary interpretations. But an awareness of the plurality of narrative perspectives may make us empathetic to the narratives of strangers, indeed even our adversaries, in so far as such cases involve overlaps between the diverse horizons of consciousness (cf. Hans-Georg Gadamer) past and present. Dialogic exchanges of narratives may also make us aware that, as Ricoeur puts it, "[t]he identity of a group, culture, people or nation is not that of an immutable substance, nor that of a fixed structure, but rather that of a recounted story." This entails a third ethical principle: narrative plurality. Narrative pluralism does not mean any lack of respect for the singularity of the event narrated by the historian or expressed by acts of public remembering. Nor is narrating and remembering differently "inimical to a certain historical reverence to the extent that the inexhaustible richness of the event is honored by the diversity of stories which are made of it, and by the competition to which that diversity gives rise."[54] On the contrary. A critical point for Ricoeur is that the "ability to recount the founding events of our national history in different ways is reinforced by the exchange of cultural memories [...] and the ability to exchange has as a touchstone the will to share symbolically and respectfully in the commemoration of the founding events of other national cultures, as well as those of their ethnic minorities and their minority religious denominations."[55]

Seen from this perspective, it may be concluded that it is not the task of the historian to defend "history" against "memory" and "myth." Rather, it is to under-

---

53. Paul Ricoeur, "Reflections on a New Ethos for Europe," in *Paul Ricoeur: The Hermeneutics of Action*, ed. Richard Kearney (London: Sage, 1996), 7.

54. Ibid., 8.

55. Ibid., 9.

stand that writing national history involves a number of social responsibilities and ethical choices.[56] It does not seem to be accidental that the revival of narrative in historiography after postmodernism has coincided not only with a new awareness of the social role of historians, but also with an interest in the ethics and the uses of history.

Bibliography

Armstrong, John. *Nations before Nationalism*. Chapel Hill, NC: University of North Carolina Press, 1982.

Aronsson, Peter et al. "Nordic National Histories," in *The Contested Nation*, edited by Stefan Berger and Chris Lorenz, 256-82. Basingstoke: Palgrave, 2008.

Beer, Samuel H. *To Make a Nation: The Rediscovery of American Federalism*. Cambridge, MA: Harvard University Press, 1993.

Bender, Thomas. "Wholes and Parts: The Need for Synthesis in American History," *Journal of American History* 73 (1986): 120-36.

Berger, Stefan and Chris Lorenz eds. *The Contested Nation: Ethnicity, Class Religion and Gender in National Histories*. Basingstoke: Palgrave, 2008.

Bhabha, Homi K. "Introduction," in *Nation and Narration*, edited by Homi K. Bhabha, 1-7. London: Routledge: 1990.

Böss, Michael. "Europas grundfortællinger" [Europe's Founding Narrratives of Nationhood and State], in *Fra modernitet til pluralisme* [From Modernity to Pluralism], edited by Jens Holger Schjørring and Torkild Bak, 29-65. Copenhagen: ANIS, 2008.

Böss, Michael ed. *The Nation-State in Transformation: Economic Globalisation, Institutional Mediation and Political Values*. Aarhus: Aarhus University Press, 2010.

Bradshaw, Brendan. "Nationalism and Historical Scholarship in Modern Ireland," in *Interpreting Irish History*, edited by Ciaran Brady, 191-216. Dublin: Irish Academic Press, 1994.

Brady, Ciaran ed. *Interpreting Irish History*. Dublin: Irish Academic Press, 1994.

Bregnsbo, Michael and Kurt Villads Jensen. *Det danske imperium: Storhed og fald*. Copenhagen: Aschehoug, 2004.

Canning, Joseph P. "Ideas of the State in Thirteenth and Fourteenth-Century Commentators on the Roman Law," *Transactions of the Royal Historical Society* 33 (1983): 1-27.

Canning, Joseph P. *A History of Political Thought, 300-1450*. London: Routledge, 1996.

Carr, David. "History, Fiction, and Human Time: Historical Imagination and Historical Responsibility," in *The Ethics of History*, edited by David Carr, Thomas R. Flynn, and Rudolf Makkreel, 247-60. Evanston, IL: Northwestern University Press, 2004.

Carr, E.H.. *What is History?*. Basingstoke: Palgrave, 2001 [1961].

Connerton, Paul. *How Societies Remember*. Cambridge: Cambridge University Press, 1989.

Connor, Walker. "Homelands in a World of States," in *Understanding Nationalism*, edited by M. Guiberneau and J. Hutchinson. London: Polity Press, 2001.

---

56. David Carr, "History, Fiction, and Human Time: Historical Imagination and Historical Responsibility," in *The Ethics of History*, ed. David Carr, Thomas R. Flynn, and Rudolf Makkreel (Evanston, IL: Northwestern University Press, 2004), 257.

Croucher, Sheila L. *Globalization and belonging: The Politics of Identity in a Changing World*. Lanham: Rowman and Littlefield, 2004.

Dumbauld, Edward. *The Constitution of the United State*.. Norman: University of Oklahoma Press, 1964.

Evans, Richard J. "Prologue: *What Is History?* – Now," in *What Is History Now?*, edited by David Cannadine, 1-18. Basingstoke: Palgrave, 2002.

Fennell, Desmond Fennell. "Against Revisionism," in *Interpreting Irish History*, edited by Ciaran Brady, 181-90 Dublin: Irish Academic Press, 1994.

Foster, Roy F. *Modern Ireland 1600-1972*. London: Allen Lane, 1988.

Foster, Roy F. *The Irish Story: Telling Tales and Making It Up in Ireland*. London: Allen Lane, 2001.

Greenfeld, Liah. *Nationalism: Five Roads to Modernity*. Cambridge, MA: Harvard University Press, 1991.

Grosby, Steven. *Nationalism: A Very Short Introduction*. Oxford: Oxford University Press, 2005.

Hastings, Adrian. *The Construction of Nationhood: Ethnicity, Religion and Nationalism*. Cambridge: Cambridge University Press, 1997.

Hearn, Jonathan. *Rethinking Nationalism*. Basingstoke: Palgrave Macmillan, 2006.

Himmelfarb, Gertrude. *The Roads to Modernity: The British, French, and American Enlightenments*. New York: Knopf, 2004.

Hintze, Otto. *The Historical Essays of O. Hintze*. Oxford: Oxford University Press, 1975.

Hobsbawm. Eric. *Nations and Nationalism since 1780*. Cambridge: Cambridge University Press, 1990.

Højrup, Thomas. *Dannelsens dialektik* [The Dialectics of Education]. Copenhagen: Museum Tusculanum, 2002.

Hunt, Lynn, ed. *The New Cultural History*. Berkeley: University of California Press, 1989.

Jensen, Bernard Eric. "Danmarkshistorie: en genre i opløsning?," in Bernard Eric Jensen, *Danmarkshistorie: en erindringspolitisk slagmark*. Copenhagen: Roskilde University Press, 1997.

Jespersen, Knud J.V. *A History of Denmark*. Basingstoke: Palgrave, 2004.

Kearney, Richard. *Postnationalist Ireland*. London and New York: Routledge, 1997.

Kidd, Colin. *British Identities before Nationalism*. Cambridge: Cambridge University Press, 1999.

Kjersgaard, Erik. *Kjersgaards Danmarkshistorie*. Copenhagen: Aschehoug, 1998.

Lévi-Strauss, Claude. *Tristes tropiques*. Paris: Librairie Plon, 1955.

Lidegaard, Bo. *A Short History of Denmark in the Twentieth Century*. Copenhagen: Gyldendal, 2009.

Lyotard, Francois. *La Condition Postmoderne: Rapport sur le Savoir*. Paris: Les Éditions de Minuit, 1979.

Mann, Michael. *The Sources of Social Power*, 2 vols. Cambridge: Cambridge University Press, 1993.

Miller, David. *On Nationality*. Oxford: Clarendon, 1995.

Moody, T.W. Moody. "Irish History and Irish Mythology," *Hermathena* 124 (1978): 7-24.

Mørch, Søren. *Den sidste Danmarkshistorie*. Copenhagen: Gyldendal, 1996.

Murphy, Brian. "The Canon of Irish Cultural History: Some Questions Concerning Roy Foster's Modern Ireland," in *Interpreting Irish History*, edited by Ciaran Brady, 222-233. Dublin: Irish Academic Press, 1994.

O'Neill, Kevin. "Revisionist Milestone," in *Interpreting Irish History*, edited by Ciaran Brady, 217-21, Dublin: Irish Academic Press, 1994.

Painter, Nell Irvin. "Bias and Synthesis in History," *Journal of American History* 74 (1987):110-11.

Poggi, Gianfranco. *The Development of the Modern State*. Stanford: Stanford University Press, 1978.

Reynolds, Susan. "The Idea of the Nation as a Political Community," in *Power and the Nation in European History*, edited by Len Scales and Oliver Zimmer. 54-66. Cambridge: Cambridge University Press, 2005.

Ricoeur, Paul. "Reflections on a New Ethos for Europe," in *Paul Ricoeur: The Hermeneutics of Action*, edited by Richard Kearney. London: Sage, 1996.

Rigney, Anne. *The Rhetoric of Historical Representation: Three Narrative Histories of the French Revolution*. Cambridge: Cambridge University Press, 1990.

Rokkan, Stein. "Territories, Centres and Peripheries," in *Centre and Periphery: Spatial Variations in Politics*, edited by J. Gottman, 163-204. London: Sage, 1980.

Schulze, Hagen. *States, Nations and Nationalism*. Oxford: Blackwell, 1998.

Scocozza, Benito. *Politikens étbinds Danmarkshistorie* [Politiken's One-Volume Danish History]. Copenhagen: Politiken, 2007.

Smith, Anthony D. *National Identity*. London: Penguin, 1991.

Smith, Anthony D. *The Cultural Foundations of Nations*. Oxford: Blackwell, 2008.

Smith, Anthony D. *Chosen Peoples: Sacred Sources of National Identity*. Oxford: Oxford University Press, 2003.

Smith, Rogers M. *Stories of Peoplehood: The Politics and Morals of Political* Membership. Cambridge: Cambridge University Press, 2003.

Soysal, Yasemin. *Limits to Citizenship*. Chicago: Chicago University Press, 1994.

Soysal, Yasemin. "Citizenship and Identity: Living in Diasporas in Post-War Europe," *Ethnic and Racial Studies* 23, no. 1 (2000): 1-15.

Spencer, Philip and Howard Wollman. *Nationalism: A Critical Introduction*. London: Sage, 2002.

Stourzh, Gerald. *Benjamin Franklin and American Foreign Policy*. Chicago: Chicago University Press, 1969.

Taylor, Charles. *Modern Social Imaginaries*. Durham: Duke University Press, 2004.

Thijs, Krijn, "The Metaphor of the Master," in *The Contested Nation: Ethnicity, Religion and Gender in National Histories*, edited by Stefan Berger and Chris Lorenz, 60-74., Basingstoke: Palgrave, 2008.

Thomson, Alistair. *Anzac Memories: Living with the Legend*. Oxford and New York: Oxford University Press, 1994.

Tilly, Charles ed. *The Formation of National States in Western Europe*. Princeton: Princeton University Press, 1975. Wertsch, James. *Voices of Collective Remembering*. Cambridge: Cambridge University Press, 2002.

White, Hayden. *Metahistory: The Historical Imagination in Nineteenth-Century Europe*. Baltimore: Johns Hopkins University Press, 1973.

White, Hayden. *Tropics of Discourse*. Baltimore: Johns Hopkins University Press, 1978.

■ Index